Tearing Down
Strongholds

Richard A. Webster

William Carey Library
Pasadena, California

Published by:
William Carey Library
P.O. Box 40129
Pasadena, CA 91114 U.S.A.
TEL: (818) 798-0819
FAX: (818) 794-0477

1st U.S. Edition, 1993

Cover illustration by Robert Ellis.

Library of Congress Cataloging-in-Publication Data
Webster, Richard A. (Richard Alvis), 1920-
    Tearing down strongholds / Richard A. Webster.
        p.   cm.
    ISBN 0-87808-240-9 (pbk.)
    1. Spiritual warfare. 2. Webster, Richard A. (Richard Al-
    vis), 1920- . 3. Missionaries—Taiwan—Biography. 4.
    Missions, American—Taiwan—History—20th century. I.
    Title.
BV4509.5.W37 1993   93-1449
266'.0095124'9—dc20   CIP

The Scripture quotations in this book are nearly all from the New
International Version or the New American Standard Bible, and
these are used by pemission. A few are from the King James Version or are the author's own paraphrase.

For her faithful efforts in
purging out the flaws of the manuscript,
seasoning it with good things,
and then feeding it all into the computer,
I dedicate this book to
my dear wife, Flo.

CONTENTS

PART THREE: MORE THAN CONQUERORS

Introduction

After twenty years of "blood, sweat and tear," involving trial and error, along with reading missionary manuals, attending church planting seminars, and seeing only a meager amount of lasting fruit in our efforts to introduce His kingdom into the dark, idolatrous villages of Taiwan, some might well ask if the title of this book is not a bit ambitious. We do not feel that it is, for "tearing down strongholds" certainly expresses the direction which gospel outreach must take in any heavily pagan situation.

When we first began our invasion into these heathen areas of Taiwan, we were filled with great confidence and anticipation. Had not the Lord Jesus declared, "I will build my church, and the gates of hell shall not prevail against it"? This statement is clear, simple and straightforward. Therefore it appeared that all we needed to do was go, claim victory, and the land would be ours.

But after two decades of employing all the approaches and techniques we knew, calling on the Lord for help, and exhausting our strength, we are by now, I believe a good bit wiser than when we began. Although we as yet haven't seen many strongholds torn down, our title still comes from God's Word. And indeed, there are areas in the world today, such as Korea, Argentina, various tribal regions, etc., where strongholds have been overcome to a marked degree, and extraordinary victories are being won.

We still expect to see a breakthrough in these Taiwanese and Hakka villages, but we realize that it may involve far more time and warfare than we anticipated. Our enemy is a cruel tyrant, and these idol-worshipping regions are truly *strong holds*. God's Word does not promise that we will be able to completely tear down all of the enemy's bulwarks here on earth during this age. That final triumph will come when the Lord Jesus returns and sets up His all-encompassing, global reign. But we are encouraged to move out now in His name as His sent-ones, appropriating the victory of His cross where He has directed us to enter.

We must go only at His bidding, under His orders each step of the way. Otherwise the "strong man" can tear us to shreds. We need not fear, but we dare not be presumptuous! We must not become proccupied with the battle itself, nor with the enemy. Our ultimate objective is alwasys the purpose for which we have been sent—to take the good news to those who are lost, and see captives set free.

The real battle has to first be waged by the unseen forces in the heavenly (spiritual) realms. When this encounter has been won through the prayers of God's people in any country, the fields will be ripe for harvest. Reapers, filled with the love and power of the Spirit, will still need to go out and gather the sheaves, but they will do so with much rejoicing (even in the face of counter-attack). My earnest desire for each of you, in your appointed area of the conflict, is that "the God of peace will soon crush Satan under your feet." (Rom. 16:20)

PART ONE:

SURVEYING THE SITUATION

1

DISCOVERING THE STRONGHOLDS

Forty years ago, with my wife and ten-month-old son, I walked up the gangplank of the *Marine Adder* to begin the journey toward my missionary career in China. After only a little more than two years, the Communists reached our western province of Szechwan, and the bulk of our ministry ground to a halt. Nearly two years passed before we managed to gain our exit and return to the States. During those months we were introduced to a good deal of the unpleasant side of missionary life. But that is a separate story of its own. Being young and undaunted, we were soon back on the sea waves, headed for Taiwan, the land of free China. By this time, we had added two little daughters to our family.

The goal of our missionary endeavors from the beginning, had been to reach Chinese students for the Lord, especially college students. For it was during my own time as a student at the Christian Fellowship of the University of California at Berkeley, that I had made my greatest spurt of spiritual growth, met my wife, and received the Lord's call to work overseas. Even today, there are seven of my fellow classmates from that group who still contribute to our missionary support.

In Taiwan we found a few of the churches thriving, and the students quite ripe for gospel ministry. We began some English-Chinese Bible classes as an attraction, and soon were off to a good start. After a few years of this elementary beginning, the Lord brought along a keen Chinese InterVarsity staff worker who helped to develop student-led cell groups throughout the island, and the student work took another great stride forward. Then catastrophe struck our family. My wife came down with malignant cancer, and after a brave but prolonged battle of many months, the Lord took her home. Two years later in 1965, the Lord gave me Flo, another Taiwan missionary student worker, to be my partner, and we set out together in the city of Taichung to establish fellowship groups in the colleges and high schools of that second largest educational center of Taiwan.

Once again the Lord prospered our efforts, and within a relatively short period a number of Christian Chinese teachers were located to serve as sponsors, and a nucleus of gospel witness was established on many high school and college campuses. The Lord gave Flo and me two little sons to add a further thrill to our lives, so we were in the waves of much blessing.

Approaching the Villages

It was about this time that I began to develop a concern to help cultivate an added spiritual dimension to the student work, that of missionary outreach. We had already from the start been teaching and training the students for witness to their fellow-students on campus, which is naturally their primary field of service. But I felt the time had come to present to them the Lord's Great Commission to the regions beyond.

This was not as simple a matter as it had been back in my own fellowship group at the University of California. For Taiwan had no Chinese mission boards, and none of our western mission agencies was set up to receive national Chinese workers. So to challenge them to give themselves for overseas service was actually quite complicated.

This problem still didn't stop the vision from growing. After all, Taiwan itself still contained many unreached areas. Outside the cities were hundreds and hundreds of villages completely void of any gospel witness. So the logical first step was to line up student teams to move out into these areas during their holidays and vacation periods.

This project was begun with great enthusiasm, much zeal, and numerous plans and ideas. The Chinese Christian community, including many pastors and well-wishers from the city churches, seemed to be excited with this new venture. So we began with great expectancy, and for the first few weeks, we covered a lot of ground. We purchased an old movie projector with a

P.A. system, and soon had visited thirty villages with what we considered to be a fair presentation of the gospel.

However, in our more quiet moments, as we had a chance to reflect on the real accomplishments of our efforts, there was a gnawing dissatisfaction, because so far we hadn't had any definite decisions to accept the Lord among the village folk, and really didn't know how we would have followed them up, even if we had.

So we decided to confine our endeavors to the students' summer and winter vacation periods, when the teams could spend at least a week in each district, and that we would work only in areas which already had a village church to serve as their base. This was a great improvement, and there was evidence of the Lord's blessing. Many students signed up to give a week of their vacation to this outreach, so there were teams averaging twenty-five to thirty students per week, for six or eight weeks during the summer, and a couple of weeks during the winter.

These were no fly-by-night operations. The first day of each of these efforts was given to training the students how best to reach these village people, but the primary emphasis was on how to spend their forenoons each day in spiritual preparation for the house-to-house evangelism in the afternoons and evenings. They were divided into small groups of three or four, and each of the students took his turn in the presentation of the message. Often one of the group would gather the children outside, and share gospel stories with them while the others gave a witness to the adults inside. Usually one would give himself to prayer while the "good news" was being announced.

The Lord singularly blessed these ventures, and in a given week there might be a hundred "decisions." I am not prepared to say that all these were valid conversions. There is always a strong tendency for eager young students to pluck unripe fruit. But a record was kept of the interest shown in each home, and these cards were left with the pastor of the village church in the area. Also, every effort was made to involve the constituency of the church itself, as much as possible, in each part of the program. The church members were especially urged to participate in the small house-to-house visitation teams. The students usually slept on the floor in the church building, and their meals were prepared by some of the church women.

Examining the Results

This type of program was continued for several years with growing interest, and what appeared to be increasing results. Then one day our steering committee decided the time had come for an examination of the real results. So we appointed one of our staff to travel through the island and visit the twenty-five or thirty areas where our teams had labored, and find out just how many of this "multitude of converts" were still actively serving the Lord in the village churches. We were shocked, almost beyond recovery, to learn that in most of the churches there wasn't one even attending the services.

Naturally it took us a long time to recover from this jolt. What does one make of such colossal failure? Even our poorest semesters in the student work produced a better record than this. As we began to lick our wounds, the tendency was, of course, to place all the blame on the lack of proper follow-up by the village churches. And no doubt a good part of the problem did rest there. But this still didn't leave us feeling at all happy in our spirits. So we cast about for other possible excuses. "After all, these are the last days, when men will turn away from seeking the truth." But that didn't help much to solve the problem, because there was still evidence of blessing in the student work itself, and in some of the city churches. "Perhaps we, and these intellectual college students, are just not the suitable ones to do village work." But that didn't bring peace either. The Lord's Great Commission still stood. And some of our best workers, whom the village people loved and respected, were the keenest intellectually. Also, if we didn't go to these unreached "uttermost parts" of Taiwan, who would? Very few others seemed ready to go, and most of those who had made some attempt soon gave up. "Maybe the areas we went to just weren't the 'good soil,' or maybe the villages of Taiwan were just not ripe anymore. For had not the standard of living risen all over the island, a factor which always dulls man's interest in spiritual things?" But the initial response, as the teams spent time in each home, had indicated a genuine hunger in many hearts!

Gaining Insight

So we began to seek the Lord and His Word, as to some clue to the real, basic problem. At such times I always return to one of my favorite passages, James 1:5-7. "If any of you lacks wisdom, let him ask of God, who gives to all men generously and without reproach, and it will be given to him. But let him ask in faith without any doubting, for the one who doubts is like the surf of the sea, driven and tossed by the wind." It wasn't long before a whole new vista of understanding began to open up. I began to see that these villages are strongholds of a powerful, sinister, and insidious force, to which we had given entirely insufficient consideration.

I had always known that there was a devil, and we had casually referred to him in our prayers for the village work, but I soon discovered that I knew next to nothing about spiritual warfare. As I began to search the Scriptures on this matter, I found them filled with the subject. In fact, I have come to see that this is the ultimate problem on planet Earth. And I have finally come to the conclusion that these village areas are Satan's strongest bastions on Taiwan. Therefore he has fortified them with all his might. He is being driven back, to a degree, in the cities and among the students, but he considers the dark, heathen, idolatrous villages to be his own, and he is not about to let them go. They are his strongholds, and he is ready to do battle with any serious attempt to invade this territory.

It became obvious then, that any future moves into the villages needed to be planned with a vital, new strategy. Not only did we need to give our student teams more specific teaching and training in spiritual warfare, but we needed to ask the Lord for some full-time workers who could establish bases out in this enemy territory, begin to do a proper job of follow-up, and see that the fruits of all our labors were sheltered, as much as possible, from the counter-attacks of these evil forces. It doesn't require much experience in village evangelism to discover that persecution from ardent, idolatrous, and ancestor-worshipping relatives and friends is the main obstacle to the growth of any new spiritual baby. In fact, without a massive amount of prayer and tender loving care, his new life will be all but snuffed out in short order. It would be ideal, of course, if the whole family or an entire clan would all turn to the Lord at the same time. But in these vicious strongholds of the enemy here in Taiwan, we dare not wait for that. For the Lord Jesus has already warned us that His gospel would not bring peace within the family, but a sword. "A man's enemies will be the members of his own household," and "Anyone who loves his father or mother more than Me is not worthy of Me" (Mt. 10:34-37).

The Lord has been gracious, and one by one and two by two, He has called in some fine, young grads (who already served on the teams) to become full-time missionaries, and to establish beachheads in four of the most needy areas in the south of the island. He also moved in the hearts of other grads and some of the concerned churches to provide their support. So eventually they formed their own little Village Gospel Mission. They are doing well, but the price they are paying to move into enemy territory is mounting as the battle intensifies. The results have not yet been phenomenal, but there are beginning to be evidences of some definite breakthroughs.

Strongholds—Neglected Areas

The Lord Jesus has been waiting a long time for the people of the villages of Taiwan to hear the good news of His gospel. It has been almost 2,000 years! Although the gospel was a long time in coming to Taiwan, it has actually been in the cities of this land for over one hundred years, but most of the villages are unreached. Why? There are, of course, many reasons. For one thing, these areas are the most superstitious, and therefore the most difficult. But when the Lord Jesus gave His Great Commission, He did not relieve us of the responsibility of the difficult areas! In fact, quite to the contrary, His directive was to the "uttermost parts" or "the ends of the earth," which specifically points to those areas which have as yet not heard.

Sometimes we are held back in the name of "strategy." Strategy is good, and we are wise to employ it in all our planning. We are cautioned in God's Word to be wise and not foolish. But is there not something wrong with our strategy when we see 2,000 churches in the towns and cities of Taiwan, most of which have been there for nearly half a century, and we still give nearly all our efforts to planting more city churches? Recent church-planting surveys in Taipei have shown that it is becoming difficult to find a spot for a new work which is not within a stone's throw of an already established nearby church.

It is true that the planting of churches in the metropolitan areas of any country is the expedient way to begin. The intellectuals, the business class, the most able leaders, need to be reached there. And we must start with leadership material. But periodically we need to rethink our overall strategy.

Of course we rejoice to see a large city church with plenty of intellectuals, business men and able leaders. But if our vision stops here, we are too shortsighted. These city churches should themselves become outreach centers with a strong missionary vision, or they will eventually become stagnant and "dead."

The people of a church get their vision from the pastor, and the local pastor often gains his vision from the missionary. So we missionaries can actually impart a higher level of spiritual life to the churches we plant if we train them from their earliest beginnings to include outreach teams as an integral part of their weekly program.

Some fifty years after the Lord Jesus had returned to heaven, He appeared to the Apostle John, and asked him to deliver messages to seven of His churches. The first message was to go to the pastor of the church of Ephesus. The Lord was happy about their hard work, their patient endurance, and their orthodox theology, but He then added some strong words: "I have this against you, that you have abandoned the love you had at first. ...I will come and remove your lampstand from its place, unless you repent" (Rev. 22:1-4). If the Lord Jesus were to come as speaker to some of our pastors' conferences, I wonder if He might not have something to say about our unreached village areas...Satan's strongholds.

Misconceptions

Another element which has held our churches back from reaching out to the village areas is a basic misunderstanding of the implications of our Lord's Commission. We seem to feel that it only applies to those who have had a special call to overseas service. And since very few individuals receive such a call, the whole missionary enterprise becomes a rather specialized effort, quite unrelated to the rank and file of ordinary Christians.

I have recently been moved by a passage in II Peter regarding the Lord's delay in His return to earth, to set up His reign. "The Lord is not slow about His promise as some count slowness, but is forbearing toward you [or "on your account"], not wishing that any should perish, but that all should reach repentance" (2 Pet. 3:9). When the Lord sets up His reign, the day of missions will be over. So the Lord keeps prolonging this grace period, hoping that His church will move out to the "uttermost parts" and give every pocket of the inhabited earth a chance to hear. It is hard for us to realize the degree to which He has committed this work into the hands of His people. Peter says, "It is on account of you" that He has had to wait so long!

The Lord's last words on the cross were "It is finished." His special part in God's plan for man's redemption was completed. But after His resurrection, He still remained here on earth for forty days. And one of the main reasons for this was the vital task of communicating His Commission to His disciples. If this failed, all would be lost. He had paid that awful price for man's salvation, but if the people of the world were not clearly informed of this precious "good news," his infinite sacrifice was in vain.

The first few generations did quite well, but then things began to slack off, and a kind of self-centeredness set in. After that, missionary endeavors came only in rather short, weak spurts. But the Lord kept patiently waiting. It has only been since about 1800 A.D. that, to any degree, His people began again to hear His Commission. And even to this day, with all the plans toward the year 2000 A.D., I fear that most of His people sitting in the pew have heard His commission rather faintly, if at all. Yet we call it His "Great Commission." Why has it failed to be great in the hearts and minds of so many of us?

Coming back again to this common misunderstanding and its implications, just who is to be involved in this commission? It is to include nothing short of every believer! This does not suggest that every Christian is to make plans to go overseas. Actually, as we have mentioned, only a small percent will receive such a "call." Of the original twelve apostles in the book of Acts, it seems that only one (Paul) received a call to serve overseas. The rest apparently remained in Jerusalem during that period, except for short visits to nearby districts. It was the ordinary, new believers whom the Lord scattered about as missionaries. "They went everywhere preaching the Word" (Acts 8:4).

If a substantial number of the 2,000 churches in Taiwan had just one gospel team, which would go regularly to some unreached village, this could cause a great impact on these strongholds. And it is encouraging that a few churches are beginning to move in that direction. (The student fellowship groups should have their teams also.) One good example is a friend of mine who is a high school chemistry teacher. Every Sunday evening he and his wife take a few other fellow Christians to an unreached coastal area an hour away to preach and teach the gospel. And interest has grown. Nearly forty young people now come to listen.

Paul's View

I wonder if we tend to look at the villages (or other "hidden people" groups) as the Jews looked at the Gentiles: as sort of a "lesser breed." "It doesn't really matter a great deal whether they hear the gospel or not! They are so steeped in their idolatry and superstition that they can't comprehend anyway. Also, they are scattered out in inconvenient, out-of-the-way places. Don't worry about them!" But the Lord is concerned about them. So a basic question is, "To what extent do I have His Spirit and His feelings filling my heart?" Paul had a hard time trying to convince the Jewish Christians of his day that the Gentiles had a right to the gospel. But where would you and I be if he hadn't given himself to the needs of us "outsiders"? The thrust of many of his epistles, especially the book of Romans, is that the Gentiles also have a right to hear. And so do the villagers!

And "how are they to believe in Him of whom they have never heard? And how are they to hear without a preacher?" The church which is pleasing to the Lord is that congregation which is sending out its people to needy areas. He says the people of such a church have "beautiful feet." Their feet are beautiful because they are going to the "uttermost parts," the unreached places.

Taiwan's church population has now reached the stage where it does not need a lot more imported, professional missionaries from abroad. Let's look at Paul's three missionary journeys. Each trip lasted about two years, and each was to a different place. On his first journey, he travelled through the province of Galatia, an area three times the size of Taiwan, and planted three churches. His second tour was in Macedonia and Achaia, another area three times as large as Taiwan. There he planted four churches. His third term was in Asia Minor, a province four times as large as Taiwan, and according to the record, he planted one church.

After these three "short terms," he makes an incredible statement in his letter to Rome, where he hoped to go next. "Since I no longer have any room for work in these regions, and since I have longed for many years to come to you, I hope to see you in passing, as I go to Spain" (Rom. 15:23,24). How could he possibly consider the job to be completed in such a vast area as the four provinces of Galatia, Achaia, Macedonia, and Asia Minor (altogether ten times the size of Taiwan), when only eight churches had been established? We find the answer to this phenomenon in his letter, a few years later, to one of those eight churches. "Not only has the word of the Lord sounded forth from you in Macedonia and Achaia, but your faith in God has gone forth everywhere, so that we need not say anything" (1 Thess. 1:8).

It would seem that Paul operated on the basis of the yeast principle, taking his lead from the Lord's little parable about making bread. "The kingdom of heaven is like leaven which a woman took and hid in three measures of meal, till it was all leavened" (Mt. 13:33). The "three measures" spoken of here is a mighty large batch of flour. It amounts to about eight gallons (twenty-two liters). It is surely meant to be a picture of reaching the whole world with the message of God's kingdom. But the main point of the parable is that "all" is to be leavened. The yeast is to be mixed into every part, a thorough penetration.

Paul knew well that he and his little band of co-workers could never manage such a complete coverage over so vast an area, but this didn't seem to bother him. He was confident that the churches he had planted were dynamic yeast. They would spread in all directions.

Another element of the yeast principle should be mentioned here. Yeast requires a certain amount of heat in order to "rise." If the dough is less than 28 degrees C. (82 degrees F.), nothing will happen. But when the temperature rises, it can work very fast. And at this increased warmth it requires but a small portion of yeast to leaven a large amount of meal. Less than 1% will do the job. Here in Taiwan we have probably a 5% Christian population in some of our larger cities, but probably less than 0.005% in many of the village areas. Not a very even penetration.

Mark begins his Gospel with a moving picture of the heart of the Lord Jesus. "In the morning, a great while before day, He rose and went out to a lonely place and there He prayed. And Simon and those who were with him hunted for Him. They found Him and said to Him, 'Everyone is searching for You.' His reply was, 'Let us go on to the neighboring villages, that I may preach there also; for that is why I came out'" (Mk .1:35-38). He didn't allow the evident blessing on His city ministry to detain Him from moving out to the unreached areas.

Luke records another picture of our Lord's concern. "After this [sending out His twelve disciples in pairs to proclaim His kingdom], the Lord appointed seventy others and sent them on ahead of Him, two by two, into every town and place where He Himself was about to come. And he said to them, 'The harvest is plentiful, but the laborers are few; pray therefore the Lord of the harvest to send out laborers into His harvest.'" Twelve plus seventy was only considered a "few" for those unreached towns and villages.

Wars take time, and they require large armies of well-trained, well-equipped soldiers. There may be some colossal defeats along the way, for our enemy is very strong, very shrewd, and very cruel. Our failures so far in the village work have taught us a great deal, and we are seeking to share some of the insights we have gathered in the following pages of this book. But our foremost longing in this first chapter is to stimulate a vision and a concern for the "hidden peoples" and the unreached areas of the world, and to rekindle in the hearts of the Lord's people something of that fire which burns and blazes in His heart.

We are not seeking to plant "guilt trips" on anyone, for this is only counter-productive. Not all have the gift of direct evangelism. Our talents and ministries are different. And certainly not all are called to "full-time service." But every Christian should be able to experience the joy and satisfaction of seeing himself involved to a meaningful degree in some operation of tearing down the enemy's strongholds, and the planting of God's kingdom in enemy territory.

2

THE TWO KINGDOMS

"One day Jesus was praying in a certain place. When He finished, one of His disciples said to Him, 'Lord, teach us to pray, just as John taught his disciples!' He said to them, 'When you pray say, "Our Father in heaven, hallowed be your name. Your kingdom come; may your will be done on earth as it is in heaven"'" (Lk. 11:1,2).

When Jesus first called His disciples, they were completely untutored in the matter of prayer. This is probably why they were so clumsy and inept in every other phase of spiritual life. For prayer is communion with God and is therefore our primary means of acquiring the strength and facility we need to live for Him.

Here in chapter eleven of Luke's gospel, the disciples just looked on awkwardly while Jesus prayed. Finally one of them had enough insight to evaluate the situation a bit, and after recalling how John the Baptist had taught his disciples to pray, he asked the Lord to give them some instruction. So He gave them lesson number one.

These same disciples did finally learn how to pray, however. In fact they developed tremendous aptitude and tenacity in prayer. In accordance with the Lord's final instructions they, plus a hundred others, "with one accord devoted themselves to prayer" for ten days before they began their ministry. This was even before the Holy Spirit came upon them. And it is a good thing they did learn to pray, for otherwise they would never have stood in the ensuing battle. In that drama of the Acts of the Apostles, there is recorded such fierce opposition and attack upon these men, their ministry, and the infant churches which they planted, that the entire enterprise would have died out early in the

17

conflict, were not they and their students skilled to do battle in prayer. (They were beaten, imprisoned, and scattered in all directions. Steven was stoned; James was beheaded; and Paul was driven out of town nearly every place he went.)

The Primary Essential of Prayer

This first prayer outline which the Lord taught them contains only the bare essentials, but they are certainly the main ones. The primary item, in the first place after worship, is: "Thy kingdom come." The implication of these three words is really quite staggering. The Lord God created the entire universe, and yet there is still one tiny part of it where *His* kingdom has not yet come. How can such a thing be?

Astronomers tell us that there are 100,000,000,000 galaxies in our universe, and that each of these galaxies contains an average of 100,000,000,000 stars. Our earth is but one of the smaller planets revolving about just one of these stars. And it is by no means in the center of the universe; actually it is quite far out on the fringe. Yet from one aspect, this little planet earth has become the very center of things. For the next phrase in that beginning prayer outline which the Lord Jesus taught His disciples reads, "Thy will be done *on earth* as it is in heaven." This would seem to indicate that God's will is being done (His kingdom has come) in all the other reaches of this vast universe, leaving only little planet earth as the last stronghold of another rebellious kingdom.

This unbearable state of affairs was and still is the matter of utmost concern upon the heart of the Lord Jesus. In the Gospels, well over a hundred times, we hear Him discoursing on the "kingdom of God," or the "kingdom of heaven." Luke therefore informs us that after His resurrection, "over a period of forty days He spoke about the *kingdom of God*" (Acts 1:3). At the end of those forty days, His disciples still didn't understand what He was talking about and asked if He at that time were going to establish the kingdom of *Israel*. But He summarily dismissed that subject and came back to their need to be filled with the Holy Spirit in order that they would have the necessary power to go "to the ends of the earth" with the gospel of *His* kingdom.

We mentioned above that in a very real sense, our earth has become the center of spiritual warfare. It is something like what happened a few years ago when enemy forces entered the Falkland Islands. These tiny little islands were way down at the tip of South America, out on the periphery of our cosmic sphere. Yet suddenly they became the center of attention of the whole world, especially of England to whom they belonged. A warfare began, and that warfare continued until the enemy was completely routed. This, in essence, was the burden on the heart of the Lord Jesus which brought Him to this earth. It was the burden which He sought to transfer to the heart of His disciples, and which He longs to implant in your heart and mine: "Thy kingdom come; Thy will be done on earth as it is in heaven"! We can, of course, in no way do justice to this burden by merely reciting these words once a week on a Sunday morning. It is good to recite them regularly as a declaration of our goal in life, but such a declaration is only the beginning.

The History of This War

It is now time to go back and take a look at the beginnings of this warfare. Whatever could have precipitated such a thing? How could anyone take over any part of the universe which was called into being by the Almighty Creator? And even if they did, how could they manage to hold onto it for these thousands of years? We will never be able to answer all the questions, but we are given some insights in God's Word which reveal bits and pieces of what happened.

The opening verse of the Bible reads, "In the beginning God created the heavens and the earth." We are not told much about the creating of the heavens. The record is mostly about the creation of the earth. However we do gather from a number of references throughout Scripture that the creating of the heavens included the creation of spirit-beings called angels. These angels have free wills just as man has, but a portion of them used their free will to rebel against God and formed a rival kingdom of their own. Their desire ever since has been to attack and destroy any part of God's kingdom which they possibly can. Evidently they failed to do any damage throughout the major expanse of the heavens, but they have had phenomenal success here on earth.

As we follow through the creation story there in that first chapter of Genesis, at the close of each major step we hear it announced with real pleasure and satisfaction that "God saw that it was good." And the conclusion in the last verse reads, "God saw all that He had made, and it was very good." All that our God does is always very good. He does nothing but that which is right, just, and for the best. Even after a time of severe testing, David cries out, "As for God, His way is perfect" (Ps.18:30).

The nature of the *enemy's* kingdom is just the opposite. He is against everything that is good and right. He is negative, hurtful and destructive. There is nothing creative or good about him. In the Scriptures the Lord calls him "Dragon," "Serpent," "Deceiver," "Liar," and "Murderer."

But how could such a vile kingdom ever gain an entrance into any part of God's beautiful and perfect universe? Why would an omnipotent God ever allow such a thing? Why were not Satan and his kingdom snuffed out as soon as they rebelled? God could have done this, of course, but in this omniscience God doesn't always do things that way. As Paul exclaims in Romans 11, "Oh the depth of the riches of the wisdom and knowledge of God! How unsearchable are His judgments, and His paths beyond tracing out!"

For His own good reasons, God decided that this perfect man and woman whom He had created, and to whom He had committed a free will, should be tested. Otherwise their free will would be meaningless. So in the beautiful garden which He had prepared for their dwelling, He planted a tree called "The Tree of the Knowledge of Good and Evil." But He warned them repeatedly that they were not to eat of the fruit of that tree, because if they did they would die. As long as they did not eat of the tree, they knew only *good*. For everything that God had made was good. And God loved them and desired only their good. But He wanted their love for Him to be a tested and proven love, and not just the forced, automatic love of a puppet or robot. God was not interested in merely creating automatons. So He allowed His enemy Satan to enter the garden and tempt them.

Satan has no love for man. He was delighted with the opportunity to introduce to these creatures whom God loved both "evil" and "death." They listened to his lie, and much evil and death has been the result ever since...not only evil and death, but war and destruction. God knew, however, that a small portion of the world's population would throughout the ages (with the help of the Holy Spirit and the Word of God) be able to see the results of sin; they would repent, turn back to God, and become His children. And as we mentioned before, it was only a portion of God's original angels which rebelled, so God still has His forces. The main conflict of the ages here on earth has therefore been between God's kingdom and Satan's kingdom.

The Nature of This War

This conflict has always been basically a *spiritual* battle. Although God is creative, good, loving and beautiful, He also is holy and righteous, insisting on self-denial and obedience. Since Satan is a liar and a deceiver, he would seek to present his kingdom as good and helpful. But sooner or later every person will discover that it is destructive, painful and ugly. Satan's approach is to argue that holiness, self-denial and obedience are forms of bondage and slavery and are therefore best to be set aside and ignored. In fact in this modern age of evolution and humanism, any such ideas as seeking God's will and living for others are readily repudiated and strongly opposed. Lust, pride, self-indulgence, superstition and materialism are the seductive "sweets" which the enemy offers, and with these he has managed to lure the whole human race into his net. The results are always blindness, fear, and eventually death.

This would naturally mean the end of the spiritual life of planet earth, were it not for God's loving provision. He of course knew ahead of time what would take place, so in the counsels of the Godhead, the Son, the Lord Jesus, declared that He would come to earth and be born as a proper, complete and perfect human being. He would become the "second Adam," resisting all of Satan's tests, and give His life, the life of God, as atonement for the sins of those who would repent and turn back to God. Satan did all he could to destroy this plan, but it was executed perfectly, at infinite price, on the cross. Our Redeemer rose from the grave, has ascended back into heaven, and sits at the right hand of God as an effective mediator for all who believe and receive Him as their Savior and Lord.

The battle still rages, but now on a different plane. The Lord Jesus has sent His followers as His ambassadors into all parts of the world with the good news of what He has done, and one by one people's eyes are being opened to Satan's deceptions. They are turning to the truth, to this Savior, and are experiencing the new life, the peace and joy, which He gives.

Satan, to be sure, is extremely unhappy about this, so his attacks are now primarily directed against these, the Lord's emissaries. The more diligent and zealous they become, the more he turns his barrages toward them. The more they grow and mature spiritually, the more he hates them and attacks their homes, their service, and even their physical health. He is especially persistent in seeking to hinder and curtail their study of God's Word and their prayer life. But what makes Satan most violent is when one of the Lord's missionaries sets up camp in the heart of one of his domains where he has held control for many years, perhaps for several hundred years, such as in one of these idolatrous villages of Taiwan. A courageous warrior certainly needs to understand what he is about. He needs to proceed with caution. He needs to gird himself with "the whole armor of God." He needs to develop a strong devotional life. And above all, he needs a corps of heavy artillery behind the lines who, on his behalf, will pray every day, "Thy kingdom come; Thy will be done on earth [on this particular village battleground], as it is in heaven."

The book of Acts pictures such a battleground. The more that early company of believers moved ahead on their knees, filled with the Holy Spirit, and "turned the world upside down," the more the enemy cut them down, imprisoned them, scattered them, beat them, killed them and tempted them to sin...anything to stop them. And when some would grow weary and settle down to become just ordinary, passive Christians, he would back off with his attacks and use his *soothing* tactics to lull them to sleep.

But thank God, there have continued to this day those attack squadrons which refuse to taper off. They remain on the front lines. They are backed and supported by the faithful, earnest prayers of a corps of their brethren, and they are taking spoil from the enemy.

How to Pray "Thy Kingdom Come"

What, then, are we to comprehend as being involved in this prayer? To answer this question, we must first ask another. What is our area of vision? What portion (or perhaps portions) of this globe of ours has He especially laid on your heart? None of us could possibly pray for all the areas of need; there are far too many! If we spread ourselves too thin, we don't pray in depth for anything. Surely the Lord would have each of us to ask Him for that definite focus which He has for us. When we do this, we will want to gather all the information we can regarding that battlefield, as a "good soldier of Jesus Christ" would do, in order that our barrages will be well-placed.

Probably the first item which should concern us as we seek to see His kingdom come is the need for *workers*. This concern has always rested very heavily on the Lord's heart, and He would have it lie heavily on our hearts also. That day, after He had sent out His twelve disciples in pairs to the unreached villages to preach the gospel of His kingdom, He then gathered seventy more and sent them out as well (a total of eighty-two). He then further shared His heart's burden with the plea, "The harvest is plentiful, but the laborers are few; therefore *beseech* the Lord of the Harvest to send out laborers into His harvest" (Lk. 10:2).

Beseeching the Lord for workers naturally means calling upon Him for the *most suitable* workers for a particular project, those with the right gifts, personalities and strengths. It includes prayers for their support, their training, their vision and their passion for the rescue of Satan's captives. After they arrive on the field, there is much need for continued intercession for their health, their protection from the Evil One, their daily fellowship with the Lord, and their anointing and empowering by the Holy Spirit. Casualties on the battlefield are many!

The next item included in praying "Thy kingdom come" is for preparation of heart for the *captives* in the area of battle. You can be sure that Satan has their eyes blinded, their ears stopped up, their hearts dulled, and their attention occupied. Until all these shackles are removed, there is little hope of much penetration by the pleas of another kingdom.

After they are freed from these impediments, there is still

need for the conviction of the Holy Spirit. "When He comes, He will convict the world of guilt in regard to sin and righteousness and judgment" (Jn.16:8). Remember, it is only when the Holy Spirit is able to work in a life that there is hope of true deliverance, of salvation, of eternal life, and of being "transferred from the kingdom of darkness into the kingdom of light."

This deliverance usually does not come easily or readily. A helpful reminder is the Lord's instruction to Joshua, to have the entire army march around the city of Jericho each day for six days and then seven times on the seventh day. These heathen villages are walled strongholds just as Jericho was. It requires a mighty working of the power of God to pull down their unseen walls. Finally, we must add that, when we ask that "thy kingdom come," we must intercede much for the *new spiritual babies* which are brought to birth in these dark areas. The Evil One immediately begins to give them a hard time. Usually a mighty counterattack of persecution sets in from their friends and relatives. As they struggle with this, there often come attacks from Satan upon their bodies, their minds, their property, or their business. That old Dragon can become extremely vicious. They need your support. They need some heavy artillery to drive back this awful enemy.

In our twenty years of village teams working in the heathen areas of Taiwan, we have discovered that proper *follow-up* is still definitely the weakest link in the chain. During a week's work in a village, there may be a good number who honestly reach out to the Lord, with the help of a praying group of workers. But after the teams leave, the mortality rate is great.

In a recent ten-day outreach, with a concentration of nearly a hundred workers in one particular stronghold, 700 showed genuine interest in the Gospel and desired further help. However, as the rather weak follow-up proceeded over the next month, less than a dozen managed to associate themselves with the church. We are extremely grateful for these, and there will probably be others come along later, and there is much evidence of a softening toward the Gospel throughout the community, yet the statistics show that the enemy's clutches can hold hard and fast to his captives.

A further and yet vital plea is to request the Lord of Hosts, our Commander, to call forth intercessors who know how to resist, bind, and drive back the enemy even before the planned advances are made into his territory. We will give a whole chapter to the need for such heavy artillery later, but we must encourage you here to include all these insights when you cry to Him for the establishment of His kingdom in the midst of Satan's precincts.

Our Vital Part in the Coming of His Kingdom

The Scriptures speak of three phases of the coming of God's kingdom here on earth. The preliminary phase is when His kingdom is established in a particular human heart. The second phase is when His church is planted within one of Satan's strongholds. And the final phase will come when the Lord Jesus returns to our globe. He will set up His headquarters in Jerusalem, and will rule the entire earth for a thousand years, and will then construct a new heaven and a new earth. It is an amazing truth, and should be a tremendous challenge to us, to realize that God's kingdom will be planted on this earth, in each of these phases, as you and I ask that it be done.

The media today is very much taken up with the activities of the various nations of the world, and this, of course, is of true significance. But basically there are only two kingdoms which are in control of things. This was the primary lesson that Jesus sought to teach His disciples in that first lesson regarding prayer. Satan's kingdom is driven back, and his captives are transported from the kingdom of darkness into the kingdom of light, as you and I really learn how to pray "Thy kingdom come, Thy will be done on earth [in Peikang, in Mexico City, in Beruit, in Los Angeles] as it is in heaven."

Our God is not in a hurry. He has waited already for thousands of years, and will continue to wait as long as he sees fit, while His people join Him in this battle of bringing in His kingdom. It was way back in chapter 3 of Genesis that God promised to Adam and Eve that their seed would crush the head of the serpent. But time was not ripe for that until many millennia had passed, and the final consummation of this has still not taken place. A few chapters later, He promised to Abraham and his seed all the land from the Nile to the Euphrates. He even took special pains to repeatedly confirm this covenant to Abraham.

Yet even to this present time, Abraham's seed hold but a fraction of this territory, and for most of the ensuing 4,000 years they did not possess any of it. They spent 400 years in Egypt, and another forty years in the wilderness. Then, shortly after their wonderful take-over of a minor portion of their Promised Land, under Joshua's great leadership, they began to lose it again bit by bit, and lapsed into 400 years of pitiful darkness during the period of the Judges.

Finally David, a man after God's own heart, was appointed as their king, and they regained a bit more of their pledged domain. But within one generation they began to lose again, and were eventually driven out of their land, and even the final remnant was taken captive for seventy years. A small band returned to their homeland and gradually rebuilt things for a time, but everything still remained under the rule of foreign powers. In 70 A.D. the Romans demolished their land, and from then on, for nearly 2,000 years, they lived as a scattered people all over the world.

Less than fifty years ago, a tiny sector of their country was given back to them, but they have had nothing but hatred and attack from their neighbors ever since. And it is almost unbelievable, but true, that ever since their Messiah (the King of their kingdom) came, they, more than any other people on earth, have been His most bitter opponents.

But God is still waiting for them to turn around, and one day they will turn around. They will begin to see Him whom they pierced and will become His most zealous, spiritual warriors. In the meantime, the Lord is hoping and longing that the rest of His people will, as a result of all this, cry out with ever more earnestness, "Thy kingdom come!"

In the Psalms David writes, "The Lord says to my Lord:'Sit at my right hand until I make Your enemies a footstool for your feet.' The Lord will extend Your mighty scepter from Zion; You will rule in the midst of Your enemies" (Ps. ll0:l,2). Why has the Lord waited so long, in seeming disgrace, for us, His weak, blind people, to finally come to see something of what is taking place here on earth, and what *should* be taking place as a result of our involvement in prayer and outreach?

In the end, it is far more glorious for a king to "rule in the midst of his enemies," with the beauties of wisdom, grace and power, than just to annihilate all his opponents at their first offense. An astute and able king will "cause even the wrath of men to praise him" (Ps.71:10). Paul tells us, "God exalted Him to the highest place and gave Him the name that is above every name, that at the name of Jesus every knee should bow, in heaven and on earth and under the earth, and every tongue confess that Jesus Christ is Lord, to the *glory* of God the Father" (Phil. 2:9-11). There is not much glory when a tyrant executes all his enemies before ample opportunity has been given to substantiate before all observers who is righteous and who is unrighteous. Competent, artful rulers are never in a hurry, especially when matters of justice and integrity are at stake.

One day every living being will be forced to admit, by sheer weight of the truth, that the wisdom and patience and love of God were absolutely right! And it will all bring Him that glory which is due to His name. Won't it be wonderful, on that day, to be able to know that we were there with Him laboring and praying, "Thy Kingdom come!"?

3

PREPARING FOR BATTLE

As I was visiting with a friend who had just returned from a year abroad, he told me of a beautiful picture he had seen painted on the wall behind the pulpit in one of the churches he had attended. It was the scene of Mt. Calvary with its three crosses. At the foot of the center cross lay the body of a serpent with its head crushed. My friend indicated that the congregation much appreciated this scene because it gave them the relaxed feeling that Satan has been demolished and that we do not have to worry about him anymore.

It would be nice if this were really true. Our lives and our world would be very different if it were so. I myself lived most of my Christian life subconsciously assuming it to be true. But in recent years, as I have become involved in some "front line" missionary work in the villages of Taiwan, I am discovering that the real truth presents a far different picture. I am finding that the Evil One, the Adversary, is involved in a lot more situations than we tend to give him credit for. Sometimes we hear this fact belittled by comments about "those who would find the devil behind every bush." He may not hide in bushes, but he and his forces are certainly present and active wherever human life is found. "The whole world is under the control of the Evil One" (1 Jn. 5:19).

We are not contending that all the blame be put on Satan, for sometimes it is our own sinful flesh which is our enemy. (It is well to recognize, however, that Satan considers our sinful nature to be his best ally.) What we are seeking to do in this chapter is to open eyes and prepare hearts for the conflict which is continually going on around us, and which will increase in intensity as our Lord's return draws near. We will discuss more fully in later chapters the vast expanse and magnitude of the enemy's operations on our planet today, but for the moment let us return to that picture of Mt. Calvary. What actually was accomplished there?

The Lord Jesus completely defeated Satan when He gave His life on the cross. He ruined Satan's plans by purchasing our salvation. He divested Satan of all his authority, and when He descended into Hades, He released Satan's captives. Then He ascended to the Father's right hand where all authority in heaven and on earth was granted to Him. Yes, the Lord Jesus delivered the initial death blow to Satan's program on the cross, and from that point on his kingdom was doomed to ultimate destruction. Satan's head (all his claims and prerogative) was crushed. But Satan himself was by no means killed, abolished, or even immobilized. It will not be until the Lord Jesus returns to establish His millennial reign that Satan will be locked up in the bottomless pit. Even after that, he will be released for a period (Rev. 20:1-3). Finally he will be cast into the lake of fire forever (Rev. 20:7-10).

The Lord Jesus could of course have bound Satan and completely destroyed him that day when He overcame him on the cross, or at any other point in history, but our God always has very good reasons for doing things the way He does. We may not understand them all, but we can be sure that He has some good in mind for His children in everything He allows. He, for instance, would far rather allow you and me the opportunity to experience some spiritual warfare, to learn some things firsthand about the conflict that has been raging in His universe, to have a chance to grow up and develop our spiritual brawn and brain, than for us to experience only ease, comfort and pleasure. There will be an infinite supply of these in heaven for us to enjoy throughout eternity, but we couldn't appreciate it all unless we had this present opportunity for exposure to some of the dark background. It is very revealing to read in the first part of the third chapter of the Book of Judges, that the Lord left a great number of enemy nations in the land of Canaan "to teach warfare to the descendants of the Israelites who had not had previous battle experience."

When we stop to think about it, the Bible is truly a book of battles, wars, and unceasing conflict. The word "war" is used 500 times; "battle" 230 times; "enemy" 500 times; "sword" 500 times; "fight" 200 times; "power" 150 times; "shield" 80 times, etc. In fact, as soon as the story of creation is completed in the first two chapters of Genesis, the title of chapter three is "Enter the Serpent." And from then on it is battle. The song of Moses begins with the phrase, "The Lord is a warrior." Two hundred eighty times in the Old Testament, God is called "The Lord of *Hosts*." From the Old Testament prophets to the book of Revelation, it speaks of the armies of heaven. David's Psalms are full of military expressions, such as "You armed me with strength for the battle" (Ps.18:39), and "The chariots of God are tens of thousands and thousands of thousands" (Ps. 68:17).

When the Lord Jesus came to earth as that seemingly insignificant little infant lying in the manger of a lowly cattle shed, the battle moved up to a new level of ferocity. Those wise men from the East had little idea of the tremendous impact of their question, "Where is He who is born king of the Jews?" Not only did it inflame Herod the earthly ruler, but it absolutely terrified the unseen "Prince of this World." The King of Kings and Lord of Lords had arrived to begin the process of repossessing planet earth. At once the enemy's machinery was put in order to destroy Him. (The book of Revelation presents a graphic picture of how the "great red dragon" tried to devour the "man child") (Rev. 12:1-5). All the boy babies of the whole district were destroyed, but He escaped. And He continued to escape until the time came to win that astounding victory by submission to death on the cross. Since that time, His plan has been that the "Ruler of this World" would be progressively dethroned by His church. And there is no way that this can take place without heavy, persistent warfare.

We know our God is all-wise and all-powerful, and we sing "Jesus never fails," yet as we examine the Scriptures and church history, we discover more defeat than victory. Adam was created perfect, and placed in perfect surroundings. He had daily communion with God, and a very clear warning from God regarding the terrible sentence of sin. Yet, at his very first temptation, he fell. Israel, God's chosen people, had the oracles of God plus the covenant promises of Abraham, yet their history is that

of repeated failure and punishment. For instance, when the prophet Elijah was so discouraged with the awful state of affairs in his day, the Lord tried to comfort him by informing him that there were still 7,000 who had not bowed down to worship Baal. But even that remnant probably didn't amount to one out of a thousand of Israel's population. Even the church with its completed revelation, including the New Testament, passed through a thousand years of the Dark Ages, and today even in most so-called Christian nations there is only a small percent of the population who are true born-again believers. We are told that in some heathen countries there are not more than one in a million who know the God who made them and the Lord who bought them.

Why? How can we possibly face up to such facts? We know that there is no defeat or failure with God. There are really two areas where we must place blame. The first, of course, is upon our enemy, that old serpent Satan, and all his forces. But the second is upon ourselves, God's children who have been insufficiently aware of Satan's presence and his tactics and therefore insufficiently prepared to cope with his attacks. We have not yet developed a battle mentality. I fear that we have been more encouraged to seek *comfort* from God's Word than to observe and apply the *challenges* of His Word. Both are needed, of course. Only a happy, contented soldier is a strong soldier. One who is too preoccupied with the enemy or the obstacles can become morose and weak. On the other hand, Satan is delighted when we are taught that he has already been destroyed, that the battle is over, and there is no need for concern. An invisible enemy is at best hard enough to deal with. But when we are convinced that he does not even exist, or that he has already been put out of commission, he has gained tremendous advantage. Satan is clever, in fact downright crafty, at concealing his identity in the thick of the battle and in the face of the very ones he is mauling.

There is much in Scripture about being strong and receiving power from the Holy Spirit. But why do we need to be strong? Why do we need this power? Because we have an enemy; because we are in a *war*!! If it were not for the enemy and the battle, all would be serene and such terms as strength and power and authority would be extraneous. If we as Christians are living a thousand miles from the front lines, we are of course wondering why all the talk about war, battle and conflict? "I am not suffering any attacks from an enemy. I live a happy, 'victorious' Christian life." But our Lord desires us to become "front line soldiers," and in the process of taking the gospel into the darkness, to really learn what it means to "overcome." When the Lord Jesus sent out His disciples, He said to them, "I am sending you forth as sheep among wolves," but then He encouraged them to "fear not" and proceeded to tell them why.

While our Lord was Himself here on earth, He certainly maintained a battle mentality. When that storm came on the Sea of Galilee and threatened to destroy them, the Lord "rebuked" the wind. When they led Him into Peter's home, where the mother-in-law was sick, He also "rebuked" the fever. He knew their source. When Peter tried to dispense with the thought of the cross, the Lord's immediate reply was "Get behind me, Satan." He knew the origin of such thinking. When the Pharisees tried to condemn His words and actions, He shocked them by informing them that they were of their father the Devil. He knew He was always in the thick of the battle.

Salvation Meant to Include Enlistment

Coming now to Paul's letters to his young disciple Timothy, we find him strongly urging his "son" to prepare himself for hardship and not to get entangled so that he might please the One who had "*enlisted* him as a *soldier*" (2 Tim. 2:3,4). Sometimes we overlook the fact that on that day when we turned our lives over to Jesus Christ, we were enlisted into His army! Satan surely didn't overlook this truth. He took down our name and address, and filed it carefully in his list of deserters, and ordered his intelligence to keep an eye on us to see how dangerous to his cause we might become!

Paul was desirous that Timothy might become very dangerous to Satan's domain. In the first chapter of his first letter, he writes, "This charge I give you...that you might wage a good warfare." Then again in the last chapter, he repeats it, "Fight the good fight of the faith." We have already looked at the appeal in his second letter, but we must not forget how he closes that letter:

"I have *fought* the good *fight*, I have finished the race, I have kept the faith." In summing up his life, item number one is his continual conflict with the adversary. Like the Lord Jesus, Paul possessed a battle mentality.

Perhaps before we go further, we should note that in every case Paul calls it a good fight, or good warfare, or being a good soldier. Ordinarily we consider war, fighting, battle and conflict all to be very negative, painful and wasteful occupations which we do our best to avoid. They conjure up visions of destruction and death, but Paul would have us understand that in the spiritual realm it is worth it all a thousand times over. For it means the deliverance of bound and blinded captives. It means beauty for ashes. It means a restoration of love, joy, peace and goodness where once dwelt sin, darkness, hate, self-centeredness and hopelessness.

In Taiwan and in many other countries today, every young man when he turns eighteen must be enlisted for training as a soldier. When I turned eighteen as a student at the University of California, I was also summoned, but it was discovered that I had a heart problem and could not undergo the rigors of boot camp. However I was still involved in the preparation of munitions. Every nation must have its standing army, equipped for active service, and the Lord's kingdom is no exception.

On the night before the Lord Jesus went to the cross, He gave His disciples a special, final warning. He first asked them, "When I sent you out with no purse or bag or sandals, did you lack anything? They replied. "Nothing." Then He said to them, "*But now*, if you have a purse, take it, and also a bag, and if you don't have a *sword*, sell your cloak and buy one" (Lk. 22:35,36). He was informing them that funds and equipment would be required in the Lord's work, but most of all, they needed a sword. Even if they had to sell their shirt to buy one, they couldn't get anywhere without a sword. He wasn't referring to a sword made of steel, for a little later that evening, when Peter sliced off the right ear of the high priest's servant, the Lord rebuked him. But in this passage we need to see and hear the Lord Jesus striving to convince us that His death on the cross far from rendered the enemy powerless. Rather, it made him a hundred times more furious. Therefore, as they went forth with the gospel, they were to be prepared for a pitched battle. The Holy Spirit had this all recorded for our benefit. We are to proceed with the Word of God in one hand, and a sword in the other.

Nehemiah's experience in rebuilding the wall of the Holy City is a helpful picture of this battle concept of our Christian life and service: "From that day on, half of my men did the work, while the other half were equipped with spears, shields, bows and armour. The officers posted themselves behind the people of Judah who were building the wall. Those who carried materials did their work with one hand and held a weapon in the other, and each of the builders wore his sword at his side as he worked. But the man who sounded the trumpet stayed with me. Then I said to the nobles, the officials and the rest of the people, 'The work is extensive and spread out, and we are widely separated from each other along the wall. Wherever you hear the sound of the trumpet, join us there. Our God will fight for us!' So we continued the work with half the men holding spears, from the first light of dawn till the stars came out. At that time I also said to the people, 'Have every man and his helper stay inside Jerusalem at night, so they can serve us as guards by night and workmen by day.' Neither I nor my brothers nor any men nor the guards with me took off our clothes; each had his weapon, even when he went for water" (Neh. 4:16-23).

One of the elements we observe in this passage is that the people were occupied in widely different facets of the project, yet each carried a weapon. Some were even altogether involved in guard duty. Now let your imagination work for a moment on the consideration of what would have been the result if everyone just ignored the enemy...if they posted no guards; if no one carried a weapon and all just worked happily on the building. The whole picture of Nehemiah's cautions is further strengthened by the fact that even after the wall was finished, and the gates were securely installed, he still posted guards around the clock (7:1-3). It could well have been that Nehemiah's strong cautions came from his reflections on what had happened to Israel when they slacked off after Joshua's great victories. As a result, they entered that despicable 400-year period of defeat and darkness...the period of the Judges.

The prophet Isaiah prophesied that the Messiah would come

as "The Prince of Peace." Yet at His first coming, that Prince of Peace announced in no uncertain terms, "Do not suppose that I have come to bring peace to the earth. I did not come to bring peace but a sword" (Mt. 10:34). There were many things about Jesus' years here on earth which seemed so contrary to that which was predicted about the Messiah that His disciples were continually baffled, and the Jews as a whole rejected Him. With all their centuries of study of the Old Testament, they never managed to come up with the distinction between His two appearings. Actually, they didn't want to. They couldn't seem to bear the thought of a suffering Messiah. They wanted only the instant, glorious victory, without all the painful battles to bring about that victory. We tend to be the same. We are eager for the victorious, abundant Christian life, forgetting that victory implies battle, and that battle implies involvement in danger

Soldiers in Service Must Avoid Entanglements

Returning now to Paul's counsel to Timothy, we read: "No soldier in active service entangles himself in the affairs of everyday life." Or, as another translation puts it: "As Christ's soldier, do not let yourself *become tied up* in worldly affairs." This is a much needed warning for all of us. It should frequently become a trumpet sound in our ears, whenever we begin to allow ourselves to "become tied up." Here again Paul is using warfare language. If an enemy can use a trap or a snare or a net to capture his opponent, he can chalk up another victory. And our enemy is incredibly skilful in his use of such methods.

In order for a snare to be effective, it must be hidden or at least not obvious. This, of course, is exactly the kind Satan uses. He has a whole assortment of traps and nets, which Paul labels here as "the affairs of everyday life." We all must be involved to a certain extent in such matters, so we hardly notice when Satan strings up a few more, and then a few more, until we are completely immobilized. And this is exactly the picture some Christians would see of themselves, if they had the time to get away alone some place and take a good look at just how "entangled" they really are. One sees this happening over and over again. No wonder Satan can manage to hold on so securely to all his dark, heathen areas, if he can so easily immobilize the Lord's soldiers. He has them so occupied with "important," "essential" duties that they aren't even aware there is a battle going on.

An example of this is a family of new neighbors who moved in next door to us when we were living in Tainan. They were new Christians and very eager to get involved in Bible study. Since they had just arrived in Taiwan, they knew very few people and were not yet involved in any community activities. So, as the husband said, "We have plenty of free time, and would like to set up a thorough course of study in God's Word." We helped them get started, but would you believe it? Within about ten days they had become so busy in "the affairs of this life" that the Bible study just fell by the wayside.

Early in the book of Acts, Satan did his best to get the Lord's apostles all tied up in some knotty problems. He brought about a bad case of friction between two cliques of widows in the assembly and the matter was brought to "the twelve." The disciples refused to deal with it, replying "It would be a grave mistake for us to neglect the Word of God in order to wait at table. Therefore, friends, look out seven men of good reputation from your number, men full of the Spirit and of wisdom, and we will appoint them to deal with these matters, while we devote ourselves to prayer and to the ministry of the Word" (Acts 6:2-4).

This may at first seem like just passing the buck to someone else. But there is an important principle involved here. You and I should accept *only* those responsibilities which we are certain that the Lord of our life would have us accept. Otherwise He is not the Lord of our life. This is why I as His soldier (if I am to be a "good" and effective soldier), must have frequent periods of waiting on Him to get my orders from Him. There are many problems in the Lord's work which have to be dealt with. But the great question is: "Am *I* the one the Lord would have to handle this matter?" A good soldier is not lazy, for there is always plenty of front-line activity. But a good soldier is very cautious to see that he doesn't get caught in a snare and become incapacitated. Our gifts and ministries are all different, and I must be slow to pick up another's assignment and try to carry it.

In the very first parable which the Lord spoke, His strongest warning was to those who allow "the cares of this life, the de-

ceitfulness of wealth and the desire for other things to come in and choke the Word, making it unfruitful." He likened such a life to a plant growing among thorns. The indication or application of such a message is naturally to encourage us to be on the alert for every little sprig of thorn that pokes its head up through the soil and uproot it immediately. This I find I have to do continually, or else the thorn patch soon takes over. A good soldier must be *taught* in the principles of war, and allow nothing to choke the Word.

Dave Wilkerson, the author of *The Cross and the Switchblade*, begins his book with a very moving testimony of how he became "unentangled," and what an exciting difference it made in his life and the lives of many others. His habit had been to watch T.V. every night from 10 p.m. until midnight, after the rest of the family had gone to bed. But one evening he began to consider what a difference it might make in his ministry if he used those two hours each evening for prayer. In order to test the idea to see if it was really the Lord's will, he decided to place an ad in the paper offering his T.V. for sale. His decision was that if the T.V. were sold by 9:30 p.m. the following night, this would indicate the Lord's will to go ahead with his plan. There were no calls all that day or evening to ask about it, but at 9:29 the phone rang, and an interested party said he would buy it sight unseen!

From that time on, Dave began nightly vigils of earnest prayer to the Lord, and very soon God gave him a concern for the gangs of New York City. This set off a mighty battle which has, through the years, resulted in hundreds and hundreds of amazing victories.

A SOLDIER

A soldier, Lord! Afresh I hear Thy call
To separate from things of earth, and all
That would entangle; thus, with single aim,
To aid Thy cause and bear Thy glorious name;
Then bring me forth to join the battle line,
Free from the world, O Lord, and wholly Thine.

The Lord's Forces Need Tough Marines

In his commission to Timothy, that old warrior Paul put it straight from the shoulder. "Suffer hardship with me as a good soldier of Jesus Christ," he challenged. And this is all recorded for your benefit and mine. When Paul said "Suffer hardship *with me*," Timothy knew what he was talking about. When the old "general" was forced to compare himself with the other apostles, he wrote, "I have worked much harder, been in prison more frequently, been flogged more severely, and been exposed to death again and again. Five times I received from the Jews the forty lashes minus one. Three times I was beaten with rods; once I was stoned; three times I was shipwrecked; I spent a night and a day in the open sea. I have been constantly on the move. I have been in danger from rivers, in danger from bandits, in danger from my own countrymen, in danger from Gentiles, in danger in the city, and in danger in the country, in danger at sea, and in danger from false brothers. I have labored and toiled, and have often gone without sleep; I have known hunger and thirst and have often gone without food. I have been cold and naked, etc. etc." (2 Cor. 11:23-27). All this was in the line of battle.

We also observe that the heros of faith in Hebrews 11 were tough marines. "And what more shall I say? I do not have time to tell about Gideon, Barak, Sampson, Jephtha, David, Samuel and the prophets, who through faith conquered kingdoms, administered justice, and gained what was promised; who shut the mouths of lions, quenched the fury of the flames, and escaped the edge of the sword; whose weakness was turned to strength, and who became powerful in battle, and routed foreign armies. Women received back their dead raised to life again. Others were tortured and refused to be released, so that they might gain a better resurrection. Some faced jeers and flogging, while still others were chained and put in prison. They were stoned; they were sawed in two; they were put to death by the sword. They went about in sheepskins and goatskins, destitute, persecuted and mistreated. The world was not worthy of them. They wandered in deserts, in mountains, and in caves and holes in the ground.

These were all commended for their faith, yet none of them received what had been promised. *"God had planned something*

better for us so that only together with us would they be made perfect" (Heb.11:32-40).

Now, just what is this "better" thing that God has in mind for us?

Is it a different kind of life...the "good life" without all that fight and warfare? That doesn't seem to be what the author is indicating. His next chapter begins: *"Therefore,* since we are surrounded by such a great cloud of witnesses, let us throw off everything that hinders, and the sin that so easily entangles and let us run with perseverance the race marked out *for us.* Let us fix our eyes on Jesus, the author and perfecter of our faith, who for the joy set before Him, endured the cross, scorning its shame, and sat down at the right hand of the throne of God. Consider Him who endured such opposition from sinful men, so that you will not grow weary and lose heart. In your *struggle* against sin, you have not yet *resisted* to the point of shedding your blood" (Heb. 12:1-11).

Actually, it would seem that the "better" thing that God has in mind for us is an even more noble and courageous warfare than those Old Testament saints exemplified. Many of them had very little of God's Word to support their faith. We have all of the Old Testament, and all of the New Testament, plus the special presence of the Holy Spirit. Therefore, it is only reasonable that God would expect better (greater) attainments in battle from us. The obvious question is, is He seeing what He is looking for in my life? How effective have I been in the battle?

In his autobiography, Bob Vernon tells of the inner and outer conflicts involved as he gradually and painfully worked his way up from a rookie cop to finally become the Assistant Chief of the Los Angeles Police Department. He dreaded each shift into a new division, for it meant a whole new set of crimes and problems to be dealt with. But in the end it was easy to see that all this confrontation with the craft and meanness of the enemy was absolutely essential if he were to learn how to combat evil.

So it is with you and me. We hate war! All this exposure to the enemy's forces is distasteful and unpleasant, and at times the battle becomes tragic and terribly destructive. But the true Christian life is a battle. There is no getting around this. The enemy exists; he is there. He crucified our Lord, and he is out to crucify

you if you are like your Lord. But praise God, there is victory to
be had.

"Let us fix our eyes on Jesus, the author and perfecter of our
faith, who for the *joy* set before Him endured the cross." The
Lord Jesus overcame Satan on that cross, and you and I can overcome him too. As a result of the cross, salvation was purchased
for all those Satan has led into sin. And as a result of our cross,
our conflict, many of those for whom the Lord Jesus died will
know about His death, His love, His victory, and they will be led
out of the kingdom of darkness into the kingdom of His marvelous light. Therefore we can sing with confidence and determination such words as: "Forth to the mighty conflict, against
unnumbered foes, let courage rise with danger, and strength to
strength oppose."

You and I may not be called upon to endure the same kind
of hardship and warfare that Paul and those other heroes of faith
met with. But if and when we set ourselves for earnest prayer and
supplication for the deliverance of the captives in Satan's domain, the arrows will begin to fly and the bombs will begin to
fall. Such intercession is a declaration of war against that old serpent, the Devil, and we must be prepared for battle. Do not forget, though, there will come wonderful results!

One day we will hear the trumpet sound, and that announce-
ment from heaven, "The kingdom of the world has become the
kingdom of our Lord, and of His Christ, and He will reign forever and ever." This will be the grand commencement of *phase
three*, the inauguration of the King of Kings and Lord of Lords,
when earth's enemy, that old dragon Satan, who brought all this
grief to our earth, will be bound with all his forces and cast into
the bottomless pit. Then our warfare will all be over, and we, the
Lord's soldiers, will begin a new regime of ruling and reigning
with Him.

4

THE ROAR OF THE LION

"Be sober, be watchful. Your adversary the Devil prowls around like a roaring lion, seeking someone to devour. Resist him, firm in your faith" (1 Pet. 5:8,9).

"Woe to you, O earth and sea, for the Devil has come down to you in great wrath, because he knows that his time is short!" (Rev. 12:12).

In his revelation of the end times, John would have us to understand that in these last days Satan's attacks against God's work and God's soldiers will become increasingly fierce, because he knows his time is short. Evidences of this buildup of the enemy's forces are apparent all over the world. But there are certain areas where his ravages seem to be particularly awesome, and Taiwan is one of these. Taiwan is an island, and it is strikingly significant to notice that John's prophecy rather pointedly draws our attention to the devil's attacks on the "sea." The Scriptures give us no suggestion that Satan has any particular interest in the ocean as such, but his strategy for some reason does seem to be focused more and more on some of these East Asian islands. Perhaps it is because they have afforded him such devout worship for so many centuries.

The explosive spread of idolatrous fever on this island of Taiwan during the last couple of decades is almost unbelievable. Shortly after I arrived here thirty years ago, the largest idol in the world was built on Pa Kua Hill right in the center of the island. Then, just a few years later, an even larger "Buddha" was put up just within a few blocks of where we were living. We must realize that these are far more than tourist attractions. They are visited mostly by caravans of ardent worshippers.

A few years ago, the *China Post* reported that a million pilgrims attended the frenzied celebration of the birthday of the goddess Matzu in Peikang. The next year the report was three million. This is one sixth of the entire population of this island. Recently when one of our village workers made a survey of that area, he reported that many of those living in the city are suffering from either physical or emotional illness. A month later, when he and his family moved there to begin a gospel ministry, they all, within twenty-four hours, became so ill they had to be taken for emergency treatment at the Christian hospital in Chiayi twenty-five miles away. They were in Peikang for two years and suffered almost continuous attack from the enemy. And when the student teams go out for their summer and winter ministries into such villages, there is often severe attack upon the families of the leaders of the group.

Heathen festivals are becoming so numerous and so elaborately celebrated, that several times recently, returning home from a meeting at night to the village where I live, masses of idolatrous worshippers have been so congested on the roads that it was impossible to drive. I had to park my car on the other side of the village and walk home, squeezing my way through the crowds.

It used to be that Thailand was known as the most idolatrous country in the world because it had the greatest number of temples. But in the last few years there have been constructed on this island so many new centers of idol worship that they now outnumber Thailand's. Yet Thailand is five times as large as Taiwan. There are now reported to be over 20,000 heathen temples in Taiwan, an average of one for every square mile (two square km.). Of course it is not just an even spread, for about half of Taiwan is rather uninhabited, mountainous terrain. And even in the plains, some areas are more densely populated than others. So in these more crowded regions the concentration of temples is unbelievable. For instance, in this village where we live, there are three large temples and several smaller ones. The idol carving business is booming at an all-time high, and shops for selling worship paraphernalia are seen everywhere. One Chinese scholar has now declared that "Taiwan folk religion is diffused in every corner of the life of the people."

It is true that an idol in itself is nothing, but we are repeatedly warned in Scripture that these are representative of mighty forces: "principalities," "powers," "world rulers of this present darkness," "spiritual hosts of wickedness in heavenly places" (Eph. 6:12). One speaker who travels all over the world holding special evangelistic meetings in various places mentioned that he feels an uncanny oppression when he comes to this island.

We (1,000 missionaries in Taiwan) can and should encourage ourselves in every gain we see in our church planting efforts in this country, but to be realistic, we (and our 2,500 churches) must admit that the kingdom of darkness is outstripping us ten to one. A few years ago when I was travelling with three fellow missionaries to a country village to attend a prayer meeting for the village work, the clutch cable broke on our car, and we were stranded on the side of the road. While we were waiting and hoping for someone to come by to tow us in, along passed *thirty bus loads* of Buddhist pilgrims on their way to visit the big shrine in Taichung. As I stood there, I could see the whole affair as a clear picture of the situation on this island. Satan's forces are moving along in huge caravans, with little hindrance, while the Lord's people are for the most part standing in little groups along the side of the road.

The Lion's Roar

When Peter described our adversary as a roaring lion, he particularly chose the most vicious beast he could think of. And when he used the verb "devour," he intended to present as strong a warning as possible. He was not just trying to frighten us, but he surely was doing his best to get our attention and move us to concern and consequent action.

Why does a lion roar? An Old Testament Scripture tells us quite clearly why he roars. "Does a lion roar in the thicket when he has no prey? Does he growl in his den when he has caught nothing?" (Amos 3:4). The implication, then, is that the lion roars when he has found some victim to devour. And here in Taiwan he is steadily devouring one after another!

Recently the *China Post* carried an article stating that 20% of the pastors of village churches have given up their work and left. Many others are so discouraged and dejected that they are about ready to leave. But it is not only the villages. When I was in Hsinchu awhile back, I was told that there are now 300 temples in that city, whereas seven of the struggling churches are without pastors. While there I visited with a missionary who travels all over the island, and he observed that many of the churches on Taiwan are growing smaller rather than larger. In a recent survey of the country districts ("hsiang"...areas which include several villages), many are listed as having no church at all, and in those which have only one church, it was discovered that most of these have closed their doors and were no longer meeting.

For some years now, casualties have been particularly alarming among pastors and missionaries attempting to do evangelism among the Hakka and Taiwanese, which are the most idolatrous groups on the island. Several of the missionaries have become so ill they have had to leave the field, and Chinese pastors have met with serious accidents or catastrophes in their families. It is not only a matter of village churches closing down, however. Even in the larger cities where many churches are still functioning, an unusual number of God's people are struggling with discouragement and depression.

Yes, the lion is roaring here in Taiwan. He is devouring his victims right and left, and the sooner we face up to what is really happening, the sooner we will take our weapons down off the wall, polish and sharpen them, and begin to use them.

Resist Him

When the Lord Jesus taught His disciples to pray "Deliver us from evil," or as most translations have it, "Deliver us from the Evil One," He had considerably more in mind than just teaching them to resist sin in a general way. That model prayer, which some call "The Lord's Prayer," was meant to be an outline for a life of prayer, not just a twenty-second recitation.

A little later on, He presented to them (and us) a very basic principle to any church planting effort, or to any attempt at evan-

gelism for that matter. He said, "How can anyone enter a strong man's house and carry off his property, unless he *first* binds the strong *man*? And then he will plunder his house" (Mt. 12:29).

It was about four years ago that our Village Gospel Mission began to consider the possibility of establishing a second outreach center in the city of Peikang. A small church there had invited one of our families to come and help. One evening I was discussing this matter with one of our co-workers, and I shall never forget his conclusion. He summed it up this way: "If we can manage sufficient prayer backing to support the work there, then we can move ahead. But if we don't have enough prayer artillery to drive back the enemy, it will be disastrous to go in. For Peikang is probably the darkest, most idolatrous of all Satan's strongholds on this island." After a few more months of deliberations and seeking the Lord's leading, we finally decided to encourage brother Lin to move to Peikang and begin to work there. We have already mentioned above the crisis he and his family experienced as soon as they arrived in the city and their harrassments ever since.

The Lord Jesus Himself several times called Satan a "strong man." And until his forces are bound, no amount of effort, planning, strategy or clever technique on our part will accomplish much. Another pastor who labored in Peikang for many years finally labeled the place as "impossible." After a couple of decades of work, the little church had seven people attending. But the purpose of this book is not just to present the negative side of the picture. Our Lord is a victorious Lord, and He intends that we become His victorious witnesses. The title of this book reads *Tearing Down Strongholds*, and that is the confident stance we must always take. After Peter gives us the sound warning regarding this roaring lion, he then urges us to *resist him.*.

Although we as yet may not be meeting with too much success in our defense and offense against the enemy here in Taiwan, there are some very encouraging examples of victory in battle in other places, so let us take a look at one of these.

Last year the pastor of a rather mediocre church in southern California handed in his resignation and left. The congregation, after some looking about, invited another man to come as the leader of their flock. He was a very wise and godly man, so one of the first things he did was to invite the elders, deacons, Sunday School teachers, youth director, and the other leaders of the church to a retreat for a couple of days up on a hill overlooking the city. There they gave themselves to evaluating the condition of the church, and to seeking the Lord as to what He had in mind for their future. As a conclusion, they decided that the pastor and the elders should take a two-week trip to Korea to observe first-hand the principles of growth in the churches there. Here is one spot where things are definitely moving head. There is no decline of church growth in Korea.

After their return, the pastor made his report, and the part which impressed him the most was that portion of Korean church life which is given to prayer. We have all heard many times of the praying Christians in Korea—of their early morning prayer vigils, their prayer mountain, prayer chapels, prayer caves, prayer chains, etc. But the activity which moved him more than all else was their regular Wednesday night prayer meetings. In the church which he visited there were about 10,000 in attendance on Wednesday evening. They began at 7:30 p.m., and the first item was three sessions of teaching from the Word of God, one hour each, by three different pastors. At 10:30 p.m. they began six hours of testimonies. The Lord is always doing so many wonderful things for them all that everyone seemed to have a thrilling account of some recent, marvelous victory. This, of course, was a beautiful preparation for their three hours of prayer from 4:30 a.m. to 7:30 a.m. At 7:30 they all left to go to work, and the students to get to school. Every Wednesday evening they just planned to spend the whole night at church in the prayer service. No wonder the "strong man" is bound! No wonder he has so little chance of holding things back in that kind of atmosphere. No wonder church growth is a vital reality in such a land!

Now thanks be to God who is also causing us to see the beginnings of the same kind of "resisting" the devil here in Taiwan. I serve on the board of two different retreat facilities here on this island, and I am delighted to report that both of these are now being used more and more for prayer retreats. Recently several churches have brought their leaders to one of these camps for

days of fasting and prayer. At the other camp, several student groups have had their first experiments in fasting and prayer. You can be sure that we will see fruit from such activity.

Firm in Faith

There is still one more part of Peter's instruction which we must consider here. He said *"Resist him, firm in your faith."* Let us never forget that "faith" in Scripture always means faith in someone other than ourselves. It means faith in someone stronger than ourselves. In Luke 11:21,22, we read "When a strong man, fully armed, guards his own palace, his goods are in peace." This should be a great challenge and rebuke to us. As long as Satan's forces remain fully armed here in Taiwan, he guards all these village areas which are "his own palace," which he has held for centuries, and "his goods are in peace." It should really shame us that we have allowed him such total and complete reign in so much of this country, for so long. For it need not be so!

The next verse begins with a "but." *"But* when one stronger assails him and overcomes him, he takes away his armor in which he trusted, and divides his spoil." "But when." When you and I, like our advancing brothers in Korea, really get involved in militant prayer, *then* "one stronger than he" comes into the picture. And by the way, this title of the Lord Jesus, "The Stronger One," is one of His *names* which is very appropriate to employ in such offensive praying.

Now let us also note what happens when this "Stronger One" enters the scene. He accomplishes four things. He assails him; he launches an attack; then he overcomes him. Satan doesn't have a chance, for that old serpent has already been divested of any real authority by the cross. The next thing the Lord will do is to "take away his armor in which he trusted." Without the removal of Satan's armor and weapons, it can be dangerous for you and me to enter his territory and attempt to establish God's kingdom. But praise God, the fourth thing He will do is to divide Satan's spoil. There will be those whose eyes will be opened, whose ears will be unstopped, who will begin to comprehend the gospel and receive it, and leave Satan's dark domain.

They will enter God's kingdom of light and life and love. Satan's spoils will be divided.

When we learn how to effectively use our Lord's names and attributes in such militant prayer, we are sure to see some breakthroughs. Paul encourages us that "At the name of Jesus every knee shall bow, in heaven, on earth, and under the earth" (Phil. 2:10).

Introducing the "Prayer Companion"

Perhaps this is the place to introduce the "Worship and Warfare" prayer material which is a companion item to this book. As students begin to develop their prayer life, they are often faced with the very practical problem of *how* to profitably and effectively spend a prolonged period of time in prayer and intercession. Most of us are not ready for a whole night of prayer or even an hour in prayer! We must grow into this prayer warfare step by step.

One set of materials which has been a great help to many is this companion called "Worship and Warfare." It consists mainly of the names and attributes of God, along with many of His promises and other helpful supports to faith and vision. It is designed to create great confidence and expectancy as we approach the throne of our mighty and loving Heavenly Father, and our resurrected, victorious Lord Jesus. It contains some forty-four pages of practical material, most of it directly from the Scriptures, to be digested bit by bit in unhurried meditation, then applied to the various situations we are wrestling with in prayer.

It should be mentioned that this material is only a starter companion to help you get under way on this rewarding adventure of victorious, militant prayer. You will want to be adding to it from your own daily Bible study.

In conclusion, let us return to Peter's first words in the passage we have been studying. "Be *sober*, be *alert*, for your adversary the Devil prowls around like a roaring lion, seeking someone to devour." Peter hoped that a consideration of the wrath, might and fierceness of our enemy would be very sobering to us, and keep us alert and always in full battle array against his ploys, his attacks, and his strongholds.

As you begin to undertake specific exploits in your spiritual warfare, may you see many specific accomplishments and the dividing of Satan's spoils. And as a special encouragement of the magnificent working of God's marvelous grace and power when we do undertake such exploits, we close this chapter with the personal account of one of the victories won from the stronghold of Manchou, near Hengchun in the southern tip of the island, during the summer of 1985.

Testimony of Mr. Lin, Taoist Priest and Spirit Medium

For over twenty years, I served in Manchou as Taoist Priest and Spirit Medium, but look at what my gods gave me! Only sickness and ill health. Although I performed healings in many cities in Taiwan, still I could not heal myself. Everyone knew who I was. Every year in Fengshan, when all the Taoist priests gathered for their annual meeting, I represented all forty of the other priests in Manchou. I regularly attended other annual conventions, and every three years when Manchou held their huge Taoist festival, I was always one of the top leaders. Formerly, I isolated myself in an extended fast and afterwards ascended the ladder of 108 swords, and communicated with the top god of the Taoist religion. I was put in charge of teaching seven other priests. So, because of all this, many of the Taoist gods gave me their approval. I knew a lot about the Taoist gods, but what I didn't know for sure was whether they were really good or not. I had read many religious books, including Buddhist, Taoist, and other religions...I studied over fifty of them. I had special powers so that I could see where I was going with my eyes closed. I heard the leading Taoist god speak to me on nine occasions. I was given special means of performing supernatural acts.

But all during these more than twenty years of serving them, my gods did not protect me or keep me from sickness. I was constantly ill. My body suffered greatly in the ceremonies where I walked without pain on knives and nails and abused my body in many countless ways. I constantly lost much blood, until my body was drained of energy. But others were unaware of my misery. The gods were heartless and cruel. When they possessed me I was full of strength, but as soon as they left, I was limp and weak. In 1983 during a big festival, I was ill in the hospital in Tainan, but they still sought me out to come to Manchou and perform.

This year, after the Chinese New Year season, although I no longer stayed in the hospital, for a period of three months I constantly visited this clinic and that clinic, spending a lot of money trying to find help for my sick body. My mother took sick as well, and we tried to care for each other. In mid-March we decided to try the Heng Chun Christian Hospital clinic. Then one night, on the evening of June 17, I had such a bad attack of asthma that I couldn't breathe. At 10 p.m. I went to the emergency room at the Christian Hospital. Dr. Cheng was very kind to me that night. He put me in the hospital, and during those days when I was dizzy, could scarcely breathe, and often didn't know what was going on around me, the nurses were all very kind to me. The second day I was in the hospital, my second son returned from the Air Force Academy and came to visit me. We discussed my will and many things of the past, and my son couldn't keep from crying. My oldest son seemed unmoved by my sickness. I told him to go out and buy poison so I could take my life.

On the eleventh day, one of the nurses asked me if I wanted to become a Christian. I agreeably said "yes," but no one guessed that this Taoist priest really wanted to become a Christian. A few days later, that same nurse asked me again if I wanted to make a real decision to receive Christ. Again I said "yes." She led me in prayer, sentence by sentence, and the next day another nurse came and taught me to pray. The doctors and nurses continued to reach out to me in loving ways day by day.

Five days later, Caleb and Suzie Chen came to visit me, and I told them my story and asked them if it was possible for a priest to become a Christian! The next day their co-worker, Mr. Chu, came to see me and I related to him the vision I had the night before:

I saw in a vision my special god come to me and say, "You must not become a Christian! In the past you have had much power. Even Christians have to see a doctor when they are sick."

But I didn't listen to him; I believed what they had told me at the hospital. Suddenly there appeared many spirits together in the room, threatening and disturbing me. But behind me a bright light shone, and when I looked around to see it better, it was gone, and so were the evil spirits.

Another five days later, during my noon nap, I had a dream. I dreamed my spirit left my body and went into the desert. I saw many people kneeling there. I asked, "Why are you kneeling here?", but no one answered me. Then there appeared a bright light again, and in the light I saw a prince, but before I could get a good look at him he was gone. Then I looked behind me, and there was the head nurse of the hospital. She said, "Follow this light, and you will not go wrong." But when she had spoken, the light disappeared, and also all the rest of the people. I felt I was falling into a deep ocean. I saw my special god riding a white horse, coming to save me. He lifted me up and took me to Hell. When we arrived at the seventh level, those there said to me, "You have already believed in Jesus; you don't belong to us any-more; you cannot come here." I answered them, "I have come here many times before; why can't I come now?" These people then got ready to kill me. Suddenly there appeared in my hand a sword, and I began to fight with them. When I was almost done in, the nurse awakened me to take my blood pressure. She asked me why I was breathing so hard. I told her I had had a nightmare. She said, "Do not be afraid; God is in this place."

The time came when I was fully convinced that Christianity was the truth. Although it has no visual images or god, I know that this light is the true light. I made my decision to follow Christ and become a Christian. I was determined to ignore the gods I had worshipped, but I was afraid I would not be able to ig-nore the people I had served. They had supported me all these years to be their priest and representative, and now I had turned to Christ. What would be their reaction? I talked these things over with Pastor Chen.

Jesus showed me that I should be baptized in the hospital on July 5, 1985. Why in the hospital? Because there I could give my testimony before all the other patients. That afternoon I was re-leased from the hospital, rested one day, and then on Sunday came to church to give my testimony. That day I took an important step; I destroyed all the idols in my home...the process took four hours to complete!

****

Mr. Lin is now with the Lord. After giving this testimony, he continued to suffer from sickness and bodily weakness, but God gave him boldness to take his stand for Christ and delivered him from fear of people and their reactions. After several months of glowing witness to all his acquaintances, God took him to his heavenly home to live with Him.

5

INTELLIGENCE REGARDING
THE ENEMY

Every army has its intelligence division. It needs to know all it can about the enemy's placement, weaponry, strategy, tactics, etc. Only an informed military knows where it is going and what it is doing. So it is in our spiritual warfare. Paul wrote, "I do not run aimlessly, I do not fight as one beating the air" (1 Cor. 9:26). And again, "...to keep Satan from gaining the advantage over us...we are not ignorant of his designs" (2 Cor. 2:11).

In our spiritual encounters, the enemy and all his forces are totally invisible, which complicates things for us tremendously and gives him a great advantage to start with. In fact there are those who even doubt his existence. Others, granting that he exists, still haven't begun to conceive of how deeply entrenched he is in this world of ours, nor have they any conception of the seriousness of his involvements.

The Scope of Satan's Activity

Three times the Lord Jesus acknowledges Satan to be "The Ruler of this World." Paul calls him "The God of this World," and another time, "The Prince of the Power of the Air." John labels him as "The Deceiver of the *Whole World*," and in another place declares that "the *whole world* is under the control of the Evil One."

These statements not only portray the magnitude of the intrusion of this enemy, but they set our minds reeling, wondering how God's people could ever have allowed such an invasion to come about. In the parable of the tares, the Lord Jesus gives us some insights into the latter question. He says that it is while people are *sleeping* that the enemy has his chance to sow his evil seeds. It would therefore seem that there has been an excessive amount of "sleeping" among God's people through the centuries.

The scope of Satan's activity should move us to do more, however, than merely wonder how it all could have reached such a state. Now we need to hear what the Lord Jesus says we are to do about it. He tells us that we who have been so privileged to hear the gospel of salvation and be delivered from the kingdom of darkness into His kingdom of light are to enlist in His attack squadrons and, armed with love and prayer, go forth to seek the release of the captives. But as we launch out on our mission to conquer and set free, we soon discover that it is not a simple task. The enemy has been around for a long while, and he has his prisoners well shackled. Most of your fellow students, or your neighbors, or the idol worshippers out in the villages, don't even realize that they belong to Satan's kingdom, and therefore it is not easy to convince them that they need to be set free. They don't realize the situation until the shackles begin to pinch and grate and become painful. Sooner or later, chains do become uncomfortable, however, and then it is easier for the captive to become aware of his enslavement.

Satan Blinds

Why can't these captives see their situation? Why can't they realize the plight they are in (until it begins to hurt)? In 2 Corinthians 4, Paul describes their condition perfectly. "Our gospel is *veiled*...to those who are perishing. In their case the god of this world has *blinded* the minds of the unbeliever, to keep them from seeing the light of the gospel of the glory of Christ."

This is a very specialized kind of blindness. For instance, many of your fellow students may do well in science, art and music, but when it comes to spiritual truth, they are totally blind and therefore not interested. The idol worshipper out in the village may be an excellent farmer, or a successful business man, but again he is utterly blind to the follies and dangers of worshipping his wooden idols. It is somewhat like a person who is colorblind.

Although he can see certain objects clearly, yet he has no idea what we are talking about when we speak of its color. What is color? To him it doesn't even exist. And yet it does exist, very much so, to the person who can see it.

An astounding development has recently taken place in the legislature of the State of California. Several of the congressmen were trying to pass a bill requiring the high school science text-books to present creation as at least one of the possible explanations for the origin of life and matter. But there were amazing repercussions. Ten Nobel Scientists wrote to the legislature declaring that creation ought not even to be mentioned. These men are, of course, extremely brilliant in their areas of study. They have reached the pinnacle in their field of research. Yet spiritually, they are totally blind. The evidences for law and design are so abundant in our universe that *many* physicists, chemists, biologists, geologists and astronomers, including the great mind of Albert Einstein, have been firmly convinced that creation is the *only* possible explanation of it all.

The Scriptures strongly speak to this point in Romans 1:20, where it states, "Since the creation of the world, God's invisible attributes, His eternal power and divine nature, have been *clearly seen*, being understood *through what has been made, so that they are without excuse.*" Yet Satan has succeeded in so blinding their eyes that they don't even realize they are blind. The conquest of the enemy here on planet earth has advanced beyond anything most of us have considered. The degree of his subjugation is really overwhelming.

His Blinding Techniques

The first parable which the Lord Jesus spoke to the multitudes was about the sower and the four kinds of soil (the various kinds of blindness). Satan has so prejudiced those in the first category against any kind of spiritual truth that there is no penetration whatsoever. Their hearts are as hard as a paved road. The seed just lies there untouched. But then, just to make sure that the seed is not left around too long (lest there might possibly come the least thought of pondering the matter later), Satan's "birds" swoop down and quickly pick up every kernel. For prejudiced eyes there is nothing there to be seen, so "let's get on with the job and forget about all this nonsense."

The second type of eyes have a bit of vision. In fact they are quite attracted to the picture of a new peace, joy, forgiveness, and eternal life. But as soon as Satan sees them being drawn away, he turns on the persecution and their eyes are soon black and blue and swollen shut. So they at once part company with this risky business, this "foreign gospel."

The third category have better vision. They begin to comprehend the gospel message, receive it, and make a good beginning, "but the cares of the world, and the delight in riches, and the desire for other things, enter in and choke the Word, and it proves unfruitful." Satan knows that the greatest weakness of most people is their love for this world. God has created a beautiful world for us to enjoy. In fact, it is so attractive that it becomes particularly easy for Satan to turn men from a worship of the Creator, to a passionate love of what He has created!

Long ago, back in the Garden of Eden, Satan won his first smashing victory by using this technique. He pointed to all the material advantages of enjoying that fruit. "The delight in riches" ["*deceitfulness* of wealth"—Greek] blinded the eyes of Adam and Eve until they forgot about everything else. As we have mentioned before, the Lord Jesus called Satan the "King of *this World*." And Paul called him the "God of *this World*." So naturally he is constantly using all his powers to keep man's focus on this world. He is so continuously advertising the benefits of this world that it becomes extremely difficult for man to have any time to allow the Holy Spirit to reveal spiritual matters.

This is why God's Word repeatedly warns us to beware of allowing ourselves to be caught up in the love of this world and become blinded. When God was ready to lead His people Israel into that wonderful promised land, He actually did so with a sad heart. He said, "When I have brought them into the land flowing with milk and honey, the land I promised on oath to their forefathers, and when they eat their fill and thrive, they will turn to other gods [who cater to the lusts of their flesh] and worship them, rejecting Me, and breaking My covenant" (Dt. 31:20).

Isaiah and the Lord Jesus both spoke of the fulfillment of this very prophecy. "This people's heart has become calloused [fat]; they hardly hear with their ears, and they have *closed their eyes*" (Mt. 13:15). Therefore, the New Testament gives us strong and repeated caution against allowing ourselves to become enamored with this world. James writes, "You adulterous people, don't you know that friendship with the world is hatred toward God? Anyone who chooses to be a friend of the world becomes an enemy of God" (Jas. 4:4). And John adds, "Do not love the world or the things in the world. If anyone loves the world, love for the Father is not in him" (1 Jn. 2:15).

Satan knows these passages well, so he pushes the love of the world on people in every way he possibly can. Another verse Satan knows by heart is 1 Timothy 6:10, "The love of money is a root of all kinds of evil." He discovered long ago that to dangle the possibility of wealth before a man's eyes can often obliterate all spiritual hunger. Just as a bright light can blind one's eyes, so the craving for material possessions and "enjoying" life, can destroy all true spiritual vision. It is a strange paradox, and yet it is so often true, that such a lovely thing as material prosperity becomes one of Satan's main tools to blind people to the blessings of God, while catastrophe or disaster in many cases are God's tools to bring man back to Himself.

Thirty-five years ago, when I first came to Taiwan, the country was filled with refugees who had lost all their lands and possessions, and their lives were difficult and pitiful. That was the period, however, when there was a great turning to the Lord in this land, and hundreds of new churches were planted. As the economy has gradually improved, spiritual hunger has waned, and the common reply is "I'm sorry, but I'm too busy!"

This last spring, my wife and I had the opportunity to visit the country of Austria, whose capitol is that magnificent, refined city of Vienna. It was with mixed feelings, however, that we toured the land of these well-bred, polished people. For we learned that probably less than one tenth of one percent really know the Lord Jesus. Satan has used their genteel culture to blind their eyes.

Religious Blindness

When we speak of Satan blinding people toward spiritual truth, we are by no means saying that he is against their being involved in a religion. Quite the contrary. Satan is very much interested in religion, for here is precisely where the heart of the battle lies. Coming back to Paul's title for Satan, we must acknowledge and wrestle with the fact that he is the "*god* of this World." That is, his primary desire is to divert worship away from the true God, to distort it and ruin it in every way he can. The true and living God, the Creator of the Universe, is really his one and only enemy. Man is merely his pawn. The more he can enslave man and blind him, leading him into eternal destruction, the more he gloats, because he has to that extent succeeded in destroying God's best purposes for man.

Satan knows very well that God has implanted in man a desire to worship. In some cases, by means of sophisticated pride and prejudice, the enemy has been able to suppress this desire, but with the vast majority of mankind, he has allowed them to worship. He has often driven them into fanatical worship, but again with such blinded eyes that they miss the truth completely.

It is amazing to observe how Satan can use religious absurdities to effectively blind even rational intellectuals. A friend of mine, who for many years was the leading professor of crystallography at Massachusetts Institute of Technology, told me of an experience he had on one of his lecture tours in the Far East. He had stopped off in India for a few days to visit some of his former students who had done their graduate work at M.I.T. and received their Ph.D. degree. They were very happy for this opportunity to entertain their former professor, so they took him around to see many of the interesting sights, and finally brought him to visit one of their idol temples. It was a ghastly, filthy place. And he could hardly believe his eyes when he saw these M.I.T. PhD.s each pick up a dirty cup of water, mix in some of the ashes from burning incense, and drink it down in an act of sincere worship.

Most of the human race are not, of course, endowed with a Ph.D. mental capacity and are therefore even more susceptible to superstition. So it is not surprising when we observe that 99% of the world's population have been blinded to the truth of the gospel by some form of false religion.

Here in Taiwan the great deception is the dragon. Most of life, business and worship is built around the dragon. Last Easter my wife and I took a trip around the northern half of the island, and it was very striking to discover how many villages include the word "dragon" (lung) in their name. This all points to a very serious state of affairs, for in Revelation 12:9, where a number of Satan's names are listed, the very first one is the "Great Dragon." It is actually a picture of the way this island is predominantly given over to Satan worship. Just recently, since returning from a year's furlough, we have seen a new tactic of the Evil One to grip his followers even tighter. It is a form of gambling tied in with their temple worship and many forms of superstition, called "Ta Chia Lo." Also, a week ago I attended a lecture on "I Kuan Tao" and learned that this religion is mushrooming to the point of a million followers within the last six years.

In many other countries it is Islam, and this is even worse, for it is much less tolerant. In some Muslim lands, the murdering of Christians is a means of obtaining merit. Actually, a study of the world's religions can be a discouraging endeavor. It exposes the crudest, most despicable elements in many cultures.

Even within Christianity, Satan has been diligently and effectively at work. Most of Israel's history in the Old Testament is dark and bleak indeed. Our Christian era since the Lord Jesus gave His life on the cross, rose from the grave, and ascended back up into heaven, is still a period of less than 2,000 years. Yet this period has included a thousand years of "Dark Ages," plus many other centuries of spiritual famine. Even today, when we see more of an advance in spiritual life in many places, we are told that the cults are growing faster than any other group. And within the mainline denominations of the church, the last century has seen the blight of modernism and liberalism wipe out the true light of the gospel in many places.

No, Satan is not afraid of religion. He loves it. It is one of his most effective tools, as long as by it he is able to blind and distort. And he seems to be extremely successful at sowing tares while men sleep. The Lord Jesus had to tell the religious leaders of His day, "You are of your father, the Devil" (Jn. 8:44).

What awful advances the Evil One has been able to make, because ever since Adam, he has been able not only to blind the worldlings with all his many devices, but also to blind too many of God's people with sleep. In many armies a soldier who sleeps at his post is immediately court marshalled and executed. God has been merciful to His people, but we can begin to see how concerned He is that we awaken and become informed as to the "intelligence" of our enemy. We need to see how deeply entrenched he is, how varied are his tactics and weapons, and how vast are his operations.

Paul's Commission

When the Lord Jesus commissioned Paul to take the gospel to the Gentiles, he spelled out a very clear job description. He said, "I am sending you to open their eyes, so that they may turn from darkness to light and from the dominion of Satan to God, in order that they may receive forgiveness of sins and an inheritance among those who have been sanctified by faith in Me" (Acts 26:18).

There are several things we should notice about this assignment, for it is His charge to us as well. First, we should observe that step *number one* is *"to open their eyes."* Then he adds, *"so that* they may turn from darkness to light," and again, *"in order that* they may receive forgiveness of sins...."* Until blinded eyes are opened, there is no hope of reaping a harvest and building a church or any kind of Christian fellowship group. Is this not perhaps the reason why many sincere efforts of pioneer missionary work or on-campus evangelism are bogged down and seeing no real response? It is very difficult to paint beautiful pictures for a blind person to appreciate!

The Cure for Blindness

Total blindness is a very difficult malady to cure. Most doctors just shake their head sympathetically, with the reply, "I'm sorry, but there is no hope." Throughout my Christian life of some sixty years, I have heard and read of a number of people who by prayer have been healed of serious diseases such as cancer, heart trouble, kidney problems, etc., but I don't recall ever hearing of many blind persons receiving their sight. I know of some who were prayed for and who did not receive their sight. It is extremely easy to blind a person's eyes, but almost impossible to restore sight. Once the delicate seeing mechanism has been seriously damaged or destroyed, a person is in a pitiful condition indeed.

There is hope for spiritual blindness, of course, but it doesn't come simply or easily. Its remedy demands a price. Even in dealing with physical blindness, although the Lord Jesus did heal several blind people when He was here on earth, each account seems to have something special about it. In one case He put mud on the man's eyes and sent him to the Pool of Siloam to wash. In another case it was a two-step process where the person first received partial vision, and then finally could see clearly. In a third case, which gives us both encouragement and challenge, He first asked, "Do you believe that I am able to do this?" When the reply was "yes," the Lord then added, "It will be done for you according to your faith" (Mt. 9:29).

The Lord Jesus is abundantly able to heal all kinds of blindness, we know. But there is a significant limiting factor here. And this limiting factor is our faith. Faith is seldom as simple as it may at first appear. If it were all that simple, then why are so few of our friends (for whom we so diligently pray) ever healed of their blindness? Why do our struggling little churches remain the same size decade after decade?

We need help. We need all the help we can get to strengthen our faith. The greatest help faith can possibly have is the Word of God. "Does *He speak* and then not act? Does He promise and not fulfil?" (Num. 23:19). Whenever we have a clear promise from God and we have met all the conditions (for all God's promises have conditions), then we are on solid ground to expect Him to act. There is, to be sure, the time factor, which we will discuss in another chapter, but there is most definitely a place for robust faith and expectancy in prayer.

Now, then, let us look at some statements from the Lord Jesus which can give us strong hope in asking Him to open the eyes of those who live in darkness, those who have been blinded by the God of this World. The very first time when the Lord Jesus stood up to speak in the synagogue of His hometown, Nazareth, they handed Him the scroll of the prophet Isaiah. He found the place where it was written, "The Spirit of the Lord is on Me, because He has anointed Me to preach good news to the poor. He has sent me to proclaim freedom for the prisoners and *recovery of sight for the blind*, to release the oppressed, to proclaim the year of the Lord's favor." Then He rolled up the scroll, gave it back to the attendant, and sat down (Lk. 4:18-20).

On that sabbath morning the Lord Jesus very simply and clearly set forth the commission which He had received from His Father. An integral part of His assignment was "recovery of sight for the blind." It is evident from the overall content of this prophecy that His commission was primarily of a spiritual nature. That is, the prisoners He came to free are spiritual prisoners, those imprisoned by Satan. The oppressed are those oppressed by the Devil. And the blind are the *spiritually blind*, those who have been blinded by Satan toward spiritual truth.

This forthright declaration by the Lord Jesus (prophesied by Isaiah) as to the purpose of His coming does give us great confidence as we begin to ask Him to open the eyes of our blinded neighbor or fellow student. We should employ His own words in our praying.

Another of His statements which we can also claim is in John 9:39. The Lord had just healed a man who had been physically blind from birth. But the Pharisees, who were always looking for a chance to condemn Jesus, rose up with great opposition because He had done this on the sabbath. The Lord's final reply to them was, "For judgment I came into this world, that those who do not see may see, and that those who see may become blind." This is certainly a two-edged metaphor. It pictures both sides. Those pitiful souls who would desire light but who have been blinded by Satan He came to heal. He came that they might see. But those whose own pride and jealousy lead them to despise God's truth He allows to be confirmed in their blindness.

"To him who has [a seeking heart] shall be given, and whoever does not have, even what he has shall be taken away" (Mk. 4:25).

These verses and others like them give us both encouragement and caution as we seek healing for the spiritual blindness of our friends. There are those who, like the Pharisees, don't really want to see, but there are many others who are groping for truth but cannot find it because Satan has blinded their eyes. In the latter case we have solid ground for asking in faith, and with persistent prayer that their eyes would be opened.

A few days ago I was reading the testimony of a young lady missionary who went to India to take the light of the gospel to those who sit in darkness in that land. She learned the language and then began her ministry of telling the good news. But she soon discovered that her message made very little impression on the people. After a couple of years she hadn't much fruit to show for her efforts and was greatly discouraged. She set aside a period to seek the Lord as to what He might have to say to her. Finally the Holy Spirit seemed to indicate that her primary ministry was to be prayer. "Not by might nor by power, but by my Spirit, says the Lord of Hosts" (Zech. 4:6).

Although at first she found it extremely difficult, almost impossible, to set other things aside and give the best hours of her day to intercession, there soon came evidence of much blessing. Blind eyes were opened and many hungry hearts turned to the Lord for forgiveness and new life. Within six months, one hundred twenty-five new believers were baptized and became faithful living stones in the church.

"The Son of God appeared for this purpose, that He might destroy the works of the Devil" (1 Jn. 3:8). But it is not automatic! He must involve us. How wonderful to be involved in this, the greatest of all professions: bringing light into darkness, and seeing people delivered from the dominion of Satan into the kingdom of our God, lifted from death into eternal, abundant life.

There must be the going and telling, but before either of these can be effective, eyes must be opened. You and I can't possibly open blind eyes, but we can come to One who can!

6

THE FIELD OF BATTLE

Before a general can determine his plan of attack and properly employ his armor and his weapons, he must have an understanding of his field of battle. During World War II, fighting was carried out on two main battlefronts, the Asian and the European. Our situation in spiritual warfare is similar, in that we also have to maintain action on two fronts, the outer world of Satan's kingdom, and our own inner struggle. We will now devote a chapter to each of these.

In speaking of the "field of battle," we are referring to the basic issue which caused this war in the first place and which has kept it going on ever since the Garden of Eden. The issue at stake is the *goodness of God*. Satan has been exhausting all his energies, all his craft, and all his forces, to discredit and distort the image of the goodness of God.

In an earlier chapter, we introduced the two kingdoms which co-exist today on planet earth. This is by no means a happy co-existence. One is the "kingdom of darkness"; the other is the "kingdom of light." One is the kingdom of sin; the other is the kingdom of righteousness. But the most lucid distinction, which so graphically pictures the field of battle, is that one is the kingdom of *evil*, while the other is the kingdom of *good*.

Back in the first chapter of Genesis, where everything on this earth had its beginning, we read of the step by step process of God's creating the universe. At the close of each step, we have the statement that God "saw [made sure] that it was good." In the conclusion to that chapter, in the last verse it is again strongly emphasized that *"God saw all that He had made, and behold, it was very good."*

God has always desired the very best for man, so He clearly warned Adam and Eve of the test which would come to them, the battle in which they would soon be involved. He wanted them to enjoy only good, so He pled with them not to eat of the tree of the knowledge of good *and evil*. The Evil One came, as God permitted him to do, and his typical scheme of attack was to question, belittle, and finally destroy their confidence in the goodness of God. He convinced them that God had not told them the real truth, that He was holding back from them something which was actually to their advantage, that He was depriving them of enjoyment, and therefore God was not really the wonderful Person He had made Himself out to be.

If we are to become strong, conquering warriors, able to overcome and defeat the Wicked One, we must first arrive at the firm conclusion that our God, in every way (whether it at first appears so or not), is absolutely and completely *good*! The battle always hinges on this point. This is truth. This is our message. Our God only does what is good, and *"every* good and perfect gift is from above, coming down from the Father of Lights, with whom there is no variation or shadow of turning [from that which is good]" (Jas. 1:17).

In like manner, it must become clearly fixed in our minds and our understanding that Satan is the *"Evil* One," the *enemy* of all good, who as the Lord Jesus denounced, "comes only to steal, kill and destroy." All our pain, all our hurts, all our sorrow, all our misfortunes, come either directly or indirectly from him. "We wrestle not against flesh and blood," but against him and his forces. It is only when we see this picture very clearly, and are unhesitatingly convinced of its truth, that the battlelines will be sharply drawn for us, and we can go forth with that might and determination which empowered David to slay Goliath.

When God's servants get sick, when His missionaries have to leave the field, when new believers fall back, when discouragement sets in, we need to see the unseen enemy "Goliath" behind it all. We need to march ahead forthright toward him, gather our "five smooth stones," and drive him back. Sometimes the Lord may allow a prolonged encounter, as He did in the case of Job. But even that will be for our *good*. We must always keep our sights clear as to who is our real friend, and who is our real enemy.

There are times when God does some destroying, punishing and disciplining, but it is always to deal with that which is *bad*. He at times steps in and completely destroys that which is incurable or rotten. There will (eventually) always be punishment for the self-centered, the unrepentant, and those who refuse the kingdom of light. And whenever His own children wander too far from the fold of righteousness, He, because of His own holiness (goodness), has to administer chastening. But even then, "He disciplines us for our *good*, that we might be partakers of His holiness" (Heb. 12:10).

The portion of Scripture which we will study primarily in this chapter is 2 Corinthians 4:3-6: "If our gospel is veiled, it is veiled to those who are perishing. In whose case the god of this world has blinded the minds of the unbelieving, that they might not see the light of the gospel of the glory of Christ, who is the image of God. For we do not preach ourselves but Christ Jesus as Lord, and ourselves as your bond-servants for Jesus' sake. For God who said, 'Let the light shine out of darkness,' is the One who has shone in our hearts to give the light of the knowledge of the glory of God in the face of Christ."

In these verses Paul lays out before us the heart of the battle, which in one word is the "*glory*" of God. We either see His glory or we don't, and this determines which side of the battle we are on. And the clarity with which we see His glory determines the degree to which we are involved. Paul, who was so infatuated with the glory and beauty of the Lord Jesus, was involved to the hilt. To present the "good news" of the gospel of Christ was the one thing he lived for. And to tear down all the enemy's obstacles was the one thing he fought for. The battlefield was very clear to him.

Paul reminds us in the above verses that Satan "blinds the minds of the unbelieving." Unbelief is insufficient confidence in the goodness of God. And this is too often a problem even with Christians. Satan is always trying to plant warped images in our minds. We would never say so, but our attitude, our lack of joy and exuberance, all too frequently betray the fact that our inner thoughts have accepted the enemy's lie...that God can at times be quite unfair, extreme, and rather a kill-joy. So we must have continual inoculations of the beauty and kindness of our God, to be strengthened in the inner man. The taproot of faith is the goodness of God. So we need to learn how to attack each of our problems from the premise that God is good. "Godly sorrow" brings good; "worldly sorrow" brings death. We each can decide which it will be on the basis of our confidence in the goodness of God. Someone has said it this way: "Faith's foundations are laid on the solid stones of the goodness of God." And when we sing "Holy, Holy, Holy, Lord God Almighty," and when we think of the righteousness of God, let us remember that holiness and righteousness mean that He is without any error or wrong doing. He is good!

Seeing God's Goodness in our Bible Study

On the night before the Lord Jesus went to the cross, He made an amazing statement. "These things I have spoken to you that my joy might be in you, and that your joy might be full" (Jn. 15:11). To speak of His own joy at such a time seems almost incongruous. For as He drew closer to the hour of His crucifixion, He sweat drops of blood and prayed repeatedly for deliverance. He knew full well the suffering that lay ahead for Him, yet after each petition He added, "Not my will but Thine be done."

Way back in the Psalms, a thousand years before, His heart conviction was pictured by the words, "I *delight* to do Thy will, O God." It seems a paradox that He could plead for release from the cup of agony and at the same time express an honest desire to do the Father's will. But this is a picture of absolute trust in the goodness and rightness of His Father's will. "On the night He was betrayed, *He took the bread* and *gave thanks*."

We don't always enjoy the experiences our Father allows us to partake of, but an unshakable confidence in His goodness is the kind of faith which will see us through with peace and great victory. And such confidence is built up within our hearts by the perpetual process of focusing on His goodness in our daily study of His Word. "These things I have spoken to you, that My joy might be in you."

The Word of God does have its "hard" portions, but our firm reliance on the goodness of God should be the enzyme which helps us digest such passages. We should train a new believer to begin his daily devotional time with some positive prayer as David did. "Open my eyes that I may see wonderful [beautiful] things in your law" (Ps. 119:18). Paul encouraged his disciples to "Rejoice in the Lord always; I will say it again, rejoice!" "...Whatever is true, whatever is noble, whatever is right, whatever is pure, whatever is lovely, whatever is admirable...if anything is excellent, or praiseworthy, think about *these* things" (Phil. 4:4,8).

For many years I was quite bothered by certain Scriptures which present so strongly the wrath of God. But one day as I discussed this problem with an older brother, he relieved all my concerns by pointing out that God's wrath is a part of His love. God cannot tolerate that which is unjust, that which hurts others unfairly, or any form of selfishness. A *good* teacher will most certainly deal with a bully in the classroom. Even God's curse on our earth which brought death, thorns, and thistles, plus the reduction of man's longevity after the flood—all these were beneficial restraints and reminders after our human race had determined to go Satan's way. The goodness of God shines through it all. Another approach to the negative passages in Scripture is to remind ourselves that all those things which our God so dislikes are actions and attitudes which make us ugly!

The painful hang-ups from which many Christians are needlessly suffering today often come from their misconceptions of God. They have forgotten about their unseen enemy. They are actually hearing his voice and are being stung by his venom, but can't seem to realize that it is *he* who is tormenting them in his torture chamber. He has succeeded in convincing them that God is their enemy. We dare not allow Satan to turn the tables on us. We must always keep it clear in our vision as to who is our friend and who is our enemy. We must put on our armor, pick up our weapons, and drive away this evil one. Instead of allowing him to pommel us, we must begin to pommel him. We must return to the firing line and become engaged again in spiritual warfare.

So our confidence in the goodness of God not only brings much blessing into our lives, but it also can generate a great deal of power and victory. In the heat of the conflict, God's goodness can become a two-edged sword. We can begin to recount all His past mercies to us, and we can remind ourselves of His promises of future rewards. "Our present sufferings are not worth comparing with the *glory* that will be revealed in us" (Rom. 8:18). Or, perhaps another way of looking at it when Satan puts us in the midst of some testing, is that the goodness of God can enable us to *pass the test*. And the quicker we pass the test, the sooner we will sing as Moses did, "The horse and his rider He has hurled into the sea" (Ex. 15:21). Also it should give us a real boost to remember that those periods of grappling with the rigors of our Christian life are usually the periods of our greatest growth. That Christian who has won a lot of victories has a lot of things to share.

Our hearts and lives need to become saturated with the goodness of God. And this is accomplished by a positive, constructive, therapeutic time of fellowship with the Lord each day in His Word. We should collect His names, His promises, His encouragement. His names are refreshing: "Bread of Life"; "Water of Life"; "Good Shepherd"; "Deliverer"; "Friend"; "Light of the World"; "Merciful"; "Prince of Peace"; "Rewarder"; "Stronghold," etc. There are hundreds of His names in the Scriptures, and they are all good. There is a long list already compiled in the "Worship and Warfare" prayer companion.

The occasion of the Lord's first miracle was to take His disciples to a wedding and produce a super-abundant supply (150 gallons) of the very best wine. This of course is also meant to be a parable of what He desires to do for us.

David was an effervescent optimist. He couldn't bear to go for very long without his cup overflowing with the joy of the Lord. He was so used to *enjoying* the Lord's goodness that it pained him deeply when something got in the way and hindered that flow. Actually, as you read the Psalms, you discover that things often got in the way, and it was usually the enemy. In fact, a great portion of David's Psalms are cries to the Lord for deliverance or references to past deliverances.

I like to look at the Psalms as David's devotional notebook. He often comes to his quiet time in great distress, but goes away with confidence and song. They are beautiful examples of what our quiet time should do for us. Just this morning I read Psalm 63. The title is: "A Psalm of David, when he was in the desert of Judah [being chased by Saul]." It begins, "O God, you are my God, earnestly I seek You; my soul thirsts for You, my body longs for You, in a dry and weary land where there is no water." But a little further on... "My soul will be satisfied as with the richest of foods; with singing lips my mouth will praise You."

David was a warrior. He was usually involved in some sort of encounter with an enemy. But he was a tremendously successful and victorious warrior. He knew his God. He knew the goodness of his God. Over sixty times David refers to the goodness of God, over one hundred thirty times to His mercy, and twenty-three times to His lovingkindness. And the Lord called David "A man after My own heart." "Those who know their God will be strong and do exploits" (Dan. 11:32).

Yes, the purpose of the Word of God is to enable us to know our God, to feed on His goodness, and in so doing, to be delivered from our hang-ups, our bondage, and our failures. James calls the Word of God "the law of *liberty*." Paul confirms this with the words, "Where the Spirit of the Lord is, there is freedom." And the Lord Jesus assures us that if we know the truth, "the truth will make you *free*." The Westminster Catechism begins beautifully in its opening statement: "The chief end of man is to know God and to *enjoy* Him forever."

So, as a fitting conclusion to this section on "beholding good things in His Word," I will leave with you a precious little jewel which a friend gave to me: "Never doubt in the dark, what God has shown you in the light."

Employing God's Goodness in Prayer

Many of us give up far too soon and much too readily when one of our prayers is not answered. Without realizing it, we hold quite a fatalistic view of God's sovereignty. If the Lord doesn't answer right away, we decide the answer must be "no," so we drop the request, forfeit the whole idea, assume we just made a mistake, and back off in weakness. This is exactly what our enemy is hoping for, so he is delighted every time it happens. It amounts to one more of his advances against the goodness of God.

"Without faith it is impossible to please God." And the next sentence defines the type of faith referred to. We must "believe that He is a *rewarder* of those who *diligently* seek Him." In a later chapter entitled "The Time Factor," we will see how answers to prayer are often held up by the unseen conflict which goes on in the heavenlies, when we give ourselves to prayer. But there are also other reasons for delayed answers.

We would learn very little about prayer if, every time we ask for something, our request was granted immediately. Children's prayers are often answered right away, for they know little about intercession, and their span of patience is naturally very limited. So the Lord is especially merciful to them. But you and I are not children. Certainly the Lord does not want us to remain babies all our lives. He desires that we become disciples (students, learners), to grow up unto "full manhood," to become strong, able warriors.

When the answer to our prayer is delayed, the easy way out is to give up. But the diligent supplicant asks "why," and strikes out to learn something more about prayer and about God's will. He may gather a few more promises, a few more of God's names, some more encouragement from the Psalms, some challenge from the parables or miracles, or ask for wisdom. There are many things he can do (all of them tied in with the goodness of God). And he will do them.

The goodness of God should become a motivating force within our spirits, driving us ever forward, with great expectancy in prayer. The Lord loves us, and He loves the people we are praying for. So there is little reason to discontinue our pleas for that which we are convinced is a good cause. The Lord is always desirous of meaningful accomplishment. He has no interest in just sitting back and watching things fall apart. He is against defeat. He is only satisfied with victory. He can't be pleased with failure. He only wants what is good.

The Lord said to Jeremiah, "Call upon Me and I will show you *great and mighty* things which you know not" (Jer. 33:3). He really wants to do "exceedingly *above* what we ask or even think." Therefore we ought not to settle for too many "no" answers from the Lord. He is not a God of "no," but a God of "yea and amen." He is good; He is positive, not negative.

The parables on prayer which the Lord Jesus gave us are all intended to strengthen our faith in the goodness of God. Twice they are reinforced by the powerful promise: "Ask, and it shall be given you; seek, and you will find; knock, and it shall be opened unto you." And this challenge is further strengthened by the repetition, "For everyone who asks receives, and he who seeks finds, and to him who knocks it shall be opened."

The man who has learned much about the goodness of God, and offers up his prayers with God's lovingkindness and mercy as the basis of his intercessions, and perseveres in this, will receive many beautiful answers. He will therefore move on from victory to victory. It becomes a cycle of encouragement and growth.

Naturally, there will be times when the Lord's answer may not be identical with our request, for His ways are not always the same as our ways. But we should firmly remember that His ways are *higher* than our ways. In fact He adds, "My ways are higher than your ways as the heavens are higher than the earth" (Isa. 55:9). This is just one more passage assuring us of His unfathomable goodness.

Emphasizing God's Goodness in Presenting the Gospel

On that first Christmas morning, the angel appeared to the shepherds with the grandest message which has ever reached human ears: "Do not be afraid, for behold, I bring you *good news* of *great joy* which shall be for all the people, for today in the city of David, there has been born for you a *Savior*" (Lk. 2:10-11).

For you and me who have come to comprehend this report and to know this Savior, the Christmas story is indeed "good news." Over 100 times in the Scriptures, this message is called the "gospel," which means "glad tidings." And whenever we preach the gospel, we call it "evangelizing," which comes from the Greek word "euaggello," which means to "announce good news."

The Lord Jesus often spoke of Himself as the light of the world. We frequently refer to our missionary efforts as bringing light into a dark place. And Paul, in the passage which we are using for our text in this chapter, speaks of "the light of the gospel," and "the light of the knowledge of the glory of God in the face of Jesus Christ."

Light is naturally a wonderful thing to someone who is groping and stumbling about in darkness. It is exactly what he needs, and what he longs for more than anything else. But the amazing phenomenon which confronts all of us who are seeking to present this glorious gospel to a world that is lost and dying in darkness is that most of them are not interested. How can this be? Paul gives us the very clear answer in our text. "The god of this world has *blinded* the minds of the unbelieving, that they might not *see* the light of the gospel of the glory of Christ, who is the likeness of God." And in the preceding verse, he states that the good news of the gospel is "*veiled* to those who are perishing."

Yes, light, even very strong and powerful light, such as the brilliant rays of the sun on a bright summer day at high noon, can be very easily blocked. If someone places his hand over our eyes or causes us to close our eyes, we can't see a thing. We are in total darkness.

This, as Paul reminds us, is precisely the situation which confronts us when we try to share our good news with the unbelievers of this world. Their ears are stopped up; they cannot hear. Their eyes are veiled; they cannot see. Their minds are sealed; they cannot comprehend. Their hearts are closed; they cannot take it in. And Paul makes it very clear, that this is all the work of "the god of this world."

No wonder the Lord Jesus did His best to prepare His disciples with the warning and challenge: "How can anyone enter the strong man's house and carry off his property, unless he *first binds the strong man*? And then he will plunder his house" (Mt. 12:29).

But the element we need to deal with in this chapter is *how* the Evil One blinds unbelievers. How could he possibly manage to veil the eyes, ears, minds and hearts of 99% of the population of the world? This brings us back to the battlefield, the theme of this chapter.

We have already seen how Satan dealt with Adam and Eve in that beautiful Garden of Eden which God in His great thoughtfulness and love had prepared for them. He destroyed their confidence in the goodness of God by blinding their eyes with materialism. He cleverly, step by step, focused their attention on what God had made, and in the process belittled the One who made it all. And this is exactly where we are today. He is "the god of *this world*." He is extremely adept at leading man to "love the creation rather than the Creator." It is really quite easy for him to fasten all their concerns on that which they can see with their physical eyes and blind them to the unseen One who put it all there for them.

"That which I am able to get hold of and enjoy now...that is *good*. I really know little about the future or the unseen realm, and it only makes me fearful when I think about it. Also, to give too much thought or attention to mystical, spiritual things takes up my precious time which I need to accumulate more of this real world's useful and enjoyable goods." So the Evil One has actually succeeded in rendering the preaching of the gospel as "foolishness," even as something objectionable in the busy lives of the worldlings. He has destroyed the image of the goodness of God. "The god of *this world* has blinded the minds of the unbelieving, that they might not see the *light* of the gospel of the *glory* of Christ, who is the image of God."

Therefore when we preach our message to those who do not yet believe, we must realize that they are not only hopeless (lost, perishing), but they are helpless. They are blind; they are living in darkness; they are in bonds; they are enslaved by the Prince of this World. He has convinced them that evil is good and good is evil. We must ask the Holy Spirit to open their eyes, ears, minds and hearts, and we must also ask Him to help us to present the gospel as truly *good news*.

In speaking of the Holy Spirit, the Lord Jesus said, "He will glorify Me." This is exactly what needs to be done. We, by our own abilities, just can't manage to convince the worldling of any spiritual values, but the Holy Spirit is our "Helper." We don't have to strive alone in our poor inadequacy. He is the Holy Spirit and has come to straighten out this whole matter of what is good and what is evil. "*He* will convince the world of sin, right-eousness, and judgment."

Our constant prayer, therefore, should be to ask the Holy Spirit to give us the simple eloquence to tell the gospel message in such a way that the "glory of Christ," the goodness of God, will penetrate all the way into the heart of the one who hears it. He must come to see that the cross of Jesus Christ is the most beautiful thing in the universe...that his own love of sin and self-centeredness are ugly things. But the Savior has come to cleanse him from all this, to forgive him, and to love him. His image of the goodness of God must be restored.

The gospel is a positive message. The penalty of sin must be dealt with and the lordship of Christ clearly presented, but I am coming to see more and more that the Lord Jesus himself preached a beautiful, winsome gospel. To the Pharisees, Sad-ducees, and other legalistic religious leaders, His message was definitely negative, because their harsh dealings with people were negative. But to the rest of the perishing world He preached "good tidings." He was the "Good Shepherd." He "came to seek and to save the lost." He gave His life out of infinite *love* for them.

As we mentioned above, the Evil One often puts a kind of fear of Christianity in people's hearts. But the apostle John gives us the solution to this problem. "There is no fear in *love*; but per-fect love casts out fear, because fear involves punishment, and the one who fears is not perfected in *love*" (1 Jn. 4:18). If our wit-ness to the gospel is given in love, the Holy Spirit (whose pri-mary fruit is love) is able to take our presentation (feeble and in-complete though it may be), and dissolve the fear which Satan has built up. People not only need to hear about God's goodness; they need to see and feel it. We must be living examples of the goodness we speak about. Perhaps we should close this chapter with a few quotations from David's Psalms:

"The Lord is good; His lovingkindness is everlasting. And His faithfulness endures to all generations" (Ps. 100:5).

"Praise the Lord! Oh give thanks to the Lord, for He is good" (Ps. 106:1).

"Give thanks to the Lord for His lovingkindess, and for His

wonderful deeds to the sons of men! For He has satisfied the thirsty soul, and the hungry soul He has filled with what is good" (Ps. 107:8,9).

7

WINNING THE INNER WAR

"The desires of the flesh are against the Spirit, and the desires of the Spirit are against the flesh; for these are opposed to each other, so that you cannot do the things you would" (Gal. 5:17).

There is a story in the Old Testament which is a helpful starting point for this chapter. After Rebekah was married to Isaac, the son of Abraham, she was barren for several years. So Isaac prayed for his wife; the Lord heard his prayer, and Rebekah conceived. In fact she soon discovered she had twins. But these two brothers, still unborn, struggled vigorously within her. This concerned her greatly, so she asked the Lord for some explanation of what was taking place. The Lord said, "Two kingdoms are inside you," and then He described how opposed to each other these two kingdoms would be. And they certainly did not turn out to be identical twins. They were as different as night and day.

This is actually quite a revealing picture of the developments which often take place within us after we receive (are betrothed to) the Lord Jesus. Many of us are rather barren for a time, until the life of the Holy Spirit begins to grow within us. Then gradually our new-found joy becomes quite shattered as we discover a real battle going on inside. Finally, through God's Word, we begin to see that two very different kingdoms are struggling within. The Holy Spirit, who belongs completely to God's kingdom, and our flesh, which has always been an ally of Satan's kingdom, can never come to terms. So we are miserable, and our misery causes all kinds of trouble. And whenever you have several miserable people together, conflict and chaos develop.

James also helps us come to grips with this problem, "What causes wars and what causes fightings among you? Is it not your passions that are at war within you?" (Jas. 4:l). So we can readily see that there is much power loss for the Lord's work when such turmoil exists within individual Christians and within the church fellowship. In fact, "fellowship," which should be a means of vital strength, deteriorates to a very low ebb, and dissension takes over.

Therefore, it becomes obvious that before we can make much headway in the outer war against Satan's kingdom in heathen areas, we must first gain victory in the inner battle. Our Captain longs to clear up all these internal maladies, in order that we might become strong, tough marines for the major warfare.

Our flesh has two close friends which are always at hand to support it and to urge it on. One of its close companions is called "the world." The other is Satan. And these three are our relentless foes. They are powerful, united enemies. James warns us, "Do you not know that friendship with the world is enmity with God? Therefore, whoever wishes to be a friend of the world makes himself an enemy of God." And then in the same context he adds, "Resist the devil."

Now let us look at Paul's testimony in Romans chapter seven: "I see in my members another law at war with the law of my mind and making me captive to the law of sin which dwells in my members. Wretched man that I am! Who will deliver me from this body of death? Thanks be to God! *Through Jesus Christ our Lord.*"

We should not be discouraged. That only makes us weak. The Lord is on our side. He is longing to help us. He is a patient, loving coach, not a fearsome drill sergeant. In the previous chapter we learned that we must saturate ourselves with the goodness of God. And this is where we begin in the inner struggle as well. Our Lord's name is "Jesus" which means "savior" or "deliverer." So there is an abundance of hope and provision in Him.

There is one other factor which should be mentioned here, and that is that our victory through Him is *not automatic.* He wants to give us help and lead us into the joy of overcoming our flesh, but it all rests on a close, continuous fellowship with Him. Like Paul, we all have this inner battle ready to flare up within us at any time, and this potential conflict will be with us until the

Lord takes us to heaven. Even the Lord himself "was tempted in all points." But at the end of His life, He said to His disciples, "Be of good cheer; I have overcome the world." He was encouraging us that if we will maintain our intimacy with Him and follow His lead, we too can overcome.

He Desires to Draw Us to Himself

Triumph in the Christian life, or peace in the inner man, begins with a *choice*. A good illustration is the story of Mary and Martha. One day the Lord and twelve disciples arrived at their home shortly before lunch, so Martha dashed into the kitchen to put together a nice meal for about sixteen people. This was a very noble intention, but something soon began to bother her and continued to upset her more and more until it pained her a great deal. Her sister Mary hadn't come to help. Martha kept working away at the various preparations, but Mary still didn't come. Finally she could bear it no longer, so she burst out into the living room, and in front of everyone reprimanded the Lord for not being aware of Mary's negligence and her own self-sacrifice, and for not doing something to relieve the situation.

The Lord's reply was very surprising. He said, "Martha, Martha, you are bothered and worried about so many things; but only a few things are necessary; really only one. Mary *has chosen* the good part, which shall not be taken away from her." Mary had to make a choice. And it wasn't an easy choice. There was a strong pull to get into the kitchen to help her sister, but also a strong desire to sit there with the Lord Jesus and drink in His words of wisdom and comfort. Once she began to enjoy the fellowship with Him, she just couldn't tear herself away. And the Lord supported her in this choice. After all, He had come to their home, not for a big meal, not to be fed, but to feed them!

He, of course, is not suggesting that a Christian shirk his valid responsibilities, but that we make room in our busy schedule for ample fellowship with Him. For some, this may be difficult to accomplish, and it may exact a price, but it is one of those spiritual essentials, just as breakfast, lunch and supper are physical essentials. To go without sufficient nourishment for long can result only in weakness, so we need to be careful that our "no time" excuse is not just a symptom of the "Martha syndrome." A balance is needed here. Our devotional life must not become a bondage to us either. Since He loves us very much, we can be sure that He is greatly concerned about our daily and weekly schedules, and desires to help us to get untangled and to unload some of the "cares of this world."

He loved Mary, and He loved Martha, and His aim, as always, was to "strengthen them with might in the inner man." Mary was strengthened. She enjoyed peace and victory within. Martha missed out on the spiritual nourishment, so she suffered defeat and frustration, though she had probably learned a good lesson for next time. Yes, He longs to draw us to Himself for those regular interviews, those times of fellowship, when He can impart the next lesson for a victorious life.

On another occasion He urged His disciples to "*seek first the kingdom of God and His righteousness, and all these other things will be provided for you*" (Mt. 6:33). The primary requisite in seeking His kingdom is to seek His kingship within ourselves, to make sure that our King is the one and only king in our life, and that He always maintains that position. Whenever the flesh takes over, or whenever our schedule takes over, and He must step down, we are in trouble. We are not to move into a legalistic bondage, but neither are we to allow our priorities to become slipshod. He still says, "seek first."

When I was in my last year of college, I was one of those eager beavers who got involved in a full spectrum of activities. I had a load of classes, with all their assignments. I attended the Christian fellowship group with its many involvements. I had a part-time job. I was active in a church plus its youth group. I was into stamp collecting. I played in a small orchestra. I signed up for an evening course in electronics in another school, and tried to keep up my tennis and social life. I was one busy person! But my Christian life was actually very barren. I wasn't really happy with it all. I was living a full but spiritually defeated existence.

One evening as I was walking home from the electronics class, the Holy Spirit began to show me how *empty* my "full life" really was, how actually useless and unproductive it was for His kingdom. And I realized that I would never see any victories, or know any contentment until I arranged for ample fellowship with Him. In short, the branch needed to be pruned.

Having seen the whole picture very clearly, I got rid of my stamp collection, discontinued the electronics course, gave up the orchestra, and cut back on some of the activities of the youth group at church. The choice wasn't really all that difficult. Actually I felt quite relieved, to say nothing of the delicious joy which came from the renewed, unhurried times with the Lord in His Word. And it wasn't long before there began to be fruit for His kingdom. To keep first things first spells peace for the inner man and victories for His kingdom.

The book of Malachi, which closes the Old Testament, presents another sad picture of frustration and defeat. And the repeated reason given is that God's people had given only their left-overs as an offering to Him. In the New Testament, the offering which He is most delighted with is our individual times of communion with Him. He has so many good things to give us, spiritual treats which will "strengthen us with might in the inner man." Then we will begin to overcome.

The Lord's first parable pointed to four kinds of soil. The good soil was that which was free of stones and briars which "choke the Word" and make it unfruitful. A couple of good verses to have in mind as we open up God's Word to enjoy a spiritual meal are those in Matthew 6, "Ask, and it will be given you; seek and you will find; knock and it will be opened to you... If you then being evil know how to give good gifts to your children, how much more will your heavenly Father give *good things* to those who ask Him." So we should make the choice that Mary made, and come with great expectancy to feed on the "bread of life" until we are strong and well-nourished inside. To go away half-full does not provide much strength to win wars!

He Desires to Help Us Maintain the Fullness of the Spirit

We are all familiar with the Lord's final words to His disciples just before He left them to return to heaven: "You shall receive power when the Holy Spirit has come upon you" (Acts

1:8). This is a wonderful promise, but as we read on through the epistles of the New Testament, we soon discover that there are various maladies which can short-circuit that power. All of these maladies come from the same source, which is called our flesh.

Paul deals with this problem over and over again. One of his strongest statements is in Romans 8:13: "If you live after the flesh you will die." But he doesn't leave us there. He moves right into the solution. "But if you, *through the Spirit*, put to death the deeds of the body, you will live." The Holy Spirit is there to help, whenever we are ready to cooperate with Him.

This brings us back to where we began. "The desires of the flesh are against the Spirit, and the desires of the Spirit are against the flesh." But now let us focus on the latter half of that verse. "The desires of the Spirit are against the flesh." They are strongly against the flesh. He is ready to help us *slay* the flesh whenever we are ready. And it is only His power which will enable us to do so. Without this help, we are entirely at a loss to rid ourselves of a life of continual failure. Without the continual full indwelling of the Holy Spirit, our life is hopeless and helpless!

This is what Paul is seeking to get across to us when he writes, "I say, keep walking by the Spirit and you will not carry out the desires of the flesh" (Gal. 5:16). This is one of my favorite verses, because it is the solution to so many of our problems. In fact it is the solution to our most basic problem. So let us give close attention to this tremendous promise.

Paul is using one of his word pictures here, that of *walking*. Walking is taking steps. He is urging us to make sure that *each step* we take in our daily lives be taken with the help and direction of the Holy Spirit. If we will do this, the flesh doesn't have a chance.

To me, "each step" means at the beginning of each day, at the outset of each project, at the first suggestion of any temptation, at the beginning of preparation for each opportunity of service, and whenever I might need His help. I ask for His special endowment of power and wisdom.

At the conclusion of the Lord's most comprehensive lesson on prayer He promises, "How much more will your Heavenly Father *give the Holy Spirit* to those who ask Him?" (Lk. 11:13). But to grasp the great significance of what He is saying here, we need to appreciate the tense of the verbs in the original Greek grammar. It really should read, "How much more will your heavenly Father *keep giving* the Holy Spirit to those who *keep asking* Him?" It is again the picture of walking by the Spirit, of inviting His fullness and His help at every step. The amount of time we spend in prayer seeking His assistance will depend on the magnitude of the step we are about to take. There were times when the Lord Jesus spent the whole night in prayer.

The means which the Holy Spirit often uses to lead us and strengthen us is to *remind* us of some relevant truth or instruction which the Lord has given us through His Word. In introducing the Holy Spirit to His disciples, He pointed out that one of the primary ways the "Helper" would help was to "bring to your remembrance all that I said to you." He, the "Counselor," is the "Spirit of *Truth*."

He Desires to Help Us Break the World's Grip

Satan knows that our flesh loves the world. The flesh and the world are great pals. Since Satan is the "Tempter," he knows how to dangle the things of the world before our eyes in a most enticing manner. He is always doing all he can to appeal to our flesh. The Holy Spirit is anxious to help us put it to death. So we are back to our battle again.

The apostle John gives strong words regarding the allurements of the world: "Do not love the world, nor the things in the world. If anyone loves the world, the love of the Father is not in him. For all that is in the world, the lust of the flesh, the lust of the eyes and the pride of life, is not from the Father, but is from the world" (1 Jn. 2:15,16).

The word for "love" here is the word "agape" which is the same kind of love the Lord Jesus urges us to have for one another. We are to maintain real concern, ready to give of our time, thought and money to a brother in need. But we are *not* to give concern, time, thought or money to the things of the world.

Now just what sort of things is it that we are not to give our precious time and attention to? John lists three items: the lust of the flesh, the lust of the eyes, and the pride of life. The word "lust," in more common English, means "desire." So what John is saying is that I am not to get overly involved in the things my flesh would desire to *do*, the things my eyes would like to *get*, and the things my pride wants me to *be*. What I want to do, to get and to be are what the world lives for. But a soldier of Jesus Christ must keep himself free from all these undue enticements. It was Sampson's lusts, Judas' greed, and Saul's pride which became their undoing.

The three verses (12-14) just preceding John's passage on "love not the world" are a noteworthy introduction to his warning. It is that section where he says six times, "I write to you." Twice he addresses himself to his "little children" who are new believers; twice to "young men" who are "strong"; and twice to the "fathers" who are mature. They all needed this loving admonition to keep themselves free from the love of the world. Our hearts love the Lord, but our flesh loves the world. One part desires to belong to God's kingdom, and the other desires to belong to Satan's kingdom, so there is a continual inner war. But John's conclusion gives us a strengthening reminder. "The world and its desires pass away, but the man who does the will of God lives forever."

That which the world strives hardest to obtain is riches. But wealth itself, and the seeking after wealth, are probably the greatest deterrents which hinder people from entering the kingdom of God. The Lord Jesus said, "It is easier for a camel to pass through the eye of a needle than for a rich man to enter the kingdom of heaven" (Lk. 18:25). No wonder Satan so strongly focuses man's attention on material possessions. And no wonder the Lord is so disinterested in our becoming rich. Any preaching, therefore, which promises material prosperity is definitely off the track. In his book *Screwtape Letters*, C.S. Lewis writes, "Prosperity knits a man to the world. He feels he has found his place in the world, but the truth is, the world has found its place in him."

If I am to be able to honestly pray "Thy kingdom come," I must be living for His kingdom and not for the world. The primary weapons in the book of Acts were self-denial, prayer, and fasting. And one of the best ways for me to maintain victory over the world and the things of the world is to keep the things of the world in their proper place.

When Paul was trying to prepare Timothy for spiritual warfare, he reminded him that "No soldier in active service *entangles* himself with the affairs of this life." And again, when Paul is beseeching us to present our bodies to God for His service, he adds, "Be not conformed to this world, but be *transformed* by a renewing of your minds" (Rom. 12:2). Soldiers of the cross are to keep themselves free from the encumbrances of the world.

As Paul put it in Philippians 3, all of us must be prepared to do some "striving" in order to keep ourselves free from the allurements of the world. It is not a simple matter. Some are pulled strongly by a desire for *pleasure*. For others it is a fascination for money, property or just *things*. And a third group are those who have a great passion for *prestige*. Pleasure, possessions and prestige are all extremely attractive to our flesh, and Satan knows this all too well. So he uses these at every opportunity to pull us off the track of our pursuit of God's kingdom. Before we know it, he has diluted our devotion to the King of the kingdom. Every Christian needs a certain amount of recreation to restore and renew his energies, but our enemy tries to get us to overdo even legitimate essentials. Yes, we must become *weaned* from the world if we are to attain to mature manhood and become soldiers.

Although the temptations may recur persistently, we need not accept defeat in this area. Let us hear these encouraging words of the Lord Jesus again: "Be of good cheer, I have overcome *the world*." And His message here is, I have overcome it and I intend to help you overcome it too! So let us see how He overcame the world.

At the very beginning of Jesus' ministry, the Tempter came to try to pull Him off course. He used all three of his schemes to entice Him: the lust of the flesh, the lust of the eyes, and the pride of life. In order to rebuff each temptation, the Lord Jesus quoted a portion of God's Word which He had memorized. He used the "Sword of the Spirit, which is the Word of God." We will discuss this sword more in detail in our chapters on armor and weapons, but here we need to see how effective this double-edged sword can be. After the Lord Jesus repelled each of the three temptations with the Word of God, it says, "The devil left Him and behold, angels came and ministered to Him" (Mt. 4:ll). And the same results are available for you and me.

Here I want to suggest a few sword verses which can be used against each of the three forms of temptation. It will be very helpful to memorize some of these. Or of course you can make up your own list. But we need to have some specific cartridges stored and ready for handy use in our ammunition belt.

To Ward Off the Desires of the Flesh

"If you live according to the flesh you will die, but if *by the Spirit* you put to death the misdeeds of the body, you will live" (Rom. 8:13).

"Put on the Lord Jesus Christ, and *make no provision* for the flesh to gratify its desires" (Rom. 13:14).

"Put to death therefore what is *earthly* in you: immorality, impurity, passion, evil desire, and covetousness which is idolatry" (Col. 3:5).

"*Abstain* from the passions of the flesh which wage war against your soul" (1 Pet. 2:ll).

To Resist the Desires of the Eyes (Material Possessions)

"You shall not *covet*" (Ex. 20:17).

"Do not lay up for yourselves *treasures* on earth" (Mt. 6:19).

"No one can serve two masters; for either he will hate the one and love the other, or he will be devoted to the one and despise the other. You *cannot* serve God and money" (Mt. 6:24).

"Seek *first* His kingdom and His righteousness, and all these things [daily needs] shall be yours as well" (Mt. 6:33).

"It is more blessed to *give* than to receive" (Acts 20:35).

"If we have food and clothing, with these we shall be *content*. But those who desire to be rich fall into temptation, into a snare, into many senseless and hurtful desires that plunge man into ruin and destruction" (1 Tim. 6:8,9).

"Keep your life *free* from the love of money, and be content with what you have; for He has said,'I will never leave you nor forsake you'" (Heb. 13:5).

To Overcome the Pride of Life

"When pride comes, then comes disgrace, but with *humility* comes wisdom" (Prov. 11:2).

"The Lord *detests* all the proud of heart. Be sure of this: they will not go unpunished" (Prov. 16:5).

"If anyone wants to be first, he must be the very last, and the *servant* of all" (Mk. 9:35).

"God opposes the proud, but gives grace to the *humble*" (Jas. 4:6).

"*Humble yourselves* before the Lord and He will exalt you" (Jas. 4:10).

David's key to winning the inner struggle has always been a great help to me. "Your Word have I hid in my heart that I might not sin against You" (Ps. 119:11). God also gave the same piece of wisdom to Solomon. "My son, keep my words and store up my commands within you. Keep my commands and you will live; guard my teachings as the apple of your eye. Bind them on your fingers; write them on the table of your heart" (Prov. 7:1-3).

It is a serious thing to realize that to the extent I love the world, to that extent I do not love God and His kingdom (1 Jn. 2:15). The next verse repeats it from another angle. The desires of my flesh are not on the side of God and His kingdom, but are fighting on the side of the world, which is Satan's kingdom. So as long as such a condition exists, the Holy Spirit is not free to do what He desires to do through me. Or, to sum it up, the spiritual man is the person whose concerns are ultimately for God's kingdom. The worldly man is the person who holds concerns for the things of the world.

In closing this chapter, we return to the basic issue of battle, which is the *goodness of God*. We might say that God's goodness points due north. The pull of the world and the pull of my flesh cause my life to drift in a wrong direction, but the Holy Spirit is continually present with me, seeking to help me to overcome these forces, in order that my life and its goodness, like the goodness of my Father, will also point only north.

PART TWO:

OUR ENABLEMENTS

8

OUR COMMISSION

One would feel that our wonderful message of salvation, delivered by hearts of love and compassion, would readily be welcomed with open arms. But the contrary is nearly always the case. When the Lord's messengers enter a dark, heathen area with this light of the gospel, a strange, sinister reaction takes place. Even though the people themselves may for the most part be friendly and willing to hear, yet it is never long before a subtle, unseen opposition begins to block any real reception of the truth.

This opposition is no minor matter. It is always there in every place, and Paul labels these areas as "strongholds." The Lord Jesus called them "the gates of hell," bearing the sign "keep out." Not only have people been blinded and deafened to the message; not only are they ensnared by the lusts of the flesh and the love of the world, but uncanny, unseen forces immediately attack any intruder who would seek deliverance for these captives. Therefore the servant of the Lord who starts out on a mission of light and life soon finds himself caught up in spiritual warfare.

Elsewhere we have referred to James Frazer's initial converts among the Lisu tribe in West China. Each one became strangely and painfully ill as soon as he believed. We have also mentioned the Lin family who, within twenty-four hours after moving into Peikang as missionaries, were rushed to the emergency ward of the Chiayi Christian Hospital with an unexplained illness. Another friend of mine who moved to the Tachia area to preach the gospel awoke one night with a terrible choking spell. He resisted this attack in the name of the Lord Jesus, and it stopped immediately. But two more times that night the same thing happened before he was finally set free. As I began preparing this book exposing Satan's schemes and calling God's people to become involved in this spiritual battle, one night I was awakened with a stifling pressure on my chest. When I rebuked the enemy in Jesus' name, it ceased. But again it came and this thing carried on for some time before it was completely warded off.

When we first began our village work twenty years ago, a number of strange attacks came upon the families of those involved. My own son, who was about four years old at the time, would cry out in his sleep with nightmares of demons. I couldn't understand how he even knew what a demon was. In a village where there had been some response, a farmer believed and the next morning his perfectly healthy ox had died. This of course terrified the other folks in the village, but the farmer was so elated with his new life in Christ that he asked the Lord to sustain him, and testified to his neighbors that forgiveness of sins and his new peace and joy were worth it all.

Sometimes the attacks are more straightforward. People become rude and threatening, and doors are slammed in the face of those bringing the gospel. In one village the local priests and some ruffians beat up one of the student team members. In other areas of the world, serious persecution, even leading to a martyr's death, is not uncommon.

Joshua met exactly the same type of opposition when he and the people of God entered Canaan. They came with full evidence of the tremendous blessing of God upon them, yet the people of the land were stricken with fear. Instead of seeking this wonderful blessing for themselves, they declared war against the God of Israel and His forces. Only one person, Rahab the prostitute, saw things clearly, and pled for mercy and deliverance. Her request was granted with an abundance of blessing, for she became a "mother in Israel," with even the Lord Jesus Himself as one of her descendants. The rest were blind and hostile to that which could have become their eternal bliss. One heathen tribe, the Gibeonites, used trickery to spare their lives but did not possess the slightest hunger for spiritual things.

This overall reaction was uncanny indeed! So much so that there is only one explanation. There was again, as always, that unseen, sinister kingdom behind it all. And the king of this kingdom was so determined to protect his domain (which he had controlled for many centuries) that he blinded them all and turned their reasoning into foolishness. He employed them as his enslaved forces to fight with all their might against the kingdom of grace and righteousness.

So when God's people arrived, there was an immediate power encounter, a declaration of war, and this is an Old Testament picture of what happens today when we begin to enter "unreached" territory. The purpose of this book is preparation for just this type of offensive. We need to hear what the Lord had to say to Joshua as He commissioned Him to enter Canaan, for our commission is really quite the same as his.

"Cross the Jordan"

Joshua's commissioning called for a supernatural mentality from the very outset. It began with an "impossible" set of orders: "You and all these people cross this Jordan." Although the Jordan River was normally only about one hundred feet wide, the account reminds us that this particular time of year was flood season when the Jordan can be a mile across and exceptionally treacherous. Also, the population of "these people," (the Children of Israel) at that stage was well over two million. Thus even the crossing itself presented a tremendous problem, and on the other side were the Canaanites who were inflamed by Satan to do their utmost to destroy these intruders! Thus Joshua, in the very opening sentence of God's commission to him, was presented with an insuperable set of orders.

Then there was another significant factor which must have caused his assignment to loom large before him. For some five hundred years, ever since the days of Abraham, the Lord had been *promising* this land of Canaan to His people. He had even very specifically marked out its four borders. And now again in this first chapter of Joshua, His promise is repeated five times. In verse 6 He speaks of it as "the land which I swore to their fathers to give them." So it has come to be spoken of even to this day as the "Promised Land." Yet as the Lord commissioned Joshua, He conditioned His promise with the words, "Every place on which the sole of your foot treads." The Lord was by no means just handing over to His people a big beautiful piece of real estate. They were going to have to fight for every inch of it. It was to be battle all the way. In fact the only two occasions when Joshua met failure were when he tried to avoid a battle. These were in the case of the first strike at Ai when he only sent a small portion of his troops, and then later when he accepted a truce from the Gibeonites.

God could very easily have sent a few angels to do the job for Joshua and saved Israel's soldiers all that blood, sweat, and tears. Once when Hezekiah was in a real bind, besieged by 185,000 Assyrian warriors, the Lord sent one angel and wiped out the whole lot in one evening. But He seldom does things that way. The Lord desires to involve us in the conflict throughout our entire Christian career here on earth. He wants us as His eternal children to get some conception of what is going on in this universe, to learn the rudiments of spiritual warfare, to develop faith, to see Him do great and mighty things, and to get a taste of the sweetness of deliverance for ourselves and others. So we don't get very far by merely waiting or pleading for Him to do it all for us.

"Be Strong and Courageous"

This second clause in Joshua's commission follows naturally upon the first and calls for a *power* mentality. It is repeated three times, with a stronger emphasis each time. The second time the Lord adds, "Be strong and *very* courageous." The third time, "Have I not commanded you? Be strong and courageous! Do not tremble or be dismayed."

The Lord is seeking to endue Joshua with a positive, move-ahead fortitude. He wants Joshua to get to the place where he eats, drinks and sleeps with the consciousness and expectancy of power. God also desires this for us and longs for us to enter into *His* strength and accomplishments. He would have us get to the place where we have iron in our blood and power in our bones. Challenges from His Word like the following can accomplish this for us:

"In the name of our God we will set up our banners" (Ps. 20:5).

"The Lord strong and mighty, the Lord mighty in battle. The Lord of hosts, He is the King of Glory" (Ps. 24:10).

"The Lord will march out like a mighty man...and triumph over His enemies" (Ps. 60:12).

"The chariots of God are myriads, thousands upon thousands" (Ps. 68:17).

"The Lord will go forth like a warrior, He will arouse His zeal like a man of war. He will utter a shout, yes, He will raise a war cry. He will prevail against His enemies" (Isa. 42:13).

During World War II General Douglas MacArthur, commander of the Allied forces for Asia and the Pacific, was sent to Australia on one occasion to give direction to the beleaguered forces on that continent. When he arrived, the leadership in charge of the Australian troops welcomed him gladly and immediately began to describe their short supply of men and materials, expecting the general to offer a large contingent of forces and armaments to help protect their country. But they were shocked beyond measure when General MacArthur informed them that he had not come merely to protect Australia, but quite to the contrary, he was ordering the Australian forces to become involved at once in the front lines on the islands at a distance from their own shores. The wise general's first duty, as he clearly saw it, was to replace the spirit of "fear and dismay" with a battle mentality.

A similar development took place in the spiritual realm when Dr. Harold Ockenga was invited to become pastor of the Park Street Congregational Church in Boston. The church was in a pitiful state at that time. They had opened up the Sunday School rooms along the sides of the busy corner where the church was located and rented them out to various small businesses in order to pay their monthly bills. But Dr. Ockenga, a man of tremendous missionary vision, would have none of this. He at once laid down his conditions for accepting their invitation to come as pastor. The church had been striving to give a thousand dollars a year to missions, but he insisted that they promise to double this amount each year. It didn't require a great deal of mathematics to realize that within seven years they would have to come up with well over one hundred thousand dollars a year for missions. They protested that he was being extremely unreasonable. Within a year or two they would not even be able to manage his salary. "Forget about my salary," was his reply. But still they couldn't even consider such a preposterous, extreme demand. "I'm afraid, then, that I will not be able to come," was his conclusion. "Oh, but we very much want you to come. How about a compromise?" ..."No. No compromise, but I plead with you to give it a try."

Reluctantly, with many misgivings, they invited Dr. Ockenga to come, and that church really began to grow. Today Park Street Church in Boston is an example of a prospering, healthy congregation. They have purchased other properties next to their original sanctuary, to put up a multi-storied Christian Education building; they are broadcasting over many stations; and they have a sizeable staff of pastors and office personnel to carry on their worldwide ministry.

There is no substitute for a "power" mentality. Paul's reminder to Timothy is very appropriate here. "God has not given us a spirit of timidity, but of power, love and a sound mind" (2 Tim. 1:7). This admonition is particularly needed when we are dealing with missionary vision. Loss of vision and drive in this vital area of our Christian commitment will soon result in spiritual deadness. We have examples all around us in churches, student groups, and individual lives.

I shall never forget the time our Village Gospel Mission invited pastor Chou Shen-Chu (leader of the thriving, twelve-story Ling Liang Church in Taipei) to speak to our staff. His message was short and simple. He had collected a number of the challenging verses on power from the New Testament, and he read them to us with confidence and great expectancy. I include a few of them here:

"May the God of hope fill you with all joy and peace in believing, so that by the *power* of the Holy Spirit, you may abound in hope" (Rom. 15:13).

"My speech and my message were not in plausible words of wisdom, but in demonstration of the Spirit and *power*...that your faith might not rest in the wisdom of men, but in the *power* of God" (1 Cor. 2:4,5).

"The kingdom of God does not consist in talk but in *power*" (1 Cor. 4:20).

"That you may know...what is the immeasurable greatness of His *power* in us who believe, according to the working of His great might" (Eph. 1:19).

"Now to Him who by the *power* at work within us is able to do far more than all that we ask or think, to Him be glory in the church and in Christ Jesus to all generations, forever and ever, amen" (Eph. 3:20,21).

"Our gospel came to you not only in word, but also in *power* and in the Holy Spirit" (1 Thess. 1:5).

"We always pray for you, that our God may make you worthy of His call, and may fulfil every good purpose and work of faith by His *power*" (2 Thess. 1:11).

Now coming back to Joshua, he *was* "strong" in his God, and the Lord gave some tremendous exhibitions of His power. He caused those formidable, impenetrable walls of Jericho to come tumbling down! He rained massive hailstones from heaven on the enemies! He even made the sun stand still! And the Lord will do some "great and mighty things" for us too. He may grant some miraculous healings. He will deliver people from demonization, and perhaps give other visible tokens of His mighty power. But He desires even more to strengthen us with the *power of proclamation*. Later we will devote a whole chapter to this vital element of our power.

Provision—"The Lord Your God is with You"

An essential part of any commission deals with the matter of provision. What makes it all possible is the source of power and supplies. Four times in Joshua's commission the Lord assures him that He will be with him. He will never leave him or forsake him. In the opening sentence He begins, "Moses my servant is dead; now you..." Twenty-two times Moses is called "the servant of the Lord." This title is used of Moses far more than of any other person. The Lord chose Moses as a very special instrument through whom He would accomplish many "impossible" feats for His glory. Moses merely had to fulfill the role of servant. Now the same Lord was speaking to Joshua in the same way He had spoken to Moses. So, rather than creating fear by the assignment being given to Joshua, this introduction made it possible for him to move ahead with great assurance.

The truth of this promise can transform our ministry when it takes hold of us. The last final reminder which came from the lips of the Lord Jesus as He left this earth was that same provision: "Lo, I am with you always, even to the end of the age." And it immediately followed His commission to us, "Go and make disciples of all nations." This commission was also preceded by the words, "All power [authority] is given unto Me in heaven and on earth. Go *therefore*..." (Mt. 28:18-20). When we learn to live and move in the confidence of this provision, a new dimension of strength comes into our service.

Now, coming back to Moses, the mighty leader of God's people. The reason for his spiritual prowess was his determination to be assured of *God's presence* with him. One example was when things got out of control in the wilderness when Aaron led the people to make the golden calf. Moses was very angry and very discouraged. He finally turned to the Lord and cried out, "If your presence does not go with us, do not lead us up from here" (Ex. 33:15). Moses was making the statement from his heart, "If I can't be assured of Your presence, there is no point in our moving another step. We also need to get to the place where we make the same resolve.

The Lord repeated His promise to His servant Moses, that His presence would indeed go with him. And this assurance rings out in the last words of Moses' farewell message to the people: "Blessed are you, O Israel; who is like you, *a people saved by the Lord. He* is your shield and helper and your glorious sword. Your enemies will cower before you, and you will trample down their high places" (Dt. 33:29).

So our study of Joshua's commission brings us to the place where we can see that the entry into the Promised Land was accomplished by two armies, the seen and the unseen. And the latter was far more vital than the former.

We must also note that there were two commanders. Joshua was the visible captain of Israel's visible forces, but just before they moved out toward their first battle, a man with a drawn sword appeared to Joshua. "Who are you? Are you for us or against us?" Joshua asked. "I am captain of the army of the Lord," was the reply. Then He commanded Joshua to remove his shoes, for he was standing on holy ground. Thus Joshua was introduced to his Unseen Captain, who was indeed the Supreme Commander.

The provisions of our commission are exactly the same. There are two armies and two commanders. Sometimes our visible army is rather small and weak. But this matters little when we know that we are surrounded and supported by the magnificent troops of heaven. As to our visible captains, even Paul had to admit to the Corinthians that he came to them "with weakness and fear and much trembling." But when it comes to our unseen Commander, it is written, "God seated Him at His right hand in the heavenly places, far above all rule and authority and power and dominion, and every name that is named, not only in this age, but in the age to come. And He put all things in subjection under His feet" (Eph. 1:20-22).

Now, with this almighty Commander leading forth His invincible armies before us into each conflict, how can we possibly fail? And yet the sad, indisputable truth is that too many times we do fail! How can this be? It is because victory is not automatic!

In one sense the Lord's presence is always with us. He has promised that He will never leave us or forsake us. But the degree to which we can count on the power of His presence with us depends on several things. In Old Testament days there were many occasions when the Lord's unseen armies did *not* fight for Israel. And yet there were other times when the Lord's presence so permeated the tabernacle that the priests were unable to enter it. Truly the blessing of His presence with us is a relative matter.

One of the Psalms expresses this truth: "He who *dwells* in the secret place of the Most High will rest in the shadow of the Almighty...Surely He will cover you with His feathers and under His wings you will find refuge; His faithfulness will be your shield and rampart. You will not fear the terror of night, nor the arrow that flies by day...*If you* make the Most High your dwelling...He will command His angels concerning you to guard you in all your ways. ... '*Because he loves Me*,' says the Lord, 'I will rescue him. I will protect him, *for* he acknowledges My name. He will *call upon Me*, and I will answer him. I will be with him in trouble. I will deliver him and honor him'" (Ps. 91).

Yes, *all* the Lord's wonderful promises have their conditions. We deceive ourselves when we try to claim a promise, and yet fail to consider its conditions. When we do meet His stipulations, unlimited provisions are available to us. Therefore, as we gather all His wonderful provisions, let's not forget to read the instructions that come with each one. Now we come to the final part of Joshua's commission.

Meditate in the Book

"This book of the law shall not depart from your mouth, but you shall meditate on it day and night, so that you may observe to do according to all that is written in it; for then you will make your way prosperous, and then you will have success.

It was as if the Lord were saying, "Now Joshua, here is your handbook containing all the 'principles of war.' It contains all the promises and provisions; it also contains all the instructions and conditions. You will need to keep up on both types of material. *Then* you will prosper and succeed."

Paul had similar words for his successor, Timothy. "All Scripture...is useful for teaching, rebuking, correcting and training in righteousness, so that the man of God may be *thoroughly equipped* for every good work" (2 Tim. 3:16,17).

For the best example of a warrior who kept himself "thoroughly equipped," we must turn again to David. Since God urged Joshua to meditate in His Word day and night, David took it upon himself to do just that. We hear him sing, "Oh how I love your law; it is my meditation all the day." And again, "I have more insight than all my teachers, for your testimonies are my meditation" (Ps. 119:97,99).

David regarded habitual meditation in God's Word as the basic preparation for his military involvements. "Teach me your way, O Lord; lead me in a straight path, because of my enemies" (Ps. 27:11). "The wicked are waiting to destroy me, but I will ponder your statutes" (Ps. 119:95). "Your commands make me wiser than my enemies" (Ps. 119:98). "Many are the foes who persecute me, but I have not turned from Your testimonies" (Ps. 119:157).

Since Joshua's time, God's handbook has grown in size considerably. It is now well over one thousand pages in any translation. In fact some versions are almost two thousand pages. The reason for such a voluminous handbook lies in the increasing complexity of battle campaigns. Ask any general about the latest developments in military science, and he will probably suggest a four-year course in one of the academies. So it is with spiritual warfare. There are, for example, over five hundred references just to the element of "faith." There are many such requisite topics, and each has its relevant subpoints.

Yet this ought not to intimidate or discourage us. To take on the awesome task of trying to master such a mountain of material could naturally be overwhelming for a beginner. But the proper attitude is to approach this book as one would a delightful, nutritious feast. A soldier doesn't try to consume a year's worth of nourishment all in one meal. But this in no way hinders him from enjoying his food day by day. And it all makes him strong for the conflict.

Another very comforting fact is that the Holy Spirit knows exactly what type of new material (or review of previous truth) each of us will need for that day. He is a marvelous, wise teacher. If we are involved in some suitable form of daily Bible study, with provision for ample meditation, He will see to it that we are "thoroughly equipped for every good work."

Reconsidering Our Commission

Here in Taiwan we are seeing some church growth, but actually quite minimal compared with a country like Korea. There are about a thousand of us foreign missionaries on this island, and I am one of them. It has cost the equivalent of about two hundred million U.S. dollars to support all of us and our projects these past ten years, and yet the actual count of active Christians on the island has *decreased* during that same period. According to recent statistical studies, church growth in Taiwan peaked in 1976. And yet since that time we missionaries have put in probably twenty million hours of work. But how many hours of prayer?

Do we need to get back and take another look at Joshua's commission? It centers around those critical words "be strong." Just how strong am I? How much of the Lord's power is truly operating through me? How can I see more of His "great and mighty" accomplishments? There is a war going on! How effective am I in battle? How can I be more effective?

We must return to that truth again, that power is not automatically bestowed on a missionary, or any person. It comes from grasping His promises and meeting their conditions. This must become a working precept for us. In most modern-day mining operations, the process includes the discharge of many thousand sticks of dynamite to break loose the precious ore. There is much precious ore here in Taiwan, waiting for God's *power* to set it free!

9

OUR ARMOR

Armor and weapons are the very stuff of war—armor for defense and protection; weapons for attack and advance. In God's Word there are several references to our spiritual armor, but the most detailed is in Ephesians 6:10-17. Twice in these few verses, Paul urges us to "put on the *full armor* of God." And three times he encourages us that if we do, we will be able to "stand firm" in the midst of the conflict. Spiritual encounter is very different from any other type of combat. As we have mentioned elsewhere, our real enemy is unseen. At times, he may mount a direct attack upon our home, our work, or our physical bodies, yet frequently it will come in the form of what Paul here calls "schemes" or "wiles" against our mind, our emotions, or our spirit. These are subtle, unexpected maneuvers which confront us before we realize it. Therefore it is good to form the habit of carefully buckling on each item of our armor at the beginning of every day.

Our encounters with the enemy are sometimes pictured as *"wrestling,"* which implies close hand-to-hand struggle. If you have never been involved in a wrestling match yourself, perhaps you have watched some on T.V. I did some wrestling in high school and college, so I learned a bit about how tricky and painful such a scrimmage can be. The whole purpose is to get such a hold on an opponent that he is pinned to the mat, or he gives up because of the pain. Another form of wrestling, called "judo," aims to catch the opponent off balance and hurl him down to the ground. The enemy's "schemes" and "wiles" can reduce even the strongest Christian to a state of spiritual immobility if he neglects some item of his armor.

Also, in describing this foe Paul does not just present him as a single individual, but in verse 12 he reminds us that "our struggle is...against the rulers, the authorities, the world powers of this darkness, against the spiritual forces of wickedness." "Forces" means armies, and Paul warns that they are powerful and they are wicked. They do not play fair; they do not abide by any rules. They are out to hurt, hinder and destroy every person involved in the expansion of God's kingdom. Therefore, you and I need to heed the admonition to "put on [daily] the full armor of God."

As we begin the study of the individual pieces of our armor, we should realize that each is designed to protect against a particular type of attack. For instance, in modern day arsenals there are anti-aircraft, anti-tank, anti-submarine, anti-missile, anti-satellite equipment, etc. Warfare becomes more complex with each decade. As we mature spiritually and become more involved in the various aspects of God's work, we discover that there are many kinds of spiritual complications in people's lives and in God's work.

Just as we come to know and understand the ways of our God by collecting and studying His names and attributes, so we can begin to comprehend the tactics of our enemy by giving attention to his names and attributes. Many are mentioned in the Scriptures. Therefore we will consider each part of our armor as it relates to certain aspects of the character of our enemy. Each piece is available for protection against some special type of assault.

The Belt of Truth

Three of Satan's names in Scripture are "Liar," "Deceiver," and "The Old Serpent." This last name is a reminder of his initial approach in the Garden of Eden. The Lord Jesus declared that the Devil has nothing to do with the truth, because there is no truth in him. When he lies, he speaks according to his own nature, for he is a liar and the "Father of Lies" (Jn. 8:44). His lies are of course the root of all the false religions, the cults, the heresies and the divisions within the church. He is a master of deception and distortion. By his mixtures of part error and part truth, he has misled the great masses of mankind into a morass of delusion.

It is not surprising, therefore, that the first component of our armor is "truth," the belt of truth. Much of the soldier's equipment is attached to his belt. So we can begin to appreciate in a new way the words of the Lord Jesus when He said, "If you *continue in My word*, you are truly my disciples, and you will know the *truth*, and the truth will make you free" (Jn. 8:31-32). In other words, step number one in our "Manual of Safety Procedures" for the Lord's soldier is to gird oneself daily with the truths of God's word. Then and only then will God's man be able to "stand firm."

The Devil is called "The Deceiver of the Whole World" (Rev. 12:9). And we are particularly warned that in these last days "many false prophets will arise and lead many astray." (Matt. 24:11) In discussing these false prophets, Paul describes them as "deceitful workmen, *disguising* themselves as apostles of Christ." Then he adds, "for even Satan disguises himself as an angel of light. So it is not strange if his servants also disguise themselves as servants of righteousness" (2 Cor. 11:13-15). These "angels of light" are cropping up all over the world. Within recent decades they have established virulent colonies in Japan, Korea, Taiwan, India, the Middle East, the west coast and east coast of the United States, and probably in many other areas.

One of the prophesies regarding the last days reads: "The activity of Satan will be with all power and with pretended *signs and wonders*, and with all wicked deception for those who are to perish, because they refused to *love the truth*" (2 Thess. 2:9,10). An unhealthy hunger for "signs and wonders" seems to be sweeping the Christian church these days. A great plea, especially for work among the heathen in the villages, and in the underdeveloped regions, is for signs and wonders. The argument is that these people can't read, and even those who can, don't, so signs and wonders are the thing which will attract them.

It is true that the Lord does desire to use some miraculous interventions on occasion. When He decides to do this, naturally we welcome it. But we must be very careful that we don't get carried away and led astray by the "counterfeiter" who is always looking for an opportunity to deceive and delude. It is the *truth* that sets free and arms against error, not signs and wonders.

The church or the fellowship group which clothes its people

with truth need not fear the disguises of the Evil One. The belt of truth is our protection against the plausible allurements of all that is diluted with falsehood. In emphasizing truth, however, we must be careful that we do not just robe ourselves with dead orthodoxy. Peter reminds us that we have been "born anew...through the *living* and abiding word of God" (1 Pet. 1:2,3). It is not just the favorite doctrines of our denomination which save us, but the truths about the living Lord Jesus and His atonement. It is knowing Him, and entering into life with Him by allowing Him to speak His truth to us regularly from His living word, the Scriptures. The word becomes particularly "living" when we meditate on it with the aid of the Holy Spirit, and then apply it practically to our daily lives.

The Breastplate of Righteousness

Six times in Scripture, Satan is called "The Wicked One" and eleven times "The Evil One." In the text which we are studying, his troops are described as "the hosts of wickedness." He and all his forces are vile indeed. The Lord Jesus often called them "unclean spirits" or "evil spirits." It becomes understandable then that one of his main objectives is to defile and putrify the thoughts and character of everyone he possibly can. In fact he has corrupted us all. Actually, man has become so used to uncleanness and impurity that many accept it as the normal way of life. Consequently the apostle John says, "the whole world lies in the lap of the Evil One" (1 Jn. 5:19). He and his hosts of wickedness are the engineers of the awful depravity which throughout history has sunk much of mankind into the mire of detestable abominations.

We are also warned that as we approach the end of this age and our Lord's return, the process of decay even within the ranks of those who call themselves Christians is going to become increasingly widespread. Paul says, "Mark this: there will be terrible times in the last days. People will be lovers of themselves, lovers of money, boastful, proud, abusive, disobedient to their parents, ungrateful, unholy, without love, unforgiving, slanderous, without self-control, brutal, not lovers of the good, treacherous, rash, conceited, lovers of pleasure rather than lovers of God. Having a form of godliness but denying its power" (2 Tim. 3:1-5).

The purpose of this long, detailed list, laid out before us by Paul, is not merely to inform us, but to alert us to make sure that we do not fall into the same quagmire.

There are two types of righteousness for the Christian. The first is *imputed* righteousness which we receive when we accept the Lord Jesus as our Savior. Our sins are forgiven; our slate is wiped clean; the pure and lovely righteousness of the Lord Jesus is credited to our account. The second kind of righteousness has to do with the quality of life which we live as a Christian. We might call it our Christian conduct. When Paul speaks of the breastplate of righteousness, it is quite evident that he is primarily referring to the latter. In the first verse of chapter 4 he says, "I therefore, a prisoner of the Lord, *beg* you to *lead a life* worthy of the calling to which you have been called." A little further down in the same chapter, he uses descriptive terms which give the picture of dressing ourselves with the breastplate of righteousness. He tells us to "*put off* your old nature which belongs to your *former manner of life* and is corrupt through deceitful lusts, and be renewed in the spirit of your minds, and *put on* the new nature, created after the likeness of God in *true righteousness* and holiness."

John spells it out very clearly in his epistle. "Little children, let no one deceive you...He who *does right* is righteous as He is righteous." And again, "by this it may *be seen* who are the children of God, and who are the children of the Devil; whoever does not *do right* is not of God" (1 Jn. 3:7,10). In other words, the breastplate of righteousness is to be a distinctly visible part of our armor. Of course, it is not there for show. Rather it is there for protection. But it should still be evident to ourselves, to others, and to our enemy, whether we have it on. If we are not wearing it, Satan can soon wound us severely. He can shoot all kinds of wicked arrows right into our hearts. After urging us to "put on the new nature," Paul follows with the caution, "and give no opportunity to the Devil."

It is an extremely dangerous risk for a Christian to go

around without the breastplate of righteousness. "By rejecting conscience [the breastplate], certain persons have made shipwreck of their faith" (1 Tim. 1:19). In the church at Corinth, there was a foolish fellow who felt he could flaunt the grace of God by living in sin. Paul ordered them to "deliver this man to Satan for the destruction of the flesh, that his spirit might be saved in the day of the Lord Jesus," and then further told them "not to associate with anyone who bears the name of 'brother' if he is guilty of immorality or greed, or is an idolater, reviler, drunkard or robber...drive out the wicked person from among you" (1 Cor. 5:5,11,13).

While a student in seminary, I received a phone message one afternoon that my best friend, a fellow student, was in the hospital with a broken leg. I immediately rushed over to see him. He had just been brought from the operating room and was awaking from the ether as I walked in. He opened his eyes and looked at me, and his first words were very pitiful. He said, "I know why this has happened to me. I have been playing with sin and God has had to chasten me."

Recently I heard of another Christian brother who had become harassed by a demon. Godly friends of his were able to cast out the evil spirit, and then they asked him when this wicked demon had begun to bother him. He confessed that it was on the day he had deliberately committed a vile sin. It is folly indeed for a child of God ever to neglect to wear his breastplate of righteousness. Satan is always looking for opportunities to get at us and wound us. We dare not tolerate even minor sins. Most major defeats grow out of an accumulation of minor lapses. So it is not very wise for a child of God to remove his breastplate and take a little stroll out into enemy territory. Our flesh at times urges our minds to saunter forth and "enjoy" such an outing. But the Evil One is eager and ready for just such a chance to get his spear into us. "A wise man [soldier] refuses to play the part of a fool!"

Perhaps we should sum up this section with Paul's words to Titus: "Show yourself in all respects a model of good deeds, and in your teaching show integrity, gravity and sound speech that cannot be censured, so that an opponent may be put to shame, having nothing evil to say of us" (Tit. 2:7,8).

Shoes of Peace

Another name which we must ascribe to our enemy is "Sifter." On that night before the Lord Jesus went to the cross, He informed His disciples that Satan was desiring to have them, that he might *sift* you (plural) as one sifts wheat. We have a graphic word picture here. If you have ever seen wheat sifted in an old-fashioned sifter, you will understand the significance of this statement. It vividly portrays another of Satan's tactics. When wheat is sifted, each grain is tossed back and forth in such a vigorous fashion that the wheat is thrown into absolute chaos.

Have you ever found yourself a victim of such treatment? Doesn't it sound familiar? If you try to stand erect, you soon have blisters on both feet. So a soldier in this spiritual warfare needs shoes, a good pair of shoes. He needs boots with cleats, made of the toughest leather, if he is to "stand firm." Can you fancy a marine going out to the front lines barefoot? Not only does our enemy desire to sift us as if the ground beneath us were shaken by an earthquake, but he strews the battlefield with thorns, thistles, poisonous adders and explosive mines. We need the best boots available for protection!

A few summers back, I took my family to the Tung Hsiao beach on the west coast of Taiwan. We arrived when the tide was out, and the long, wide beach was covered with a kind of pointed shells cast off by the crabs. It was probably a hundred yards down to the surf, and we found it so painful walking over these shells in our bare feet that it was impossible to get even half-way to the water's edge. As we were gingerly picking our way back to the boardwalk with our sore, bleeding feet, we saw another vacationer briskly heading out for a swim. He walked along as if there were no shells there at all. As he passed us, I noticed that he was wearing a pair of sturdy, transparent plastic shoes. What a difference!

Have you ever stopped to think that the legacy which the Lord Jesus left His disciples was a pair of shoes? On the night before His death He said to them, "*Peace* I leave with you; My peace I give you. I do not give to you as the world gives. Do not let your hearts be troubled and do not be afraid" (Jn. 14:27). In speaking of our Christian armor, Paul labels this particular part of it the "shoes of peace," or shoes which are "the preparation of the gospel of peace." First we need the gospel of salvation, but after we are saved, we also need the preparation (some translate it "equipment") of the message of peace, for our enemy soon begins to sow our pathway with all kinds of painful harassments.

The typical legacy which a wealthy parent leaves his children includes land or money or jewelry or some other tangible items of value. But the Lord Jesus said, "I do not give to you as the world gives." He left us no land, money, or material jewels. But He did leave us a vast supply of spiritual blessings. And the one which He particularly singled out as especially precious was peace, the message of peace. A little later on that evening, He brought up the matter again and said, "I have told you these things, so that in Me you may have *peace*. In this world you will have trouble. But take heart! I have overcome the world" (Jn. 16:33). In the world we have trouble. In Him we have peace. Trouble and peace are enemies, but the Lord thoroughly intends our peace to win out and overcome the trouble.

Note how He said, "I have told you *these things, so that* in Me you may have peace." As we have mentioned before, every promise has its condition. The condition for enjoying the protection of our shoes of peace is to put them on! We are to have our feet "shod," or fitted, with the preparation (equipment, readiness) of the good news of peace. When the Lord Jesus said, "I have told you these things, so that in Me you may have peace," "these things" refers to a substantial body of instruction which He gave them that night, recorded in the five chapters of John 13-17. A certain rather simple formula for peace emerges as we follow through what the Holy Spirit says about peace in the epistles.

We might put it this way: every soldier needs two shoes, one for his right foot and one for his left. As we survey the provisions for heart peace in God's word, there seem to be basically two. One is *asking for wisdom* to know how to handle the problem which is at the heart of our frustration. The other is *offering up praise* to God for His love, His understanding and ability, which are sufficient for any situation. The latter must include specific thanksgiving for the benefits and blessings He has been granting me recently, and for those special deliverances from my perplexities in the past. These two exercises, asking for wisdom and offering up praise, are meant to be firm supports and comforting cushions under our feet. They are indispensable pieces of our armor.

One of the "things" which the Lord had previously said to His disciples was, "Behold, I have given you authority to tread upon serpents and scorpions, and over all the power of the enemy, and nothing shall injure you" (Lk. 10:19). Discouragement and depression seem to be two kinds of "serpents and scorpions" which Satan is employing in ever-increasing measure these days to bite and sting God's people and remove them from the battlefront. Sometimes severe depression may be in part due to a chemical imbalance, but often it is nothing other than a pit or trap which Satan has set to immobilize one of God's soldiers. The passage of Scripture which most quickly brings me out of the doldrums is the encouragement provided in Philippians 4:6-8: "Do not be anxious about *anything*, but in *everything*, by prayer and petition [for wisdom] *with thanksgiving*, present your requests to God. And the *peace* of God, which transcends all understanding, will guard your hearts and minds in Christ Jesus. Finally, brothers, whatever is true, whatever is noble, whatever is right, whatever is pure, whatever is lovely, whatever is admirable...if anything is excellent or praiseworthy ...*think on these things*."

Much discouragement and depression come from thinking on the negative, the problems, the hurts, the lack of gifts and talents, etc. Satan is a very negative being. He majors on that which is ugly, contrary, and deadening. His whole realm is called "the kingdom of darkness." God is the Lord of light, love and beauty. He desires His children to have no contamination from the kingdom of darkness. If you are constantly being "sifted" back and forth in dejection, gloom and heaviness, I suggest that you read the book on God's *Favor*, by Bob Buess. God has a pair of shoes for you; they are just your size, and they are labeled "peace"!

Shield of Faith

Now we come to a particularly essential part of our armor,

the shield of faith. Paul says, *"Above all,* taking the shield of faith, with which you can quench all the flaming darts of the Evil One."* The primary name of our enemy is "Satan," which means "adversary." The Lord Jesus also called him a "murderer," and Peter describes him as a "lion," seeking some victims to devour. Although Satan our adversary is to be charged with many physical and bodily murders, he is primarily interested in spiritual murder. When Peter referred to him as a lion, he added, "Resist him, strong in your *faith."*

In describing the function of our shield, Paul says it is to "quench all the *flaming darts* of the Evil One." What are these flaming darts? If they are to be quenched by faith, then they must be the opposite of faith. They must be flaming, burning *doubts,* a kind of incendiary shells which would destroy our confidence in God and in what He has said. Hebrews 11:6 is a verse which Satan knows well. "Without faith it is impossible to please God. For whoever would draw near to God must *believe* that He exists and that He rewards those who diligently seek Him." The Devil knows that if he can shoot us full of doubts, he can tear apart our Christian life.

In the very beginning, he seriously wounded Adam and Eve with one of his fiery darts. Before they realized what had happened, their hearts had been pierced with disastrous doubt as to what God had said. That chapter begins with this fearsome statement: "The serpent was more crafty than any beast of the field which God had made."

We might class the questioning of God's assertions as "intellectual doubts." Satan hates the Scriptures so he is always looking for any opportunity to weaken one's confidence in that book. If he can't persuade us to disbelieve its authenticity, he will so manipulate our schedule that we neglect the study of God's word. Consequently our faith becomes weak, because we don't actually know, or have forgotten, some of the essential shielding materials that God has given us. Satan not only hurls darts of doubt, but he is also eager to *remove our shield.*

Another one of his fiery darts of doubt is to get us to blame God when things go wrong. We question God's love for us or His wisdom in ever allowing such a catastrophe to happen. Why wasn't He in control of things? Such doubts are indeed "fiery." They are painful for us, and they set fire to God's integrity in our eyes. This of course pleases Satan immensely, for he has won another victory.

"Resist him, strong in your faith." This means, don't forget that he [Satan] is the Evil One. All doubts are "fiery darts of the *Evil One*." All evil really comes from *him*! So don't blame God. Blame *Satan* when things go wrong! "Every *good* and *perfect* gift is from above, coming down from the Father of lights, who does not change" (Jas. 1:17). "God is love." He is only the author of good. He has nothing to do with evil. "In Him is no darkness at all." Hold up your shield of faith. Ward off all those ugly thoughts which blame God. Turn them back onto Satan. Blame him for all the evil attacks on your life, and turn to your loving heavenly Father with *faith* in His promises, faith in His love, faith in His wisdom, and faith in His power. Soon you will be praising Him, and soon you will be singing. Yes, the shield of faith is a vital piece of equipment. David's favorite song was, "His mercy endureth forever." Such confidence makes a beautiful, impenetrable shield.

A few choice reminders from God's word may help us to maintain a firm grip on our shield of faith:

"I have come that they may have life, and have it to the full" (Jn. 10:10).

"As the heavens are higher than the earth, so are My ways higher than your ways, and My thoughts than your thoughts" (Isa. 55:9).

"As for God, His way is perfect" (Ps. 18:30).

"We know that in all things God works for the good of those who love Him" (Rom. 8:28).

"Did I not tell you that if you *believed*, you would see the glory of God?" (Jn. 11:40).

"Call to Me, and I will show you great and mighty things which you know not" (Jer. 33:3).

The Helmet of Salvation

Our helmet is to protect our head, our thinking apparatus,

our self-image. Much depression comes from poor self-image. A depressed Christian with a poor self-image is not a strong soldier. Our enemy is fully aware of this, so he hurls accusations at God's people right and left. In fact his name, "The Devil," means "accuser." And in Revelation 12:10 he is specifically called "the Accuser of the Brethren...who accuses them day and night."

Some Christians are particularly vulnerable to this type of attack. If I am not as gifted as others, if I don't possess an attractive, out-going personality, if I am held back with a physical handicap or a low income bracket, I may be an easy target for the enemy's accusations. I may suffer much from deep feelings of poor self-worth. My head, my whole thought pattern, having been badly injured, I naturally withdraw from any front-line encounters and spend my time in the valley called "no hope."

My own personal experience has been that when I am in such a state of "low tide," the Holy Spirit, the Comforter, often brings relief by reminding me that Satan is a liar. That is, whenever he can plant the thoughts of "no hope" or "no worth" in my mind, he has succeeded in bridling me with some of his lies. Our God is the "God of Hope," and every one of His children are of great value to Him. He paid a tremendous price for each one. As Paul closed his letter to the Christians in Rome, his prayer for them was: "Now may the God of *hope* fill you with all joy and peace in *believing*, that you may *abound in hope* by the power of the Holy Spirit (Rom. 15:13).

There is another type of accusation, however, which can inflict wounds on those who are the very picture of success. These are the direct darts of criticism or condemnation from either friend or foe. The successful person may have such a positive image of himself that the least blow can send him sprawling, and he doesn't recover for days or weeks. His pride has been badly hurt. His head is bleeding profusely, so he too must retire from the battle.

A perfect example is the prophet Elijah after his great victory on Mount Carmel. The wicked queen Jezebel severely criticized his accomplishments and threatened his life, so he ran away and hid. After tramping a day's journey into the wilderness, he flopped down under a juniper tree and asked the Lord to let him die. "It is enough, O Lord, take my life, for I am not better than my fathers." After lying there under that tree for a few days, he trudged another forty days out into the hills until he came to Mount Horeb and found a cave to stay in. When the Lord asked him what he was doing there, he replied, "I have been very zealous for the Lord, the God of hosts; for the sons of Israel have forsaken Your covenant, torn down Your altars, and killed Your prophets with the sword. And *I alone am left*; and they seek my life to take it away." He told the Lord all about how hard the spiritual warfare had become, but here he was, three hundred miles from the front line, hidden in a cave. One rebuke from his favorite enemy had also caused him to completely discount the tremendous victory which the Lord had just won back on the battlefront. All he could think of now was how bad things were, instead of how much better things had become. God's army had lost its main general because he hadn't strapped on his helmet of salvation (deliverance).

A third type of situation where a child of God can have his self-esteem badly wounded is when a parent, a teacher, or an employer continues to belittle or mistreat a person who is under their control. Such treatment can be devastating to one's sense of worth, and if prolonged, may lead to emotional illness or even suicide. Such victims are in dire need of a helmet.

We must now give thought to what constitutes our "helmet of salvation" and how we put it on. "Salvation" in Scripture often means "deliverance," and deliverance from blows on the head by the Accuser are surely essential when we move in to assault his kingdom.

If we return to the passage in Revelation 12 where our enemy is specifically named the "Accuser of the Brethren," we find the description of our helmet in the next verse. It reads, "And they overcame him by the blood of the Lamb and by the word of their testimony, and they loved not their life even until death."

A helmet has several parts to it. There is usually a soft cushioning material for the lining inside. There is also the hard outer casing, and there is the strap and buckle to hold it on. It would seem that we really have a reference to each of these functions in the verse before us. The blood of the Lamb, which was shed two thousand years ago for my sin, is the most soothing, comforting antidote to any accusation which could possibly come my way. Even if the accusation is just; even if I have made a mistake; even if I have sinned badly; I can turn again to the Lamb of God for forgiveness and cleansing. This tender cushion is by no means intended to replace the breastplate of righteousness, or to grant license to my flesh. Not in the least! But when I fall, as a soldier sometimes does when tripped up by the enemy, the blood of the Lamb which was shed for our transgressions is there to cushion our fall. The apostle John puts it beautifully in his epistle when he says: "My little children, I am writing this to you so that you may not sin; but if anyone does sin, we have an advocate with the Father, Jesus Christ the righteous." (I Jn. 2:1) Whenever I hold up the blood of the Lamb as my plea to forgiveness, Satan's accusations lose all their validity, their sting, and their venom.

The second part of my helmet, the hard outside covering, is termed "the word of their testimony." Satan's testimony is always negative. His accusations are always distorted, usually painting a far blacker picture than the facts of the case really allow. The word of your testimony should be the hard facts of the situation. When we get "down," we tend to let Satan pound us on the head until he even stomps us into the ground. There may be some validity to his accusations, for they usually contain partial truth. Our testimony, however, should consist of a *true* analysis of what happened, squarely facing up to our wrong, and then with complete truthfulness confessing it to the Lord and asking His forgiveness and cleansing. Again, John gives us wonderful protection in the promise: "If we confess our sin, He is faithful and just, and will forgive our sins and cleanse us from all unrighteousness." This is the strong fiberglass casing which will ward off all of the Accuser's blows.

There may be some need for confession of wrong to another person (or persons), and certain situations may call for an amount of restitution. But even here we must be careful that our enemy does not get in and make things worse. Some *over-sensitive consciences* can be driven to confess openly things which would best be unburdened only to the Lord. And none of us could ever make compensation for all of our misdemeanors. A portion of Scripture which has often been a helpful guide to me is Paul's counsel to the Ephesians: "Therefore be careful how you walk, not as unwise men, but as wise, making the most of your time, because the days are evil. So then do not be foolish, but understand what the will of the Lord is."

I have observed cases where "The Accuser" has driven hyper-conscientious Christians almost to distraction over some past offense which it would be almost impossible to correct. Counsel from a mature, loving friend can help us to "walk as children of light." But even after our common sense has been assured that the issue is to be dismissed and forgotten, the Accuser will at times return and harass us. We must learn to refuse his attacks by turning our thoughts to more profitable occupations. Our minds can never stop thinking, but we can ask the Holy Spirit to enable us to divert our introspections to things of more value. Satan may accuse you of stifling the voice of the Lord. But God's messages to us are always clear and reasonable, never fuzzy or foolish. Our enemy is also fond of bringing up again and again guilt feelings regarding those things which are *in the past*, and which we have already dealt with. The Holy Spirit is much more interested in our *present* walk with the Lord.

There is still another essential part to a helmet: the strap and the buckle. Without these, a helmet soon falls off. Our verse spells out this element with the expression, "and they loved not their lives even until death." The word for "love" here is quite significant. It is "agape" in the original Greek, which refers not to emotional love, but to deep concern. Often, the cause of a prolonged illness due to a blow on the head is what we call a "concussion." This malady is "a severe agitation of the brain." If the Devil, by one or more of his accusations, can so turn us in on ourself that our agape love, our deep concern, becomes focused on ourselves rather than on others, then our helmet has fallen off; we are in a state of concussion; and we are completely vulnerable. In other words, the sooner we get our eyes off ourself and begin to get involved in the needs of others, the sooner our own injuries will be healed. "They loved not their [own] life even until death [as long as they lived]." This is the mark of a healthy soldier...one who is out there fighting for others; one who keeps his helmet buckled on; one who refuses to indulge in self-pity. The helmet of salvation not only assures our own deliverance, but the deliverance of others. It is a "hard hat," dealing only with the true facts of the case in any accusation. It is well-cushioned with forgiveness, and it is well-fastened because the one who wears it refuses ever to become engrossed with himself.

Our Sword—the Word of God

God's Word has many functions. It provides our spiritual food and drink; it gives the light we need for our walk and our decision making; it is good medicine for all our spiritual ills; and it is a sharp, two-edged sword to be used in every form of spiritual combat. In our next chapter we will study the use of God's word as an aggressive weapon, but in the passage we have before us here, Paul is urging us to learn how to employ our sword in defensive warfare.

Five times in Scripture, Satan is called the "Tempter." His first piece of work on planet earth was to approach Adam and Eve with a subtle, yet powerful temptation to sin and disobey God. Even the ministry of the Lord Jesus was attacked at the very beginning with this clever enemy's standard, threefold allurement to indulge the lust of the flesh, the lust of the eyes, and the pride of life.

The Lord Jesus was a skillful swordsman, however, so His enemy was soon put to route. It will be a great help for us to observe how the Lord Jesus wielded His sword. He met the first temptation with three simple words, "*It is written.*" And then He quoted an appropriate verse from the written Word of God. He struck down the second temptation in similar manner. "Jesus said to him, 'Again, it is written,'" then quoted another verse. He countered the third temptation with the decisive blow, "Begone, Satan! for it is written," and He recited the relevant passage from the Scriptures.

The Lord Jesus placed tremendous confidence in the word of God. He also knew that Satan himself was aware of the mighty power and authority of God's written word. So He wielded it with decisive strength. And He desires that we as His soldiers also become skilful in the use of this sword.

How can we who are His disciples develop such skill? There is really only one way, and that is to commit to memory key passages which will enable us to handle the enemy's temptations. This was old warrior David's practice. "Your Word have I hid in my heart, that I might not sin against You" (Ps. ll9:ll).

When Gideon marched into battle, he called out, "The sword of the Lord *and Gideon.*" Paul calls it the "sword of the Spirit," but he urges us to "take" it, which means learn how to use it so we have it ready for immediate use when the enemy presents his temptation. For even those Christians who do have some sort of sword at their side are not always all that agile in using it and often can hardly draw it out when desperately needed.

Memorizing Scripture for use as a sword is not as simple as it first appears. Anyone can memorize a verse of Scripture in a few seconds, but repeating it two hours later is another matter! Therefore, to really fix a passage in one's memory requires much review. This means the development of a specific *system of review.* Flash cards, a memory list, a memory partner...these can all be helpful. But diligence and persistence must be added as well. Don't let Satan rob you of your sword! It is a weapon you and I *must* have available at all times. Learning how to handle our sword well demands more than casual efforts of "on again, off again" attempts to learn a few verses. It calls for an effective, disciplined memory system that is really affording us a firm grasp on God's Word.

A country lady who used to work for us a few mornings each week, was completely illiterate. "She couldn't read half a large character," as the Chinese say. But when she became a Christian she realized her need for God's word. So my wife began to teach her certain key verses, and then review them with her each time she came to our home. Her determination soon enabled her to be able to recite dozens of verses. She became a skilled swordsman and told us how these verses were a great help to her in times of temptation.

There is one other reminder we need to give here, and that is Paul's counsel to use our sword to "resist" the Tempter. When

Satan tempted Eve, the temptation was so strong that she couldn't muster enough will to resist it. She had her sword. That is, she had memorized the very words God had said to her, and even quoted them directly to the serpent in the midst of the temptation. But it was a very weak endeavor. She didn't really wield her sword with force. Her flesh really wanted what Satan had to offer. Our flesh will also want what Satan has to offer. This is always the case, else there would be no temptation involved. So we need to remind ourselves during the memory process that we must link our wills and action with the Scripture we memorize. It is not child's play.

When we began our outreach into these heathen, idolatrous villages of Taiwan, our youngest son Sam was about three years old. He knew nothing of what was going on, but night after night he would be wakened with nightmares and scream out that the demons were after him. I don't know how he even knew what a demon was, but this made me all the more concerned because it was evident that something supernatural was taking place.

Each night I would go into his bedroom and comfort him and pray with him, but the situation continued. Finally I realized that what this little boy needed was his own sword. So I began to help him memorize a few simple verses such as "The Lord is my shepherd"; "Jesus is Lord"; "God is love," etc. In short order, these attacks ceased and did not return. Our sword is a mighty sharp and powerful instrument. How vital it is to develop skill in using it!

We close this section as we began it, with Paul's thrice-repeated challenge to "stand firm." Even before we discuss our weapons (in the next chapter), we need to remind ourselves that we have sufficient armor to protect us from *all* our enemy's attacks. Our God is a God of victory. He Himself tolerates no note of defeat. And since He has equipped His soldiers with adequate armor, He expects them to tolerate no defeat.

Whenever things begin to go wrong, the situation looks bad and the future seems dark and grim, tell the Lord, yourself, and your enemy that you refuse to accept defeat! Declare that you are prepared to entertain only victory, no matter how long or how costly the battle may be. As you begin to wield your weapons, you will often be amazed at how quickly the enemy backs off.

10

OUR WEAPONS

In some places the Scriptures urge us to "resist" Satan, but the Word of God also goes further than that. Paul not only instructs us regarding our armor. He also gives attention to our *weapons*. "Though we walk in the flesh, we do not war according to the flesh, for the *weapons* of our warfare are not carnal, but are mighty through God for *tearing down strongholds*" (2 Cor. 10:3-4). Tearing down a stronghold involves more than merely resisting.

God's warrior, David, actually refers more to his weapons (sword, bow, spear) than he does to his armor. And more often than not, he is speaking of these in a spiritual context. For he is very much aware that his *spiritual* weapons are the ones which really count. The Psalms are full of such expressions as "the God who girds me with strength" ... "He trains my hands for battle" ... "For You have girded me with strength for battle," etc. etc.

The Lord Jesus certainly took a much more aggressive stance than merely that of resisting the enemy. "How can anyone enter the strong man's house and *carry off* his property unless he first *binds* the strong man? And then he will *plunder* his house" (Mt. 12:29). And again, "When someone stronger than he *attacks* him and *overpowers* him, he *takes away* from him all his armor on which he trusted, and distributes his plunder" (Lk. 11:22). And in speaking of His own ministry, the Lord declares, "He has sent me to proclaim *release* to the captives...to *set free* those who are downtrodden" (Lk. 4:18).

On His cross, the Lord Jesus triumphed over Satan, but He has not yet cast him into the bottomless pit or bound him. So when the Lord sends us forth with the good news of the gospel, He is sending us out as soldiers into battle to obtain deliverance

121

for those who are still in the grip of the Evil One. The basic concept of the Great Commission is that of aggression. "As the Father has sent Me, even so send I you." Those missionaries who realize that they are on an attack mission and therefore go forth with both armor and weapons are those who will see captives delivered.

In this chapter we will be discussing the five main weapons which I feel are the most essential. These five are: the Word of God; warfare prayer; worship; the names of God; and the cross of our Lord Jesus, which includes the blood He shed on that cross. Other weapons could also be suggested. Some are more skilled in wielding one battery of weapons, while others are more agile with perhaps a somewhat different set.

The Word of God as a Weapon

Several times in Scripture, the Word of God is referred to as a sword. In our last chapter we discussed the use of our sword as an implement of defense against the "Tempter." Now we are ready to consider its function as a weapon for invasion. We should remind ourselves, though, that the purpose of our aggressive exploits into these unreached, enemy-held "strongholds" is not primarily to fight with the evil forces. We can get ourselves into all kinds of trouble if we pursue the wrong objectives. We are going forth with the good news of the gospel, with love, patience, kindness, and all the other fruits of the Spirit. We are taking light and life into a dark place. We are not warmongers eager for battle, but we must nevertheless expect it and be prepared for it.

The enemy will defy us and stir up his forces against us, but God's Word will become his deterrent. We must never lose our consciousness of the fact that God's Word is the Word of *God*, and all the enemy's forces must bow before it.

One of the earliest stories of the Old Testament is the account of Satan's attack on Job. At each stage, when God spoke, Satan had to obey. At that time Job didn't possess any of the written word of God. But today we possess over a thousand pages of it. We must learn to use it freely and with great confidence as we enter enemy territory.

The bow, the sword and the spear were about as far as an arsenal of weapons extended in Bible days. If the New Testament were written in our modern age, I would expect our weapon, the Word of God, to be likened to a Sherman tank or a ballistic missile. It is a powerful entity which is designed and empowered to overcome all the enemy's obstacles. Few of us adequately appreciate the vitality of God's written word, and therefore we often use it far too weakly.

The great missionary Paul, however, wielded the Word of God with mighty power. I am moved when I read the nineteenth chapter of Acts. Paul argued daily in the hall of Tyrannus, "so that all the residents of Asia heard *the Word of the Lord*, both Jews and Greeks. And God did extraordinary miracles by the hands of Paul, so that handkerchiefs or aprons were carried away from his body to the sick, and diseases left them and the evil spirits came out of them. ...So *the Word of the Lord* grew and prevailed mightily" (Acts 19:10-12,20).

It is no wonder that our most effective evangelists, such as Wesley, Finney, and Billy Graham, were all men of the Word. They employed it with great expectancy, and they were not disappointed. They quoted it as if they were quoting the words of *God*. And the people therefore received it as the words of *God*. We are here touching one of the most vital elements of faith. As Paul said, "I haven't the slightest shame in presenting the gospel message, because it is the *power* of God for the salvation of everyone who believes, first for the Jew [as hard as they are to reach], and then to the Gentiles [even those who are blinded and bound by Satan]" (Rom. 1:16). And again, "For this gospel I was appointed a preacher and apostle and teacher, and therefore I suffer as I do. But I am not ashamed, for I *know* whom I have believed, and I am convinced that He is able to guard until that day [the fruits of the message which I have preached] which I have committed unto Him" (2 Tim. 1:11,12).

Every time we have opportunity to share some portion of God's Word with a needy soul, we need to do it with the full confidence of His wonderful promise to Isaiah. "As the rain and the snow come down from heaven, and do not return without watering the earth and making it bud and flourish, so that it yields seed for the sower and bread for the eater, so is My *Word*, that goes forth out from My mouth. It will not return to Me empty, but will accomplish what I desire and achieve the purpose for which I sent it." Then He adds, "You will go out in joy and be led forth in peace; the mountains and hills will burst into song before you, and all the trees of the field will clap their hands" (Isa. 55:10-12). No enemy can stand up against such a declaration!

One evening in a student meeting in Tainan, a graduate engineer gave his testimony. He had come to know the Lord as a student on the mainland. He had been a sophisticated intellectual with many objections to Christianity. But one of his friends who was a believer suggested he go have a talk with that famous pastor Wang Ming-Tao. So, on a Saturday afternoon, he went to see him and began by asking some of his most weighty questions. When Pastor Wang had an opportunity to reply, he stated that he was really quite weary that afternoon and had a big day coming up on Sunday, so that he would not be able to enter into such a heavy discussion, but that he would be glad to share with him some verses showing God's promise of salvation. The young man couldn't do much else than be polite and accept the offer. But he left that home a born-again believer.

Soon after I heard that testimony, a young teacher came to visit me in my home one evening. He also had many of the typical doubts and criticisms of Christianity. Instead of arguing with him, the Holy Spirit led me to just share portions of the Word with him. I handed him a Bible, and as he posed a question, I had him turn to a relevant reference. I was amazed at the way one verse was usually sufficient to answer each of his queries. After an hour or so, although he hadn't yet accepted the Lord, he got up and left in a much more humble and pensive attitude than when he had come. It was evident that the Word of God had overcome the voice of the enemy in his heart.

"The Word of God is living and active. Sharper than any two-edged sword, it penetrates even to dividing soul and spirit, joints and marrow; it judges the thoughts and attitudes of the heart." And the next verse is closely related. "*Nothing* in all creation is hidden from God's sight. *Everything* is uncovered and laid bare before the eyes of Him with whom we have to do" (Heb.

4:12-13). The "nothing" and "everything" and "all creation" surely include all His enemies. Their schemes are all "laid bare" and under the control of His Word. Jeremiah likens the Word of God to a "hammer which shatters a rock" (Jer. 23:29. Satan has his strongholds walled with impenetrable granite, and he seeks to vitrify men's hearts until they are as hard as stone. But there is a sledge which can break down the heaviest resistance. And that weapon is the Word of God.

We close this section with an encouragement from the elderly apostle John: "I write to you, young men, because you are strong, and the *Word of God* lives in you, and you have *overcome the Evil One*" (1 Jn. 2:14).

Prayer as a Weapon

"And when you go to war in your land against the adversary who attacks you, then you shall sound an alarm with the trumpets, that you may be remembered before the Lord your God, and be saved from your enemies" (Num. 10:9). When we consider prayer as a weapon, it may be that we need to adjust our thinking. It is not prayer itself which is to be equated with power. And yet prayer is one of our greatest means of power in this warfare. Prayer is sounding the trumpet before the Lord (which He has invited us to do), in order that *He* might call His mighty arsenal of weapons and forces into action. When the Lord asked Joshua and his army to march around Jericho for seven days, the armed men are mentioned five times; the Ark of the Covenant (God's Word) is mentioned nine times; but the sounding of trumpets made of ram's horn (calling on God) is referred to twelve times.

David was a mighty man of prayer. Most of his Psalms were prayer Psalms. For he, most of the time, was in the thick of some battle. For instance, we find a whole spread of verses throughout Psalms 59-64 in which David is linking his praying to God's deliverance.

"Deliver me from my enemies, O my God. Set me securely on high, away from those who rise against me...for behold they have set an ambush for my life...Arouse Yourself to help me.

"O my strength, I watch for You. You, O God, are my fortress.

"God will go before me, and let me look triumphantly upon my foes.

"Scatter them by Thy power, and bring them down, O Lord, our shield....That men may know that God rules in Jacob, to the ends of the earth.

"Save us and help us with Your right hand, that those You love may be delivered.

"Give us aid against the enemy, for the help of man is worthless. With God we will gain the victory. It is He who will tread down our enemies.

"Lead me to the rock that is higher than I. For you have been my refuge, a strong tower against the foe.

"My soul finds rest in God alone; my salvation [deliverance] comes from Him. He alone is my rock and my salvation [escape]; He is my fortress, I will never be shaken.

"My salvation [rescue] and my honor depend on God; He is my mighty rock, my refuge. Trust in Him at all times, O people, pour out your hearts to Him, for God is our refuge.

"Power belongs to God.

"My soul clings to You; Your right hand upholds me. They who seek my life will be destroyed.

"Hear me, O God, as I voice my complaint; protect my life from the threat of the enemy.

"God will shoot them with arrows; suddenly they will be struck down.

"Let the righteous rejoice and take refuge in Him."

And on and on he goes, sounding the trumpet and watching the Lord deal with the enemy. Yes, prayer is a mighty weapon, for it calls forth the battalions of God. When the Lord Jesus taught His disciples to pray, He began with the trumpet call, "Our Father who is in heaven," and He concluded with "Deliver us from the Evil One."

The Lord gave us much instruction on prayer, and much of this teaching is to encourage us to develop militant intercession. One parable was about a besieged widow. The passage begins: "Jesus told His disciples a parable to show them that they should always pray and not give up." Then He describes the widow's plea as "Avenge me of my *adversary*." And finally He closes the parable with the challenge, "Shall not God avenge His own elect who cry out day and night to Him, though He bears long with them? I tell you that He will avenge them speedily. Nevertheless, when the Son of Man comes, will He really find faith on the earth?" (Lk. 18:7,8).

The Lord's particular reference to "faith" here would seem to indicate a despairing lack of faith during this period just prior to His return, which really implies a lack of prayer (militant prayer). For that is what He has just been speaking about. And this deficiency will, of course, mean more of a free hand for the adversary. This is exactly the situation we find ourselves in these days.

I recently read an article on militant prayer written by a godly British author. In his treatise were these painful words: "Christianity in the United States is 3,000 miles broad, but only a half inch deep." And in another recent report was the statement that the average U.S. pastor spends seven minutes a day in prayer. This pitiful condition of spiritual anemia is precisely what the Lord was speaking about in the conclusion to His parable.

The story of the widow, however, was not primarily intended to be a negative condemnation, but to stimulate us to equip ourselves with a vital weapon against our adversary.

Now we come to Paul's most famous passage on dealing with our enemy in prayer. It follows immediately his reference to the sword of the Spirit. "Pray at all times, in the Spirit, with all prayer and supplication. And with this [spiritual battle] in mind, keep alert with all perseverance, making supplication for all the saints" (Eph. 6:18).

We really need to dissect this verse and look at it piece by piece. Paul's first admonition is to develop the habit of prayer "at all times." A soldier on active duty carries his weapons with him at all times, especially when he is on the front lines. He doesn't just fire a volley of shot once a day. There may be a certain period of the day when he does set off a concentrated barrage, but the "guerrilla" which the enemy fears most is the man who keeps himself dressed in full battle attire, including all his gear and weapons. Prayer is like his portable telephone by which he can continuously call forth and direct the fire from his supporting forces. Paul put it very simply when he wrote to the Colossians: "*Devote* yourselves to prayer."

Paul's next descriptive phrase regarding militant praying is that it should be "in the Spirit." He elaborates on this more fully in his letter to the Romans. "The Spirit also helps our weakness, for we do not know how to pray as we should, but the Spirit Himself intercedes for us with groanings too deep for words" (Rom. 8:26). Most of us would readily admit that in ourselves, our praying demonstrates more weakness than power. Instead of that confidence which causes us to feel that we are rending the heavens, our feeble efforts too often leave our spirits in neutral. Paul definitely included himself in this problem, for he uses the first-person plural: "*We* do not know how to pray as *we* should." But he had found the solution to the problem. "The Holy Spirit helps our weakness."

He is really urging us to invite the Holy Spirit to join us, as our prayer partner, at the very outset when we begin each of our prayer times. It makes all the difference between a mediocre stab at the enemy and a complete rout! We can rise from our period of intercession with a joyful assurance rather than wondering if anything really was accomplished. During our pleadings, the Spirit may lead us into concerns "too deep for words." There may be tears; there may be fasting; there may be unexplainable longings. And they will not be in vain, for God says "the effectual, fervent prayer of a righteous man [a man right with God] avails *much*" (Jas. 5:16).

Now we come to the words "with all prayer." The indication here is that *all kinds* of prayer are beneficial in this spiritual warfare. Group prayer meetings, prayer retreats, prayer partners interceding together, nights of prayer, and of course personal prayer.

I would like to share a testimony I heard from a fairly new Christian. He told about the first time he spent a whole night in prayer. A godly friend called him on the phone and asked if he had the evening free. When he replied that he did, his friend asked him to locate a couple of sleeping bags and be ready to leave at 8 p.m. His friend finally arrived, and they went out into the hills to spend a night in prayer.

They drove out to a quiet spot, climbed halfway up the hill, snuggled down into their sleeping bags, but did no sleeping that night. They first began to share areas of concern for their families; then they prayed unhurriedly and in great depth for those needs. Then came the problems at work, in the church, on the various mission fields they knew of, etc. Their inner longings grew deeper and deeper as they lay there under the stars and wept before the Lord. And before they realized it, it was daybreak.

But this is only the first half of the testimony. The second half was the report of the results. This young Christian was absolutely thrilled as he related the amazing answers that he had seen to the intercessions of that night. "All prayer." How many kinds are you and I regularly involved in?

The word "supplication" is used twice in this verse. It brings out the element of humility in prayer. The word "supplicate" means "to ask for humbly, or to entreat." This word is used over fifty times in the Scriptures, so we know it is a quality which the Holy Spirit deems vital in our intercessions.

Sometimes we tend to become rather cocky when we discover how to see our God do things in answer to our petitions. But whenever a bit of pride and self-glory enter the scene, the Lord turns His attention and His listening ear to someone who is more meek and lowly. "God resists the proud, but gives grace to the humble" (Jas. 4:6). And the next verse reads, "Submit yourselves therefore to God. Resist the devil and he will flee from you." Further on, James adds, "Humble yourselves in the presence of the Lord, and He will exalt you." If the devil can manage to engender even a small measure of spiritual pride into our prayer life, he knows that this will have a crippling effect.

Next comes the charge to "keep alert." A soldier standing guard in the blackness of night is alert to every movement, every sound, every crackle in the bushes. He is not about to allow the enemy any sneak approaches. Our enemy is very clever at sneak approaches. When we least expect it, here comes an onslaught from another direction!

The soldier who begins to yawn and get sleepy because it's "business as usual" is easy prey for the hungry lion lurking nearby. The alert man of prayer will at once put down on his prayer list each indication that the enemy is making an advance against the Lord's kingdom or toward any one of the Lord's people. There is a great difference between the heart of an alert soldier out on the front line, and the heart of a relaxed citizen a thousand miles behind the lines. Paul is seeking to direct our aim in this prayer challenge to "all the saints." The saints are the ones the enemy is hard after. We need to keep a watchful eye on the areas of spiritual need in each other's lives.

And now, finally, we come to the call for "*perseverance*" in prayer. The function of prayer as a weapon, and the essential of perseverance in our praying, is presented in a gripping illustration back in the book of Exodus. The story of Moses up on the mountain interceding for Joshua and Israel's army as they fought against their attacking enemy, the Amalekites, is a perfect example of spiritual warfare. (We will study this passage more fully in a later chapter, but we need to consider one facet of the story here.)

Moses stood there with his hands lifted up to God, the picture of a man who knew the source and means of power. But Moses had to learn the indispensability of *perseverance* in prayer. Moses' arms naturally became tired and sank down. When this happened, the tide of battle immediately turned. While Moses was reaching up to heaven for supernatural help, Israel was winning but when Moses became weary, the thrill of victory soon turned to the pain of defeat.

The kind of prayer which involves earnest, vital intercession is definitely an exhausting endeavor. Paul even likens it to the labor of "travail." Therefore any of us, like Moses, while giving ourselves to earnest prayer, can reach the point of fatigue. In fact, "fatigue" is a common military term which applies particularly to a soldier during battle. What do we do about this?

Two things are called for. The first is the element of perseverance which Paul is urging upon us. We can begin to see that perseverance is really a type of sacrifice. And sacrifice is always a weighty factor in prayer. It is not that our Father, or the Holy Spirit, is seeking to make prayer a difficult, grueling task. Not at all! However, whenever a child of God is willing to "pay a price" in some spiritual exercise, it is much appreciated by all the celestial beings in heaven. This world is full of needy people and pitiful situations, but the level of concern in the heart of most of us is not very high. When the Lord sees a man or woman who is deeply concerned about His kingdom which is built on love, when He sees a soldier who cares enough to spend some hours in heart-broken intercession, the Lord will bend the heavens and come down to listen to that person's prayer.

This is why fasting, giving of ourselves and our means, losing some of our sleep time, or any other form of self-discipline which is offered up to the Lord from a heart of loving concern, is a precious sweet savor to Him.

When Moses became weary, they gave him a stone to sit on and propped up his arms until sundown. We don't necessarily need to hold our arms up all the time we are praying, nor do we need always to pray until the sun goes down. We are at liberty to adjust our manner and period of prayer according to our own wishes. As it is when we give our offerings, Paul said: "According as every man has purposed in his own heart." But we can certainly pick up some pointers from this story recorded for us in Exodus. There is a place for sacrifice, and there is a place for the wise extension of our prayer vigils beyond just the comfortable minimum. We have a lot to learn from our Korean brothers in this matter.

The second thing we can learn to do is to intersperse our heavy intercessions with praise and worship. And this will bring us to our next section. But before we leave this story of Moses up on the hill interceding for Joshua and his army in the valley, let's take another look at the picture of Aaron and Hur standing on either side of Moses, helping to hold up his arms. I feel that these two helpers can be likened to *sacrifice* and *worship*, which are the two main supports to persevering prayer. Perhaps one of the major contributing factors to the voluminous and effective prayer life of our Korean brethren is the joy and delight in worship which they weave into their earnest supplications. "They who sow with *tears* shall reap with *joy*" (Ps. 126:5).

One final word now on our weapon of prayer. Distractions can fritter away much of the quality of our prayer time, and thus ministering in a battle situation requires special effort in prayer.

We must plan ahead for sufficient time, be prepared to exercise self-discipline, and deal firmly with distractions. Sufficient rest (before and after) and a quiet secluded place also need to be arranged for. We should give serious thought to the logistics of our militant intercessions. We will discover it to be tremendously worthwhile. Our Heavenly Father, who listens attentively to our supplications, will reward each such resolute venture with the most gratifying results and victories.

Worship as a Weapon

We don't usually think of worship as a weapon, and in one sense, we shouldn't. When we focus our attention on the greatness and goodness of our God in order that we might really worship Him in Spirit and in truth, our adoration ought not to be diluted or distracted by attempts to employ it as a tool to defeat our enemy. It is out of order to merely use praise as a battle ax to chop down Satan or as a means to manipulate God. Satan cannot bear to hear us give glory and thanksgiving to our God (his enemy), so he will soon make his departure, but let us strive to keep our worship pure and beautiful, a sweet-savor unto Him.

We worship our God because He is worthy. In fact, the word "worship" comes from the old English expression "worth-ship." He is infinitely worthy! First, because of His position as God; next, because of His greatness as Creator of all things; then, because of His goodness in the control of it all; and finally, because of His love for you and me.

We have already seen in previous chapters that the goodness of God is the fundamental field of man's battle here on earth. Therefore, whenever we by our singing or sharing or personal devotions enter into an exaltation of the goodness of our God, we are actually taking over the field of battle. We don't have to worry about using praise as a weapon. It naturally, and yet very forcefully, works out that way. We just need to keep free and abounding in our spirits as we worship the Lord and tell Him how we love Him.

I have been greatly helped in this by observing the purity of David's worship in the psalms. Although David was a mighty warrior and almost always involved in some fierce battle, we never find him trying to employ his praises of God as a weapon against his enemy. Of course, David's worship is one of the great reasons for his consistent victory, and it will be for us too, but we want to keep our hearts pure and filled with a simple, strong love toward *Him*.

I attended a very interesting Sunday evening sharing service in a live and growing church some months ago. After singing several beautiful hymns of worship, the pastor asked the congregation, *"Why* should we praise the Lord?" One person after another gave excellent, well-thought-through answers. And as they did so, you could feel the spirit of faith and expectancy rising higher and higher. One replied that praise is incense to God, but a poisonous vapor to Satan. Another said, "Praise changes the atmosphere from negative to positive." A third added that praise is the foundation of confidence. Another noted that "praise drives back Satan's cloud and allows God's sun to shine through." And they went on and on. I was wonderfully edified. Yes, the main thing about praise is that it exalts our God, and Satan simply cannot tolerate that. He soon packs his bags and moves elsewhere.

In a book I have been reading, there were several other very helpful quotes regarding praise. "There is no other way to remain airborne, except by praise." "Praise works, because it reverses the prevailing *rulership* in an earthly situation." And we could add here, that one of the magnificent byproducts of worship is the soothing effect it has on our own spirits and the way it *lifts* us and reinforces our confidence during our periods of strenuous intercession. Without these periods of restorative worship, our supplications can become heavy indeed.

I recently heard of a group of young Christians who gathered every Saturday evening for two hours on a street corner in a crime-ridden section of New York City to sing praises and magnify the Lord. This area was so corrupt that the police reported a murder or a major crime on an average of one every seven minutes. After a few weeks, a police officer came up and informed them that an amazing thing was happening. Each time they came to sing their praises, the crimes diminished amazingly during that period. Praise is a powerful weapon! It acknowledges God's greatness and control when Satan's forces are making a real bid for the victory. So we need to become accustomed to interspersing our prayer times with robust periods of praise to our Father and our Lord. This is a mark of Holy Spirit-led prayer, for in His teaching about the Spirit, the Lord Jesus states, "He will glorify Me."

Thanksgiving is the basis of praise; therefore sometimes we may need to begin with simple, specific thanksgiving and work our way up into the atmosphere of praise. Thanksgiving is showing appreciation for something which the Lord has done for us. Praise is expressing an awareness of how great He is. David does a great deal of both in the psalms. David is a real artisan when it comes to thanksgiving and praise. A very profitable Bible study would be to work one's way through the Psalms and pick up some pointers from him on how to worship.

Coming back to the matter of thanksgiving, we should probably remind ourselves that the Scriptures speak of three levels of thanksgiving, and the second and third levels are not quite so simple. The first level is quite easy. It is merely saying "thank you" for the blessings, the good things, which our Heavenly Father has poured out upon us. The second level requires a bit more effort. Paul says in I Thessalonians 5:18, "In *everything* give thanks." He of course is referring to those times in our lives when some things are not so pleasant. However, the implication of his statement would seem to be that even though some things aren't going well, we can always find other areas (if we look for them) where God has been blessing. So thank Him for these!

The third level is most difficult of all. In the original Greek text of Ephesians 5:20, it reads, "giving thanks *for* all things." This requires some spiritual muscle, but it is an essential and helpful exercise. To thank our Father for allowing some disagreeable event to happen is never easy. But proper faith will soon rise to assure itself that God makes no mistakes, and that even though Satan and his forces may be the author of the tragedy, our Lord has His "better" plan in mind and is well able to turn it all out for good. Otherwise He would never have allowed it to happen. So I can offer up a genuine "thank you." And when I do, I begin to feel much better and can soon rise again into the realm of praise. God's attributes...His majestic qualities...are not in the least affected by any negative attack Satan brings against me, and I should tell Satan so, tell God so, and tell myself so. And as soon as I do, the enemy's scheme is punctured.

Job was a very righteous man. In all the grief which Satan brought upon him, Job never once accused God or blamed Him, but the Lord was still not entirely pleased with Job. The Lord was disappointed because Job was not able to see how God could possibly have any positive designs in what had happened. Therefore, all Job could do was grovel in the dirt. He just couldn't rise to the level of thanksgiving, let alone praise. Here is a great difference between Job and David. Job had no weapons of thanksgiving or praise. David was a master with both. Let us take another look at how he handles his weapons of praise and gratitude.

"I love you, O Lord, my strength. The Lord is my rock, my fortress and my deliverer; my God is my rock, in whom I take refuge. He is my shield and the horn of my salvation, my stronghold. I call to the Lord, who is worthy of praise, and I am saved from my enemies" (Ps. 18:1-3).

In Psalm 28, David is really in the thick of the battle, yet he plows through to a beautiful victory in verse 7. "The Lord is my strength and my shield; my heart trusts in Him, and I am helped. My heart leaps for joy and I will give thanks to Him in song."

"May the praise of God be in their mouths, and a double-edged sword in their hands" (Ps. 149:6).

But David's most classic piece of oratory, which always strengthens me in a conflict, is his adoration of the Lord in the last half of his 24th Psalm. "Lift up your heads, O you gates; be lifted up you ancient doors, that the King of Glory may come in. Who is this King of Glory? The Lord *strong and mighty*, the Lord *mighty in battle*. Lift up your heads, O you gates, lift them up you ancient doors, that the King of Glory may come in. Who is He, this King of Glory? The *Lord of Hosts*, He is the King of glory."

We know that many of these Psalms were songs which David sang, accompanied by one or more instruments. Singing and music are some of the greatest means of refreshment for a weary soul. Many times, when I have felt at low tide, I have turned on one of our tapes of worship hymns and have been quickly lifted back into the invigorating current of delight and gladness, renewed and ready to rejoin the attack squadron.

There are many fine, fresh choruses of praise and worship today. We will do well to obtain some of these and introduce them to our churches and fellowship groups. We must become a people of worship and praise. Then we will become a people of power.

We have so many things to help us in this matter of worship. We have all of David's psalms. We have all the Old Testament, plus all the full and complete blessing of the New Testament. We live in this age of grace and gospel (good news). We have many books on worship and many song books of praise, with new editions coming off the presses every month. We hear messages on worship and thanksgiving regularly, and yet for many years my own personal worship of our tremendous God and glorious Savior didn't rise much above the three words "Praise the Lord." No wonder Satan didn't fear my weapons! They were too dull and blunt.

I never cease to be amazed at the astonishing spiritual insight which the shepherd boy David possessed regarding worship and warfare. He lived in the Age of Law, before even most of the Old Testament was ever written. He didn't have any of the Psalms. He had to write most of them himself. Yet when he got started praising the Lord, he could hardly stop. And this element of song was one of his main supports.

Let us share again a few of his insights:

"I am in pain and distress; may your salvation, O God, protect me. I will praise God's name in song, and glorify Him with thanksgiving. This will please the Lord more than an ox, more than a bull with its horns and hoofs. The poor will see and be glad. You who seek God, may your hearts live! The Lord hears the needy" (Ps. 69:29-33).

"He who looks at the earth, and it trembles, who touches the mountains and they smoke. I will sing to the Lord all my life; I will sing praise to my God as long as I live. May my meditation be pleasing to Him, as I rejoice in the Lord. Praise the Lord, O my soul, praise the Lord" (Ps. 104:32-35).

"Deliver me from my enemies, O God protect me from those who rise up against me...But I will sing of Your strength; in the morning I will sing of Your love; for You are my fortress, my refuge in times of trouble. O my Strength, I sing praise to You; You, O God, are my fortress, my loving God" (Ps. 59:1,16-17).

Although David called to the Lord for deliverance and recognized God as his fortress and his refuge, his praise to God was pure praise. He made no attempt to use it as a means to manipulate God. His love for God was too genuine and too strong for that. But this caused the enemy to tremble even more.

David gives us another noteworthy picture in Psalm 8. "From the lips of children and infants You have ordained *power*, because of your enemies, to silence the foe and the avenger." The Lord Jesus used this verse to silence His enemies when the children were shouting "Hosanna" during His triumphal entry into Jerusalem. And it is interesting to observe that when the Lord Jesus quoted these words of David, He used "praise" as His substitute for the word "power." The praise of "children" carries power against the enemy, because a child's praise is pure praise. And pure praise is death to the designs of the Evil One.

One helpful and acceptable means of worship is to use the Lord's *names* to praise Him. This is surely pleasing to Him, for His Word encourages us to do so. "Through Him then let us continually offer up a sacrifice of praise to God, that is, the fruit of lips that acknowledge *His name*" (Heb. 13:15).

It is not surprising to discover that David was also skilled in using God's names in worship. And he strongly urges the rest of us to become fluent in this practice.

"I will cause *Your name* to be remembered in all generations; therefore the peoples will give You thanks forever and ever" (Ps. 45:17).

"*As is Your name*, O God, so is your praise to the ends of the earth" (Ps. 48:10).

"Ascribe to the Lord, O families of the peoples, ascribe to the Lord glory and strength. Ascribe to the Lord *the glory of His name*" (Ps. 96:7-8).

"Bless the Lord, O my soul; and all that is within me, *bless His holy name*" (Ps. 103:1).

In ourselves, we have a hard time making much progress in magnifying our Lord. Our spring soon runs dry. We need help. But one dear fellow missionary here in Taiwan, who is now retired, prepared a list of about 300 of the Lord's names and attributes and entitled it, "Names with Which I can Praise the Lord." A portion of that list is in the "Worship and Warfare" prayer companion, accompanying this book. She suggests that you meditate on each name, until a fountain of adoration begins to spring up deep in your soul. We shouldn't have much problem worshipping our Lord and Savior with a list like that. What a rich treasure!

Now we come to the challenge of employing some of the Lord's names as weapons in our warfare.

The Lord's Names as a Weapon

The name of the Lord is referred to over five hundred times in the Scriptures. So it is certainly a vital entity which He would have us appreciate and comprehend more and more. If we would feed these five hundred references to His name into a computer and begin to categorize their use, we would discover that one of their major functions is in the realm of authority and power.

The names of God as our weapon carry with them tremendous authority. Just before the Lord Jesus returned to heaven, as He was sending forth His disciples into all the world (which meant sending them into enemy territory), He prefaced His commission with the assurance: "All authority in heaven and on earth is given to Me; therefore proceed on this basis." And several times during those last few hours before He went to the cross, He extended to them the provision: "Whatever you request *in My name*, it shall be granted." Naturally, to requisition something in His name presupposes that you are petitioning according to His will and for the establishment of His kingdom. His name becomes the key which opens the arsenal for dispatching His forces.

Let us look at a few of such instances.

Jeremiah states, "No one is like You, O Lord; You are great, and *Your name* is mighty in power" (Jer. 10:6).

Solomon tells us, "*The name* of the Lord is a strong tower;

the righteous run to it and are safe" (Prov. 18:10).

Luke mentions that the seventy-two disciples whom the Lord sent out "returned with joy and said, 'Lord, even the demons submit to us *in Your name.*"

One of Paul's many references to Jesus' name is in Philippians 2:9-10: "God has highly exalted Him, and bestowed on Him *the name* which is above every name, that at *the name* of Jesus every knee should bow, in heaven and on earth, and under the earth."

Then, there are the examples of how David uses the name of the Lord as he goes into battle:

"Those who *know your name* will put their trust in You, for You, O Lord, have never forsaken those who seek You" (Ps. 9:10).

"We will lift up our banners *in the name* of our God. ...Some trust in chariots and some in horses, but we trust *in the name* of our God" (Ps. 20:5,7).

"Because he has loved Me, therefore I will deliver him. I will set him securely on high, because *he has known My name*" (Ps. 91:14).

"All the nations surrounded me, but *in the name of the Lord* I cut them off. They surrounded me on every side, but in the name of the Lord I cut them off. They swarmed around me like bees, but they died out as quickly as burning thorns; *in the name of the Lord* I cut them off" (Ps. 118:10-12).

"*Our help is in the name of the Lord*, the maker of heaven and earth" (Ps. 124:8).

This last reference is particularly significant, because it is one of the numerous instances where David actually *uses* one of the Lord's names. David had quite a list of militant names for his God, which we can also employ as our weapons. His list included such titles as: "the Lord of Hosts"; "Deliverer"; "Refuge"; "Shield"; "Our strength"; "Fortress"; "Mighty One"; "Most High"; "The Lord mighty in battle," etc. During a battle, the Lord revealed Himself to Moses as a "Banner," to Joshua as "Captain," to Isaiah as a "Strong Arm," to Luke as "The Stronger One," and to Paul as "Triumphant."

How do we utilize these battle names of the Lord in our

spiritual warfare? David again gives us some practical help. He shares with us his own practice. "We wait in hope for the Lord; He is our help and our shield. In Him our hearts rejoice, for we trust in His holy name" (Ps. 33:20-21). We need to notice the three key verbs of these verses, "wait," "rejoice," and "trust." They suggest unhurried *meditation* on His names, until we reach a point of *rejoicing* in His greatness. Then our faith begins to take over, and we expect Him to accomplish exploits. When we have reached this point, victory is right around the corner.

The Cross as a Weapon

The cross of Christianity is of far greater significance than just an emblem which we affix to the top of our church steeple, or use as a carving to decorate the pulpit or as an ornament to hang about our neck. Most Christians, and a few non-Christians, do see it as the reminder of the Lord Jesus' sacrificial death, picturing the only means of salvation from the penalty of sin. But do we see the full measure of victory and triumph which are meant to be portrayed by that cross? It is the symbol of the Conqueror's victory in the spiritual realm. It means that the Victor has prevailed over the enemy! In our spiritual warfare, we are therefore to maintain the confidence that we are facing forces who themselves are well aware of the fact that they are now but usurpers—illegal occupants here on planet earth. So we hold up the cross boldly as we move in to declare our position, and to remind them that they have no rights here!

The Lord Jesus' first reference to the cross was during His talk with Nicodemus about the kingdom of God. In His discussion, He referred back to the occasion 1500 years before when the children of Israel in their wilderness journey were being bitten by poisonous snakes as punishment for their sins and rebellion. He stated, "As Moses lifted up the serpent in the wilderness, so must the Son of Man be lifted up" (Jn. 3:14).

Moses had been told by God to make a serpent of bronze, fashioned after the snakes that were biting the people, and fasten it to a standard for the people to see. "And it shall come about, that everyone who is bitten, when he looks at it, he shall live"

(Num. 21:8). The bronze serpent was a clear picture of the penalty and suffering brought on by their sin, which is also a picture of the whole program of Satan's kingdom. It is therefore a perfect portrayal of the Lord Jesus taking upon Himself all the punishment for man's transgressions and nailing it to His cross. The "lifting up" (the cross) of the Son of Man is hereby declared, by the Lord Himself (even before it ever took place), to be the visible exhibition of readily available victory over the pain and death inflicted by the "Serpent."

After that initial talk with Nicodemus, the Lord spoke of the cross a number of times. And one of those occasions, which we should mention here, was at the close of His ministry, just a couple of days before He was to be crucified. Philip and Andrew had come to report that a company of Greeks were desiring to "see Jesus." The Lord made a rather unexpected reply. His thoughts were so pulled toward that which was looming before Him that He immediately began to speak of His death.

"Unless a grain of wheat falls into the ground and dies, it remains alone, but if it dies, it bears much fruit." Then He added, "Now my soul is troubled. And what shall I say? 'Father save me from this hour?' No, for this purpose I have come to this hour. ...Now is the judgment of this world, *now shall the ruler of this world be cast out* and I *when I am lifted up* from the earth, will draw all men to myself.' He was saying this to indicate the *kind of death* by which He would die" (Jn. 12:24-33). Here once again, the Lord Jesus vitally links the cross with His victory over the enemy.

The cross is the central point of the whole *process* of the redemption of this *world*. "God so loved *the world* that He gave His only begotten Son" (Jn. 3:16). Not every person in the world will avail himself of this salvation which God has provided. In fact, most will not. But "God was in Christ reconciling *the world* to Himself" (2 Cor. 5:19). It was the process of recovering the world from the rulership of enemy Satan and his forces. "The Son of God appeared for this purpose, that He might destroy the works of the Devil" (1 Jn. 3:8). He left heaven and came to earth to rid our planet of the curse of enemy domination.

This process of redemption was comprised of many parts. It

included His incarnation, teaching, ministry, crucifixion, resurrection, ascension and glorification. All of these steps were involved. In fact, the operation is still not complete and will not be until He returns to set up His worldwide kingdom. But it is still very much under way, and we His people, in obedience to His Great Commission, are also a very vital increment in it all. It is the process of repossession.

The book of Hebrews, in speaking of this process, specifically points to His death as the event where the crucial victory was won. "Since the children share in flesh and blood, He Himself likewise partook of the same, that *through death*, He might *render powerless* him who had the power of death, that is, *the Devil*" (Heb. 2:2-4). So again, the cross is designated as the point where the legal subjugation of the enemy was consummated.

Now let's move in even closer, and hear once again His final words on the cross. "It is finished," He cried. And when He had said this, "He bowed His head and gave up His spirit" (Jn. 19:30). That instant marked the greatest accomplishment of all history. Not only was the work of procuring our salvation completed, but the whole basic rulership of our planet changed hands. This transaction is magnificently celebrated in the fifth chapter of the Book of Revelation of Jesus Christ. The chapter opens with a picture of God sitting on His throne holding a sealed scroll in His hand. But no one in heaven or on earth or under the earth could be found who was worthy to open the scroll. So John, who was observing the revelation, began to weep. But then he writes, "One of the elders said to me, 'Do not weep, look, the *Lion* of the tribe of Judah, the Root of David, *has triumphed. He is able to open the scroll* and its seven seals. Then I saw a *lamb*, looking as if it had been *slain*, standing in the center of the throne....*He came and took the scroll* from the right hand of Him who sat on the throne. And when He had taken it, the four living creatures and the twenty-four elders fell down *before the Lamb*....And they sang a new song:

'*You are worthy* to take the scroll and to open its seals, *because you were slain*, and *with your blood* you *purchased men* for God from every tribe and language and people and nation. You have made them to be a *kingdom* of priests to serve our God, and they will *reign on the earth.*'"

There could not be a clearer picture manifesting how the death of the Lord Jesus entitled Him to reclaim the deed to planet earth. In that event of being slain as a lamb, He conquered as a "*lion.*" So, from yet another view, the cross is presented as the insignia of the Overcomer.

Paul too states it with mighty force which engenders absolute confidence, when he wrote, "Having *disarmed* the powers and authorities, He made a public spectacle of them, *triumphing* over them by the cross" (Col. 2:15). Paul was certainly one to exalt the cross.

We have already mentioned that our Lord's death on the cross was the central point of the process of retrieving the world back from Satan's dominion. We must keep in mind, however, that the other steps in the process were also of great importance. For instance, His very incarnation was a mighty blow to Satan. He came! Yes, He came! And at His birth He was given the name Jesus (Savior). And Satan did all he could to destroy Him even in His infancy. Next, His sinless life and victory over Satan in the wilderness equipped Him to become the second Adam. This was the ultimate threat to Satan because only another sinless Adam could seize his kingdom. Then, the Lord's teaching and ministry were also the death knell to Satan because He repeatedly subdued and cast out Satan's demons. We, therefore, can and should employ all these truths in our warfare maneuvers.

After the cross came the resurrection—that mighty confirmation that the victory of the cross was complete and valid. The Lord Jesus' references to the cross were often tied to the phrase, "and be raised again on the third day." In the book of Acts, as the apostles preached the gospel message of the Lord and His cross, they almost always included the phrase, "whom God has raised up." This was their incontrovertible proof and assurance of salvation and victory. Yes, we need to repeatedly remind ourselves and Satan's forces of all this. The resurrection was followed by His ascension, which was one more powerful stroke of victory. "When He ascended on high, He led captive a host of captives" (Eph. 4:8). And His ascension was followed by His exaltation. This enthronement is specifically denoted as that special glorification by the Father which will cause every living creature (including His enemies) to bow before His name. "He humbled Himself, and became obedient to death, even death on a cross. Therefore God *exalted* Him to the highest place and gave Him the name that is above every name, that at the name of Jesus *every knee should bow*, in heaven, on earth and *under the earth*, and every tongue confess that *Jesus Christ is Lord*, to the glory of God the Father" (Phil. 2:8-11).

Paul longed that the effectiveness of all this victory would become operative in our own lives, ministry and spiritual warfare. He wrote to the Ephesians: "I pray that the eyes of your heart may be enlightened, in order that you may know...His incomparably great power for us who believe...which He exerted in Christ when He raised Him from the dead and seated Him at His right hand in the heavenly realm, far above all rule and authority, power and dominion and every title that can be given, not only in the present age, but also in the age to come. And God placed all things under His feet, and appointed Him to be head over everything *for the church*, which is His body" (Eph. 1:18-23). All this incomprehensible triumph has been accomplished by His cross!

Before we conclude this section on the cross as a weapon, let us return to one of the Lord's statements which we referred to earlier. "But I, when I am lifted up from the earth, will draw all men to Myself" (Jn. 12:32). The cross as a weapon not only forces Satan and his hordes to back away, but when properly and powerfully employed in our preaching to exalt the Lord Jesus and His infinite grace, it will be used of the Holy Spirit to *draw* people of every kind out of the enemy's camp into the kingdom of the Son of God. Therefore, the cross should certainly hold a prominent place in our praying, preaching and singing.

It was on that cross that He vanquished His enemy, and His enemy knows it full well. We also need to know it well, and confidently employ this truth as a weapon against all the attacks of our defeated foe! We are to remind him that he has no rights, and therefore we forbid him to operate against us.

Satan not only hates to hear about the cross, where he lost his rulership, but it also binds his efforts when we claim the efficacy of the *blood* of the Lord Jesus which was shed on that cross. By that blood, mankind was *purchased* from Satan's dominion. He therefore has no warrant whatever to interfere with our preaching of the gospel message, and we must tell him so. All five of these weapons can be used in combination with each other, and this should often be the case. For instance, to lift up the cross, and use God's Word, praise, and the Lord's names in prayer and song is an invincible approach. Yes, we His soldiers are to *enforce* the victory of the cross.

In closing this chapter, we must make mention of David's powerful warriors. He called them his "mighty men." I am challenged and exhilarated every time I read of their astounding exploits, standing their ground and accomplishing unbelievable victories against impossible odds (1 Chron. 11:10-25). God's Word refers several times to these courageous heroes. In one place it describes them: "they were armed with bows, and were able to shoot arrows or to sling stones right-handed or left-handed. ...They were brave warriors, ready for battle and able to handle the shield and spear. Their faces were the faces of lions, and they were as swift as gazelles in the mountains" (1 Chron. 12:2,8).

I sometimes wonder how a description of my battle capabilities would read. I'm afraid much of it wouldn't look very impressive in print. But the Lord has recorded all these sketches in His word, not to condemn us or to discourage us, but quite the opposite, to challenge us to become strong. When we read about the *beginnings* of David's militia, it is not a very glorious picture. "All those who were in distress, or in debt, or discontented, gathered around him, and he became their leader" (1 Sam. 22:2). I'm sure that to begin with they were known as "David's ragtag army." But David trained them and they became "mighty men." And the Son of David, Jesus Christ Himself, yearns to train us also, until we become "mighty men" of God!

11

OUR AUTHORITY

Paul, in three of his letters (Ephesians, Philippians and Colossians), uses the oratory at his command to assure us of the absolute supremacy of the Lord Jesus. He states that after God the Father raised His Son from the dead, He "*seated* Him at His right hand in the heavenly realms, *far above* all rule and authority and power and dominion, and every name that is named, not only in this age, but also in the age to come. And He put all things in subjection under His feet" (Eph. 1:20-22). And in Philippians, "God exalted Him to the *highest place*, and gave Him the name that is above every name, that at the name of Jesus every knee should bow, in heaven and on earth and under the earth, and every tongue confess that Jesus Christ is Lord, to the glory of God the Father" (Phil. 2:9-11). And again in Colossians, "He is the image of the invisible God, the firstborn *over all creation*. For by Him all things were created: things in heaven and on earth, visible and invisible, whether thrones or powers or rulers or authorities; all things were created by Him and for Him. He is before all things, and in Him all things hold together. ...So that *in everything He might have the preeminence*. ...For in Him all the fullness of Deity dwells in bodily form" (Col. 1: 15-17; 2:9).

And then, in the same context, Paul makes some remarkable statements regarding us poor redeemed mustard seeds. He says, "God appointed Him to be head over all things to the church *which is His body*, the fullness of Him who fills everything in every way" (Eph. 1:22-23). And a little further on, "God raised us up with Christ and *seated us with Him* in the *heavenly realms* in Christ Jesus" (Eph. 2:6). The Greek word "to sit" or "to be seated" used here appears over forty times in the New Testament, and over half of these instances refer to sitting on a throne or judgment seat. It is so used of the Lord Jesus in the reference

146

above where God "*seated* Him at His right hand in the *heavenly realms, far above* all rule and authority and power and dominion, and every name that is named—and put all things *in subjection* under His feet" (Eph. 1:20-22). "Heavenly realms" is the term used five times in this book of Ephesians in speaking of the unseen spiritual realm all about us, where spiritual warfare is being carried on. We should also note that God has *already* "seated us with Him in the heavenly realms." It is past tense. We believers are there now, in the place of authority *with Him*.

And in the next chapter of this book of Ephesians, Paul adds: "To Him who is able to do immeasurably more than all we ask or imagine, according to *His power* that is at work *within us*, to Him be glory *in the church* and in Christ Jesus throughout all generations, forever and ever, amen" (Eph. 3:20-21). With this staggering collection of marvelous truths as a backdrop, we begin our examination of those sections which have to do with *binding and loosing*.

The Chief Cornerstone

The most notable reference is in Matthew 16. The passage begins: "When Jesus came into the region of Caesarea Philippi, He asked His disciples, 'Who do people say the Son of Man is?'" It is significant that Matthew names the district where this took place. Caesarea Philippi was the famous city built by Philip, the son of Herod the Great, and named after himself and Augustus Caesar. So it was a spot which radiated royalty and authority and commanded the respect of all in the area.

The timing is also of importance. The Lord Jesus was nearing the end of His three years of ministry and the climax of His training of the disciples. So He begins by questioning His disciples as to who people considered Him to be. He is getting ready to plant the cornerstone for the building of His church, the establishing of His kingdom here on earth. The first step in inaugurating a kingdom is to introduce its king.

They answered that most considered Him to be either John the Baptist, Elijah, Jeremiah, or one of the other prophets risen from the dead. These were the greatest spiritual giants that they could think of. But they were not great enough. None of these, fine as they were, came anywhere near the qualifications required for the foundation stone of God's kingdom.

So He then asked them, "Who do *you* say that I am?" Peter, anointed by the Holy Spirit, gave the right answer: "You are the Christ, the Son of the living God." The Lord immediately declared this to be a special revelation to Peter from His Father, for He said, "Blessed are you, Simon, son of Jonah, for this was not revealed to you by man, but by My Father in heaven." And here we have the foundation stone for His church. "You, the Son of the living God, are the Christ, the King. *You* are the *King of God's kingdom!*"

The time and place were right for setting the cornerstone. Prince Philip had set a monument there in that region for Caesar, the emperor of the mighty Roman Empire, which ruled the whole earth at that time. His monument was in the form of a city, Caesarea Philippi, in order that the fame of these great rulers would be remembered forever. But his city did not stand. It was conquered and reconquered several times, renamed, and finally today is merely the little-known town of Banias. But the kingdom of the King of Kings and Lord of Lords, which was introduced to twelve feeble mustard seeds in that same area 2,000 years ago, is alive and growing! One of these days soon, the King will return and His kingdom will encompass heaven and earth forever and ever.

Now we must move on. The Lord continued to look at Simon, and reminding him of the name He had given him three years before when they first met, He said, "I also say to you, that you are "Peter" [rock], and on this rock [the declaration you have just made] I will build My church, and the gates of hell shall not prevail against it." This great insight which Peter had just manifest, was the central, solid truth of Christianity. That is, that Jesus is the Christ, the Son of the living God. And on *this rock* He would build His church. He *himself*, as *"the Christ"* (which means the anointed King), would be the cornerstone of the church, God's kingdom on earth.

There are those who would try to interpret this passage as if the Lord were going to build His church on Peter. But the Lord didn't say, "On you I will build My church." That would mean the planting of His kingdom on a very tiny, little stone (which cracked and crumbled several times). Mustard seeds don't make very good foundations for lofty stone cathedrals. At best they can become "living stones," as we will see later from Peter's own words.

Isaiah, 700 years before, used powerful language to point to the Lord Jesus as this cornerstone. "Thus says the Lord God, 'Behold I am laying in Zion a stone, a tested stone, a precious cornerstone for a sure foundation; the one who trusts will never be dismayed'" (Isa. 28:16)

Peter himself, later on in his first epistle, quotes Isaiah's prophecy and adds quite a little commentary of his own: "As you come to *Him*, the living Stone, rejected by men, but chosen by God and precious to Him, you also, as living stones, are being built into a spiritual house, to be a holy priesthood, offering spiritual sacrifices acceptable to God through Jesus Christ. For in Scripture it says: 'See, I lay a stone in Zion, a chosen and precious cornerstone, and the one who trusts *in Him* will never be put to shame.' Now to you who believe, this stone is precious. But to those who do not believe, the stone the builders rejected has become the head of the corner" (1 Pet. 2:4-7).

Paul also refers twice to the Lord Jesus as the foundation, the cornerstone upon which the church is built. In Ephesians 2:20, he concludes his long treatise on God's household, "*with Christ Jesus Himself* as the chief cornerstone." And in 1 Corinthians 3:11 he writes, "No one can lay any other foundation than the one already laid, *which is Jesus Christ.*"

Then there is another reference we must include, and that is where the Lord Jesus Himself quoted David's prophecy to establish His authority before the chief priests and elders. He asked them, "Have you never read the Scriptures:'The stone the builders rejected has become the chief cornerstone; the Lord has done this, and it is marvelous in our eyes'" (Mt. 21:42). So "this rock" upon which the church is built is the Lord Jesus Christ, the Son of the living God, the King of God's kingdom.

Not only the time and place, but the tone of the Lord's words here mark these verses as some of the most crucial of any in Scripture, "I will build my church, and the gates of Hades shall not prevail against it." Once again, we find the Lord referring to the two kingdoms which exist on planet earth. Actually what He is saying here is, "I will establish My kingdom, and Satan's kingdom shall not be able to hold it back." This is the King of God's kingdom speaking. And He is speaking with force and power and authority.

He uses a graphic illustration here which clearly pictures the true situation in your neighborhood, on your campus, and in the villages of Taiwan. These areas are enclosed with invisible walls and locked up tight behind heavy gates which are guarded by fierce and cruel gatekeepers. So there is needed no meager element of power and authority to approach these fortresses and to overcome the enemy's forces. It requires the right key to unlock each gate to set the captives free.

The Lord Jesus would soon be leaving this earth to return to His position at the Father's right hand. He, by His "Great Commission," would be turning over to Peter, the others of the twelve, and to you and me the mammoth enterprise of taking the gospel into enemy territory and all the way to the ends of the earth. So there was need for adequate enablement. And just such ample provision came forth in His next sentence. He promised the keys necessary to unlock the gates and the authority needed to bind the gatekeepers.

"I will give you the keys of the kingdom of heaven, and whatever you bind on earth shall have been bound in heaven, and whatever you loose on earth shall have been loosed in heaven." The Lord is doing an amazing thing. He is deputizing His disciples, and you and me, to act on His behalf in binding enemy forces and unlocking the enemy's gates, in order to see His church built and His kingdom established in all areas which are still occupied by the enemy.

Since He had been speaking to Peter, He addressed these words to him. But it is evident that He intended to include all the rest of us His disciples, for a little further on in chapter 18 He used exactly the same words about binding and loosing, but the "you" is in the plural. His Great Commission was always given in the plural and extended "even to the end of the age" (Mt.

28:20), which includes you and me. So His provisions were designed to be available until His return. In His revelation to the apostle John some sixty years later, He again reminds us that He holds "the keys of death and Hades" and that "what He opens no one can shut, and what He shuts no one can open" (Rev. 1:18; 3:7).

Exercising Authority

We have now come face to face with a triple paradox. On the one hand, *He* holds the keys, and what *He* opens no man can shut, and what *He* shuts no man can open. And yet He is offering us the keys to do the binding and loosing. The second paradox is that in one place He speaks of them as the keys of the kingdom of heaven, and in another place as the keys of "death and Hades." The third paradox concerns this whole concept of authority. At one time He says, "All authority in heaven and on earth is given to *Me*," and as Peter wrote, "All authorities and powers are subject to *Him*" (1 Pet. 3:22). Yet, at other times He seems to be delegating a measure of authority to us.

These paradoxes are meant to present two sides to our employment of authority. They encourage us to move ahead without any fear, for we are backed by all the authority in heaven and on earth. And yet they are to be a continual reminder that we have no authority of our own. We must always retain the stance of humble, powerless mustard seeds. We go forth "*in the name*" of the King of Kings and Lord of Lords. We are seated "*with Him* in the heavenlies." And it is "*His power*" that is at work within us.

So the phrase, "In the name of Jesus," which should become an essential and prominent part of our warfare mentality, carries with it dual implications. It embodies infinite power and authority, but also stands as a caution against taking things into our own hands. This twofold truth is clearly included in the original Greek text of both references dealing with binding and loosing. They each read, "whatever you bind on earth *shall have been* bound in heaven; and whatever you loose on earth *shall have been* loosed in heaven." And this is exactly the way these verses are translated in some versions of the New American Standard Bible, which gives special attention to the tense of all Greek verbs. The Lord is reminding us here that when we apply His authority to a given situation, we must be sure that we are doing so according to *His* will, according to *His* desires and *His* plans, the plans of the King of the Kingdom of Heaven.

In other words, the delegation of His authority to us is by no means a wholesale license to bind or loose any and every situation we come upon. Even the Lord Himself did not do that. One example is the way He dealt with Peter's testing on the night before His crucifixion. He said to Peter, "Satan has desired to sift you as wheat." But instead of binding Satan, or his desire to do this, the Lord allowed Satan to go ahead with the test. He added, "I have prayed for you that your faith might not fail." Peter miserably failed the test, but his faith was preserved in the end, and he became a stalwart apostle, much used by His Lord. Actually, he became much stronger because of this experience. So His way, His wisdom, His strategy, His timing are always best. We must accept this basic tenet in all our warfare.

We do well, therefore, to think twice before we reach out to employ the Lord's mighty authority in any and every circumstance. In chapter 18 of Matthew, immediately following His statement on binding and loosing, He adds, "Again I say to you, that if two of you *agree* on earth about anything that they may ask, it shall be done for them by My Father who is in heaven." He seems to be suggesting a safeguard. If, after we have sized up a certain state of affairs, and are not quite sure what the Lord would have us do about it, we can discuss the matter with our prayer partner, or some other mature warrior, and pray about it together. Then finally, if we are in agreement as to His will, we can, in His name, bind or loose whatever we are convinced is bound or loosed in heaven. In most situations, there should be little question. A mature soldier usually is pretty well assured of what his captain's will would be. Also, when we have acquainted ourselves with His names and attributes, His ways and working principles, we can generally be quite certain as to what He would have us do.

Many, and possibly most of us, are too hesitant because of inexperience to step forth and bind the enemy's forces when we really ought to do so. It is obvious, all about us, that the Evil One is getting away with far more than he should. Individuals are bound and being attacked. Churches, fellowship groups, campuses and villages are walled in, and the Lord's work has stagnated, sometimes for years, before someone awakens and realizes what has really been happening.

Some may tend to feel that this whole matter of binding and loosing is best left up to the Lord. Or they assume that the most we can do is to ask *Him*, in prayer, to do it. There is a certain reticence to speak directly to Satan and his forces (evil spirits), to bind their insidious attacks. But in the name of the Lord Jesus Christ, there is nothing to fear, and He definitely commissions us to so employ His authority. He uses the word "you" throughout these passages. I have recently heard and read a number of testimonies of fellow believers who prayed for years for certain painful situations, but when they complied with the Lord's provision for directly binding and loosing, there were immediate results. The last few years I have been experiencing many encouragements in this new bold venture myself.

Another part of the picture, which perhaps we need to point out here, is that when Christians do commence to exercise authority against these opposing spirits, they often become more occupied with the binding than with the loosing. But both are essential. We bind the enemy's efforts, but we loose his grip on those who are bound. The Lord would have us see it as a two-fold operation.

Perhaps a good way to sum up this section is to recall that the apostle Paul repeatedly reminds us in his letters that we are *"in Christ."* This truth contains many significations. As long as I am "abiding in Him," nothing outside His will can touch me. To be in Christ means that I march forth as His deputy, His representative, His ambassador, carrying His authority. But to be in Christ also carries the responsibility of the ambassador, to promulgate only those dictums which are the will of our Commander in Chief. In the introduction to his primary passage on spiritual warfare, Paul begins, *"Be strong in the Lord."* This little phrase brings together the two halves which delineate our authority. Another of Paul's similar statements is that God *"causes us to tri-*

umph in Christ." And another, "*He* is head of *all things* to the church."

Practical Applications

Every author who writes on this subject has his own suggestions as to the manner of *how* to go about exercising authority. I am not advocating that we follow one particular formula. I feel that each person needs to develop the practice with which he feels confident. There are certain factors which might be brought to mind here, however, which can be of help in strengthening our faith and assurance as we proceed with this phase of our warfare.

At the outset (as we have been emphasizing above), one should present his demands on the basis of the power and authority of the Lord Jesus Christ. These are our resources. Also, we make it clear that we are coming in His name and for the sake of His glory and His kingdom. In fact, it is good preparation for our own confidence, and for the enemy's disarming, to first have a time of joyous praise and worship.

At some point, we will want to hold up before ourselves and before our adversary our banner, the cross of the Lord Jesus, whereon He won the victory over all of Satan's kingdom, and plead the blood which He shed as the price to purchase us and those for whom we will claim release. I have found it helpful and effective to actually name or identify the spirit or type of attack which is to be bound. And then I use several of the Lord's names to bring it all into sharp relief.

Finally, it is always essential to employ the sword of the Spirit, "it is written." There are clusters of Scripture passages which can serve as strong cords to bind the Evil One. One such cluster pictures the Lord Jesus sitting at the right hand of the throne of God. The author of Hebrews informs us that the main point of his book is that we have a high Priest, "Who is seated at the right hand of the throne of the Majesty in heaven" (Heb. 8:1). There are eleven references in the New Testament which accord such a position of power and authority to the Lord Jesus. In order to have ample, available supply to use as "it is written," I will list the other ten: Matthew 26:64; Mark 16:19; Luke 22:69; Acts

7:55-56; Romans 8:34; Ephesians 1:20-22; Colossians 3:1; Hebrews 1:3; 10:12-13; 12:2.

Another cluster are those verses which reiterate the truth that the Father has committed all things to the authority of the Son. In addition to those at the beginning of this chapter, are: Matthew 11:27a; John 3:35; 1 Corinthians 15:27a. This latter reads, "God has put all things in subjection under His feet."

And then there is the cluster presenting the Lord Jesus' victory which He won on the cross: Colossians 2:15; 1 John 3:8b; 4:4b; and Revelation 12:11 which reads, "And they overcame him because of the blood of the Lamb and because of the word of their testimony, and they loved not their lives even unto death."

Finally, we can align ourselves with the binding and loosing activity of the Lord Jesus Himself. Such a cluster would include Luke 4:18, where He quotes the prophecy of Isaiah, "He sent Me to proclaim release to the captives, and recovery of sight to the blind, to set free those who are downtrodden, to proclaim the favorable year of the Lord," plus Matthew 6:11 where He taught us to pray, *Thy kingdom come, Thy will be done* on earth as it is in heaven," and Luke 11:21-22. (There are other sword verses and militant names of the Lord in the warfare section of the Prayer Companion accompanying this book.)

Therefore, a typical approach of mine, in a move to bind the activities of the enemy in a given situation, might go something like this:

"In the name of the Lord Jesus Christ, the Son of the living God, the Maker and Creator of all things, the King of Kings and Lord of Lords, the King of Glory, the Lord of Hosts, the Lord; mighty in battle; and in His infinite power and absolute authority, which includes all authority in heaven and on earth, before which every knee shall bow in heaven and on earth and under the earth... In His name and power and authority I now come against all of you evil forces of _____ and _____ which are attacking or planning to attack, hurt or hinder the work of the Lord Jesus being done by _____ at _____. I also now bind all the efforts of you spirits of _____, _____, and _____ which are attacking, hurting, or hindering the person of _____. All that is bound in heaven I now bind here on earth at _____, and in His name, power and authority I loose your grip on _____. I hold up against all of you the cross of the Lord Jesus, on which He won complete victory over all of your rights and powers. And I hold up before you the blood which He shed to purchase _____ as His own, and to purchase me and my family. You have no right to attack any of us, apart from His will, so I command you to go where He would send you."

"It is written that God 'raised Him from the dead and seated Him at His right hand in the heavenlies, far above all rule and authority and power and dominion, and above every name that is named, not only in this age, but also in that which is to come.' And He has made me to 'sit with Him in the heavenlies.'"

"I do this binding and loosing for His sake, and for His glory, and according to His will. Amen and Amen."

And again, after such a declaration and employment of His authority, I may sing some songs of praise and victory. Sometimes there may be a tendency on our part to repeat all this, if we don't see immediate results. But I don't feel this is wise or necessary. It only weakens our case. Once we have bound our enemy through this type of prayer in a particular situation, we must "be strong in the Lord, and in the strength of His might...and having done all, to *stand*." I have discovered that my standing firm on the binding and loosing which I have done is often the final blow to the Evil One.

I recall the testimony of a missionary in South America who had been asked to pray for the deliverance of a demonized girl. After prayer, and finally commanding the demon to leave, nothing seemed to improve. But the missionary replied, "Take her home. The demon will leave her." And on the way home, the demon departed and the child was completely restored.

If any of the enemy's attacks do continue for a time, my next step is to refer the problem to the Lord Jesus Himself, praying directly to Him as in the case of the father with his pitiful harassed son in Mark 9, when the disciples were not able to cast out the deaf and dumb spirit. The Lord said, "Bring him here to Me," and then He added, "This kind comes out only by prayer." So I then continue the battle by intercessory prayer to the Lord.

If, after a reasonable time, there still is no relief, I then accept the situation as a matter of testing, permitted by the Lord (just as He allowed Satan to test Job, Peter, Paul, etc.). But this is by no means a rationalization. In many such instances there have been valuable lessons learned. The attacks have eventually been bound, and the individual loosed. I am willing to accept any trial which my Lord sees fit for me or my brothers to pass through, but I refuse to accept that which comes only from the enemy. In fact, when one is dealing with an unusually distressing situation, it may be wise to accompany the prayer with fasting.

After a particular attack on a person, a family, or a ministry has been bound and release has been gained, it is quite possible that before too long a similar and perhaps even more fierce barrage will come. In warfare, the enemy often sends in wave after wave of his forces to mow down his opposition. In a recent war in Korea, a certain hill was named "Heart-Break Ridge" because it had to be captured and recaptured many time. This situation is especially true for soldiers out on the front lines. In such cases we may need to periodically repeat our binding and loosing. And when we resort to "bring him to Me," as the Lord encouraged us to do in those extra difficult cases, we may have to persevere for a time to deal with these recurring attacks.

This leads us to the matter of *written* warfare prayers. And I probably should begin with the confession that up until a couple of years ago, my attitude toward any such thing as a written prayer held nothing but disdain. Prayer was meant to be a free, spontaneous, unencumbered pouring out of one's soul to the Lord. But it didn't take long to completely change my proud and foolish notions. The first few times I read through a couple of warfare prayers written by others, I was amazed at how my heart and spirit moved right along with the petitions and the comprehensive, stirring manner in which they were put together. I immediately began to find them extremely helpful. So, needless to say, I am now thoroughly sold on this means of doing battle against our adversary. I have no hesitation in saying, "Amen" to any Holy Spirit-prompted prayer. And actually, the Holy Spirit can often lead us into a more discerning and forceful effort of intercession when we spend some unhurried time, waiting on Him to do so, than if we always just speed along trying to compose a prayer as we offer it up.

It recently dawned on me that there are a number of written prayers in the New Testament, and that David's Psalms are written prayers. Some of these latter are to be classed as hymns of praise, but a good many are nothing other than warfare prayers. And his collection of written supplications has been a blessing to many, many people.

We have included a few samples of various types of this kind of material in the warfare section of the Prayer Companion. And we would highly recommend the warfare prayers in Mark Bubeck's two books, *The Adversary* and *Overcoming the Adversary*.

Before we move on, it would probably be in order to explain a bit more as to what is implied by "warfare praying." Actually, such an expression at first appears to be a contradiction of terms. We pray to God, but we certainly don't do warfare with God. We do warfare with Satan and his forces, but we surely do not pray to them. As you read over some of the prayers in the warfare section of the Prayer Companion, you will see that both of the elements, of calling on the Lord and binding the enemy, are woven together in a powerful offensive against our opposition. Warfare praying includes direct orders to the enemy to retreat. In fact, it includes such words as "command," "bind," "forbid," "tear down," etc. However, these bold assaults are done in close union with the Father, the Son and the Holy Spirit. All is done in the name, authority and power of the Lord Jesus, and all is based on God's written word.

And here we must emphasize again the need to rest all our weight on the word of God. Some Christians can become quite emotional and call out with a loud voice as they seek to bind their foe. But it is not our shouting, nor even our sincere earnestness, which has any effect on our enemy. He backs away only when we employ the word of God, which is the "Sword of the Spirit." Although fasting is often a helpful factor, even this is no substitute for a confident application of God's word.

Gates and Keys

Before closing our study of the Lord's messages regarding binding and loosing, we must give some attention to His word pictures of gates and keys. Both words are in the plural. This broadens the imagery considerably and indicates that the Lord is desiring us to think in terms of the many locked gates which will confront us as we move forth into enemy territory. And since each gate will require its own special key, we will need quite an assortment of keys!

The word for gates here sometimes refers to the gate of the garden surrounding a home and sometimes to the large city gates which were often made of iron, or the most impervious material possible. As we mentioned above, the Lord's very tone of voice in speaking of the gates of Hades (Satan's kingdom) portrays fortresses which to men are absolutely impregnable and fastened with locks which are far too complex for you or me to ever undo by ourselves. But the Holy Spirit is a wonderful locksmith. He can pick any of Satan's locks. Or, to come back to the Lord's parable, He has a key for every one of Satan's gates. And He is prepared to make keys available to us when we come to Him in humble, earnest concern.

This matter of keys is not simple, however. The key to the front door of my neighbor's house who lives on my left will not open the door of my neighbor's home on the right. And if I have lost the key to my own home, I cannot get in. A key is a very specific, definitive opener. Without it, we remain outside and cannot proceed another step. So the Lord Jesus was speaking of an indispensable requisite when He promised keys.

In one place He calls them the keys of the kingdom of heaven, and in another, the keys of death and Hades. Both are needed. The gospel message in its various forms of presentation is our set of keys to the kingdom of heaven. The keys to death and Hades are not so plain and straightforward. But we must learn to come to Him with confidence and expectancy when we need the key to unlock a closed village, a closed home, a closed campus, or a closed heart.

In our outreach into the villages, the Lord has beautifully

provided some of His keys. In one area, the breakthrough came when the members of the gospel team pooled what money they had and bought a three-wheeled cycle for a young man who was crippled from polio. In another case, an elderly grandmother who had spent her all on offerings to the various temples in hopes of deliverance from her long-standing infirmity was marvelously healed. As a result, her whole family and many others turned to the Lord.

On one occasion, when two of the team members approached a home, the man who answered the door slowly but graciously opened the door and invited them in. After they had sat down, he proceeded to tell them that the night before he had seen these two young men in a dream and had been instructed that, when they came to his door, he was to invite them in and take heed to their message. After listening intently to the gospel story, he accepted the Lord.

In some villages, the Lord has led to present the gospel by using puppets, which has been very effective. At other times, it has been posters or gospel movies. In one situation, the hearts of the parents were opened when several hours each day were given to helping their junior high sons and daughters with make-up classes for their school studies.

Several times it has been discovered that hearts have been prepared by a recent tragedy which has struck the home. When I was a teacher at Christ's College, one of my finest students suddenly passed away the night before her graduation. A few days before, in loving appreciation for four years of college support, she had presented to her unsaved father a beautiful leather-bound Bible. Her father's business had gone on the rocks, and he was in deep despair. Before his daughter's death, he had not yet opened the Bible she gave him. But the passing away of his only daughter whom he esteemed so highly caused him to treasure this gift with all his heart. He began to read it, was soon marvelously converted, and became a zealous servant of the Lord. His business began to flourish, but he turned it completely over to the Lord and joyously ran the enterprize for Him.

Many of you have read the book *Peace Child* which tells how the Lord provided Don Richardson with the key to the Sawi tribe in Netherlands New Guinea. For years he could not seem to penetrate even one heart. But once the Holy Spirit presented him with the right "opener," almost the whole area turned to the Lord. And as we read through the book of Acts, we can see how everywhere Paul went, he was given the keys to unlock closed doors. It has always amazed me how he was able to establish so many strong churches in such a short time. Often he was in a place for only two or three weeks. Actually, it doesn't take long to open a door if you have the right key! But without the key, it can take a lot of blood, sweat and tears to have to *break down* a heavy iron gate. So we do well, as we approach an enemy fortress, to first spend adequate time with the Lord seeking from Him the proper key.

We close this chapter with the reminder that our goal in binding and loosing is not merely to chalk up some spectacular victories. This can be a subtle form of pride and will result in failure and defeat. "God resists the proud, but gives grace to the humble."

Love operates on a very different wave length from pride.

12

OUR RESOURCES

War is a very costly ordeal, both in men and materials. World War II cost the United States 339 billion dollars. That was nearly fifty years ago. In present currency value, and cost of more sophisticated munitions, etc., the amount would be at least a hundred times as much, or thirty-five trillion dollars. The same war cost other countries even more than it did the U.S. And since some of them did not possess such economic strength, they are still struggling with huge war debts. The United States also had to recruit an army of eleven and a half million of its finest young men.

When we enter the realm of spiritual warfare, we soon discover that this enterprise also requires tremendous resources. Our own strength and wisdom is just not enough. We are dealing with genuine "super-powers." And some of these enemy forces have been entrenched in their dark, idolatrous, heathen fortresses for centuries. To dislodge them is certainly no small undertaking! (I am thinking of one village church, planted in the heart of such a stronghold by a team of godly missionaries. But after thirty years, with missionaries still working there, this church boasts only seven members.)

In Matthew 17 (also Mk. 9 and Lk. 9) is the record of the Lord's disciples striving to cast the demon out of a young boy, and seeing nothing but miserable failure in the face of a large crowd of skeptical onlookers.

In our last chapter we dealt with the matter of our authority, and shortly before the events of this present story, the Lord had especially granted to His disciples a full slate of what appeared to be an unlimited supply of both power and authority (Mt. 10:1; Lk. 9:1). They were given the authority, but soon discovered that they ran short on resources.

We must make a clear distinction here between authority, power and resources. When authority has been bestowed upon a person, it continues to be his until it is revoked. Power is quite different. It depends on his resources. As long as his resources hold out, he has power. But as soon as those resources run dry, his power is gone. A general in the army possesses a high degree of authority, but if he doesn't have the men and materials (the resources) to back it up, he is weak (without power). And this is precisely where the disciples found themselves in this story.

It would seem that a good alternate title for the story which we will examine in this chapter might be "Mountains, Mustard Seeds and Galaxies." My reason for suggesting such a title is the conclusion to the story. When the disciples got away from the scene of their failure, they asked why they were not able to handle this situation. The Lord replied, "Because of your little faith. For truly I say to you, if you have *faith* as a *mustard seed*, you shall say to this *mountain*, 'move from here to there,' and it shall move, and nothing shall be impossible to you" (Mt. 17:20).

Mountains

It seems quite evident that the Lord chose the illustration of moving a mountain because the disciples had just had a mountain before them which they were unable to move. Mountains come in various sizes, but no mountain is easy to move. In fact the very word "mountain," as it is used here, refers to a huge, immovable obstacle.

When the Lord spoke of "this mountain," it indicates that at that particular time they were standing near the base of a large mountain. The Lord Jesus and three of His disciples had just come down from the "high mountain" of His transfiguration. Some scholars have decided that it was probably Mt. Tabor, while others feel it was Mt. Hermon. If it were Mt. Tabor, we are thinking of a crest rising to 600 meters (2,000 feet) in height. If it were Mt. Hermon, we must picture a much higher peak of 2,800 meters (9,300 feet).

To even make a small dent in a mountain requires a massive amount of dynamite. When I came to Taiwan over thirty years ago, a cement company was digging away at a small limestone hill near Kaohsiung. Since that time, several other companies have joined them. This hill is probably not more than a couple hundred feet high, but they are still hauling out thousands of tons of material every day and have a huge supply left.

High mountains are usually composed of granite or much harder rock than limestone. That is why they have not eroded, and still remain mountains. So when the Lord spoke of moving mountains, He was talking about impossible situations. The disciples had just met such an impossibility, and you and I will meet such too as we move into enemy territory.

When missionaries enter the villages of Taiwan to represent the gospel, one factor which often causes their efforts to be ineffective is that there is little concept of the size and hardness of the mountains they are facing. Taiwan is an island with a terrain which is covered mostly with mountains, both visible and invisible. Consequently, it is possible to spend decades pounding away with our small hammer and wonder why there is so little accomplished. We need to hear again Paul's reminder, "Our struggle is *not* against flesh and blood, but against the rulers, against the powers, against the world forces of this darkness, against the spiritual forces of wickedness in heavenly places" (Eph. 6:12).

Some mountains even have volcanoes inside of them. Paul met a number of these. When he arrived at Lystra he encountered a spiritual volcano. It wasn't long before he was attacked with stones and dragged outside the city as dead. In Philippi he and his co-worker were beaten with rods and locked up in the city jail. In Thessalonica and several other places he was run out of town. In Jerusalem he was almost torn limb from limb.

In our village work we have met a measure of this type of opposition. In one area an irate temple priest beat up on two of our workers. In another town the pastor of the church was smitten with a strange incoherence after he had helped remove an idol shelf in one of the homes.

I feel we are up against some enormous mountains here in Taiwan. I recently read a testimony written by an American InterVarsity staff worker who visited the Philippines and was greatly moved by the spirit of revival which he saw there. People were turning to the Lord both in the cities and in the villages. Before returning to the States he also visited one or two other countries here in the Far East which have longstanding idolatrous backgrounds like Taiwan. What a difference! Results were very few by comparison.

Mustard Seeds

When the Lord spoke of mustard seeds, He was referring to His disciples and to you and me. What is a mustard seed in comparison to a mountain? How could a mustard seed ever move a mountain? A mustard seed is a pretty helpless little commodity. It has no hands, no feet, no eyes, no brains or money. It really doesn't have much of anything! Even its size is "the smallest of all seeds."

So when the Lord chose to compare you and me to a mustard seed, He certainly didn't intend us to get an exalted opinion of ourselves. But right here is where the crux of the whole matter lies. The potential strength of a grain of mustard seed does not lie in itself. So the reliance of a mustard seed surely cannot be on itself.

This brings us to one of the most important truths of the Word of God. Every time the Lord Jesus speaks of faith, He is speaking of faith in Himself (or faith in God). *Every time!* He never is encouraging us to place our faith merely in the *results* of something we would like to see accomplished.

But here the disciples made their big mistake. Without realizing it, they had begun to assume that *they* could heal the sick, *they* could do miracles, *they* could cast out demons. So the Lord had to allow them to be brought up short, to realize that it just doesn't work that way. Mustard seeds just can't move mountains (even small ones). They can't even move a grain of sand.

But if a mustard seed possesses *faith*... confidence in *Someone* who can move mountains ...then that mustard seed is in a position to see tremendous things accomplished. "Nothing shall be impossible to you." So, without faith a mustard seed is helpless and hopeless. But with faith (in the right Person) there is no limit to the possible results.

Therefore, when the Lord said "If you have faith as a mustard seed," He was not speaking quantitatively, but qualitatively. A tiny little bit of faith, "the size of a mustard seed," as some incorrect translations read, does no one any good. The faith of a mustard seed is tremendous faith. It is glorious faith. It is effective faith, the kind of faith God is looking for. It is faith in God's Son, to whom all authority in heaven and earth has been granted, and before whom every knee shall bow, in heaven, on earth and under the earth. It is the faith which will see mountains moved!

But remember, it is only a mustard seed which can have such faith. As long as we have not yet come to see ourselves as a mustard seed sees itself, we still have too much self-reliance. And that means we are not seeing things straight. We are not seeing the magnitude of the mountains, and we are not seeing our great inadequacy. It is a mustard seed Christian who prays earnestly. It is a mustard seed Christian who seeks the Lord and who places his full confidence in the Lord. A mustard seed has no other recourse or resource!

Now let us take a look at a related incident which will help to bring these truths into sharp relief. When the Lord sent forth His disciples on this very preaching circuit, He endued them with special power and authority to handle any situation they might come across. In fact, He charged them to "heal the sick, raise the dead, cleanse the lepers, and cast out demons" (Mt. 10:8). In Luke's account He makes it even stronger, "He called the twelve together, and gave them power and authority over *all the demons*, and to heal diseases" (Lk .9:1). And Matthew adds "every kind of disease and every kind of sickness" (10:1).

For the first few days, this all worked out very well. They were thrilled with the breath-taking results. But because things were going so well, without realizing it they began to assume that they were very able people. They began to utilize this power as if it were some special quality of their own. This is always the precursor of failure. So the Lord had to withdraw the special powers and authority which He had granted them. And later when they asked why they had failed, His reply, according to Matthew, was lack of faith, and according to Mark, lack of prayer.

Lack of faith and lack of prayer are really the same thing. If I am convinced that I have *no* spiritual powers or authority of my own but believe that He has ample power and authority, then I will come to Him continually, not only when I see things out of control. This again is the picture of mustard seed faith. The person who prays little is a person who does not yet see himself as a mustard seed and therefore does not place his total confidence in the Lord Jesus and call on Him for the needed resources for each undertaking.

In our previous chapter we dealt with the matter of authority, but let us take note here, that the endowment of unlimited healing powers and unrestricted authority over evil spirits was a *very special* grant made to His twelve disciples at that time. "He called the *twelve* together, and gave *them* power and authority" (Lk. 9:1). Then He did the same thing a little later for seventy more (Lk. 10:1,19). I mention this, for some too quickly assume that these special enablements belong to all Christians in all situations, and that all we need to do is just *claim* them. I feel there is a tendency to overwork this word "claim." The word "claim" is never used in Scripture, and we must be careful in trying to claim something that might not be ours. I have seen too many cases where it has just not worked out. It also is a practice which tends to lure us away from the more secure and more effective status of the mustard seed. So we shouldn't feel badly if we don't always possess that unique endowment "to heal every disease and every sickness...raise the dead, cleanse the lepers," etc. This exceptional empowering was granted with a very definite and specific selectivity. We will speak more of this a little later.

Galaxies

Although the text does not use the word "galaxies," it still seems the only adequate term to express the main point of this chapter. We have already discussed mountains and mustard seeds; now it is time to turn our attention to the astronomer's heavens. We compared mustard seeds with mountains from the standpoint of size. So let's look now at the galaxies and consider their size.

A mustard seed can't begin to move a mountain, but the One who made the galaxies can move any mountain. Let's begin with the largest mountain on this earth, Mt. Everest. It is about 9,000 meters tall (over 29,000 feet), the highest peak, the greatest challenge to all mountain climbers. In fact, very few professional climbers have ever made it to the top. How far would any one of them get, or even the most brilliant engineer, in trying to *move* Mt. Everest?

But let us now look at Mt. Everest the way God sees it. On a world globe the size of a basketball, Mt. Everest would be about one tenth of one millimeter in height. You couldn't even feel it if you moved your finger over it. Now let's move out into space. Our sun is a million times the size of our earth, and the star Betelguese is a million times the size of our sun. A galaxy is composed of about 100,000,000,000 such stars, and there are an estimated 100,000,000,000 galaxies in our universe. The Lord Jesus made all these! (Jn. 1:3). So we ask the question, could He move Mt. Everest?

With this as background for our thinking, let us now return to verse 17 (of Mt. 17), the key verse of the passage we have been studying. "And Jesus answered and said, 'O unbelieving and perverted generation, how long shall I be with you? How long shall I put up with you? Bring him here to me.'" It is quite evident that the Lord Jesus was very angry when He spoke these words. We do not often see Him angry. But on this occasion something was disturbing Him greatly, and we need to see what it was and comprehend the lesson He is seeking to teach us.

Why does He here speak of His disciples and everyone else gathered around as an "unbelieving and perverse generation"? "Unbelieving," of course, means lacking in faith. "Perverse" means "off the track." His disciples in this matter of faith had gotten off the track and led everyone else into wrong thinking. They had drawn attention to themselves. They had forgotten that they were only mustard seeds, but rather had begun to see themselves as quite spectacular somebodies. They had forgotten the *Source* of their power and authority, and so they found themselves without resources.

Then the Lord asked two questions. "How long shall I be

with you?" and "How long shall I put up with you?" The first question would seem to ask, "How long am I going to have to carry on this training course until you understand what true faith really is?" The second question carries a tone of warning. There are two wrong concepts of "faith" which have always been somewhat common, but both are definitely "perverse." And both are pictured as such in this story.

The first wrong concept is what we might call a glorified form of self-confidence. "If I can just cause myself to believe hard enough that it will happen (even visualize the end result), then it will surely come to pass." But this is just the *opposite* of true faith. Proper faith is *never* directed toward what *I* can manage to do, but it always is a focus on what *He* can and will do. The Lord's disciples were utterly confident that they could cast out this demon. They had been casting out many demons without any failures and healing all kinds of diseases. So they were really quite astounded when they asked the Lord, "Why couldn't we cast it out?" His reply was, "Because of your little faith." They certainly had no idea of what true faith really was.

The second "perverse" view is an over-confidence in our *gifts*. We all possess certain gifts which God has given us. These are very helpful and very useful. But of themselves, they are not sufficient to handle all the exigencies of spiritual warfare. The disciples also learned this lesson. "This kind can come out by nothing but by prayer" (Mk. 9:29).

The Lord gave a strong word which ties it all together. "Bring him [the sick, possessed boy] to *Me!*" This is the solution. "You people standing around, you must learn that my disciples have no power or authority of their own." "And you disciples, I am very disappointed in you, that you did not give credit to Whom credit is due." This is perhaps a paraphrase of what He is saying. Jesus then rebuked the demon and it "came out of him, and the boy was cured at once."

We will not leave this story, however, with our focus on the Lord's various rebukes. Rather, we must look at the beautiful way the disciples learned their lesson. Some months later, after their Lord had ascended back into heaven, and the disciples had been filled with the Holy Spirit, things were much different. One day as Peter and John were going up to the temple for prayer, a lame beggar sitting at the gate of the temple asked them for some money. In a humble manner, Peter replied, "I don't have any silver or gold, but what I do have, I will give you. *In the name of Jesus Christ of Nazareth*, walk" (Acts 3:6). Then Peter helped him up, and the man began walking and leaping and praising God.

Naturally, a crowd gathered, but as soon as Peter saw them looking at him and John, he was prepared to handle this situation. He turned to the people and said, "Men of Israel, why do you marvel at this, *as if by our own power* or piety we made this man walk?" And then he began to introduce them to his Lord and Savior.

While Peter and John were presenting Jesus to the people, the priests sent their guards to arrest them and put them in jail. The next morning at the trial, Peter began his defense again with a fine combination of power and humility. "If we are on trial for a benefit done to a sick man, as to how this man has been made well, let it be known to all of you, and to all the people of Israel, that *by the name of Jesus Christ* the Nazarene...*by this name* this man stands here before you in good health." And again, he preached to them his Lord and the gospel of salvation. The Lord can and will do "great and mighty things" when we come to see that all our resources are in Him.

When Moses, at the end of his days, was giving his final instructions to the people, he said, "When you go to war against your enemies and see horses and chariots and an army greater than yours, do not be afraid of them, because the Lord your God, who brought you up out of Egypt, will be with you. When you are about to go into battle, the priest shall come forward and address the army. He shall say, 'Hear, O Israel, today you are going into battle against your enemies. Do not be fainthearted or afraid; do not be terrified or give way to panic before them. For *the Lord your God is the One* who goes with you to fight for you against your enemies to give you victory'" (Dt. 20:1-4). They were reminded that they had ample resources, and so do we.

David was always aware of his resources. Even though he was a very talented warrior and led a very able army, yet he refused to place his trust in any human strength.

"*To You,* O Lord, ... put to shame" (Ps. 25:1-3).

"You are my king........your name forever" (Ps .44:4-8).

"I will say of the Lord, *He* is my refuge and my fortress, *my God, In whom I trust*" (Ps. 91:2).

"*Praise be to the Lord* my rock, who trains my hands for war, my fingers for battle. *He* is my loving God and my fortress, my stronghold and my deliverer, my shield in whom I take refuge" (Ps. 144:1-2).

And wise old Solomon learned from his father a lot of truth regarding resources for war. One of his proverbs reads, "The horse is made ready for the day of battle, but *victory rests with the Lord*" (Prov. 21:31).

Tapping our Resources

Though there is an infinite supply of resources for the humble little mustard seed, he must learn how to avail himself of these provisions, or he is in a bad position. Without continual access to this reservoir of vital support, the tiny mustard seed doesn't really amount to very much. Sad to say, the Lord's disciples were quite blind to this truth. Before the Holy Spirit came, they were actually weak as weak could be. Though the Lord Jesus had allowed them a special temporary grant of miraculous power for healing the sick and casting out demons, they were weak as water in every other way. Time after time He had to deal with their pride, their spiritual dullness, their lack of faith, and their lack of love.

When they asked, "Why couldn't we cast out the demon?", His reply (in Mark's account) was simply, "This kind comes out only by *prayer.*" A few days later, "as He was praying in a certain place," they stood around and waited until He had finished, and finally "one of His disciples said to Him, 'Lord, teach us to pray.'" He gave them a very thorough lesson on prayer, concluding with the words: "If you then, *though you are evil,* know how to give good gifts to your children, how much more will your Father in heaven give *the Holy Spirit* to *those who ask Him*" (Lk. 11:1-13). And yet there is no evidence that before His ascension back into heaven they did any praying at all. After the Holy Spirit came on Pentecost, they became men of prayer. But during those three years while they were with the Lord, their track record was mighty poor.

A few chapters back, we considered God's commission to that military general Joshua. We looked especially at the thrice-repeated *command* to "*be strong.*" And we find the same emphasis in Paul's introduction to his famous warfare passage. "*Be strong* in the Lord, and in the strength of His might" (Eph .6:10). These admonitions are phrased in the imperative case. They are in the form of a strong injunction. But this of course brings up the question, "How are we to be strong?" It is simple to tell a person to be strong, but he needs to know *how*! It is like the old-fashioned cards which were sent to a sick person saying "Get well soon!" It sounds great, and that is exactly what he would like to do, but he needs more help than that.

God's Word, of course, never asks us to be strong without giving us the formula for acquiring that strength. At first it might seem that Paul was pointing to our Christian armor as our means of strength, for he immediately begins to urge us to protect ourselves by putting on our armor, and then goes on to describe each piece. But armor is not really a source of strength. It is merely our safeguard against the enemy's attacks on us.

We have already had a chapter on weapons, but in the conclusion of Paul's treatise on spiritual warfare he seems to single out one particular weapon as our chief means of amassing a backlog of strength. "With all prayer and petition pray at all times in the Spirit, and with this in view, be on the alert with all perseverance and petition for all the saints" (Eph. 6:18).

In our chapter on weapons, we thoroughly analyzed this verse on prayer, but I feel we need to come back to it here and look at it from the standpoint of our *resources* for battle. In the previous section of this chapter, we have seen how unimaginably great are the resources of the Lord Jesus. All the strength that a mustard seed could ever need to move any mountain is there with Him, and with plenty left over. But mustard seeds (we weak disciples) must become adept at stockpiling a quantity of these resources for our expeditions into enemy territory. We must learn that spiritual warfare must be begun by prayer; it is to be carried on by prayer; and all victories are won by prayer. So we can "be strong in the Lord" by appropriating the "strength of His might" in prayer (Eph. 6:10). (And to be sure, all this praying is to be carried on with an abundance of fragrant adoration, thanksgiving and praise.)

This is why some missionaries are coming to the place where they give the best hours of their day to prayer, plan regular nights of prayer, involve themselves in fasting with prayer, maintain maximum prayer support from their home base, and train their new converts in prayer. Certainly the Lord Jesus meant to include these "invincible" strongholds we meet on the mission field when He said, "*This kind* cannot come out by anything but by prayer." And though He was the very Son of God, He Himself had just come from another of His prayer vigils up on the Mt. of Transfiguration with three of His disciples.

In times of war, a nation will begin to accumulate and store up extra supplies of many vital commodities: all the essential metals, fuels, chemicals, and even nourishing food stuffs. They will stockpile munitions and greatly increase their inventory of planes, tanks, ships and vehicles. I myself was in the thick of all this during World War II, and along with all other Americans, endured the rigors of austere rationing.

When the Lord Jesus informed His disciples that "this kind can come out only by prayer," He was not referring to the simple "whisper a prayer in the morning" type of approach. He was encouraging something of the order of His own prayer life. Though He was the Son of God and possessed infinite authority, He still gave careful heed to building up and maintaining ample resources of spiritual power through prayer. As we mentioned above, He had just led three of His disciples up on a mountain to witness another of His vital prayer watches. It was while He was there, praying to His Father, that He was magnificently glorified before them.

He had begun His ministry by spending forty days of fasting out in the wilderness. Moses twice spent forty days up on Mt. Sinai, and on one of these occasions Joshua went at least partway up the mountain with Him for the forty days (Ex. 24:13). Joshua also spent much time in Moses' "Tent of Meeting" (Ex. 33:7-11). Also we have the picture of the Lord's command to Joshua and his army to march around Jericho for seven days before their attack on the city.

After Paul's conversion, he spent three years in Arabia before entering upon his ministry. And he became a great proponent of intercessory prayer in all his epistles. Then we have (the finally mature) Peter's firm decision, in the midst of one of his conflicts, "We will *give ourselves to prayer* and the ministry of the Word" (Acts 6:4).

I am discovering that the men and women whom God is using are those who periodically "disappear" from the scene of battle to build up their reserves of power. If you search for them you would find them in the "Holy Place," communing with their Lord. In a book I once read, written by a great woman of God, one of her chapters began something like this: "Today I turned fifty years of age, and have had another wonderful day alone with the Lord, looking over the past half century, and once again seeking His direction and enabling for the days ahead.

Another friend of mine, who for many years was director of a thriving, worldwide student work, visited us for a week here in Taiwan. Naturally I filled his schedule to the full with meetings, interviews, travels, etc. Then as he was leaving for the plane to Hong Kong, I asked what his schedule looked like for that next week. He remarked that again it would be very full. But he added, "I must, however, have the first day free to recharge my spiritual batteries."

Foothills

Oftentimes the way up to a high mountain leads through several tiers of foothills. And it is possible for us to lose our way and become altogether stranded before we ever get to the real mountains themselves. We individual mustard seeds may be giving ourselves to prayer and fasting as best we know how and still see relatively little accomplished. There is of course the time factor, which we discuss in a later chapter. But sometimes there are other considerations that may help us to begin to make headway.

For instance, it is always beneficial for a *group* of us mustard seeds to come together regularly for a few days of seeking the Lord's empowering. This was the common practice in the book of Acts. In fact, that book begins with the account of 120 of the Lord's disciples "joined together in prayer" for ten days. But then to turn the coin over, it has been my experience through forty years on the mission field that whenever our body of co-workers has begun to *miss out* on those days together for worship, prayer and fasting, our effectiveness has dropped, and ugly problems have arisen.

There are still other ways we sometimes get waylaid in the foothills. When Satan gets a foothold within the body, we can't proceed with any power. One of the most common obstructions which hampers the Holy Spirit's working is dissension and discord. We should fear this impediment like we fear the plague. It is disastrous! When the Holy Spirit is grieved, He retreats. And when He retreats, even a whole batch of mustard seeds can be divested of power. Unresolved anger, resentment and unforgiveness are poisons to the Lord's work. "Anyone who does not love, remains in death," and "Whoever does not love, does not know God...For anyone who does not love his brother whom he has seen [even though that brother is not perfect], cannot love God whom he has not seen." And "Whoever loves God *must* also love his brother" (1 Jn. 3:14; 4:8,20,21). God's Word warns us that one person holding onto a root of bitterness can defile a whole group. (Heb. 12:15)

It is also possible for the various individuals in the group to get lost in the foothills through any one of a number of other enemy pitfalls. Though we give a great deal of attention to praying for our co-workers' physical and emotional health, these are not their most important needs. If one begins to dabble in any form of sin, if he allows a mass of hustle and bustle activity ("the cares of this life") to crush his devotional life, if he, on the other hand, gives in to sloth (frittering away his time), or if he allows some form of pride to take over, any of these can keep him from ever being able to deal with the "mountains" themselves. He will just remain sidelined in the foothills. Even the improper respect for one's wife can "hinder your prayers" (1 Pet. 3:7).

So we can understand the plea of warrior David when he cried out, "Search me, O God, and know my heart...See if there is any offensive way in me" (Ps. 139:23,24). To David, warfare was very serious business. In fact, warfare is usually a life-and-death matter, not only for the whole army but for those they are fighting to rescue. So we dare not ignore or lightly accept periods of delay or regression in the battle. It may be that our Commander in Chief is trying to point out some area of weakness we have overlooked.

We should probably add here, however, a word of comfort. Our Lord does not wait until we are perfect to use us. Then He would never be able to use any of us. But this truth must always be balanced by the fact that we never get far when there is deliberate sin, careless living, or unwholesome attitudes holding us back.

On the mission field we constantly find ourselves calling on the Lord of the harvest to send out workers into His harvest field. But sometimes He may not be too eager to send us a contingent of new workers when those we already have remain bogged down in the foothills. New workers will often find themselves caught up in the underbrush. But if we who are supposedly more mature can help them get extricated and teach them how to keep themselves free from such tangles (the enemies, traps and snares), then perhaps the Lord of the harvest will give attention to our cries for additional fellow laborers.

A positive illustration of victory in the foothills is a fellow missionary family here in Taiwan. They are becoming increasingly involved in an effective warfare and deliverance ministry among Satan's captives. They received advice from their godly parents who were much exercised about the dangers they might be bringing upon themselves and their children through these involvements. The father said, "We are glad for your willingness to enter the front lines, but we fear serious counterattacks." And well might there be concern, for this missionary couple have already had their car stolen, and their two daughters have been in accidents with bones broken and teeth knocked out. They have encountered financial crises, plus other disappointments and discouragements. But they entertain no thought of retreat! Rather, they are seeking the Lord's plans for even greater advance. They are working their way through the foothills. And you can be sure they will see some mountains moved and some strongholds torn down!

Humility and Worship

Coming back once again to the story of the disciples' failure to heal the demonized boy, it would seem that there were several reasons why the Lord was so unhappy with them and allowed them to fail. In urging them to maneuver themselves into the position of a mustard seed, He also was no doubt seeking to develop more humility on their part. For at several other times, when He spoke of mustard seeds, He particularly described these as "the smallest of all seeds." Therefore, when anyone begins to see himself as a mustard seed and to see the Lord Jesus as the Creator of all the galaxies, the Maker of heaven and earth, the universe, the atoms, all life, and everything that exists—when his eyes are opened to comprehend something of his own smallness and His Lord's greatness—a spirit of humility will surely settle upon him.

A standard platform for our daily Bible reading might well be the simple phrase, "Behold Him." Mustard seed faith comes from observing how majestic, how gracious, how wise and how able He is, and how needy and unworthy we are by comparison. Though our loving God and Father has "raised us up with Christ and seated us with Him in the heavenly realms," we minute mustard seeds will do well to be every aware that the chasm between His abilities and ours is an expanse so vast that we can never fathom it. It is like a mustard seed trying to comprehend the infinite. The tiny little mustard seed can only look on with amazement, humility and worship. It is when we tend to drag Him down to our size, or exalt ourselves to be compared with Him, that our faith becomes weak. But mustard seed faith is powerful, for it maintains an infinitely exalted view of *His glory*. It is an amazing truth and an unfathomable privilege that we have been "seated there with Him in the heavenly realms." But let us not forget that our position is *"with Him"* and by no means equal to Him.

On a previous evening, after the Lord Jesus had stilled the storm for His frightened disciples out in the middle of the lake, He said to them, "Where is your faith?" And they were fearful and amazed, saying to one another, "*Who then is this*, that He commands even the winds and the water, and they obey Him?" A mustard seed Christian, with awe and worship, never ceases to ask, "Who then is this, who does all these marvelous things?"

"When pride comes, then comes disgrace, but with humility comes wisdom" (Prov. ll:2). It is when we come to realize that spiritually we are still blind little mustard seeds, that we begin to make a bit of progress. And true mustard seed faith will say "thank you" for anything and everything that He is pleased to do for us or through us. Mustard seeds are great on worship. They are always aware of that infinite gap between themselves and their glorious Lord. So a mustard seed is one "overflowing with thanksgiving."

There seems to be no record up to that time of the disciples ever being grateful or thanking their Lord for any of the miracles He was doing through them. They were thrilled and excited when they were riding high with all their spectacular powers. But when they were confronted with failure, their only concern was their own loss of face. How often we miserable little mustard seeds forget to say "thank you." And in the Lord's eyes, this is actually a position even lower than a mustard seed. For a mustard seed has life. A thankless heart is more like an inanimate grain of sand or dirt. So we can begin to see why the Lord gets upset with us at times. He surely has to be a God of mercy. And sometimes He has to let our pride wrestle with some disgrace.

The apostle John was one of the disciples to whom the Lord Jesus had granted those special gifts of power and authority. But six decades later, when he wrote his five books of the New Testament, he never once referred to these. He had by that time grown up to become a true mustard seed. We have mentioned above the conclusion to his gospel where he pointed only to the signs which "*Jesus performed* in the presence of His disciples."

John's record of the life and labors of his Lord is often called the "Gospel of Belief," for it uses the word "believe" over ninety times. And his conclusion sums it all up: "*These* [signs which *He* did] have been written that you may believe." Occasionally today, some special "sign," done by the Lord through one of His servants on the mission field is just what is needed to convince and draw a hungry, seeking heart to Him. But more often than not, such miraculous workings in a heathen area can actually have a negative effect. I have recently heard of several situations where people were healed and then delightedly returned to their sinful ways, without any particular regard for the mercy of the Lord upon them. And in the end, their superstitious acknowledgement of spiritual power is all too frequently still directed to the human instrument through whom the Lord did the healing.

We still should be prepared to pray for the sick when a suitable opportunity presents itself, and we should do so with love and expectancy. But mustard seed faith will leave the results to Him, and above all, will handle things in such a way that all glory and recognition, power and authority goes to Him. For all our efforts are to build *His* kingdom, not our project!

Just a week ago, I heard the marvelous testimony of a medical doctor from mainland China. His teenaged daughter and five other young people had become asphyxiated with carbon monoxide poisoning. She had been in the hospital for five days in a coma and was steadily growing weaker. Tests showed that her brain function had definitely been destroyed. Three of the other victims had already died. Her father and mother had been praying night and day for her healing, but there was no improvement. Finally, the father said to his wife, "We are not praying correctly. We must pray according to the Lord's will." So they began to tell the Lord that if He preferred to take her home, they were ready to accept that. If it were His will for her to remain merely a vegetable all her life, they would gladly and lovingly care for her. As they commenced to pray in this vein, they obtained a peaceful release in their own spirits, and their daughter bit by bit showed improvement. She continued to progress until within a few days she was out of the hospital and living a healthy, normal life.

It reminds us of the lesson the Lord Jesus had to teach Mary and Martha. Their brother Lazarus became very ill, so they sent messengers to tell the Lord and to invite Him to come and heal their brother. But the Lord remained in this distant place for several days. Lazarus' condition grew worse, and he finally died. They had the funeral, and Lazarus had been in the tomb for four days before the Lord arrived. Naturally, Mary and Martha were greatly distressed. But the Lord's reply was in the form of a question: "Didn't I say to you that if you would believe, you would see the glory of God?" Mustard seeds who believe (in Him)—who trust in His wisdom and allow Him to do it His way—will always see the glory of God. In that instance, He even raised Lazarus from the dead. "'My thoughts are not your thoughts, neither are your ways My ways,' declares the Lord. 'As the heavens are higher than the earth, so are My ways higher than your ways, and My thoughts than your thoughts'" (Isa. 55:8-9).

Proper Motivation of Mustard Seed Faith

Probably another reason why the Lord's disciples failed so completely was that they had forgotten their primary assignment. When He sent them out on these preaching missions, their first order of business was to proclaim the *kingdom* of God. In fact it was only a couple of days before this miserable disgrace took place that He had asked them, "Who do people say that I am?" They replied, "Some say John the Baptist, others say Elijah, and others Jeremiah, or one of the prophets." And then He moved in closer and asked, "But who do *you* say that I am?" Peter answered, "You are the *Christ*, the Son of the living God."

Peter didn't really know or realize what He was saying, for the Lord replied, "Blessed are you Simon Bar-Jona! For flesh and blood has not revealed this to you, but my Father who is in heaven." In acknowledging that the Lord Jesus was the Christ, Peter saw Him as the Messiah, the long-awaited King of the Jews. What he hadn't yet comprehended was that this Person sitting there in front of him was the King of a much broader kingdom than merely that of the people of Israel. He was the King of Kings and Lord of Lords, the King of the *Kingdom of God*. And none of the disciples seemed to realize that their assignment to proclaim "the kingdom of heaven is at hand" was meant to introduce and exalt and prepare the way for the acceptance of the

King of the kingdom of God, not just exciting personal successes. This is surely another basic reason why they failed.

In Luke's account, the very next event is the ugly record that "an argument came among them as to which of them was the greatest" (Lk. 9:46). They seemed to have pretty well forgotten the purpose of their commission. This is all the more amazing and distressing when we consider the fact that it had been only a matter of hours prior to this colossal defeat, that three of His disciples had been with Him on the Mount of Transfiguration and beheld His "magnificent glory." And yet they were probably the ones who brought up the question of "who was greatest," for naturally they were very sure that they were quite a cut above the others. We could ask ourselves, how often does our reasoning and planning wander off in this direction? What a tragedy when a mustard seed allows the focus of its vision to become distorted and its motivation to become self-centered. And yet this all too readily occurs when a mustard seed is granted an abundance of special gifts and powers.

Both before and after all this, Jesus had given His disciples training in prayer. In His "Sermon on the Mount" at the beginning of His ministry, He said, "Pray then like this, 'Our Father which is in Heaven, *hallowed be Thy name*, *Thy* kingdom come, *Thy* will be done...'" (Mt. 6:9-10).

It is very significant then to look again at the conclusion to Mark's account of their failure. "He said to them, 'This kind cannot be driven out by anything but *prayer*" (Mk. 9:29). And what He is surely pointing to here is not just an amount of prayer, but a kind of prayer. He is hoping for that kind of prayer which longs for *the Father's* name to become hallowed (exalted and extolled) by those who now are living in darkness and know nothing about Him, the kind of prayer which cries out for *His* kingdom to come, with all its beauty and glory in those areas still being ruled now by the Evil One. When a mustard seed prays in this fashion, it possesses great faith, for this type of prayer God is quite prepared to answer. (Of course it will still be in His time and in His way).

These days there is a great deal of energy given to promote church planting. This is fine and good, and I am sure the Lord Jesus is much pleased with such efforts. And yet, I wonder if sometimes there is not a certain missing element, which could be rather painful to Him. The great emphasis seems often to be on the quantitative aspect—the number of churches each group can plant by the year 2000. Little is heard of the qualitative prayer, "Father, Your name be hallowed [in every part of it], and Your kingdom [the rulership of Your king] come [among all these hidden peoples]." I realize that these elements are "understood" to be the basic purpose of it all. But that which is stressed by the literature does pose the question, "To what degree is it understood?"

There are of course many factors involved in successful church planting. But my observation is that those operations which have as their clear and primary motivation the establishing of His kingdom (rulership, glory) are the ones most enjoying His blessing. In introducing the Holy Spirit, the Lord Jesus said, "He will glorify Me." Therefore, that missionary endeavor which, in setting goals, upholds as number one the qualitative aspiration that *He* might "be exalted among the heathen" will surely experience the Holy Spirit's help. Subconscious competition appeared to be one of the underlying causes of that pitiful downfall of His disciples, and it is all recorded (three times) for our learning. To what extent is our praying an effort to call forth His blessing on *our work* and our statistics, and to what extent is it a genuine desire for His name to be extolled and His King to be recognized and accepted as king?

We close with these words from the Psalms: "I will lift up my eyes to the mountains [unmovable as they may be]; where does my help [my resources] come from? My help comes from the Lord who made [not only the mountains, but all of] heaven and earth" (Ps. 121:1,2).

13

OUR POWER

"You will receive power when the Holy Spirit comes on you; and you will be My witnesses in Jerusalem, and in all Judea and Samaria, and to the ends of the earth" (Acts 1:8).

These were the last words of the Lord Jesus before He left this earth. They not only constitute one more final reminder of His commission, but they also contain a reminder of His promise for ample means to carry it out. Since these last few decades have seen a new revival of missionary zeal, there has also come a new emphasis on this matter of power. We now often read articles and books on "power evangelism," "power encounter," "signs and wonders," etc. All of these help to keep a power mentality before us, and that is good up to a point. But let us be careful not to fall into an unbalanced emphasis on one particular aspect of this topic. In previous chapters we have in some measure dealt with our need for power, but now we would like to examine more comprehensively some of what God's Word has to say on this subject.

Paul introduces his great warfare passage in Ephesians with the admonition, "Be *empowered* in the Lord, and in the *might* of His *strength*" (Eph. 6:10). He here puts together three different Greek words of real dynamic potency, which are meant to thoroughly encourage and equip us for all our advances into enemy territory. The first of these, the predominant Greek term for power in Scripture, is "dunamis," from which we derive our English words "dynamic," "dynamo," and "dynamite." In the New Testament it is used about one hundred times as the nouns "power," "strength" or "mighty work," and another two hundred times in such verb forms as "can," "be able," "be possible." So we can see that it is intended to portray no small degree of enablement.

In the Old Testament we have the story of Jacob spending

the night wrestling with God for special deliverance and blessing on his life. In the morning his name was changed to "Israel," which means "power with God and man." From then on God called His chosen people the "Children of Israel." Much of the time they were not people of power, but a thousand years later, when the Lord Jesus met Nathaniel, who had been spending time under his fig tree, the Lord declared, "Here is a *true Israelite*" (a man of power).

Before we proceed further, let us draw attention to the fact that there is in God's Word a clear distinction between the concepts of power, authority, gifts and ministry. We mention this in order to avoid confusion later on. We all need spiritual *power* in every phase of our service, and there will likely be times when every Christian will be called upon to exercise *authority* over some aspect of Satan's work. But our *gifts* and *ministries* are all different. So there is room for caution that we do not obscure or oversimplify this matter of spiritual power.

Primary Condition of Power

"You will receive power *when* the Holy Spirit comes on you." It is not our purpose here to discuss the issue of the external evidence for a Pentecostal experience. Rather we desire to probe much deeper and deal with the more vital matter of maintaining the right kind of *spirit* in all we say and do. This is what the Lord and the Holy Spirit are most concerned about. And this is the basic *condition* of being granted spiritual power. It is very dangerous to allot power into the hands of a missionary with the wrong spirit. This was a great problem with the disciples before the Holy Spirit came. One particular example was the occasion of their being boycotted by the Samaritans. James and John asked, "Lord, do you want us to call fire down from heaven to destroy them?" But Jesus rebuked them! Power in the wrong hands, or more pointedly, with the wrong spirit, can do a mighty lot of damage.

We all need the Holy Spirit to create and maintain a holy spirit in us. He desires to continually carry on a cleansing work, daily "taking out the garbage." It is so common for even missionaries to be contaminated with all kinds of *wrong spirits*. (We are not speaking of demons here.) We can find ourselves polluted with a critical spirit, impure thoughts, a spirit of unforgiveness, pride, backbiting, moodiness, etc. And these are monstrous hindrances to power.

The third Person of the Trinity is called the *Holy Spirit*. Let us now give some consideration to why He is called by such a name. We have already touched upon the significance of His holiness. But let us proceed further and give a bit more thought to the actual meaning of His first name "Holy." It designates that which has been "set apart" as belonging to God and His kingdom. It implies something very special, not ordinary, pertaining to the kingdom of heaven as opposed to the "kingdom of this world" (which is Satan's kingdom). So the *Holy* Spirit is nothing short of God's own Spirit.

Now let us examine the second part of His name, the *Spirit*. His primary area of operation is with man's spirit. A good example of His work is to look at the Lord's disciples before and after the Spirit came. They had received three years of the finest seminary training possible. The Lord Jesus Himself was their full-time professor, giving them a full course of both lecture and demonstration. But none of it went any further than their ears, eyes and superficial intellect. They were dull, blind, without faith, proud, unkind. Even at the end they were engulfed with fear, unbelief and hardness of heart. (Mk. 16:14) But when the Holy *Spirit* came, He took the instruction in "grace and truth" which they had received from their Master and moved it from their minds down into their spirits. So we can begin to comprehend why, at the end of His three years with them, our Lord made that phenomenal statement, "It is for your good that I am going away. Unless I go away, the "Helper" [Holy Spirit] will not come to you; but if I go I will send Him to you." And then later on, "You will receive *power* when the *Holy Spirit* comes on you." In like manner, you and I also very much need this Holy Spirit to continually restore and renew a holy spirit within us, in order that we might receive power for our ministries.

After David had fallen so badly in his involvement with Bathsheba, he not only confessed his sin with much agony of soul and pled for forgiveness, but he then cried out, "Create in me a *clean heart*, O God, and renew an *upright spirit* within me. ...Do not take Your *Holy Spirit* from me. ...Then I will teach transgressors Your ways, and sinners will be converted to You" (Ps. 51:10-13). He knew that spiritual power in his life depended on a right spirit within his heart.

Just as I have been putting together the material for this chapter, our village outreach has been passing through another dry spell with a seeming absence of power. This has of course concerned us all a great deal, so we together and individually have been looking to the Lord to show us what might be wrong. It wasn't long before He pointed out some wrong attitudes which had been smoldering inside some of us. Once these were cleared up, a new sense of His power returned.

The fullness of the Spirit and power are not only related, but they are both relative. That is to say, power and the fullness of the Spirit are not elements which are guaranteed us for the rest of our lives just because we may have had a certain experience of the Spirit coming upon us at one point in time. Not at all! Sometimes we are filled to a greater degree with the Spirit, and thus possess a greater measure of power. At other times we may run on low voltage, as it were, because of some spiritual impediment. We will deal with this a bit more in a later section of this chapter, but we need to remind ourselves here that power can fade, and fade badly.

The Purpose of Power

"You will receive power when the Holy Spirit comes on you, and you will *be My witnesses*." There are several things to be observed about the grammatical construction of this statement in its original Greek wording. First, we should note that this promise was given to the disciples in the future tense. "You *will receive* power when the Holy Spirit comes on you." In other words, there was a kind of power in store for them which was to be something other than that which they already possessed. They had already been granted authority to cast out demons and power to heal the sick (Mt. 10:1; Lk. 9:1), so now the Lord is referring to a more essential power which they would need. "You will be My witnesses." This part of His statement is also future, which suggests that they hadn't been very good witnesses so far, even with all their special ability to do signs and wonders. And they surely hadn't done a very scintillating job of exemplifying His kingdom.

The next thing we need to point out is the presence of the verb "to be." "You will *be* My witnesses." He did not say "You will witness for Me," though that action is certainly included. Greek grammar often leaves out the verb "to be" when it is not particularly needed. But when it is included, it draws attention to itself. So when the Lord Jesus told His disciples that the presence of the Spirit would enable them to *be* His witnesses, it would seem that He was pointing especially toward a *quality of life* which the Holy Spirit would enable them to live as His witnesses. We can probably say it this way: the Holy Spirit has come primarily to empower us to live out the "fruits of the Spirit" (Gal. 5:22,23).

Now coming back for a moment to the matter of bearing witness for Him by our message. We recognize that preaching is an integral part of His commission (Mk. 16:15; Lk. 24:47). But even here, we discover that there are two kinds of "power" which can be employed to preach the gospel. There is the energy of our flesh, and there is the moving power of the Spirit's fruit: love, joy, peace, patience, etc.

When God's people, whether they be missionaries, students, businessmen, or housewives, begin to grasp the significance of the Lord's statement in John 16:7, it should produce tremendous changes in their lives and ministry. He said, "I tell you the truth: it is for your *good* that I am going away. Unless I go away, the Helper will not come to you; but if I go, I will send Him to you." The word "good" here (in the Greek) means "benefit," "profit," "advantage." Second Peter 1:3 puts it: "His divine power has given us everything we need for life and godliness."

To be His witnesses, or to proclaim His gospel, we need not become pushy, nervous, mechanical or stilted, but trust the manifold enablements of the Holy Spirit. His work is to empower us. He even desires to help us with clearing out all the obstructions.

"If you *by the Spirit* put to death the deeds of the body, you will *live* [an abundant, fruitful life]" (Rom. 8:13). And the Lord's promise in John 16:7, which we quoted in the preceding paragraph, is followed by His added declaration that the Holy Spirit will also prepare the hearts of the people with whom we share our message. "He will convict the world of guilt, in regard to sin and righteousness and judgment." He will open their eyes to see their *need* of our loving Savior. All of these helps from the Helper constitute the purpose of His empowering.

Visible and Invisible Power

We are often encouraged these days to expect visible demonstrations of power to regularly accompany our evangelism. Miraculous healings and deliverance from demons are the two manifestations most commonly suggested. These can be beautiful exhibitions of the Lord's might and authority, but such ministries have not been bestowed upon all of us.

Let us come back again to the Lord's promise, "You shall receive power when the Holy Spirit has come upon you." The first great evidence of the Spirit's power was when the weak, discouraged, hiding Peter stood up to *preach* on the day of Pentecost, and three thousand scoffers were "cut to the heart," repented and were baptized. He performed no visible miracles for them to see but was mightily anointed with the invisible power of *proclamation*. It is true that his sermon was preceded by the special manifestation of his fellow disciples speaking forth the wonders of God in the many different languages of the crowd. These observing Jews had gathered in Jerusalem "from every nation under heaven" to attend both the Passover and the feast of Pentecost. They were now soon to return to all their many regions to tell what they had seen and heard during their days in Jerusalem. But an amazing part of the whole picture is that the *visible* part of the happenings of that day, namely the concurrent speaking in so many different languages, seemed to actually have quite an adverse effect, for when Peter stood up, his first words were, "Fellow Jews...these men are not drunk as you suppose." So it was not the visible, but the invisible anointing power for proclama-

tion, plus the convicting work of the Holy Spirit, which overcame all the barriers and brought about the great harvest. It is the
anointed message, the gospel of Christ, which is "the power of
God unto salvation" (Rom. 1:16).

The gift of evangelism is the primary gift which the Holy
Spirit uses to plant churches. Therefore every church planting
team certainly needs to have one or more evangelists. And these
evangelists must have the power of the Holy Spirit resting on
them. Such invisible provision of power is our primary need on
the mission field. And this hidden power is generated in our hidden chamber where we are alone with God.

An additional supply of invisible power can come from invisible dynamos hid away behind closed doors, perhaps miles
away, calling upon the Lord on our behalf. We all have electrical
outlets in our homes which supply power to the appliances we
plug into them. But sometimes we forget that it is only because
of the generating plants, which cannot be seen, out in some secluded valley, operating day and night, that we are able to enjoy
this wonderful "unlimited" supply of energy. We have already referred to Finney's Nash and Clary who were the dynamos sup-
plying the power for his evangelistic campaigns. And most of
God's great evangelists have been granted such invisible sources
of power.

Power Paradoxes

In one sense, it is good to think through this whole concept
of power at a time when we seem to be rather low on power. For
then we are driven to consider all the various factors involved.
One of these factors is what we might call a power paradox. That
is, there are times when we may feel weak but are not necessarily
weak. If we have searched our heart and find nothing to condemn
us, it may be that the Lord is allowing us a seeming lean period
to help us develop new strengths.

Paul had the experience when the Lord permitted him to undergo the "thorn in the flesh." The Lord encouraged him by stating one of His amazing paradoxes. He said, "My grace is sufficient for you, for My *power* is made perfect in *weakness*."

Paul's reaction was, "Therefore I will boast all the more gladly about my *weaknesses,* so that Christ's *power* may rest on me. That is why, for Christ's sake, I delight in *weakness,* in insults, in hardships, in persecutions, in difficulties. For when I am *weak,* then I am *strong*" (2 Cor. 12:9,10).

Another time Paul cried out, "I want to know Christ and the *power of His resurrection,* and the fellowship of sharing in His sufferings, becoming like Him in His *death,* and so, somehow, to attain to the resurrection *from the dead*" (Phil. 3:10,11). Paul here is not concerned about his future resurrection. That was already settled, but he longed for more resurrection power in his life and ministry. Resurrection power is that which overcomes all forms of deadness (which is weakness). Though Paul was one who regularly experienced a magnificent moving of the Spirit's power in his ministry, he also had his times of weakness in prison, and most of his churches had their periods of drought.

As I am writing this chapter, I am also working my way through a most interesting book entitled *Liberating Ministry from the Success Syndrome,* by Kent and Barbara Hughes. This book is a powerful example of *strength* existing in the midst of a ministry fraught with "weakness." It reminds one of Noah who preached for one hundred twenty years without a single convert. It deals with the common but erroneous concept that success is to be measured by numbers. Statistics seem to rule our minds these days. We often tend to evaluate our work, and that of our colleagues, from the viewpoint of numbers. But this book does a masterful job of liberating God's people from the tyranny of tallies and figures.

The Lord Jesus is the greatest example of the paradox of power. During the first two years of His ministry, the crowds increased to enormous proportions because of His merciful and beneficent miracles. But as He spoke to the people more and more about truth and righteousness, the throngs fell away until one day He even had to ask His twelve disciples if they too were going to leave Him. The night before He went to the cross, they finally did all flee and left Him alone. Yet later on that same night, as He gave Himself to prayer, He said, "Father...I have brought You glory on earth by completing the work You gave Me to do" (Jn.

17:4). He was not ruled by the success syndrome.

Once we are delivered from the despotism of numbers, we can view this element of power from a much more realistic stance. Power is a wonderful and necessary component in all God's work. The Holy Spirit came to provide us with power. And God intends that we possess it in great measure. But He never intended that a wrong concept of power lead us into bondage.

Potential Power

When I studied physics in college, we had a section on "Potential Energy." Potential energy is a form of *stored up power* which can be utilized either gradually or instantaneously. While this potent force is being accumulated, it may not give much evidence of being a type of power. But when it is released or discharged rather suddenly, a deluge or explosion can occur. Examples of potential energy would be the water in a reservoir behind a dam, a battery which has been well-charged, a flash gun which is ready to fire, or an atomic bomb which is being stored in its bunker.

We also have a number of illustrations of potential power of a spiritual nature in Scripture. John the Baptist spent a good bit of the first thirty years of his life in fellowship with God, hid away in the wilderness. But when he suddenly appeared on the scene, even though his ministry lasted a mere six months, his message was so powerful that people went out to hear him "from Jerusalem and all Judea and the whole region of the Jordan" (Mt. 3:5). And the Lord Jesus declared, "Among those born of women there has not risen anyone greater than John the Baptist" (Mt. 11:11).

Another example is the mighty ingathering which took place on Pentecost. The Lord Jesus had spoken much about the coming of the Spirit, and one hundred twenty of His disciples had spent ten days in prayer preparing themselves for that day. We could also refer to Paul's three years in Arabia before he began his mighty, empowered service.

In missionary history there are hundreds of cases of storing up potential power. We have previously referred to Frazer's nine years of calling on the Lord before the break came among the Lisu. There was Malla Moe's grand harvest after years of prayer and fasting in Africa. The recent breakthroughs in Argentina have come after an accumulation of concerted prayer vigils, etc.

Actually, our God operates most of the time on the principle of "potential energy." He waits until we have done an amount of spiritual preparation before He pours out His power. Most of the great times of revival have come as a result of His people making up their mind to give themselves to intercession *until* the reservoir is full and the dam breaks. And He has *encouraged* us to labor with just such patience and hope. "If My people, who are called by My name, will humble themselves and pray and seek My face and turn from their wicked ways, *then* will I hear from heaven and will forgive their sin, and will heal their land (2 Chron. 7:14).

Paul desires to strengthen us with these words, "Let us not become weary in doing good, for *at the proper time* we will reap a harvest if we do not give up" (Gal. 6:9). There are several references in God's Word which hold before us the parable of a farmer who plants his seed, waters and cultivates his field, and then finally enjoys the season of reaping.

But the most applicable examples to keep in mind here are those which have to do with war, battle, and tearing down strongholds. Our enemy has stored up a lot of munitions in his citadels, and we have to accumulate a mass of firepower to confront these fortresses. As we have heard many times, "Wars are not won in a day." In fact there is one conflict in European history known as the "Hundred Years War." So let us never "grow weary and lose heart," but rather endure all the rigors of battle until some of those enemy strongholds are toppled. "Do not cast away your confidence; it will be richly rewarded" (Heb. 10:35).

Before closing this section, we should refer to a situation which happened to the Israelites during their wilderness journey to the promised land. They came to a place called Raphidim and set up camp there but could find no water to drink. Instead of clinging firmly to their faith in the Lord, however, and trusting all the backlog of His previous faithful provision, they began to murmur and complain and cry out, "Is the Lord among us or not?" The Lord did give them water to drink, of course, but their attitude was very displeasing to Him. Sometimes in the thick of the battle, when our prayer vigils seem to have little effect, we may be tempted to ask, "Is the Lord among us or not?" But rather we should train ourselves to declare with all our might, "Even though it may not appear so, my God is here with me in power, and I know that in His time, He will bring a marvelous victory!"

Relative Power

The Lord Jesus does not always view power the way we do, nor does He view weakness as we might see it. We can gather some illuminating insights from His messages to the seven churches of Asia when He spoke through His servant John in the Book of Revelation some sixty years after He had returned to heaven. Two of the little, struggling churches which others probably would have labeled "weak" received heartening reassurance, whereas that congregation which considered themselves to be "rich and not in need of a thing" He declared to be "wretched, pitiful, poor, blind and naked."

Let us look for a moment at the comforting words which He spoke to the two "weak" churches. To the assembly in Smyrna He said, "I know your afflictions and your poverty—yet you are rich!...Do not be afraid of what you are about to suffer. I tell you the Devil will put some of you in prison to test you, and you will suffer persecution...Be faithful *even to the point of death*, and I will give you the crown of life" (Rev. 2:9,10).

And to the church of Philadelphia He said, "I have placed before you an open door that no one can shut. *I know you have little strength*, yet you have kept my Word and have not denied My name...*I have loved you*. Since you have kept My command to endure patiently, I will also keep you...Hold onto what you have, so that no one will take your crown. Him who overcomes I will make a pillar in the temple of My God" (Rev. 3:8-11).

Just as a person's giving of monetary gifts to the Lord is a relative thing and cannot be judged by the visible amount, so is the measure of a person's spiritual power. The widow who dropped two pennies into the offering box received high acclamation from the Lord because that was all she had. In like manner, it is easy for us to confuse spiritual gifts with spiritual power. Some possess very visible gifts and may thus exhibit what men would call power, while others who are not so gifted are concluded to be weak. But the Lord does not always look at things that way. He defined His criterion of evaluation when He said, "You will know them by their *fruits*" (Mt. 7:20). And when He designated "fruits," He certainly was not pointing to statistics. I have pretty well come to the conclusion that our Lord is much less quantitatively oriented than we often tend to be.

My thoughts sometimes turn to a little, unknown, retired schoolteacher in a small town in southern California who taught a small Sunday School class in a very ordinary community church. I got to know her quite well, for she mailed out our prayer letters for several years. She was an unassuming servant of the Lord, but was one of those hidden spiritual dynamos who possessed a good measure of invisible power. Though she held little claim to greatness, the Lord rewarded her in His own ways. One of the naughty little boys who attended her Sunday School class was Dawson Trotman, who later founded the worldwide "Navigators" organization. This mighty army of God's soldiers has reached thousands upon thousands of servicemen, students, and in more recent years, people in other realms of society.

In one of his references to the Lord Jesus, Paul says, "He was crucified in weakness." Yet those hours of weakness have brought about the greatest accomplishment of all history. So weakness and power are relative terms. The Book of Hebrews, when presenting its list of the heroes of faith, mentions those who "out of weakness were made strong." From a position of weakness, strength came.

When all is moving ahead well in our missionary work, there is the tendency to become "drunk with power," and we can find ourselves riding rather roughshod over others who may be passing through a period of weakness. But it is at just such times that we must be careful lest we fall flat on our face, while they "out of weakness are made strong." "God opposes the proud, but gives grace to the humble" (1 Pet. 5:5). We don't get far when God Himself begins to oppose us!

Maintaining Power

There are any number of factors which can cause an automobile to lose its power. Even a tiny bit of dirt in the carburetor can strangle its efficiency. So it is in our lives and ministry. There are several long lists in God's Word, reminding us of the various kinds of "dirt" which can hinder the flow of His power through us.

On the Lord's last night with His disciples, He gave them many hours of both instruction and warning in order that they might "bear much fruit." He spoke of how essential it would be to abide in Him, of asking in His name for what we need, of washing one another's feet, of preparing for persecution, of expecting help from the Holy Spirit, and of His plan to prepare a wonderful place for us. Finally, He urged them to "keep watching and praying that you may not enter into temptation." The Evil One is a wicked tempter. He knows that whenever he can draw us into some wrong thought, word or deed, there can come a substantial loss of power. And if he can keep us off the track, we become as powerless as a derailed locomotive. "The prayer of a *righteous* man is powerful and effective" (Jas. 5:16).

However, we don't want to dwell on the negative aspect of power loss. What a tremendous contrast is the spectacle of a properly functioning locomotive! Now let us come back to our original text. "You shall receive power when the Holy Spirit comes on you." Just prior to His saying that, He bid them remain in Jerusalem until they were "clothed with power from above." This little one-word parable of being "clothed" should lead us to picture what is involved in maintaining our spiritual power. Clothing is something we put on afresh every day, and likewise a fresh anointing of power is something we do well to obtain from the Lord each day.

We have mentioned in one of the sections above that it is very easy for power to fade or to be drained out of us. Even the strength of an ox or a lion can wane after a period of exertion. Isaiah reminds us that "Even the youths grow tired and weary, and young men stumble and fall; but those who wait on the Lord will *renew* their strength. They will mount up on wings like eagles; they will run and not grow weary; they will walk and not faint" (Is. 40:30,31).

Sometimes the Lord has to thin the ranks of His army as He did for Gideon. Those who give insufficient attention to spiritual power and as a result *persist* in their weakness, He may weed out of His attack squadrons. Especially when He is looking for men whom He can send forth on special "guerilla" missions as His "Green Berets." Such heavy assignments are not for the casual Christian. They are for those who keep themselves spiritually fit, who keep their knapsacks filled with rations and their belts filled with ammunition, who keep themselves clothed with power! A soldier without sufficient water in his canteen, provisions in his pack and charges for his weapons doesn't last long in the battle.

When two great kings are at war, namely the "king of this world" and the King of the Universe, it is not child's play. Things are going to happen! And we need masses of power. At the same time we must keep in mind that in this age we will by no means be able to demolish all of our enemy's fortresses or forces. In fact most of those will still be standing even at the end of the seven years of tribulation and God's wrath when we arrive at the grand finale of this era. That does not mean, however, that our warfare prayers and our penetration now into enemy territory are wasted or hopeless. Not at all! We have been sent on these missions by our King. They are part of His present strategy, and they do demonstrate His power and victory by piercing the enemy's bastions here and there. Our King will abolish every vestige of Satan's activity when He sets up His rule here on earth. But He desires us to be making some inroads now and setting up pockets of His kingdom.

I feel that in Taiwan we are on the threshold of the heaviest fighting and yet the greatest advance so far into the enemy's territory. The churches and the para-church organizations are gearing up for many strategic moves forward during the next ten years, as we approach 2000 A.D. The enemy knows this, you can be sure, so he is readying his forces and strategies as well. Just these last few days I have received several phone calls from various ones out on the front lines, reporting unusual counterattacks and asking for special prayer.

If we maintain all our various forms of power—our supply of hidden power, our accumulation of potential power, the anointing of invisible power on our message, love power, and the convicting power of the Holy Spirit, and if we keep ourselves free from all that would bring about power loss, we are going to see some strongholds torn down.

I would like to close this chapter by going back again to the Lord's introductory words in His commission to Joshua: "Now then, you and all these people get ready to cross the Jordan River, into the land I am about to give them. I will give you every place where you set your foot" (Josh. 1:3). There are two ways for a soldier to set his foot. He can walk about the field leisurely, suggesting a few "good ideas," or he can "wait in the city until he is clothed with power," and then firmly set his foot on the spot where the Lord sends him, and "having done all to *stand*."

"You shall receive *power* when the Holy Spirit comes on you, and you will be My witnesses...to the ends of the earth." If we become people who live by this power, *the day will indeed come* when we in our various fields of labor will exclaim, "The people living in darkness have seen a great light; on those living in the land of the shadow of death a light has dawned." And some of *them* will rejoice and exclaim, "He has rescued us from the dominion of darkness and brought us into the kingdom of His beloved Son."

14

OUR CONCERN

Offhand, the word "concern" may not sound like a military term, but it should be the heart attitude and the motivation undergirding every military operation. The right kind of concern is the element which makes all the difference between a merciful campaign of deliverance or a miserable war of aggression.

In spiritual warfare, loving concern should be the driving force which sends a man into battle, which keeps him there, and puts iron in his blood and tenderness in his heart. It should be the strength of his prayer life and the beauty of his message. Without compassionate concern, all our weapons, authority, power, faith, etc. become but a "noisy gong" or a "clanging symbol." (I Cor. 13:1-3) Coming back to military terminology, without the right kind of concern he may find himself shooting the wrong "enemy" and stabbing his fellow soldiers.

The primary content of our praying should be, "Thy kingdom come," and the primary quality should be Holy Spirit-generated concern. We have already discussed the content of our intercessions in the chapter on "Thy Kingdom Come." Now it is time to consider the element of proper heart attitude.

Not only should our prayer life be developing quantitatively from year to year, but there should also be qualitative growth. We should be aware of a continuous deepening of this element of concern in our supplications. Recently a verse has been much in my thoughts. It is the Lord's word to His people through Jeremiah. "You will seek Me and find Me when you seek Me with all your heart." (Jer. 29:13) God's message here seems to point to this vital ingredient of concern in several ways. The repeated use of the word "seek" would imply a decided measure of longing, and the key phrase "with all your heart" is speaking of the very

198

highest kind of yearning. The main point of the declaration is that it is *"when"* we reach a real level of concern that the Lord is prepared to give His special attention to our asking.

What does it basically mean to seek the Lord? Our main interest is usually to seek His blessing upon our home, our work, and our lives. And He is happy to give this. But the Scriptures seem to indicate that the Lord Jesus holds a much higher desire for His disciples. He longs for us to mature to the point where "with all our heart" we seek the welfare of others and the establishing of His kingdom.

The Scriptures list quite a number of conditions to answered prayer. Several of the main factors are given in the "Worship and Warfare" prayer companion. It is significant that several of these revolve around the matter of concern. One condition which often tends to hold us back in our praying is that perennial problem, "Is it His will?" But I have come to the conclusion that there are many things that are His will which He is *longing* to do and for which He is only waiting until a sufficient longing develops in my heart. I imagine that He must at times become weary of my passive, casual attitude in prayer.

Jesus' Demonstration of Concern

One day the Lord led His disciples up into the region of Tyre and Sidon to get away from the persistent crowds for a much needed rest. Just as they got settled down, a Canaanite woman from that vicinity came to Him, crying out "Lord, Son of David, have mercy on me! My daughter is suffering terribly from demon possession." (Mt. 15:21) Then came a series of eight "high hurdles" which she had to cross over before her request was granted.

In the first place, the Lord and His disciples were exhausted and did not want to be bothered. In the second place, she was a total stranger. She had no point of entrée. In the third place, she was a Gentile, which made her detestable to any Jew. Fourth, she was a woman approaching a group of thirteen men, which meant many strikes against her. Fifth, they gave her no reception. "The Lord did not answer her a word." The sixth hurdle was a high one. The disciples, ignoring her, urged the Lord to "send her away." Hurdle number seven was higher still, for when the Lord did answer, His reply was, "I was sent only to the lost sheep of the house of Israel." But this woman still would not leave. She came and knelt before Him, crying, "Lord, help me." Then, finally, the last hurdle was the highest of all. The Lord replied, "It is not right to take the children's bread and give it to the dogs."

Dogs in those days were about the most despised creatures in the community, probably even lower than swine, for they were the scavengers who cleaned up all kinds of refuse. The Lord Jesus did not actually call this woman a dog, but His words could easily be taken that way. She was a phenomenal person, however, for her reply was a phenomenal reply. She answered, "Yes, Lord, but even the dogs eat the crumbs that fall from their master's table." Her meaning was, "Yes, even the lowdown curs are allowed crumbs from their masters, but *You* are *my* Master (she had just called Him Lord), and I am certainly not a dog! I am someone You love very much." She completely ignored the questionable treatment which she had received and persisted in pleading her case on the basis of *whom* she knew Him to be...the loving "Son of David," the Shepherd King (for this is how she had addressed Him).

The Lord Jesus (after she had soared over the eighth hurdle) then praised her very highly by saying, "Woman, great is your faith! Your request is granted." And her daughter was healed at once. Only one other time did the Lord acclaim a person for his faith. That was the Roman Captain, and he also was a Gentile, an outsider to the Jews. The Lord never once complimented His disciples for their faith. It was usually, "O you of little faith," or "Where is your faith; why did you doubt?"

Faith and concern really go hand in hand. We commonly think of faith as confidence in His ability or His wisdom. And this is surely part of it. But probably the greatest element of faith is trust in His unfailing and ever-present *mercy*. Mercy is another word for concern. Twenty-six times (at the close of every verse) in Psalm 136, this phrase is recorded: "His mercy endures forever." "God is love," and His "agape" love is not merely a passive attitude, but an active concern. Therefore He greatly honors an active concern when He detects it within us. And this should strengthen our faith.

The woman we have been speaking of was a mother. A mother's concern for her child is the highest form of love to be found in nature. She couldn't bear the thought of her daughter remaining in the clutches of the Evil One. And this is exactly the kind of concern the Lord looks for in our hearts when we come to Him in prayer for the lost. When we get to the place where we can intercede for our fellow students, our neighbors, or those in the unreached areas of Taiwan, with the kind of concern that this Canaanite woman had for her daughter, and the kind of concern she knew was filling the heart of the Lord Jesus, we will begin to hear His words spoken to us, "Great is your faith! Your request is granted."

Why Concern is Essential

Concern is the most fundamental form of love. It moves us to action. It prods us to pray. And it will keep us moving and praying and battling the enemy until victory is secured. The theme of God's Word is loving concern. So, as our Heavenly Father sees things, this sympathetic caring is the bedrock on which His kingdom is built.

Therefore, concern in prayer is by no means just an effort on our part to try to persuade Him to show consideration toward a given need. He is already well aware of the need and is already far more concerned about it than we are. But He longs for our love to mature and flourish to the point where we begin to share something of *His* concern. He is desperately concerned for the people on planet earth. "God so loved the world that He gave His only begotten Son, that *whosoever* believes in Him should not perish, but have everlasting life." (Jn. 3:16) Two things hold Him back from reaching out and pulling everyone into His kingdom. First, He respects every individual's free will, and second, He has determined that His kingdom shall be established *through* the loving concern of His church. So we can begin to see why He is so eager for a measure of longing and yearning in your heart and mine.

In Isaiah's day He bared His heart of concern to His people. "On your walls, O Jerusalem, I have appointed watchmen. All day and all night they will never keep silent. You who remind the Lord, take no rest for yourselves; and give Him no rest until He establishes and makes Jerusalem a praise in the earth." (Is. 62:6,7) He is very sad when such intercession is not taking place. "He saw that there was no man, and was astonished that there was no one to intercede." (Is. 59:16) And again, "I looked, but there was no one to help, and I was appalled that there was no one to uphold." (Is. 63:5) The kind of people He was looking for were rare indeed. "I searched for a man among them who should build up the wall and stand in the gap before Me for the land, that I should not destroy it; but I found no one." (Ezek. 22:30) So at times, it becomes evident that among God's people there is a distressing lack of concern.

But we can thank the Lord that some of His people, as a result of these revelations of His deep longings, are responding, and are entering into earnest intercession. As a result we are seeing Him do some marvelous things.

When Hudson Taylor, the founder of the China Inland Mission, was a young man, he had drifted away from the Lord and was caught up in the things of the world. His mother was a very godly woman, so this departure grieved her beyond measure. Once when she had to leave home for a few days to be with a relative for the birth of a child, her heart became so concerned for her son that she could bear it no longer. When the time came for her to return, she remained on for a time, locking herself in her room and telling the Lord that she would not leave until she had the assurance that her son was restored. Toward evening the release came, and she knew that the transaction had taken place in her son's life.

With a free and happy spirit she returned home. At the front door, Hudson greeted her with a big smile, saying he had good news for her. Yes, she replied, she already knew. Surprised, he asked if his sister had revealed his secret. "No," said his mother, "God told me!" Together, then, they rejoiced in the marvelous thing God had done.

The answer for us may not come that readily, for sometimes

the Lord desires to test our faith and teach us other lessons as He did for Abraham, Job, David and others. But He will always honor deep, loving concern in any heart. Sometimes before He actually solves the problem, He will grant us the assurance and the release in our spirits in order that we might move on to other needs.

The Kind of Concern He Desires

We should point out here that there is a distinct difference between anxiety and the type of concern which our Father is looking for. Anxiety is a form of fear and comes from the enemy's kingdom. The Evil One would try to bring us into panic and into all sorts of negative unrest. But God's Word repeatedly encourages us to "be anxious for nothing." Our Father loves us and has only good things for us, and He is delighted when we strongly desire others to be able to share all these good things too.

So the kind of concern which He longs for is that fatherly compassion which He has for His own children and also that yearning which He has for those who are not yet His own. "Behold what manner of love the Father has bestowed on us, that we should be called the children of God!" (I Jn. 3:1) And the more we "behold" that limitless love of His in His Word, the more it will capture our own spirits and create His heart of concern within us. This is what the Holy Spirit is seeking to do. This is to be the basis of spiritual warfare...to see other pitiful captives (blind and bound) delivered.

It was this kind of concern which caused the Lord Jesus to leave His glorious throne in God's majestic presence, amid the myriads of angels, and come to this sin-cursed earth to give His all for us helpless, hopeless prisoners of Satan's kingdom. The prophet Isaiah was allowed a vision of all this seven hundred years before it actually happened. "He poured out His life unto death, and was numbered with the transgressors. For He bore the sin of many, and made intercession for the transgressors." (Is. 53:12) Later, as the Lord Jesus drew near to the actual ordeal of the cross, it was that *concern* for us which carried Him through with it all. John heard Him pray, "Now my heart is troubled, and what shall I say? 'Father, save me from this hour'? No, it was for this very reason [to save the lost] I came to this hour" (Jn. 12:27). And Paul holds up before us the same picture. "God demonstrates His own love toward us, in that while we were yet sinners, Christ died for us" (Rom. 5:8).

It was also this nature of concern within the heart of Moses which brought deliverance more than once for Israel. In Psalm106:23, we have this very moving pronouncement: "He said He would destroy them, had not Moses, His chosen one, stood in the breach before Him to keep His wrath from destroying them." At first it might appear that Moses possessed more loving concern than God did. But this is never the case. We must not forget that the bottom line of all theology is that "*God is love.*" Therefore we approach every paradox in Scripture from the vantage point of the goodness of God. The purpose of the above reference is to point out how pleased God was with Moses. In fact, this very verse describes Moses as "His chosen one." And Moses more than any other Bible character is called "The servant of the Lord." Twenty-two times he is called by this title. In the New Testament, Paul and James are each once spoken of in this way.

These two titles, "His chosen one" and "The servant of the Lord," clearly indicate again the Lord's pleasure in finding one who is so like Himself. Moses' actual words of deep concern for Israel, when they had sinned so detestably by worshipping the golden calf, remind us of the heart of the Lord Jesus, who was willing to sacrifice Himself for sinners. Up on the mountain, Moses pled with God. "O Lord," he said, "Why should your anger burn against your people, whom You brought out of Egypt with great power and a mighty hand? Why should the Egyptians say it was with evil intent He brought them out, to kill them in the mountains and to wipe them off the face of the earth? Turn from Your fierce anger, relent and do not bring disaster on Your people." Later on Moses went back again and prayed, "Please forgive their sin...but if not, then blot me out of Your book" (Ex. 32:11-12,32).

God is love, but He is also just. The death of the Lord Jesus,

His beloved Son, satisfied both infinite love and complete justice. Moses' concern was so great that he too offered himself as a sacrifice for deliverance. This concern was so pleasing to God that "the Lord relented and did not bring on His people the disaster He had threatened" (Ex. 32:14). And when Moses came down from the mountain, the Lord had so crowned him with a radiant glory that all the Israelites, even Aaron, were afraid to come near him and had him wear a veil on his face. This marvelous, supernatural glory which the Lord bestowed on Moses at that time, was God's way of manifesting His great delight in the marvelous, supernatural *concern* which Moses had shown for those who had been led astray by the enemy.

Although God is just and holy and therefore must deal with sin, He is also infinitely merciful and yearns for the growth of merciful concern in us. He will take care of the final justice. Only He is wise enough for that. Our part is to manifest concern.

Another moving example of limitless concern is Paul's passion to see his fellow Israelites saved. Although he was sent to the Gentiles and gave all he possessed of strength and fervor to see the Gentiles come to the Lord, he also wrote, "I have great sorrow and unceasing anguish in my heart. For I could wish that I myself were cursed and cut off from Christ for the sake of my brothers, those of my own race, the people of Israel (Rom. 9:2-4).

And Paul's caring did not slacken after a group of people had turned to the Lord. In fact it increased. For now they were his own children in the faith. For instance, when the churches of Galatia got off the track, he writes to them, "My dear children, for whom I am again in the pains of travail until Christ is formed in you" (Gal. 4:19). In using the word "travail," he had chosen a very strong expression, for travail in those days was an agonizing experience. It was a tremendous price a mother had to pay to bring her baby into the world, another part of a mother's love.

I have recently been reading the biography of Malla Moe, one of the first missionaries sent out by Fredrick Fransen (the founder of the Scandinavian Alliance Mission which is now The Evangelical Alliance Mission). This little woman was absolutely driven by a concern for the lost. No one could keep up with her. But it was not just fervor. It was also love. In fact the "key" which the Lord seemed to place in her hand was the giving of thoughtful little gifts to people. She was truly led of the Holy Spirit in this, for time and again the very item she gave was that which unlocked a heart's door. People loved her wherever she went, and she led great numbers of people into the kingdom. Concern, of course, manifests itself not only in prayer, but also in service and plenty of just plain, hard work.

Necessity of the Holy Spirit's Help

"You shall receive power when the Holy Spirit has come upon you, and you shall be witnesses unto Me" (Acts 1:8). I realize that what we have plowed through so far in this chapter is enough to weigh us down beyond measure if we attempt to manage such concern with merely our own faculties. We just do not have what it takes to carry around such a load. We are simply not made out of that kind of stuff, that kind of concern. We have spoken a good bit about power in this book, and we are now dealing with still another realm in which we desperately need help.

Our Father and our Lord and Savior are both well aware of this, so they have sent a Paraclete, a Helper, to walk along beside us and assist us in these particular areas of our frailty. The Holy Spirit's number one fruit is love, and His number two fruit is joy. We greatly need both of these. When we have lost either one, we begin to sink.

Let us come back to the matter of prayer, for instance. This is where things begin. We have a wonderful promise of the Holy Spirit's help in prayer. "The Spirit helps us in our weakness, for we do not know how to pray as we should, but the Spirit Himself intercedes for us with groanings too deep for words" (Rom. 8:26).

When our prayer is assisted by the Holy Spirit, it will carry a beautiful quality of involvement. It will be invested with "groanings too deep for words." And the next verse brings even further encouragement, for it reads, "And He who searches our hearts knows the mind of the Spirit, because the Spirit intercedes for the saints in accordance with God's will."

"The Spirit intercedes." This expression is used in both

these verses. One of the great longings of the Holy Spirit is to be able to carry on His work of intercession through God's people. He earnestly desires to develop this ministry within the church. The Lord doesn't just urge us to do it, but He provides an ideal, qualified, supernatural Helper.

But there still is our part. Why does it here refer to God as "He who searches hearts"? It would seem that Paul is bringing us back to consider that basic qualification for receiving the Holy Spirit's help. God searches our hearts to see just how much concern of our own is there. (The word for "search" used here in the original Greek text implies an investigation.) The Holy Spirit never starts from zero. God doesn't work that way. "To him who has shall more be given." And God's Word repeatedly asks us to periodically examine our own hearts in regard to spiritual hunger and impetus.

Next, Paul reminds us that "God knows the mind of the Spirit." These words spell results and fruitful accomplishment. God is really tuned in to our praying when the Holy Spirit is in the lead. For the Holy Spirit will tune our pleadings to God's wavelength. That is exactly what Paul is saying in the next phrase. "Because the Spirit intercedes for the saints in accordance with the will of God."

We can and should make out our prayer list as best we can. But we still can't be too sure of exactly what is going on in the hearts of those we have decided to pray for. The Holy Spirit, however, is keenly aware of precisely the situation in each heart. He knows which individual is "ripe" and ready for harvest. He knows which brother is in despair and needs support. He knows which parts of the Lord's work are under attack and need forces sent in to drive back the enemy. He knows who needs a "key" to unlock an iron gate. He knows all the strategy. So it is a great economy of time and effort to be led of the Spirit in our intercessions.

Concern in prayer is a quality of our intercession which the Holy Spirit desires to develop and increase as we *draw near* to God's heart of concern. And this exercise of drawing near requires a measure of time. This is why we should seek to arrange unhurried periods, so that the Holy Spirit is free and unhindered in generating His concern within our hearts.

But the Holy Spirit not only desires to help us with our pleadings in prayer. His number one fruit is love, and concern is also a part of active, practical love. "His command is that you *walk* in love" (2 Jn. 6). Walking in love means taking every step throughout the day in love. It is relatively easy for us to drum up a good bit of concern for some project which we are promoting. But it is also easy, if we are not careful, for such concern to degenerate into self-centeredness or pride. Walking in love is the antidote to all this. But here again we must have the Spirit's help. This is where I so often find myself falling short. Sometimes at the end of the day I can look back and wish I had shown more loving concern for John's problem, for the barber's needs, for that downcast look in someone's eyes.

"That which is born of the flesh is flesh, and that which is born of the Spirit is spirit." There are two types of concern: that which is born of the flesh and that which is born of the Spirit. We can push along a project with a measure of fleshly concern, but after a time we will be sitting beside the road lamenting, "Why? Why no fruit?" But "You shall receive power when the Holy Spirit is come upon you." Whenever He is alongside, directing, reminding, and filling our hearts with loving concern, there will be advance, there will be lasting fruit.

I shall never forget an evening meeting when I had to speak to a certain youth group here in Taiwan. I had spoken to this group before but found them to be rather cold, distracted and unresponsive. It was the youth fellowship of a rather denominational church, and the pastor who led their meetings was quite ritualistic in his manner. I didn't really relish going to this meeting. It was just before their final exams, so I didn't expect many to be there either. Also, I had difficulty deciding on a suitable message.

Finally, I began to feel convicted of my negative attitude and asked the Lord to fill me with a Holy Spirit-generated concern for those young people and their pastor. The Lord is always happy to answer such a prayer, so I went to the place with a real measure of expectancy.

That night there were a good number of students who came. I had liberty, love and power in my speaking, and at the close several amazing things happened. The pastor did some things which I feel sure he had never done before. His techniques were rather awkward, but his heart was very earnest and sincere. First, he asked the students to all gather in a big circle around the outside of the seating area. Then they held hands, sang a worship chorus or two, he led in prayer, and then he asked them to divide into small groups, share their heart concerns, and have a time of prayer.

In the small group which I attended, one young man and a young lady, both seniors, spoke up immediately and announced that they soon were to graduate and yet were still not sure if they were truly Christians. It was a perfect invitation to pray with them the prayer of receiving the Lord. It was a tremendous evening.

Now let us come back for a moment to the picture of the Lord looking and longing for someone to "build up the wall and stand in the *gap*." It would seem that God is pointing to a missing link in the chain of concern between Himself and those He longs to reach. The Father's heart of love sent His only Son to be man's Savior. The Son gave His life at infinite cost on the cross. The Holy Spirit yearns to plead through someone for the lost. *But where is that someone?*

Charles Spurgeon put it this way: "There is no contradiction between God's promises and the delay in His answers, nor is it any mystery. When we remember how those men and women prayed who received overwhelming answers, we can see that the art of real praying and wrestling against the powers of darkness is largely a lost art. But thanks be to God, the door to this type of praying is wide open.—No, not *wide* open, because this 'way is narrow,' and sad to say, few there be that actually seek it." Somebody has to pay a price for revival. But the price is worth every penny. Or to be more precise—worth every minute of compassionate intercession.

We close this chapter with that beautiful last verse of Psalm 126. "He who goes out weeping, carrying his bag of seed, will return with songs of joy, bringing sheaves with him." The Christian life is by no means all weeping. In fact, actual tears may be rather rare for some of us. But there should be periods of deep Holy

Spirit-prompted concern. These are the drive of effective spiritual warfare. Such "groanings," however, should be interspersed with periods of Holy Spirit-energized praise and worship. These provide the exhilarating morale for spiritual warfare. Such a warrior will surely return from his battles "with songs of joy, bringing sheaves [freed captives] with him."

15

OUR TRAINING

The Lord Jesus gave us a number of military parables for our consideration. Most of these are short, terse, and presented in the form of a question. Let us begin this chapter with one of these challenges: "What king, going to contend with another king in war, will not sit down first and take counsel whether he is able with ten thousand troops to meet him who comes against him with twenty thousand?"

The chief matter for consideration here is, of course, the *quality of training* which the king's soldiers have received. As the Lord indicated, it is not just the number of recruits we have, but how well they are equipped and prepared. Victory often hinges on this point in the battlefields of the world and also in the spiritual realm. *All* Christians need to be taught the rudiments of offensive and defensive battle. This is the prominent message in all of these military parables.

So our primary question here is, how and where are the Lord's forces to get this training? Not every believer is privileged to attend a seminary. And it is actually questionable how many seminary students receive much training in spiritual warfare. No, the place for such training of God's army is in the church. In one sense, of course, the church is God's house. In another sense, however, it is to serve as a military academy, preparing and sending forth warriors of the cross. One of its theme songs should be "Onward, Christian Soldiers!"

The Church at Antioch

A perfect example of just such a body of believers was Paul's spiritual home, the church at Antioch. This group of disciples were an amazing lot, sending out such stalwarts as Paul,

211

Barnabas, Silas, and Mark. The Scriptures seem to set them forth as a shining model for the rest of us to aspire to. They were surely the leading congregation of their day. Therefore, let us take a close look at this church.

Acts 11 tells of the founding of their fellowship. It was formed as a result of persecution. When the attacks became so fierce against God's people in Jerusalem after the stoning of Stephen that the believers could no longer remain in that area, they fled in all directions. But not just to hide and save their lives. No, it was also to take the good news of the gospel to new, unreached places. One of these places was Antioch.

You can be sure that a church planted under conditions of heavy warfare would be a live, warm-blooded organism, alert and battle-ready. And it certainly was just that. They were a *training institute*; they were a *spiritual body*; and they were a *sending base*. Let us examine these aspects.

They Were a Training Institute

When the apostles who remained in Jerusalem heard of this group of believers, they sent Barnabas up to see what was going on. Barnabas was so delighted with what he found that he never returned to Jerusalem but went on to Tarsus to find his friend Paul and invite him to come help set up a training school for these zealous, new disciples. "And when he had found him, he brought him to Antioch. For a *whole year* they met with the church, and *taught* a *large company* of people" (Acts 11:25-26). The picture here is of something far more than merely the Sunday morning service and the Wednesday night prayer meeting.

When I first arrived in Taiwan nearly forty years ago, conditions were actually quite similar to those in Antioch. A million refugees had just arrived from the mainland. They were unsettled, discouraged, and very hungry for some form of comfort and security. A large portion of the churches now in Taiwan had their beginning at that time. They sprang up all over the island. Privation and turmoil certainly did not hurt God's work.

I hadn't been here long before I received a letter from a fellow missionary in another town, asking me to come to his church two nights a week to help with an evening Bible school which he was beginning for his people. I went for a semester and was delighted to see the hunger for spiritual training in God's Word. This was producing Christian soldiers who were ready to go to the front. And in a short time that church began a daughter church in a village a few miles away.

As the story of the Antioch assembly is picked up again in chapter thirteen of Acts, it continues: "Now in the church at Antioch there were prophets and teachers." The prophets were the preachers; the teachers were the trainers. Certainly the Lord is quite prepared to provide each of our churches with teachers and trainers. We can be certain of this because there is so much in His Word indicating that He desires His people to be taught and trained, and trained in such a thorough and effective way that they in turn can pass it on to others. Paul made this very clear to his student Timothy. "What you have heard from me before many witnesses, entrust to faithful men who will be able to teach others also" (2 Tim. 2:2).

We are not just to plant churches; we are to plant virile, reproducing churches. One group in the Philippines takes twenty or thirty of their college students to a small island for nine weeks each summer to give them concentrated instruction in how to study and teach God's Word. And a young teacher in a village of central Taiwan began a spiritual training course for his middle school students at 6 a.m. each morning. At first only two or three came, but in a few weeks, thirty to forty were attending. We must ask the Lord to give such gifts to His church.

Since the church at Antioch was brought into being as a result of persecution, we can know that the content of their training included plenty of instruction on how to do spiritual battle. There were, no doubt, courses explaining the two kingdoms, our strategy, our resources, binding and loosing, wearing one's armor, employing one's weapons, etc. I'm sure that the graduates of their school were a fearful battalion to the enemy, and that they moved out from victory to victory, releasing many captives and establishing other churches of like confidence and strength. Archaeological excavations have unearthed over twenty churches in the environs of Antioch, but there were probably many more than that. As Paul mentioned in Ephesians 4:12, they "equipped the saints for ministry"; they didn't just expect some professional clergy to do it all. This church really had their priorities straight.

The Three Priorities of Ministry

For the first ten years of my student ministry in Taiwan, I gave myself primarily to evangelism. After all, I was a missionary. And a missionary's first and foremost work should be evangelism. But should it?

About that time, I returned to the States for furlough and found that the pastor of our home church was laying a new emphasis before his flock which he called "the three priorities of ministry." The first was worship; the second, fellowship; the third, evangelism. Worship, he explained, is ministering to the Lord. Fellowship is ministering to the body. And evangelism is ministering to the world.

He remarked that some of us get carried away with evangelism to the neglect of the first and second priorities of ministry to the Lord and to His body. These three priorities soon caught on in our home church, and advance began to take place in every area. Evangelism did not lose out by being put in third place. Rather, the growth of the church commenced to pick up in a most encouraging manner.

Another church not far away took note and its pastor attended one of our "Three Priority Seminars." His poor little group had been working away for thirty years but was still small and unpromising. It took this pastor some weeks to become convinced that there were things other than evangelism which should occupy first and second place. But he finally decided to give top priority to worship and second priority to meaningful fellowship for his flock and equipping them for ministry. Within ten years his church was up to 4,300, is now over 10,000, and is still growing and planting daughter churches in other areas.

There are three ways to do missionary work. The first and least effective is to do it yourself. The next best is to help the nationals to do it. But the most fruitful of all is to *"equip"* the nationals to do it. And the way to equip anyone to be productive in the Lord's work is not just to train him how to do evangelism but to immerse him in the first two priorities of worship and fellowship.

When I began to grasp some of this and to join others in applying it to our student work in Taiwan, the whole picture changed and things took off in high gear. The students do a much better job winning their classmates on campus than we as foreigners from the outside ever could. But even for them, there are two items which are more important than evangelism. These are worship and fellowship. And this is the model which is set before us in the church of Antioch.

They Were a Spiritual Body

The next few verses describe this marvelous church: "While they were *ministering to the Lord* and *fasting*, the Holy Spirit said, 'Set apart for Me Barnabas and Saul, for the work to which I have called them.' Then, after fasting and praying, they laid their hands on them and sent them off. So, being sent out by the Holy Spirit, they went..." (Acts 13:2-4).

Some versions translate the phrase "ministering to the Lord" as worshipping the Lord. Ordinary worship is surely included, but the original word for "ministering" here, is "leiturgo" from which we get our English word "liturgy." It carries a much deeper significance than our usual concept of worship. It includes the whole realm of devotion to the Lord. The word is used several times in the book of Hebrews to denote the service of the priests in the Holy Place and the Most Holy Place. It depicts a very godly, spiritual tone at the church at Antioch.

I fear that many of us are not very familiar with the thought of ministering *to* the Lord. We know about ministering *for* the Lord or asking the Lord to minister to us. But just what sort of thing is it to minister to the Lord?

I, for instance, finally had to come to see that self-centeredness was so ingrained in my being that even my "devotions" were about 99% designed for my own benefit. It was a case of seeking for the Lord to minister to Dick Webster, rather than this tiny little creature seeking to minister to the Lord. I primarily came to my quiet time to receive the Lord's blessing on my life, my family and my ministry, and naturally to enjoy that wonderful "lift" which I knew the Holy Spirit had for me.

These expectations are certainly to be valid fruits of one's "devotions." But the word "devotion," as it is used in Scripture, or even in its ordinary sense, implies a giving of one's self to something or someone other than himself. The leaders of the church at Antioch had grasped this practice of "ministering to the Lord," and you can be sure that they taught it to their people.

Holy Spirit-led "devotions" will produce real devotion to the Lord. The Scriptures speak of it as "drawing near" to God. And the book of Hebrews refers several times to the picture of the Old Testament Tabernacle and encourages us to move, step by step as it were, from the outer court (of the common man) to the Holy Place, and finally into the Most Holy Place, which is introduced by the altar of incense. The flame on that little golden altar filled both the Holy Place and the Most Holy Place with a sweet, fragrant aroma to the Lord. A standard platform for our daily Bible reading could therefore be: behold Him, worship Him, serve Him.

Now let us come back to this word "liturgy." For many of us evangelicals, it conjures up the impression of a lifeless formalism which we would at once label as a waste of time. We are so eager to enjoy the warmth and blessing of the "service" that we want to quickly dispense with all this unnecessary procedure and get on with partaking of all those good things the Lord has for us.

When we think of a "service," we subconsciously have in mind the Lord's service to us. We are great on "enjoying the goodness of the Lord." But how strong are we at "ministering to the Lord"? We mustn't forget that the word used here in the original Greek text is still "liturgy."

We would all agree that anything of a dead or dry routine has no place in either the service of the Lord or in service to the Lord. "In Him was *life*, and that life is the *light* of men" (Jn. 1:4). But some of us need a basic overhaul in our consciousness as to who should primarily be serving whom. To develop the "liturgical" first part of our meetings to the degree that the major portion of our "service" is "ministering to the Lord" could become a whole new pattern of worship for some of us. And such a modification of our little, fixed routine could bring a whole new element of life to our long-held traditional ways.

It was quite a shock to me one day, after I had spoken at a meeting where several European friends attended, to hear one of the ladies remark that she quite missed the depth of spiritual worship in our services because of the abbreviated liturgy. This person was by no means a liberal. She was a very godly woman who was used to a bit more "ministering to the Lord."

Though we need to be careful of formalism and routine, we also need to be careful of the opposite extreme of self-centered emotionalism and of hypnotic repetition in singing the same little chorus over and over again, a dozen times non-stop. The Holy Spirit longs to lead us forth in ever new, heart-warming experiences of genuine ministry to our God.

I have recently attended several gatherings where things began with quite an extended period of praise and meditation on the greatness and goodness of the Lord. In some cases, the program of participation was well planned. In others, it was quite unplanned. But in each instance, things were done "decently and in order," and I found it all to be very refreshing and uplifting. I believe the Holy Spirit was pleased. I would suggest that many of us can enter some new spheres of creative worship.

To focus on this matter of "ministering to the Lord" is not just an effort to over-emphasize some obscure passage. Rather, this is the very thing for which we were created. It is meant to become the "first priority" of every man's life and labor. "Worthy are You, our Lord and God, to receive glory and honor and power, for You created all things, and by Your will they existed and were created" (Rev. 4:ll).

There is a little chorus which we should sing often, that states: "The greatest thing in all my life is knowing You...loving You...serving You." There are two types of Bible study, two types of prayer, and two types of singing, etc. One type is to feed and strengthen one's self, which is good and necessary, but the mature Christian (like those leaders in Antioch) will see these benefits as secondary. When the three disciples were on the Mount of Transfiguration with the Lord Jesus, Peter spoke up and said, "Lord it is good *for us* to be here..." Then "a voice came from the cloud: *'This is my Son whom I love*; *listen to Him'*" (Mk. 9:5-7).

We will certainly never lose out by keeping "ministry to the Lord" as our top priority. "Seek *first* the *kingdom of God* and His righteousness, and *all these other things will be added to you*" (Mt. 6:33). When we ask anything according to His will, we should remember that we are basing our request on "the *good and acceptable and perfect* will of God." And never forget, the two keys in worship are: He is worthy, and He is good.

Yes, the best way to keep our own cup filled is to minister *to Him* in our devotions. The 23rd Psalm which we all love so much was written by the man who probably knew more and did more in ministering to the Lord than anyone else. After several verses describing the abundant life of a lamb who has the Lord for his shepherd, he then goes on, "*You* prepare a table before me in the presence of my enemies. *You* anoint my head with oil; my cup overflows. Surely goodness and mercy will follow me all the days of my life, and I will dwell in the house of the Lord forever."

So once the Holy Spirit has been able to teach and train us to minister to the Lord, He then can move on to the second and third priorities and help us to minister to the body and to do warfare against the enemy in our ministering to the world. The thing that often holds us back in all this is that we so easily lapse into the totally unacceptable position of allowing our pride to focus our attentions on the *success of our work* as our first priority. Then the enemy gets into the act and all begins to deteriorate instead of advance. Motives are hard things to keep pure, so we very much need to keep asking the *Holy* Spirit to continuously sanctify and purify all our incentives and ambitions. Actually, I find a joyous release in my spirit when I devote the basic concerns of my praying to the advance and welfare of His kingdom, rather than indulging in anxious pleas for help in "*my work.*"

Spending time ministering to the Lord is certainly vital and indispensable, and top priority, for equipping the Lord's soldiers. It insures *His presence* in all our maneuvers. When Moses was about to lead Israel out across the vast, treacherous wilderness, he cried out to the Lord, "If your presence does not go with us, then do not send us up from here." He knew that to enter the battle field with anything short of the Lord's mighty presence would mean only disaster.

But there is no need of disaster. Moses had the habit of going regularly outside the camp to a place which he called his "tent of meeting." And "as Moses went into the tent, the pillar of cloud would come down and stay at the entrance, while the Lord spoke with Moses. Whenever the people saw the pillar of cloud standing at the entrance to the tent, they all stood and worshipped, each at the entrance of his own tent. The Lord would speak to Moses face to face as a man speaks to his friend." And one day the Lord said to Moses, "My presence will go with you, and I will give you rest" (Ex. 33:7-15). There were still battles along the way, but each one resulted in glorious victory.

The Village Gospel Mission here in Taiwan has established a very wise custom for their workers. They strongly encourage them to set apart the entire forenoon every day for spiritual preparation and "ministering to the Lord," each in his own "tent of meeting." This, I am convinced, is the most effective equipment there is for spiritual warfare. It should be held as first priority. And each new convert should be taught how to minister to the Lord.

With Fasting

Another item of notable prominence in the church at Antioch was the element of fasting. It seemed to be woven into the very texture of all they did. As they ministered to the Lord, they fasted. Before they sent out their missionaries, they fasted. Yet I gather that fasting is an exercise which is rather foreign to many of us. I myself gave very little attention to this practice until I was nearly fifty years of age. I considered it to be an extreme measure promoted by people who were trying to be "super-holy." But in His wisdom and mercy, the Lord used a rather startling development to get me started.

I received a letter from a certain student group asking me to be their speaker at a three-day retreat where they hoped to make a study of, and take a venture into, the matter of fasting along with some extended praying. I was disturbed, because I knew nothing about fasting myself! My first thought was to reply that I would not be able to attend and to ask them to find another speaker. But the Lord gave me no peace to send such a letter. Rather, He seemed to indicate that the time had come for me to undertake a thorough investigation of this whole issue. So I began to read articles, talk to others, and do some research as to what God's Word really has to say about it.

I soon found that the Scriptures have some seventy references to the subject, but that these were almost altogether limited to accounts of people who did fast, and what happened as a result. In other words, we are never commanded or even directly urged to fast. And yet it was quite common for God's people, in times of distress or weakness, to give themselves to fasting. Some even practiced it regularly, as did John the Baptist and his disciples, and probably the leaders of this church of Antioch.

Although God's Word does not require us to fast or give us instructions about how or when to fast, yet it seems to strongly imply that here is something we would do well to look into and experiment with. It seems to fall into the category of *"proving what is pleasing to the Lord"* (Eph. 5:10).

Probably the reason why so little direction is given to us regarding this form of spiritual devotion is that our spiritual maturity and our physical strength are so varied. For some who are not physically strong, much fasting can be harmful. For others who are not spiritually robust, it can easily induce pride and other unhealthy traits. The Lord Jesus particularly warned us about this latter danger.

There are many different patterns of fasting. Some find that to forego eating for one meal, or for a full day, once a week or once a month, is a good way to begin. I know of a group of workers in one village area who recently began to fast at noon each day. Just last night I had a call from one of them who was excited about a marvelous breakthrough they were experiencing in their work. Another organization which has seen "rivers of living water" flowing out to many has a number of visitors coming to their headquarters each week. In the list of explanations as you enter, it says "no meals will be served on Wednesdays, since it is the custom of all our staff to have one day each week for fasting and prayer." Their practice has been a means of elevating many growing Christians into a new atmosphere of blessing both for themselves and their ministry.

For some, it seems best to follow their physical and spiritual inclinations. When Daniel was an older man, he involved himself in a *semi-fast* for three weeks. He probably didn't feel he had the strength to go without any nourishment at all. To quote his words, he said, "I did not eat any tasty food, nor did meat or wine enter my mouth, nor did I use any ointment at all until the entire three weeks were completed." (Dan. 10:3) Some people reserve their fasts for times of pressing need but may continue their abstinence of food for a longer period. In any case, we should "not be foolish, but understand what the will of the Lord is" (Eph. 5:17). Each soldier must decide for himself what his own system will be and be prepared to adjust this pattern either forward or backward as needs indicate and as his own physical constitution dictates. There should be no room for bondage, but neither should there be just a giving in to laxness. He also is to keep his decisions to himself and seek to cover up any evidence that he is involved in fasting.

Though people who are older may need to take care in the matter of fasting, yet there are some in their later years who can have an especially effective ministry in this area. Anna at age 84 "served night and day with fastings and prayer" (Lk. 2:37). So even we senior citizens would do well to give some consideration to this challenge.

Our thoughts in regard to this matter should revolve around our *yearning for something more* by way of a breakthrough from our weary routines. When we get to the place where we long to see more lasting fruit in His work; when we hunger and thirst to see the glory of God permeating His tabernacle, then our fasts will be meaningful and we will see fresh accomplishments.

A few days ago I was challenged by a message from the pastor of a thriving church in Canada. He remarked that "dissatisfaction is the key to spiritual progress." It is when we are content to move along smoothly, accepting the status quo, that nothing happens. It is one thing to *wish* something would take place, but it is quite another to resolve to seek the Lord with humble determination and at whatever cost *until* His Spirit begins to do "great and mighty things."

There are many examples of this brand of fasting in Scripture, and the Lord greatly honored it in each case. We have referred to Daniel's exploits and their phenomenal outcome. Another reference pictures his approach to these ventures. "I gave my attention to the Lord God, to seek Him by prayer and supplications, with fasting, sackcloth and ashes" (Dan. 9:3). Then there was the Lord's much used servant Nehemiah. "When I heard these words, I sat down and wept and mourned for days; and I was fasting and praying before the God of heaven" (Neh. 1:4). One more instance was the action taken by the people of Ninevah after Jonah's message to them. "When the word reached the king of Ninevah, he arose from his throne, laid aside his robe, covered himself with sackcloth, and sat on ashes. And he issued a proclamation...'Do not let man, beast, herd, or flock taste a thing. Do not let them eat or drink water. But both man and beast must be covered with sackcloth; and let men call on God earnestly'" (Jnh. 3:6-8). This was followed by one of the greatest revivals of all history.

Now what should we make of these references to sackcloth and ashes? I myself have never resorted to wearing sackcloth, or putting ashes on my head, or sitting in ashes. And we find no reference in the New Testament to any who employed such measures in the early church. Yet I am convinced that the Word of God is seeking to say something to us by including a number of such accounts in the Old Testament. What was the significance of such extreme action? The people who did this had reached a state of desperation. And they had decided to underscore the longings of their heart in some exceptional manner before the Lord.

There is one New Testament reference in the book of Revelation which I feel is of no small consequence in this regard: "I will grant authority to my two witnesses, and they will prophesy for 1260 days, *clothed in sackcloth.*" When we look over the record of achievements for these two witnesses, it is truly phenomenal. The hand of the Lord was certainly upon them.

I still am not sure that the Lord is encouraging us to manifest our earnest concerns by putting on literal sackcloth, but it would seem that there is a place for exhibiting to the Lord (not to man) that we are prepared to pay a price to see His kingdom established in needy areas and in blinded hearts. To wear sackcloth next to one's skin, as was usually the case (2 K. 6:30; Job 16:15) was certainly not comfortable, for it was a coarse material made from goat hair. Some of us spend half our lives trying to get comfortable in the Lord's work, and it results in much frustration. But a tough marine out on the front lines cannot afford to give much thought to comfort. And so it is that when we give up our efforts to achieve an easy life and orient our attitude toward His challenge to "endure hardness as a good soldier of Jesus Christ," the frustration is usually over, and we actually discover a release.

To go a step further, what are some of the substitutes for sackcloth and ashes which we in this day might engage in to accentuate our deep desire to see new breakthroughs? The Lord Jesus on occasion spent the whole night in prayer. (He gave up His usual quota of sleep.) I have heard of several who have sold any gold or silver objects they possessed and given the proceeds to an urgent shortage in the Lord's work. Others have imposed a stringent frugality upon their lifestyle for a period of time in order to aid some phase of His harvest. Some retreat to a mountain cabin or a motel room for a few days to do business with the Lord. Hudson Taylor subsisted on bread and water for a time. Some have given up marriage for the Lord's sake, and the Scriptures speak of married couples foregoing their intimate pleasure for a season, "that you may devote yourselves to prayer" (1 Cor. 7:5).

In the Old Testament, the rather rigid restrictions regarding the *sabbath* seemed to be a measure to encourage personal discipline toward the Lord's cause. "If because of the sabbath, you turn your foot from doing your own pleasure on My holy day, and call the sabbath a delight, the holy day of the Lord honorable. And shall honor it, desisting from your own ways, from seeking your own pleasure, and speaking your own word, then you will take delight in the Lord, and I will make you ride on the heights of the earth; and I will feed you with the heritage of Jacob your father, for the mouth of the Lord has spoken" (Isa. 58:13,14).

I would suggest that each mature Christian give some serious thought as to various ways whereby he can gain release for his burdened spirit, when the weight of some need for God's glory and His kingdom is heavy upon him. A mighty man of God once remarked that "whereas gluttony reduces spiritual power, the various forms of fasting can generate a whole new level of blessing and spiritual attainment for His enterprises."

As Paul and Barnabas, the missionaries from the Church of Antioch, went about their church planting ministry, they certainly introduced fasting to every group. "When they had appointed elders for them *in every church, having prayed with fasting*, they commended them to the Lord in whom they had believed" (Acts 14:23). Yet Paul also taught them that any type of personal sacrifice which merely brought dullness or deadness was not a *"living* sacrifice."

They Were a Sending Base

"While they were ministering to the Lord and fasting, the Holy Spirit said, *Set apart* for Me Barnabas and Saul for the work to which I have called them.' Then after fasting and praying, they *laid their hands on them*, and *sent* them off. So, being *sent* by the Holy Spirit, they went."

There are two basic concepts regarding missions. One is "go"; the other is "send." For many years, the emphasis of my preaching was "go." Is that not how the Lord presented His Great Commission in Matthew and Mark? True, in most translations it is a simple imperative, "go." But in the original text, "go" is a participle. The actual wording would be more accurately put as "going, therefore, make disciples of all nations" (Mt. 28:19). And "going into all the world, preach the gospel to the whole creation" (Mk. 16:15). It assumes the command "go," of course, but the emphasis in the Lord's mind seems clearly to be on His sending them forth.

The commission as it is presented in the Gospel of John is much more clear as a *commission* or a sending. "As the Father has *sent* Me, even so *send* I you" (Jn. 20:21). The Lord's commission to His disciples is a continuation of the Father's commission to Him. There are no references in Scripture of the Lord Jesus Himself deciding to come to this earth, but *seventy times* He refers to Himself as being *sent*. Seven times it speaks of the Holy Spirit being sent, and thirty times the Lord refers to *sending* His disciples.

I feel we would see a tremendous advance in our worldwide project of missions if we approached the element of thrusting forth laborers more from this aspect. The individual must be aware of God's call, God's will for him to go, but the great emphasis of Scripture is on the sending, which the Lord does *through His church*, as in the case of Antioch.

If each church would come to look upon itself as a sending base, rather than waiting for some individual to feel called, the picture could be very different. It seems the focus needs to be reversed. The basic responsibility and vision should rest on the church. Every member of that church should see himself as a vital part of a sending body. The Lord's Great Commission is primarily to the church. They are the ones to "pray the Lord of the harvest that He would *send* out laborers into His harvest" (Lk. 10:2). And as the Lord sends them forth, two by two, the local church (not just a mission board) should "lay their hands on them and send them off," as did the brothers in Antioch.

If each local church keeps the Lord's commission constantly before *all* its believers, if all are continuously involved in sending, the missionary enterprise will surely move forward. If each church in Taiwan would send out just one of its members each year, this would mean two thousand new missionaries every twelve months, or 10,000 in five years. Think of what could have taken place during this century, even here on this small island!

We are not talking about extreme or impossible dreams here. It has been proven many times that the church which catches this vision and proceeds to become a channel of blessing to other unreached areas is always a body which enjoys unusual blessing from the Lord.

The leaders of a church will reproduce their own kind. If they genuinely possess this vision, their people will catch this vision. If the leadership is a godly, spiritual group, the missionaries who are sent out from their fellowship will be a powerful, moving force. For missionaries commissioned by any church with the spiritual qualities of that congregation at Antioch will be "sent forth by the Holy Spirit." The missionaries who went out from the church at Antioch "turned the world upside down."

16

OUR SUPPORTING ARTILLERY

When my son Larry was a student in high school, one day he brought home from the library a book entitled *The U.S. Frogmen of World War II*. That evening I noticed it lying on the living room couch, so I picked it up to have a look. It was one of the most fascinating books I have ever read. It was the story of the significant and vital role carried out by the young swimmers who surveyed the approach to each of the occupied islands in the Pacific before the invasion of that island. The navy soon discovered that such an investigation was strategic and absolutely essential to a successful landing.

But to approach a heavily armed, enemy-held island by a team of defenseless swimmers clad only in a pair of khaki trunks was not a simple venture. In fact it proved to be an extremely perilous assignment. The enemy, becoming aware of what was taking place, naturally desired to blast each of these frogmen out of existence. There was one provision, however, which made it possible for these young men to move across the reefs, proceed clear up onto the very beaches of these island, make their investigations, and even attach packs of explosives to certain obstacles to clear out a path for the landing craft. How could they possibly accomplish all this in the face of enemy fire? The answer is that the enemy fire was driven back by a cover of bombardment from the U.S. Navy's *heavy artillery*.

There is a beautiful story in the Old Testament (Ex. 17:8-16) which is a perfect picture of the very thing we are talking about here, as it takes place in the spiritual realm. There are many battle passages in Scripture, and each has its own significance, its own special spiritual lesson to teach us. As we examine these accounts, it becomes quite clear that many, if not all, of these are intended to be studied as spiritual parables, even though they are actual historical events. So now we want to take a close look at Joshua's encounter with the Amalekites.

Amalek was Israel's perpetual enemy. In fact, the closing verse of the passage reads, "The Lord has sworn; the Lord will have war against Amalek from generation to generation." It sounds somewhat like our unseen enemy, doesn't it?

When Moses learned that Amalek was mounting an attack against God's people, he called Joshua and asked him to lead the army of Israel out against the enemy, and then he added, "I will station myself on the top of the hill, with the staff of God in my hand." So what we see here are two interrelated battles taking place simultaneously. One is seen; one is unseen. One is being fought in the valley; the other is being fought up on the hill. But the crucial point to the whole story is that the outcome of the battle in the valley is being controlled by the progress of the battle on the hill. We will discuss this factor more a little later, but we must consider another matter first.

Prayer Warriors—The Ministry of Prayer

Although the heavy artillery up on the hill determines the results of the battle in the valley, yet the little group on top of that hill are by far in the minority. There are only three men up there: Moses, Aaron, and Hur. With Joshua in the valley are perhaps a hundred thousand soldiers. So we are reminded that prayer warriors have a very specialized ministry. Certainly not everyone is called to this position in the Lord's work. But every church, every mission, every Christian organization needs a few pieces of artillery. Although the percent of men operating the heavy artillery in any army or navy is relatively small, yet no general could possibly do without them. He would never win any wars without his cannons and mortar fire.

Perhaps the reason why real, devoted prayer warriors are so scarce that such ministry is a hidden work. Actually, those "up on the hill" are usually shut up in their bedroom or cloistered away in some little closet. Nobody sees them or even knows what they are doing. It is not like a public ministry which gives clear evidence that we are really busy for the Lord.

How shall we describe a "prayer warrior"? Let us begin with a consideration of what constitutes artillery. The smallest rifle which is ever used for hunting small game, such as rabbits or squirrels, has a bore of about 5 mm. Most military rifles are probably 8 to 10 mm. However, when we speak of artillery, we are referring to guns which can fire shells of larger sizes. There are three grades of artillery: light, medium and heavy. Light artillery ranges from 25 to 50 mm., medium from 50 to 100 mm., and most heavy artillery from 100 to 300 mm. These latter are huge projectiles. A 300 mm. shell is as big around as a man and weighs 350 lbs.

In World War I, the Germans had a huge gun called the Big Bertha, with a bore of 420 mm. It could fire a projectile weighing nearly half a ton 15 miles high to reach a target at a distance of 76 miles (115 km.). That is almost as far as from Taipei to Taichung, or clear across the island of Taiwan, from Taichung to Hualien. This mighty weapon was, of course, the only one of its kind.

It has occurred to me that we might think similarly of artillery in the spiritual realm, as those who have been called to spend say 25 to 300 minutes a day in prayer for the Lord's work. Those spending 25 minutes a day will be more numerous, of course, than those spending 100-300. But so it is with the army and navy. Three hundre millimeter guns are less numerous, but there still are some warships and field artillery equipped with such weapons. In God's kingdom, we don't find many who have the ability to spend two to five hours a day in prayer, but the Scriptures speak of some, and occasionally we hear of a Praying Hyde, a David Brainard, or men like Finney's Clary and Nash. And of course there are others that you and I know nothing about.

At first, such a concept may really seem foreign and unreasonable to us, but it is not foreign or unreasonable to the Christians in Korea. Regular, prolonged periods of prayer are quite common among God's people in that land, and they are surely seeing the results of it. It is not impossible, if the Lord *calls* a person to this ministry. The problem with most of us in the rest of the world is that we haven't even begun to think in terms of heavy artillery. It is just too far out, too extreme, too "impractical." Consequently we move along year after year in our crippled, weakened state, satisfied with a mediocre ministry. Should we not begin asking the Lord to raise up men and women and equip them to replenish this desperate need?

Where are we likely to find the caliber of people we are talking about here in this chapter? They will probably be some of the unassuming jewels among our senior members. These people are retired; they don't have to go to work eight hours a day. Their families are grown and out of the nest. Also, they are often the more spiritually mature ones in the congregation. There are a number of retired Christians these days who have not yet found their spiritual niche and may feel somewhat "put on the shelf." But that period of life which is given to prayer can be the most productive of all.

The Scripture pictures some heavy artillery for us when it refers to Anna and others of her kind. She had been a widow for a good many years. "She did not depart from the temple, worshipping with fasting and prayer night and day" (Lk. 2:36-37). Also, in the church at Ephesus they had a corps of elderly widows who "continued in supplications and prayers night and day" (1 Tim. 5:5).

As we began one of our previous furloughs, we asked the Lord to give us a few of these very special, choice servants of His to support our ministry out here in Taiwan. He did this by calling a half dozen mature retirees from several different churches. They accepted from Him the vital assignment of driving back enemy forces and upholding the needs of the work before His almighty and loving throne. You can be sure that this has meant a marked advance in His kingdom.

Prayer Support—The Controlling Factor in Spiritual Warfare

As Paul was moving west on his second missionary journey to begin work in the province of Asia, he was stopped at the border by the Holy Spirit. So he turned north to open up the province of Bithynia. Again he was stopped at the border by God's

Spirit. That night he had the vision of a man pleading for him to come to Macedonia. The next day he and his fellow-workers proceeded toward the city of Philippi, which was the capitol of the province of Macedonia. As soon as they arrived, they learned of a small group of prayer warriors who were meeting regularly down by the river. Now they could understand why the Lord had led them to this area. Their corps of artillery was already in place, so they could move in and begin operations.

More than once God spared the Israelites from destruction because of Moses' long vigils with God up on Mt. Sinai. But one day a thousand years later, the Lord confided in Ezekiel His great sorrow of heart because there were no such intercessors in the land at that time. He said, "I searched for a man among them who should build up the wall and stand in the gap before Me, for the land, that I should not destroy it; but I found no one" (Ezek. 22:30).

It is indeed a strange phenomenon, and yet it is true, that prayer support is always the controlling factor in spiritual warfare. Coming back to Joshua's encounter with the Amalekites, we read that "when Moses held his hands up, Israel prevailed, and when he let his hands down, Amalek prevailed." We have already mentioned that Joshua had perhaps 100,000 soldiers with him, and Amalek probably had more than that. Yet here is Moses with his two companions up on the hill controlling the tide of nearly half a million mighty fighting men. The key which unlocks this mystery is the truth that even a billion mighty fighting men are nothing compared to God's power. When the Lord is ready to send forth His unseen forces, no earthly army will stop Him. The Scriptures are full of such examples. We must learn how to enter into more cooperation with Him and His forces.

We frequently read more recent illustrations of how this principle has been applied. Moody had his men who spent an hour in a little room beneath the platform, crying out to God every time Moody preached in his big church in Chicago. I know of another church which has a half dozen deacons waiting in prayer in a back room during every Sunday morning service. Finney had two men who gave themselves to prayer all day and part of the night during his campaigns. And this sort of intercessory support is quite continual in the thriving churches in Korea and South America. It is indispensable to the winning of spiritual battles.

I have already twice referred to the two men who maintained that position of heavy artillery for the great evangelist Charles G. Finney. And I feel it would be helpful for us to hear one of these mighty warriors described by Mr. Finney himself: "I must introduce the name of a man, whom I shall have occasion to mention frequently, Mr. Abel Clary. He was the son of a very excellent man, and an elder of the church where I was converted. He was converted in the same revival in which I was. He had been licensed to preach, but his spirit of prayer was such; he was so burdened with the souls of men, that he was not able to preach much; his whole time and strength being given to prayer. The burden of his soul would frequently be so great that he was unable to stand, and he would writhe and groan in agony. I was well acquainted with him, and knew something of the wonderful spirit of prayer that was upon him. He was a very silent man, as almost all are who have the powerful spirit of prayer."

We need to be reminded again here that periods of intense supplication need to be interspersed with ample times of praise and worship. The Holy Spirit desires to keep all things in a wise and beautiful balance (Eph. 5:15,17; 1 Thess. 5:21). Even Anna, who spent all those years in fasting and prayer night and day, did so with "worshiping" (Lk. 2:37).

Prayer support for any given work can also be likened to the function of muscles in the human body. A friend of mine who is a medical doctor for many years operated a polio clinic. One evening I heard him speaking to a group of university students, telling what the disease of polio actually does to a person. He explained that it atrophies the muscle tissue of the legs, so that the patient cannot walk or run or sometimes even stand without crutches or braces.

When the undergirding of prayer has dried up for any church, fellowship group or mission, there is little strength left, so the great tendency is to substitute programs, activities, entertainments and other attractions as crutches and braces to help support the work. But we find none of these in the book of Acts. They were in the midst of heavy warfare and what they needed was not crutches and braces, but strong muscles. In chapter 12 we read that "King Herod killed James the brother of John with the sword; and when he saw that it pleased the Jews, he proceeded to arrest Peter also...And when he had seized him, he put him in prison, and delivered him to four squads of soldiers to guard him. ...So Peter was kept in prison, *but earnest prayer* for him was made to God by the church."

You remember the awesome conclusion to the story? "The very night before Herod was to bring him out, Peter was sleeping between two soldiers, bound with two chains, and sentries before the door guarding the prison, and behold, an angel of the Lord appeared, and a light shone in the cell; and he struck Peter on the side and woke him, saying, 'Get up quickly.' And the chains fell off his hands. ...And he went out and followed him. ...When they had passed the first and the second guard, they came to the iron gate leading into the city. It opened to them of its own accord, and they went out and passed on through one street, and immediately the angel left him. And Peter came to himself, and said, 'Now I am sure that the Lord has sent His angel and rescued me from the hand of Herod and from all that the Jewish people were expecting.' When he realized this, he went to the house of Mary, the mother of John... where many were gathered together and *were praying*."

Heavy artillery will stir things up today as it did then, but it will also drive back enemy forces today as it did then. How determined are we to call on our God for such advances?

Why Tenacity Is So Essential

When Moses was up on that hill he discovered that every time he let his hands down, Joshua's forces began to lose ground, so naturally he then did his best to keep his hands held up before the Lord. But the story tells us that his hands began to get heavy. So "they took a stone and put it under him, and he sat on it; and Aaron and Hur supported his hands, one on one side and one on the other. Thus his hands were steady until the sun set."

Two kinds of tenacity in prayer are needed for results in spiritual warfare. First there is the heavy investment each day, and secondly there is the faithful continuance from day to day until battles are won. Not all battles are won in a day. In fact, later on in the book of Joshua, after one of Joshua's major campaigns, it reminds us that "Joshua waged war a *long time* with all these kings" (Josh. 11:18).

It is also encouragingly significant to recall how Joshua's first campaign in the land of Canaan was begun. As soon as they had crossed the Jordan River and entered the land, a man with a drawn sword appeared to Joshua. "Are you for us or against us?" Joshua asked. "I have come as Commander of the Lord's army," was the reply. Then he commanded Joshua to remove his shoes, for the place where he was standing was holy ground. Joshua fell down with his face to the ground and asked, "What message does my Lord have for His servant?"

Then the Lord gave Joshua the strategy for the beginning of his first campaign. Before he did any fighting, he and his soldiers were to march around Jericho once each day for seven days, and then seven times on the seventh day. God would then tear down the walls and give them the city.

My wife Flo has a wonderful testimony of how this very strategy worked out in her first spiritual campaign here in Taiwan. She had been sent to the small city of Chaochou in the south of the island to study the Chinese language and to learn something of the culture of the people. Her living quarters were just across the street from the Chaochou High School. Since her heart's burden was primarily for students, she longed to be able to communicate with those young people, but her language was not yet sufficient. There was one thing she could and did do, however, and that was to ride her bicycle around that campus every afternoon praying and pleading with the Lord to open a door to those young lives. Before long she was transferred to the city of Taipei in the north of the island.

In Taipei she became a sponsor of the fellowship group of the Teachers' College. One of the young lady Christian students there became very interested in learning how to study God's word. So Flo began to give her regular training in inductive Bible study methods. This young Christian grew very rapidly, and upon graduation the Lord called her to teach in the Chaochou High

School down in the south of the island. He used her there in establishing a fruitful student fellowship group.

Just a few weeks ago, as we were ministering at a Christian Teachers' Retreat, we made a thrilling discovery. One of those Christian teachers now being much used by the Lord heard the gospel for the first time and accepted the Lord in that very student group in Chaochou High School! The strategy of surrounding any given work for God with a saturation of prayer is always an effective approach.

The time factor may involve years, as we have pointed out in a later chapter, but God's Word encourages us to "cast not away your confidence, for it will be greatly rewarded" (Heb. 10:35).

I would like to share again with you here two other references which have been a strong challenge to me in this matter of tenacity in prayer. The first is in Isaiah 62:6,7: "I have posted watchmen on your walls, oh Jerusalem (or whatever place He has burdened you to intercede for); they will never be silent day or night. You who call on the Lord, give yourselves no rest, and give Him no rest, *till* He establishes Jerusalem (or your special concern), and makes her the praise of the earth." The other passage is the Lord's familiar parable of the persistent widow, which He gave to urge us to "always pray and not give up." His conclusion was in the form of a question, plus the answer to that question. "Will not God bring about justice for His chosen ones, who cry out to Him *night and day*? Will He keep putting them off? I tell you, He will see that they get justice, and quickly. However, when the Son of Man comes, will He find *faith* [tenacity] on the earth?" (Lk. 18:1,7,8).

How to Spend Effective Time in Prayer

Artillery is effective, not just because of the size of its projectile, but mainly because of the *content* of that projectile. These mammoth bullets are also called *shells*, because they are actually containers filled with powerful explosives. When they strike, their target is totally demolished.

Spiritual artillery must be of the same make-up. Not just the amount of time one spends in prayer, but the quality of intercession is also important. The Lord has made it clear to us that He is not merely looking (or listening) for "vain repetition," as a zealous heathen fills up his prayer time. It is not counting over again our "prayer beads" or spinning our "prayer wheel." He is looking for genuine concern, and intelligent content...humble yet powerful supplication.

The first thing we need to do, in preparation for an effective prayer vigil, is to collect information on the area the Holy Spirit is leading us to pray for. Most missionaries put out regular prayer letters. Thus they equip their prayer warriors with identification of their targets. We need to collect all the data we can on the objects of our concerns. We need a prayer notebook, which includes a prayer list.

The second area of preparation is the collecting of helpful Scripture passages. This includes many of His promises, His names, His attributes, His instructions, His encouragements, and sample prayers. We have attempted to provide a starting sample of all these various aids in the "Worship and Warfare" prayer companion, which is a companion piece to this book.

The third item to deal with here is the scope of concern which the Lord would have you to include in your prayer ministry. Many people spread themselves so thin that they are not able to intercede in depth for anyone or any project. It is helpful to ask the Holy Spirit to lead you to focus particularly on one or two areas of the world and to do everything you can to become knowledgeable and effective in prayer for those. Others you may want to keep on your list but perhaps pray for less frequently.

As one proceeds in this ministry of intercession, the Holy Spirit will guide us to develop many effective new skills and concerns in reaching out to the needs of the lost and the enabling of the laborers of our particular area of the harvest field.

For many, a great help and strength to intercession is to join regularly with another for joint prayer. This is also pictured for us in the passage we have been reviewing. Aaron and Hur went up on the mount with Moses and helped to hold up his hands. The Lord Jesus also encourages us in such *agreed* prayer. "Again I say to you, if two of you agree on earth about anything they ask, it will be done for them by My Father in heaven. For where two or three are gathered in My Name, there am I in the midst of them" (Mt. 18:19,20).

In another chapter we have introduced the very helpful concept of written warfare prayers. We might add here that for two people to read aloud together through these prayers, alternating from paragraph to paragraph, is a very effective way to utilize this material.

The missionary Paul was certainly one to make sure that he had plenty of artillery to support each of his evangelistic tours. We find his pleas at the end of almost every one of his letters. Perhaps we should again remind ourselves of a few of them. "I appeal to you, brothers, by the Lord Jesus Christ and by the love of the Spirit, to strive together with me in your prayers to God on my behalf" (Rom. 15:30). "Pray for me, that whenever I open my mouth, words may be given me so that I will boldly make known the mystery of the gospel, for which I am an ambassador in chains. Pray that I may declare it fearlessly, as I should" (Eph. 6:19,20). "Pray for us, that God may open to us a door for the Word, to declare the mystery of Christ, for which I am in prison, that I may make it clear, as I ought to speak" (Col. 4:3,4). "Brothers, pray for us" (1 Thess. 5:25). "Brothers, pray for us, that the Word of God may speed on and triumph, as it did among you, and that we may be delivered from wicked and evil men" (2 Thess. 3:1,2). Paul was always operating in the thick of the battle.

A few years ago the United States sent an unescorted reconnaissance ship to survey the coast of North Korea. The ship was soon captured. Then a plane was sent over the area and it was shot down. Single, unprotected vessels of war are pitifully vulnerable objects for destruction. A missionary without prayer support is also a vulnerable target. And yet many mission boards tend to neglect this vital item of missionary equipment. For instance, when a candidate whom I know well made application to a certain mission board, he had to work through a long checklist of preparations. He had a very thorough physical examination. He had psychological tests. He had to receive a number of immunization shots. He had to acquire a passport and visa. He had to seek a sufficient amount of financial support, plus various other requirements. And yet hardly any mention was made of the need for specific prayer backing. On the other hand, one other mission board I know of urges each of their missionaries to ask the Lord for a dozen mature fellow-laborers at home who will definitely stand behind them as regular artillery support. Financial support is usually more easy to come by than effectual co-laborers in prayer, but it is well worth the effort to acquire a responsible corps of faithful artillery. One simply cannot afford to go forth vulnerable to the enemy at every turn.

A doctor has nurses to assist him; a mason has his helpers; an airline pilot has his ground crew. Likewise, a missionary needs supporting fire from his home constituency, or he is at a great loss. It is indispensable! Without it, he will see little accomplished. In fact, he may soon find it necessary to return home from the field himself.

John the Baptist, of whom the Lord Jesus declared there was "none greater," built his spiritual career around prayer. In fact, he spent his youth, until he was thirty years of age, in the wilderness alone with the Lord (Lk. 1:80). When he began his ministry, his first order of business was to gather some disciples and teach them to pray (Lk. 11:1). His ministry only lasted a few months, but the Lord Jesus testified of him that "he was a burning and brilliant lamp" (Jn. 5:35).

We have a few examples from more recent days as well. In one Asian country, a very scholarly missionary with a Ph.D. went to a tribal village to plant a church. He worked there for several years and finally returned home extremely discouraged because of his very meager results. Several years later, a simple, poorly educated tribal pastor went to that same village and taught the people how to pray, and now there is a large, thriving church in that spot. In fact, the latest report stated that every Friday night there is a prayer meeting until about three o'clock in the morning, and on Saturday evening the Junior High young people spend most of the night in prayer. The Lord surely chooses the weak things of this world to confound the mighty (if they are wise as to their source of power).

I recently came across a little tract entitled "Intercessory

Guerrillas," published by the Overseas Missionary Fellowship. I have their permission to close this chapter with a few paragraphs from its moving challenge:

"Many years ago, a young missionary worked among the animistic tribes of the great mountain ranges of southwest China. Living in a little house of plaited bamboo strips, trudging for miles along narrow, precipitous paths, eating and sleeping in the same rough conditions as the people themselves, there were times when he felt so oppressed, so defeated, that he wondered whether or not he should go on. It was not the hardships, nor even the loneliness, that depressed him, but the sense of impotence, pitting his puny strength against an army of dark spirit beings of whose reality and power he was becoming increasingly aware. He was learning from experience what anguish the fiery darts of the wicked could inflict on his own spirit, for instead of delivering the Lisu tribespeople from bondage, there were times when he himself seemed in danger of being taken captive by the great enemy of souls.

"It was to his mother in England that he turned for aid. That she prayed constantly for him, he knew. There were times when his spirit was strengthened and his heart lightened. This buoying of his spirit, he knew to be God's answer to her prayers. But he longed for something more than personal blessing. It was for the thousands of Lisu tribesmen scattered over the mountains that he yearned. Without a spiritual battalion in this remote battlefield, how could he hope to deliver the captives single-handed? So he wrote to ask his mother if she could enlist recruits. Their age and sex did not matter. Their health report did not matter; nor did their lack of academic qualifications. The recruits he wanted were men and women who could pray.

"'What I want is not just an occasional mention of my work and its needs before the Lord, but a definite time (say half an hour or so?) set apart for the purpose every day...Can you give that time to me—or, rather, to the Lord?'

"There were those who could—and did. J.O. Fraser, the young missionary, was in the field alone no more. The host of intercessors turned the tide, and the grip of the spirits of evil on the minds and hearts of the people was loosened. The story of how the Lisu turned to God in their hundreds has been told by Mrs. Howard Taylor in *Behind the Ranges*. And the secret of that spiritual victory has not been forgotten. The CIM (OMF) makes no appeals for money, but it does make appeals for intercessors! Its success or otherwise in the countries of Southeast Asia to which it turned after China was closed to western missionaries, largely depends on them.

"In those countries missionaries are confronting spiritual legions of wickedness as powerful as those which faced J.O. Fraser on the mountains of Lisuland. The Buddhist temples, the Mohammedan mosques, the Shinto shrines that rear their spires and cupolas from Thailand and Malaysia to Japan, are but the outward symbols of the organized, invisible armies at the command of the prince of this world.

"A spiritual host at the command of the Lord of Glory is needed to drive them back—a host of men and women who understand, in some measure, what it is to 'come to the help of the Lord against the mighty.'"

One final reminder for all of us should be that it is not prayer itself that carries any weight or any power. It is our loving and almighty Heavenly Father who hears our prayer and honors our concern and importunity. But (we say it again), our concern, even though it be with groanings which cannot be uttered, must be a *loving* concern, or it is only "sounding brass and noisy cymbals." Through this kind of prayer we can enter into and share His heart of urgent yearning and compassion for those in unreached areas, which is surely the most beautiful thing in all the world.

PART THREE:

MORE THAN CONQUERORS

17

DAVID AND GOLIATH

Now that we have had chapters on our armor, our weapons, our authority, resources, power, concern, etc., it would seem wise to insert a couple of chapters on the practical application of it all and see how it worked out in real life for two of God's warriors. First we will take a look at David's approach to the giant Goliath, and then in the next chapter we will examine the encounter of King Jehoshaphat and his army with the hordes that attacked them from Syria.

The account of David's victory over Goliath (recorded in 1 Sam. 17) can be rather naturally divided into four parts, which we will consider one by one.

The Situation Before David's Arrival

The story begins with the statement that "the Philistines gathered their armies for battle at Socah *which belongs to Judah.*" So again we have the same, typical picture of the enemy's forces usurping territory which is not theirs. As we become engaged in each spiritual battle, a first step should be to remind ourselves and to remind the opposing forces that since the Lord's victory on Calvary, they now have no rights to any property on this earth, and wherever they stand and whatever they attempt, they are entirely out of place.

The army of Israel had evidently forgotten all the promises and all the abundant provisions which their God had laid down for them in His Word. For forty days they had been held at bay by just one of the enemy's soldiers. Of course if you were to face them with this humiliating fact, they would immediately invite you to come have a look at the size of this giant. "He was over nine feet tall. He had a bronze helmet on his head and wore a coat of scale armor of bronze weighing 125 pounds (sixty kilograms). On his legs he wore bronze greaves, and a bronze javelin was slung on his back. His spear shaft was like a weaver's rod, and its iron point weighed fifteen pounds (seven kilograms). And his shield bearer was ahead of him."

He came out each day and defied the army of Israel *for forty days*. This was not only extremely embarrassing; it was downright disgraceful. For their name "Israel" means those who possess "power with God and power with men." Also, their history as God's chosen people was replete with accounts of all kinds of miraculous victories. Their deliverance from Egypt, their provisions for forty years in the wilderness, their marvelous entrance into their "Promised Land"—all stood as their rear guard to make them invincible. Even the spot where their enemy was camping was part of their inherited promised land.

But before we fling too much mud at them, perhaps we should take a glance at our situation here in the villages of Taiwan. These villages have been in the hands of the usurper for not just forty days, or even forty years, but for 400 years! The next logical step is to ask why Israel was so weak at this juncture. And the answer is that they were weak for the very same reason we are weak. They knew too little about spiritual warfare.

David's Arrival at the Scene of Battle

David had a warrior's spirit, so he quickly surveyed the situation and was at once ready to go and deal with this taunting giant. "Who is this uncircumcised Philistine, that he should defy the armies of the living God?" he demanded. Notice that David spoke of God's "armies" in the plural. Saul's visible army, which wasn't doing much good, stood there wringing their hands and wondering what possibly could be done. But David knew that God had another invisible army with plenty of firepower and no fear of Goliath.

We must be careful, however, that we do not picture David as a young enthusiast who "rushed in where angels fear to tread." There are missionaries who have plunged ahead when they lacked sufficient insight and experience and wound up paying a heavy toll for their imprudence. In our village work we have had our fingers burned more than once. We will be writing more about this aspect in the next chapter.

There were several reasons, however, why David could justly feel so ready to move ahead with his attack. He had a strong *assurance* within himself that this was exactly what the Lord would have him do at this time. "Faith is the *assurance* of things hoped for, the *evidence* of things not seen" (Heb. ll:l). And David not only possessed this firm inner assurance, but he also had a backlog of experience which served as *evidence* that the Lord was able and willing to use him in such a situation. And he readily and convincingly presents this evidence directly to king Saul himself. He said, "Your servant has been keeping his father's sheep. When a lion or a bear came and carried off a sheep from the flock, I went after it, struck it, and rescued the sheep from its mouth. When it turned on me, I seized it by its hair, struck it and killed it. Your servant has killed both the lion and the bear. This uncircumcised Philistine will be like one of them, because he has defied the armies of the living God."

This last phrase brings out David's third basis of confidence for surging ahead. The enemy had overstepped himself and had begun to defy and blaspheme the living God. Whenever this happens, we can be quite sure that the Almighty is already lining up His forces to do battle.

David's own brothers, the king, and probably a good many others tried to hold him back and pound some sense into his head. And this lack of faith and understanding on their part is a very common trait today. But it didn't frighten or hinder David. He had had dealings with the Lord which they knew little about, and he had experience to back him up and make him strong. So there was an unmistakable certainty encompassing his spirit. "The Lord who delivered me from the paw of the lion and the paw of the bear will deliver me from the hand of this Philistine."

David's Primary Weapons

At first it might appear that armor and weapons were the very things David didn't have. King Saul tried to fit him out with a heavy coat of armor, plus a sword, but David's final reply was: "I cannot go in these, because I have not tested them." So he took them off. It was a case of *not* relying on unproved, borrowed suggestions from others.

I tend to feel that the "simple" items of equipment which David did take with him can well be looked at as parables of our own spiritual weapons. First it mentions that he took his staff with him. Another of God's warriors who made great use of his staff was Moses. Many great and mighty things were accomplished with Moses' staff. David also used his staff to slay the lion and the bear. In our spiritual warfare today, a parallel might be drawn between the staff and our Lord's cross. Certainly this is one of our weapons. It is the absolute and final sign to Satan and all his forces that he is a usurper. His authority is finished! His rights are now null and void! All his ownership is over! He is bankrupt of any property of his own! We should always go forth with His cross as our vanguard.

The next sentence reads that he "chose five smooth stones from the stream, put them in the pouch of his shepherd's bag, and with his sling in his hand, approached the Philistine." So here we want to take a good close look at these weapons.

Let us begin with the fact that he chose five smooth stones from the stream and put them into his shepherd's pouch. This is not the way a modern day military man would approach his enemy, but I wonder if it is not meant to say something to modern-day missionaries about the way we should approach our enemy. We know (from Eph. 6:17) that the Holy Spirit's primary weapon is the Word of God. When the Lord Jesus did battle with Satan in the wilderness, He chose three smooth stones and slung them at His adversary with mighty power, using His sling, "It is written."

If, each time we prepare for a session of warfare praying, we first take time to choose out a few suitable stones from God's Word and prepare to sling these at our enemy, I think we will discover that the Holy Spirit can use them to accomplish some encouraging victories. This is becoming my experience.

I say that this is "becoming" my experience, for at first I was very awkward at using my sling, and I find this to be the common case with others too. I don't know if you have ever put together an actual sling of the type David used. I made one when I was a boy and found that with a bit of practice I could hurl stones with tremendous force. My main problem was controlling the direction!

It is interesting to note that David's original ragtag army of 600 men were Benjamites who could sling stones as effectively with their left hand as with their right (1 Chron. 12:2). And in another place it speaks of the Benjamites as being able to sling stones so accurately that they could hit their target to a hair's breadth (Jdg. 20:16). These warriors of David's became an awesome lot who never seemed to lose a battle.

When we learn to choose suitable stones and sling them with force and accuracy at the enemy and his forces, we will begin to win more battles and to win them more quickly. Therefore I feel it is in order to share a few suggestions from my own experience.

I now have five smooth stones which I keep in my "shepherd's pouch" at all times. They are the following verses from God's Word, which I always sling with that effectual power of "It is written":

1. All must bow before *His name:* Philippians 2:9-10.

2. I am invited to trust *His power:* Ephesians 6:10.

3. He is head of all *authority:* Colossians 2:10.

4. He has triumphed over all His enemies on *His cross:* Colossians 2:15.

5. He holds the position of highest *glory:* Revelation 19:16.

You may, of course, choose a different set of stones to keep in your pouch, and that is fine, but I suggest that you get together your basic collection. (In the section of the Prayer Companion entitled "Warfare Prayers," we have included one example of a prayer employing these "five stones.")

Now, apart from what I have termed a "basic collection," one needs to give special thought to the *more specific* needs of each particular encounter. For instance, I recently felt very compelled to go to battle for the need in the lives of two of my friends who seemed to be overcome by the spirit of "time-wasting." As I thought about how this malady was really wrecking their ministry, the Holy Spirit seemed to lead me to think of

that verse in Ephesians 5:16: "Making the most of your time, because the days are evil." In my praying I began to order any of
the spirits of the Evil One which might be involved in the problem to retreat. "For *it is written* that we Christians are to be making the most of our time. It is therefore not according to our
Lord's will for time to be wasted, so I command any such hindering spirits to go where He would send you, and cease your attacks on _____and _____."

Perhaps another example is in order. One of the adversary's
most common tactics is to bring discord between a couple of the
Lord's soldiers, or even divisions between ranks at higher echelons. This, of course, is very displeasing to the Holy Spirit and
can slow down a whole section of His operations. There are a
number of "smooth round stones" from God's free-flowing
stream of living water which could be fitted into our sling at such
times, and hurled at our enemy. But one I have found especially
effective is Ephesians 4:31. I remind the Evil One and his forces
that "It is written we are to 'get rid of all bitterness, rage and anger, brawling and slander, along with every form of malice,'
therefore I command all of you involved in this attack of disharmony to back away and go where He says you are to go."

When we are quoting Scripture, we know we are giving orders according to His will and therefore can with confidence
"stand firm against the schemes of the devil." Yes, stand firm
then, and expect him to "be gone"! For surely if we, God's children, must abide by that which "is written," the forces of evil
even more so are controlled by His Word. And this brings us to
our next step, which I will introduce with a question. How can a
group of students or village workers most effectively use their
sessions of warfare praying when they gather to prepare for some
special assault into enemy territory?

This past summer the Village Gospel Mission scheduled
seven such offensives into their various areas of outreach. There
were twenty to thirty college students and other mature young
people as well who signed up for each of these maneuvers. The
plan was to begin each ten-day campaign with two or three days
of fasting and prayer. This was an admirable plan, but the first
couple of ventures showed up two major problems. First, those

participating in these preliminary periods of warfare prayer
didn't really know how to deal head-on with their unseen opponents and were therefore quite reluctant to do so. The second
problem was related to the first. Since they were so unskilled in
wielding the weapon of the Word, their efforts of outreach which
followed resulted in more counterattacks from the enemy than
deliverance of his captives.

From then on they began to practice building their sessions
of warfare prayer and praise around some portion of God's
Word, and the results were very different. A real entrance was
made into the enemy's grounds, and in each case some solid fruit
was gathered into the little village church.

Although we have four other major weapons: prayer, worship, His names, and His cross (which we should also learn to
utilize in battle), we must never forget that our primary implement of warfare is the Word of God. There is no substitute for
His written Word skillfully wielded by His child in battle.

For the benefit of those who might appreciate knowing
which portions of Scripture they chose as the groundwork for
their warfare prayer sessions this summer, I will list them below.
Please note that each of these passages is not just a single verse,
as were the "smooth stones," but they are more extended portions
of several paragraphs, which include much vital material.

1. "It is written...": Matthew 4:1-11.
2. "All is under His feet...": Ephesians 1:15-23.
3. "Every knee must bow...": Philippians 2:5-22.
4. "All was made by Him...": Colossians 1:9-20.
5. "He is worthy to reign...": Revelation 5:1-14.

Each of their sessions was composed of an hour or so of
worship, followed by an hour and half of verse by verse working
their way through one of these passages in attack-prayer,
...slinging stones!

It is worth noting that a warrior wielding his sling doesn't
just hurl stones broadside at the whole attacking army, hoping to
strike one or two of the enemy's troops. Rather, he picks out a
particular target and aims well to strike him down. It is much
simpler and easier to pray in general for the Lord to drive back
all the forces of evil in a given town or village. But we will find

our prayers much more effective if we aim our missiles precisely.

For instance, in our various sessions of warfare praying for a particular area, we could first direct our attack on those forces controlling the school. Even more specifically, we could pray against those powers of the Evil One which are holding back the principal, the teachers, the students and the parents. Another time we could focus on those which are hindering the village magistrate and other individuals in positions of authority. Other targets are those tough demonic rulers controlling the temples, priests, sorcerers, and the whole retinue of heathen spiritism. None of these are too difficult for the Lord of Hosts. More than one Buddhist priest or sorcerer has turned to the Lord in Taiwan. We need to move out with confidence as David did against Goliath!

David's Other Weapons

Now we must come back to the story of David and Goliath and make a few other observations. As David and his enemy approached each other, the giant "looked David over and saw that he was only a boy, ruddy and handsome, and he despised him."

There are very good reasons why David was ruddy and handsome, and there are equally good reasons why Goliath despised him. David was in the pink of health. And an even greater factor was that he was in top spiritual health. We don't have to read very many of David's psalms to get a picture of David's devotional life. He spent much time in the Holy Place and in the Most Holy Place. "One thing I ask of the Lord, this is what I seek," he said, "that I may dwell in the house of the Lord all the days of my life, and gaze upon the beauty of the Lord and to seek Him in His temple" (Ps. 27:4).

The more David gazed upon the beauty of the Lord, the more he worshiped Him. David was a master at the art of worship. This was one of the unseen weapons which was always part of David's kit. The Philistine couldn't see this invisible weapon, but he could see David's ruddy, handsome face.

This of course made Goliath very angry, for he knew that by comparison he himself was very ugly. Though he towered over everyone else at nine feet in height and was very strong, yet he carried no beauty on his face. Our enemy too, is extremely powerful and to many very fearful, but there is nothing of elegance or loveliness to attract those who appreciate true beauty. And he knows it. He therefore fears and disdains those who, by virtue of a life of worship, are ruddy and handsome. He can't bear it. Worship becomes a potent weapon which he cannot and will not abide.

Then a few verses further on we are introduced to another of David's weapons. David said to the Philistine, "You come against me with sword and spear and javelin, but *I come against you in the name of the Lord of Hosts*, the God of the armies of Israel, whom you have defied. This day the Lord will hand you over to me, and I will strike you down and cut off your head." David was very clear as to the source and nature of his power. He often employed the names of the Lord in times of battle. And he knew *how* to use the Lord's names as a weapon. We will discuss his use of this weapon a little later.

First we should notice his straight forward attack. "*I come against you*." He did not just sit in his tent and pray that the Lord would deal with Goliath. Probably a good number of the Israelite soldiers were doing just this type of praying, but they were discovering that it brought no response from the Lord. God could have wiped out Goliath the first time he strode out to make his blasphemous boast or the first time anyone prayed and asked Him to. But the Lord waited for forty days for a David to come along and take the matter directly in hand. Fifty thousand Israelite soldiers, plus you and I, needed to learn this basic lesson in spiritual warfare.

We need not be afraid to speak out to our unseen harassing opponent with the forthright words, "I come against you," and "I command you." In fact this is the stance we *must* take if we are to see any kind of prompt results. Otherwise things can be drawn out over a long, discouraging period, which may cause us to give up altogether as the Israelite army was being forced to do. With all the backing we have in God's Word, we who are seated with Christ in the heavenly position of rulership are to be as definite and forceful as David was. We of course make our demands according to the will of our Commander-in-Chief. But once we are convinced that a given attack of the enemy is a thing which would surely have been "bound in heaven," then we are to be bold to "bind it on earth."

There is one caution here which should be mentioned. Even though our enemy may be vile and cruel, we are not to *rebuke* him. That is not our prerogative. All rebuke belongs to God. In Jude we are warned not to "slander celestial beings." For "even the archangel Michael, when he was disputing with the devil...did not dare to bring a slanderous accusation against him, but said, 'The Lord rebuke you'" (Jude 8,9).

It is imperative to keep in mind that there is a great difference between a command and a rebuke. Some Christians are too timid to do either, while others are so rash as to attempt both. Our proper posture should be that of a commanding officer who himself is under a higher command. Our objective in all our spiritual warfare is the glory of God and His kingdom. So we must be careful that we do nothing in a manner which would detract rather than add to that glory.

Now we look at the rest of David's statement. "I come against you *in the name* of the Lord of Hosts, the God of the armies of Israel." What he is really saying (in using God's names) is, "I come against you in the authority and the power of the almighty God, and with the backing of His unseen armies." The names of God were very meaningful to David, and they stood for exactly what they meant. They were reliable, vital and usable. David makes much use of God's names in his prayers and in his worship in the Psalms.

I fear that much of the time our enemy is more aware of the potency of the names of God than we are. James tells us that the demons most definitely believe in all the powerful aspects of God's being, and tremble every time they think of it. We need to learn how to seize upon this truth and employ it in our attacks against them.

Many of God's names carry a military significance. (There is a list of these in the Warfare section of the Prayer Companion.) And each of these is meant to equip us with a certain area of confidence and competence. We can brandish these names before our enemy with great expectancy and authority. The Lord will stand behind His own name, and He will accomplish His will. We may not always understand all the details of His plan, but we can and should expect to see "great and mighty things" take place.

After David's weapons (visible and invisible) brought Goliath down, David ran up and cut off his head with the giant's own sword. Our enemy's sword is *fear*. He holds his subjects under control by fear, and he holds back many of God's people by fear, just as Goliath held back God's people by fear. This, of course, is not at all the way things ought to be. Our adversary should be the one to fear us. Paul begins his primary passage on spiritual warfare with the words "be strong in the Lord, and in the power of His might." In other words, we need to develop the acumen and bravery in our approaches to the point of such assurance that we can actually slay the enemy with his own sword.

Before proceeding further, we should probably deal with the problem some might have as to "How effective are our weapons at long range?" David's encounter with Goliath, all the Old Testament battles, and all the spiritual conflicts faced by the Lord and His disciples were at close range. And since neither Satan nor any of his subjects are omnipresent, how can we do battle with them at a distance, several miles away, or even halfway around the world?

I certainly do not claim to understand the communications system of the spirit world, but we do find several relevant indications in Scripture. Since we are assured that Satan's emissaries are fallen angels, we conclude that they are endowed with the same qualities as God's angels. The book of Hebrews describes these by quoting from the Psalms: "He makes His angels winds" (Heb. 1:7; Ps. 104:4). Other passages as well give the impression that these spirit beings can move about almost instantaneously and that the transmission of information by their telegraph network is almost immediate. In fact, the word for angel in the original Greek text means "one sent," or "messenger." And the verb form means "to tell" or "announce."

Coming back to the first chapter of Hebrews, which has a good bit to say about angels, we find the conclusion in the last verse: "Are not all angels ministering spirits sent to serve those who will inherit salvation?" In other words, it appears that when we issue our commands to any of the evil spirits, God's angels will see to it that they get the message, no matter how far away they are geographically.

Now, to finish off this chapter, we must look at the two-part conclusion. "When the Philistines saw that their hero was dead, they turned and ran. Then the men of Israel and Judah surged forward with a shout and pursued the Philistines to the entrance of Gath and to the gates of Ekron. Their dead were strewn along the Shaaraim road."

Victory is a very contagious thing. Once the enemy is driven back in one village, we become brave to chase him back in other villages. And once he has lost ground in one area, he knows he is likely to lose ground in another. So our goal and plan should be to keep him in retreat. Another encouraging way to view it all is that victory begets victory. The battle may become extremely fierce for a time, but we must never give up. We are most certainly on the winning side.

The second half of the conclusion is better still. When the Israelites returned from chasing the Philistines, they plundered their camp. And this is always our final objective—to plunder the enemy's camp, to collect the spoil, to see the captives freed. In other gospel terminology, it is to reap a harvest and gather in the fruits of our labors.

It is thrilling to be able to experience a well-won victory, and this is intended to be one of the joys of the Christian life. Not only did the Lord mean for David, Joshua and a few others to enjoy such triumph, but He desires you and me to likewise be victors in our conquests.

Perhaps another of the reasons David was victorious so much of the time was that he remembered all the encouragements God had given His people in regard to their previous battles. We close with one of these from Moses' challenging farewell:

"Hear, O Israel. You are now about to cross the Jordan to go in and dispossess the nations greater and stronger than you, with large cities that have walls up to the sky. The people are strong and tall—Anakites! You know about them and have heard it said:

'Who can stand up against the Anakites?' But be assured today that the Lord your God is the one who goes across ahead of you like a consuming fire. *He will* defeat them, He will subdue them before you. And *you will* drive them out and destroy them quickly, *as the Lord has promised you*" (Dt. 9:1-3).

18

JEHOSHAPHAT AND THE SYRIANS

The story of king Jehoshaphat's encounter with the Syrian hordes (2 Chron. 20) is one of the most moving episodes in all of Israelite history. I feel it contributes some very helpful insights to our arsenal of spiritual warfare principles. The account begins: "After this, the Moabites, Amonites, with some of the Meunites came to make war on Jehoshaphat." We should pause right here and look at those first two words: "after this." We are of course being led to check back into the previous chapter. When we look at chapter 19, we find that king Jehoshaphat had just instituted some wide-sweeping reforms to draw his people back into a righteous walk with the Lord.

"He went out again among the people from Beersheba to the hill country of Ephraim and turned them back to the Lord, the God of their fathers. He appointed judges in the land. ...He told them, 'Consider carefully what you do, because you are not judging for man, but for the Lord, who is with you whenever you give a verdict. Now let the fear of the Lord be upon you. Judge carefully, for with the Lord our God there is no injustice or partiality or bribery.' In Jerusalem also, Jehoshaphat appointed some of the Levites, priests and heads of Israelite families to administer the law of the Lord, and to settle disputes. ...He gave them these orders: 'You must serve faithfully and wholeheartedly in the fear of the Lord....You are to warn them not to sin against the Lord; otherwise His wrath will come upon you and your brothers...Act with courage, and may the Lord be with those who do well.'"

Reading these lines enables us to see why Jehoshaphat's unseen enemy laid out such a massive attack against him. All that spiritual departure which the Evil One had been accomplishing among God's chosen people was being halted and turned completely around. So this evil monster set himself to show the world, and especially Israel's weak believers, that too much righteousness is not good. It doesn't stave off trouble. In fact it rather will bring trouble. He was determined to see that this revival effort spread no further. And he knew that a good way to halt any spiritual advance is to embroil the whole regime in war. This would certainly destroy their preoccupation with the virtues of God's kingdom and divert their attention to the more urgent issues of self-preservation.

But it didn't work out that way for a man like Jehoshaphat. True, he was very fearful when he heard of the threatening disaster, but he was one who knew at least the preliminary steps to take. When all seems about to be hopelessly lost, what should God's child do?!

Jehoshaphat—Spiritual Engineer

Modern military strategists make every possible use of all the latest research and developments in science and engineering. In fact, they unceasingly carry on research of their own to supply their armies with the most powerful and effective weapons possible. So actually, much of modern warfare is carried on around the scientists' conference table, in the drawing room, and in the laboratory. Progress in these efforts has made unbelievable advance in warfare power and technique.

When I first came to Taiwan nearly forty years ago, most everything in the construction realm was done by hand, employing only human force and strength. Cement was mixed by hand and transported even to the upper stories by laborers with carrying poles. Every piece of lumber was sawed and planed by hand. Foundation trenches and basements were dug by hand, etc. Even empty freight cars at the railways depots were moved about by calling together twenty or thirty "coolies." Today the picture has changed. Powerful machines do all the heavy work. Men merely operate this equipment.

In the realm of warfare, it was not too many centuries ago that soldiers fought with swords and spears. Today they use tanks, planes, missiles and atomic bombs. Enemies think twice before they attack one of the superpowers. In like manner, our spiritual enemy should be fearful of attacking us or our ministry, because we should be to him a superpower. But too often this is not the case. Instead of waiting on the Lord to align ourselves and equip ourselves with His infinite might and know-how, we barge ahead in our own strength and try to tackle the "Strong One." But this doesn't accomplish much, and never will!

However, wise old Jehoshaphat didn't go at it that way. He was a spiritual engineer. He knew that the very limited strength of his physical troops was no match for the enemy's "vast army" (seen and unseen), which was facing him. He didn't immediately issue an order for his men to march out to battle and then hope the Lord would undertake and give some measure of victory. No, Jehoshaphat was much too aware of the facts of the situation, (the intelligence report regarding the enemy's strength). He was too wise and experienced to be satisfied with weak, human weapons. He was determined to align himself and his forces with those hosts which are almighty and all-knowing (even though it might slow things down a bit, and perhaps appear overly pious for a respectable confident leader and strategist to operate that way).

"Jehoshaphat was afraid and set his face to seek the Lord. He proclaimed a fast throughout all Judah. So Judah gathered together to seek help from the Lord; they came from all the cities of Judah to seek the Lord."

It is always good to give special notice to those words which the Holy Spirit uses *repeatedly* in any given passage of Scripture. In the above two verses, the term "seek the Lord" is used three times. Therefore, like Jehoshaphat, the spiritual engineer, we will do well to make this the first step in each of our campaigns. Let us now turn our attention to this vital, basic, first step of seeking the Lord.

We need to give some serious study to this item, for there are several factors which should be involved in seeking the Lord, and there are varying degrees of seeking the Lord. Then, too, the very concept of seeking the Lord means different things to different people, and for some it may even be merely a vague term. I readily acknowledge that I am still a learner myself. However, as a starter, we would no doubt all agree that the first and primary factor is prayer.

The Size of Jehoshaphat's Prayer Meeting

Let us begin here with a quantitative analysis of the number of people involved in Jehoshaphat's prayer meeting. We have all heard it stated that the most essential element in bringing revival is for masses of God's people to band themselves together to plead for His special intervention. In the verses before us it mentions that Jehoshaphat sent out his notice to "all Judah," and that "indeed they came from every town in Judah." Then as we look on down a few verses it is repeated that "all the men of Judah, with their wives and children and little ones, stood there before the Lord." This could have been well over a million people.

In a recent testimony describing the Lord's mighty working among the "impossible" areas of Argentina, my attention was drawn to one statement which I feel had no small significance. The speaker mentioned that in preparation for one of their most difficult and yet strategic spiritual battles, they called together people from all the different denominational groups to seek the Lord. The response was most gratifying because it was almost complete. Even the separatist bodies joined in. The Lord is especially pleased when His body can join together and function with such unity of concern. This is a sure sign that something extraordinary is about to take place.

We must not forget that when any kingdom begins to speak of an all-out war, they are talking about something of enormous magnitude. Often several nations are involved, as was the case with Jehoshaphat. And even one nation of any size usually has several armies. An army is usually composed of two or more corps. And each corp consists of several divisions. A division is made up of brigades or regiments, which are composed of battalions. Battalions include several companies, which are divided into platoons, and these are made up of squadrons. Each squadron has perhaps a dozen or so individual soldiers.

God's Word would have us understand that our enemy Satan also has his "princes," "armies," "rulers," "hosts," "authorities," "powers," "forces," "demons," etc., which surely correspond to the systematic military organization of a modern kingdom. So when we contemplate the "tearing down of strongholds," we must think in terms of mega-strength. A small squadron of individual soldiers doesn't tackle a whole regiment or division of enemy troops.

I feel this perhaps points up one reason why so many of our well-intentioned times of prayer seem to accomplish so little. All prayer is certainly heard by God and will therefore not go wasted. But I am beginning to wonder if one of the main reasons we so seldom see a massive breakthrough is that we so seldom have massive prayer meetings. Jehoshaphat did! "He who sows sparingly shall also reap sparingly; and he who sows bountifully shall also reap bountifully" (2 Cor. 9:6) Though this verse was originally used in regard to giving to God's work, it can also be applied to prayer.

I realize that we seldom can manage to assemble a million people together to seek the Lord as Jehoshaphat did. In fact, on the mission field our possible contacts may number only in the dozens. But still there is a salient principle here which is too often overlooked or minimized. The Lord desires His people to become a people of organized, corporate prayer. There is, of course, a place for individual prayer, the more the better. But He tells us that when two or three get together it is better still. And many Scriptures indicate yet more results can be expected when a group gets together, and still more power when the group is a large one.

Therefore, a missionary should cry unto the Lord, and "give Him no rest" until He supplies an abundance of prayer support on every level. A missionary's corp of prayer warriors, plus his on-the-scene prayer partners, and his backing of a praying church, should be held onto as his most valuable assets. It is easy to say that numbers don't count, but in some battle situations numbers (of the right kind) are the very essence of victory.

In one of the Taiwan village outreach ventures this past summer, the teams (even after their beginning days of prayer and fasting) were seeing very meager results. The leader decided to have one team remain back at headquarters and give themselves to united prayer while the others were in the field. From that very hour the whole picture changed, and captives began to be released.

We here in Taiwan have discovered in our encounters with

the enemy that when the battle gets hot, one of our enemy's first goals is to knock out our prayer meetings. He can interpose a dozen hindrances to keep people occupied and shackled. But this we must anticipate and utterly refuse! He has no rights to do this, and we must tell him so. We need to bind him and compensate for all his attacks by developing every kind of Spirit-led strategy God shows us to keep our heavy artillery functioning with full effectiveness.

Several times we have made reference to the Christians in Korea as prime examples of those who make much of prayer and fully enjoy the bountiful results. Korea is now a land brimming with a wonderful supply of the largest churches in the world. Brother Paul Cho, pastor of a church of half a million, has made the statement that probably the reason for such an outpouring of God's blessing upon their land is the great emphasis on prayer. The Christians in Korea are a people who for decades have banded themselves together daily for church-wide or even city-wide prayer sessions. They have early morning prayer vigils. They have prayer mountains, prayer caves, nights of prayer, and much prayer with fasting. No wonder the enemy's strongholds have been torn down in Korea.

But coming back now to the type of situation we face in a totally unreached field, such as the villages of Taiwan, we must realize that there exist strongholds of all sizes and on all levels. These stretch all the way from the demonized individual to the "gates of hades" which control a whole village or even a whole "hsiang" (a large cluster of towns and villages). And every one of these strongholds is a *strong*-hold, armed to the teeth and patrolled by powerful demons or legions of powerful forces. We dare not underestimate the enemy's strength. We have already written in another chapter about the failure of the Lord's disciples to cast the demon out of just one boy. The Lord replied, "*This kind* comes out only by prayer." And it is becoming evident that we have many of "this kind" here in Taiwan. This brings us to our next point, the time factor.

The Duration of Jehoshaphat's Prayer Meeting

"Seeking the Lord" can mean anything from thirty seconds to thirty days. And again (particularly in the realm of spiritual warfare) you pretty much "get what you pay for." Before the day of Pentecost, 120 people had gathered in the Upper Room to seek the Lord for ten days. This is something very few of us are used to. What do you do, hour after hour, for ten days? They didn't just divide up into a series of discussion groups, or insert a few tours around Jerusalem and its environs, or work out other novel ways of filling up the time. No! it says, "These all with one mind were continually devoting themselves to prayer" (Acts 1:14).

We love to read about all the wonderful things the Holy Spirit did in the Book of Acts. But as we do, we also need to do some reading between the lines. Those early believers knew something about quantitative and qualitative prayer which we rarely observe today. And we can't just bypass these references. For they are an integral part of the picture. To wittingly or unwittingly close our eyes to a primary means of power simply means less power. And "less power" in spiritual warfare can be a dangerous thing.

Now coming back to Jehoshaphat's prayer meeting, we probably must assume a period of several days (if not several weeks) of seeking the Lord. The land of Judah covered a sizeable territory. This prayer meeting was held in Jerusalem, but it clearly states that "they came from every town in Judah," and a good many of the towns of Judah were 100 miles (150 km.) distant. Since there were no telephones, cars, trains or buses, it took some time for the initial message to reach all the people, and another good while for them all to gather in one place. We can be sure that the first arrivals (from Jerusalem itself) did not just stand around waiting for the others to get there.

With such a fearsome enemy approaching, the people were not only eager but anxious and desperate to give themselves to seeking the Lord as soon as possible. For a heavy spirit of fear and intercession had come upon them. The latter half of the story presents a great emphasis on singing and rejoicing, but we must be careful that we do not too quickly skip over the first half of the chapter which lays the foundations for all the delightful results. There were those days (perhaps weeks) of earnest seeking the Lord before the break came.

As to the consideration of how to profitably spend a prolonged time in prayer, we can again pick up some helpful pointers from the basics of Jehoshaphat's prayer, which is very similar to the outline the Lord Jesus gave to His disciples. I well remember a very meaningful whole night of prayer which I attended a few years ago in Taipei. There were perhaps a hundred people present, and the leader used the "Lord's Prayer" as a guide. Like Jehoshaphat, we began with the rudiments of worship. "O Lord, God of our fathers, are you not the God who is in heaven? You rule over all the kingdoms of the nations. Power and might are in your hand, and no one can withstand You." Then he proceeded with a review of the wonderful things the Lord had done, moved into God's promises, and finally applied it all to our present need. Yes, the best way I know of to confidently, effectively, and with unflagging persistence maintain an extensive prayer vigil is to employ and apply portions of God's Word. (There are many such aids in the Prayer Companion which accompanies this book.) And this brings us to the consideration of their earnestness.

The Fervency of Jehoshaphat's Prayer Meeting

Jehoshaphat employed the most vital and effectual approach he knew of. He proclaimed a fast for all Judah. Then when they had all gathered before God's sanctuary, the temple, Jehoshaphat reminded them and the Lord of the words God had spoken to his predecessor, Solomon, when he dedicated that temple fifty years before: "If My people, who are called by My name, will humble themselves and pray and seek My face and turn from their wicked ways, then will I hear from heaven and will forgive their sin and will heal their land" (2 Chron. 7:14).

They had been turning from their wicked ways and now they were humbling themselves, praying and seeking His face with the self-abasing dimension of fasting. Jehoshaphat had assimilated the essential elements of spiritual warfare and now the

Holy Spirit was helping him to bring them into effective operation. So he was on the verge of seeing some tremendous developments. God promises, "Call unto Me, and I will answer you, and show you great and mighty things which you know not" (Jer. 33:3). One can "call" with various levels of intensity, depending on the magnitude of the problem.

Jehoshaphat faced a situation of life or death for perhaps millions of people, and we know that it included far more than just physical life or death, for the approaching armies were actually being propelled by Satan's forces. So Jehoshaphat chose the highest level of earnest supplication. I wonder if sometimes we missionaries who declare our concern for the *eternal* life or death of those held by the enemy today might not gain some helpful insights from this aspect of Jehoshaphat's prayer meeting.

I have recently read some very challenging sentences from the monthly prayer letters of a young missionary couple in a difficult spot on the east coast of Taiwan. They began their work in that area with a number of encouraging responses. But then in a few months it all fell apart, and they were back to square one. So they are now really crying out for help and in one letter concluded with these words: "What we need is a day-in, day-out, bombardment of prayer."

Previously they had asked for forty people to commit themselves to pray five minutes a day. This is not to be belittled, for forty times five equals more than three hours a day. But now they are realizing that even this is not enough. Their next letter entreated: "Pray your hearts out." They were getting desperate! And I feel they are on the right wavelength, being taught by the Spirit.

I realize that the emphases we have presented so far in this chapter may at first appear to be rather crass or mechanical:

Number of people multiplied by number of hours compounded by *degree of concern* = Results. But such an approach seems to be very significant to our Heavenly Father, for to Him it all implies a depth of *love* for the lost and perishing. Really, when you get down to it, only a genuine, Holy Spirit-generated *love* is going to bring a volume of people out to a prayer meeting to intercede for people they have never seen and keep them there for hours, crying out for mercy and deliverance. Jeremiah recorded what the Lord said to him: "You shall seek Me, and find Me, when you search for Me with *all your heart*" (Jer. 29:13). It all boils down to a matter of the *heart* of God's people. Where, actually, is the *heart* of each member of our church? Our student fellowship? Our missionary team?

We all know well that it is only the Holy Spirit who can burden the hearts of the many neutral Christians. But this truth can be accepted in either of two very different ways. Some accept it as an excuse for hopelessness and helplessness. But a wise leader will do all in his power to provide the Holy Spirit with the proper and most effective opportunities to change hearts. Jehoshaphat was just such a leader. Instead of just giving up and sending out his army in all their weakness, he "*resolved* to seek the Lord, and he proclaimed a fast for all Judah."

Some years ago when one of the student fellowship groups here in Taichung was at quite a low ebb, their sponsor left, so they had to invite another. This new advisor was strong on "seeking the Lord," so his first suggestion was that each week before their evening meeting, they give their supper hour to waiting on the Lord in prayer for His direction and anointing for the service. And of course this new sponsor was himself crying out to the Lord throughout the week for the Holy Spirit to implant a vital concern for "seeking the Lord" in the heart of each student. The results were astounding! These pre-service prayer entreaties grew to a half dozen sizeable groups; the meetings themselves were soon attended by well over a hundred students; and the spiritual tone of their meetings was exhilarating and heart moving.

This summer I attended a week-long discipleship training camp for three hundred college students. One element of their training was to gather in the meeting hall and spend half an hour quietly waiting on the Lord before each evening meeting. They had other small group and individual prayer times during the day, but to bring together three hundred earnest students in a thirty-minute exercise of "seeking the Lord" caused a spirit of great expectancy to rise over that whole camp and for their coming semester's on-campus outreach as well. We can be sure they will not be disappointed.

It all comes down to a matter of well thought-through priorities. Jehoshaphat was just such a leader. He was one who put first things first. And he had received great stimulus for all this from his great-great-grandfather, Solomon. For as Jehoshaphat continued reciting King Solomon's prayer of dedication for the temple, he came to that part: "If calamity comes upon us, whether by sword of judgment, or plague or famine, *we will stand in your presence* before this temple that bears your Name *and will cry out to You in our distress, and You will hear us and save us.*" And then on his own, Jehoshaphat added, "We have no power to face this vast army that is attacking us. *We do not know what to do*, but *our eyes are upon You.*" And this brings us to our next consideration.

Jehoshaphat Seeks God's Strategy

Seeking the Lord for deliverance in the throes of a spiritual battle must include the seeking of His strategy. In fact, this part of our preparation for a major spiritual assault is absolutely vital. Someone has stated it poignantly: "If you don't know what you are doing, Satan will eat you for breakfast." We not only need the Lord's power and the support of His unseen forces to assist us as we move into a given conflict; we also must have His battle plan.

This past summer in the various village outreach endeavors here in Taiwan, great progress was made in earnestly seeking the Lord. Before each assault the teams spent two to three days in worship, fasting and prayer. Yet in most villages there were only a few captives set free, and the counterattacks were extremely heavy. In other words, the conclusions to their approaches were very different from Jehoshaphat's.

In one area the wife of a new believer, on the verge of joining her husband in his new joyous faith, was struck by lightning. This brought great fear upon the rest of the villagers, causing them to draw back and become quite belligerent against the gospel. In another area the enemy focused his attacks on the family of one of the workers and "tore them to shreds." In one situation, two workers were disabled with broken bones and serious bruises. Several of the district prayer meetings on the island were completely shot down. The people just stopped coming. In other districts some of the staff experienced such stress that they thought of leaving.

Warfare is not child's play. It is for real. If our seeking the Lord only results in angering our enemy and calling forth his great wrath upon our efforts, we haven't gained a great deal. We must seek the Lord for His wisdom, direction, protection and the necessary cautions. "Therefore be careful how you walk, not as unwise men but as wise, making the most of your time, because the days are evil. So then do not be foolish, but understand what the will of the Lord is" (Eph. 5:15-17). In a previous chapter we have mentioned how even the Lord Jesus refused to get into conflicts with Satan which were not ordered of His Father.

We today, with the whole of the Old and New Testaments, are in quite a different situation from Jehoshaphat. We are expected to do more than merely ask for a direct revelation to tell us in a few words precisely what actions we are to take. The written Word of God is our handbook on the principles of war. On certain occasions the Lord does speak to His people and inform them of His specific will, but far more often it is "study to show yourselves approved unto God, workmen [or soldiers] who need not be ashamed, rightly handling the Word of Truth" (2 Tim. 2:15). Then we will not be shot down so readily.

We have already dealt with many of the warfare passages in the Scriptures, but since the clobbering received this summer here in these dark, idolatrous villages of Taiwan, chapters 10 and 11 of Luke's gospel have begun to open up to me. I feel these two chapters (with their related sections in Matthew's gospel) give us some much needed insights. In fact I am beginning to look upon those very familiar verses of Luke 11:9-10 as perhaps the primary key to spiritual warfare. I write them out here in an expanded form which fits in with the context and the meanings listed in Moulton's Greek Lexicon:

"I say unto you, 'Keep on asking [for the power and fruits of the Holy Spirit] and they will be given you; keep on seeking [searching after, pursuing, striving for His strategy and principles of warfare], and you will keep finding [detecting, discovering, acquiring, gathering new light]. And to him who keeps on knocking [at the gate of a given village or situation], the door will be opened [by the "Stronger One," who holds the keys of death and Hades]. For everyone who keeps on asking keeps receiving, and he who keeps on seeking keeps finding, and to him who keeps on knocking the doors and gates will be opened."

Now we need to go back and examine these amplifications piece by piece. The emphasis to "keep on" asking, seeking and knocking comes both from the tense of the Greek verbs and the Lord's parable of the importunate, persistent friend, which immediately precedes these verses. Also, the marginal note in the New American Standard Bible states that the passage should read "keep asking," "keep seeking," and "keep knocking."

The "asking" may primarily refer to the power and fruits of the Holy Spirit since the very next three verses stress the Father's willingness to give *the Holy Spirit* to those who ask Him. When we come to the next admonition to "keep on seeking" and we will "keep finding," we discover that the lexicon has an abundance of very descriptive synonyms for "seeking" and for "finding." These seem to present a strong indication that our warfare strategy comes, not usually from an instantaneous revelation, but from a continual perusal of the relevant passages in God's Word. Another reason for our so readily applying the "seeking" and "finding" to warfare strategy is that, as mentioned above, these two chapters, 10 and 11, have so much to do with this very issue, and the humility needed to obtain His strategy. "You have hidden these things from the wise and prudent, and revealed them to little children" (10:21). Also, there is the warning that we must not proceed without His strategy. "He who is not *with Me* is against Me, and he who does not gather with Me *scatters*" (11:23).

Therefore, it would seem that one place where the Taiwan village teams were in error this past summer was that even though they gave themselves at the beginning to a period of fasting and prayer, there was no "seeking" for His strategy, and then of course, no "finding" of His strategy. This was not the case with Jehoshaphat. The conclusion of his intercession was, "We have no power to face this *vast army* that is attacking us. *We do not know what to do*, but *our eyes are upon You*."

It is easy for us eager, ambitious beginners to bite off too quickly more than either our limited prayer support or our lack of God-given strategy can handle. Someone put it: "Never initiate more than you can saturate with prayer." I remember one young missionary, new to the field of Taiwan some years ago, who stated that he was praying that all the temples on this island would be closed down. But the number of temples has actually increased greatly since that time. What do we say to this? His sincere heart desire was indeed admirable, and our God is infinitely able, but we dare not over-simplify things. I know that this young man is now well aware of many of the factors involved in tearing down enemy strongholds. And Jehoshaphat knew one thing well. He knew that the enemy facing him amounted to a "vast army." In fact, this expression of a "vast army" is used repeatedly throughout the story. It greatly intensified their incentive to seek the Lord.

The Lord's Response

After Jehoshaphat's massive, extended and intense prayer session, the Lord responded with everything they needed. His response included quieting encouragement and clear directives, based on His wise and faultless strategy. He said, "Listen, King Jehoshaphat and all who live in Judah and Jerusalem! This is what the Lord says to you: 'Do not be afraid or discouraged because of this vast army. For the battle is not yours but God's. Tomorrow, march down against them. They will be climbing up by the pass of Ziz, and you will find them at the end of the gorge in the desert of Jerual. You will not have to fight this battle. Take up your positions; stand firm and see the deliverance the Lord will give you, O Judah and Jerusalem. Do not be afraid; do not be discouraged. Go out to face them tomorrow, and the Lord will be with you.'"

One of the significant items to be observed here is the triple repetition of the charge to *go*. Though He had assured them that "the battle is not yours" and "you will not have to fight this battle" and you will see "the deliverance the Lord will give you," it was still coupled with the thrice-repeated command to move out into the battle lines themselves. "Tomorrow, march down against them." "Take up your positions and stand firm." "Go out to face them tomorrow."

It is another graphic picture of the dual nature of His Great Commission. "All authority in heaven and earth is given to Me. *Go therefore,* ...and surely I am with you always, to the end of the age" (Mt. 28:18-20). True, He is the Lord of Hosts and has an infinite array of mighty, unseen armies at His command. And surely He can, and occasionally does, speak directly to the un-reached heathen by an angel or in a dream. But still, He has cho-sen as His primary mode of operation to send out human dis-ciples to be His visible troops. "As my Father has sent Me, so I am sending you" (Jn. 20:21).

Now let us come back again to that special promise of no need to fight in this battle. This was really a superabundance of extra grace. Joshua and his army certainly had to fight in their campaigns. David and his men had to fight hard in their en-counters. And so did most others who were God's men. Likewise do you and I, in the majority of our penetrations into enemy ter-ritory.

What then was so special about Jehoshaphat's case? Well, there was something unique about his approach. Neither Joshua, David, nor any one else had ever had such a prayer meeting, such a massive seeking of the Lord, as Jehoshaphat did. We can say what we will, but the fact seems to remain that our God par-ticularly honors that magnitude of turning to Him which involves all His people and all they've got. "You shall search for Me and find Me, when you seek Me with all your hearts [plural]" (Jer. 29:13). Or, to put it in a different way, the "Stronger One" takes over as we, His people, "keep on asking, seeking and knocking."

Jehoshaphat's Response

As we move ahead now to examine Jehoshaphat's response to the Lord's wonderful, encouraging word to His people, we have further opportunity to observe the spiritual stature of this man of God. He stood tall as a mountain. And the reason he was tall even in God's eyes was that he, being a king, was not hesitant to bow down with his face to the ground before all his subjects and give himself to worship.

"Jehoshaphat bowed with his face to the ground, and all the people of Judah and Jerusalaem fell down in worship before the Lord. Then some of the Levites from the Kohathites and Korahites stood up and praised the Lord, the God of Israel, with very loud voice.

"Early in the morning they left for the desert of Takoa. As they set out, Jehoshaphat stood and said, 'Listen to me, Judah and people of Jerusalem! Have faith in the Lord your God and you will be upheld; have faith in His prophets and you will be successful.' After consulting the people, Jehoshaphat appointed those who sang to the Lord and those who praised Him in holy attire, to go out before the army, and said, 'Give thanks to the Lord, for His lovingkindness is everlasting.'"

Jehoshaphat all along, made much of worship. Way back at the commencement of his big prayer meeting, he began his initial intercessions with the highest form of worship, acknowledging the Lord's transcendence, His sovereignty, and His mighty power. Now again, even before the victory has been won, he leads his people into such an atmosphere of glorifying God that they themselves move out in loud voices of praise. Then he appoints a special male chorus as a vanguard at the head of his army. Three times before the battle and twice afterward, he involves his people in worship.

In my own experience, I have found the two elements of worship and the Word to be the greatest aids to my prayer life. They are the greatest supports to faith. Proper, full-orbed worship directs our focus toward His majesty, greatness, wisdom, power and love. And this always creates a wonderful atmosphere of expectancy and triumph.

Quoting portions of God's Word, and prefacing each quotation with the firm, muscular grip of "Lord, You said..." or "It is written...," dispels all kinds of doubts and fears and greatly heightens one's confidence. When Jehoshaphat said, "Listen to me, Judah and people of Jerusalem! Have *faith* in the Lord your God—have *faith* in His *prophets*," he was putting a sword in their right hand and a shield in their left hand. For faith is our shield, and God's prophets (His Word) is our sword.

And that particular hour was a very crucial moment in the

whole sequence. They had received a marvelous encouragement from the Lord, and yet the "vast army" of the enemy was still headed for them with great fury. You can feel the inner struggles as Jehoshaphat does his best to reassure them all.

When he spoke to "Judah and all Jerusalem," he was not just seeking to build the morale of his army but to strengthen the supplications of all their beloved families who would most certainly be interceding for them as they marched forth to meet the foe. All the mothers would be praying for their sons; the wives would be praying for their husbands; sisters would be praying for their brothers; betrothed young maidens would be praying for their fiancees; children would be praying for their daddys, etc. It goes without saying that all these prayers would carry the deepest concern and lay full claim to the words of the prophet Jehaziel which had just been given to them.

In our missionary work, we often find ourselves in just such tense circumstances. We have by the Holy Spirit been reminded of some remarkable, amazingly applicable promise from God's Word which spurs us on, and yet the victory has not yet been won. The enemy is still very much there! At such times it is essential to know that there is a back-up army of mothers, sisters, brothers and children, who are crying out to God with the unfeigned concern of beloved kin. God's wonderful promises still need their prayer support.

In fact, the reason for so much spinning of wheels, so many stalemates, and so few actual breakthroughs in idolatrous areas is often due to insufficient teamwork on the part of the prayer constituency. And this is frequently the fault of the missionary himself. Unlike Jehoshaphat, he comes to the field with little understanding of what he is really getting into. He graduates from a sound seminary, attends cross-cultural seminars, raises his financial support, and leaves for his overseas assignment with perhaps even a hero's send-off. But the great problem is that when he says "goodbye" to his friends and supporters, it is actually too much of a goodbye. He is often spiritually quite on his own from that moment and therefore much weaker than he ever realizes.

I am coming to feel that when the Lord charged us to pray that He would send forth laborers into His harvest, He had no intention that the prayers for those laborers should cease or slacken off when they left for the harvest field. Rather, their departure for the front lines should cause a measure of almost painful concern to fill our hearts, as when a young lady's sweetheart, or a mother's son leaves for the battlefield. And this concern should manifest itself in daily earnest pleas for protection, spiritual strength, the Holy Spirit's fruit, and many victories.

The Great Commission was not given just to those few who go, but primarily to the rest of the body who send them. It is just as important, in fact more so, to be supported by a continuous undergirding of prayer when you go, as it is to go in the first place. It is just as important, in fact more so, to acquire your prayer backing before you leave home than to acquire your financial support.

Actually, in these last days, when the enemy is operating with "great wrath because he knows his time is short," there is mounting evidence to substantiate the conclusion that it is probably better not to send out a missionary to a heathen field if he does not have an ample supply of prayer partners. It is becoming a more and more common phenomenon for missionaries to find themselves so harassed by depression and frustration that they require special medication, counseling, or even repatriation back home.

Just as I have been writing this chapter, I have had two S.O.S. phone calls from a dear brother in a dark area crying out for help. The idol worshippers in his district (nearly the whole population) had begun a nine-day special series of heavy demonic "pai-pai." His first call came on the second day of these fanatical celebrations, and already his family had come under a very oppressive cloud. Four days later he called again, and he was filled with such strong, dark emotions that he could hardly speak. It was so unlike him, I was quite frightened. After some of us had a time of earnest prayer for his deliverance, binding again these new waves of the enemy's attacks, he called again to say that he now had release and was back at his work.

We may very well discover that when we begin to grasp the principle of buttressing our missionaries with enough prayer reinforcement, the Lord will send more out. Their material needs are by no means to be our primary consideration. Therefore, assembling prayer concern should probably be the most vital part of presenting the Great Commission. And if this is true, then we must conclude that the Holy Spirit is just as ready to place a burden for prayer in the hearts of the senders as He is to put a call to "go" in the heart of those being sent. Our problem seems to be that for some reason we place our emphasis on "going," and are almost blind to what is involved in "sending."

Neither we missionaries nor anyone else can, to any degree, manufacture prayer concern in the hearts of our senders. Only the Holy Spirit can do this. Therefore, this being the case, a young missionary preparing to leave for the field needs not only to pray in his financial support, but he also urgently needs to "keep on asking" until he "receives" a bountiful supply of genuinely committed co-laborers in prayer. And if at all possible, he should appoint one of them as convener and challenge them to get together periodically to stimulate and encourage one another in praying together for him and his work.

In the apostle Paul's main treatise on spiritual warfare, he begins with the words, "Be strong in the Lord, and in the strength of His might." (Following this, he urges us to protect ourselves with the various pieces of our armor.) Then he finally concludes with the *means* of being strong in the Lord. "With all prayer and petition pray at all times, in the Spirit, and with this in view, be on the alert with all perseverance and petition for all the saints" (Eph. 6:10,18).

Paul was a missionary who was always out in the thick of things, so he was very diligent about keeping up his backing of faithful prayer warriors. We have previously mentioned a number of his calls for help in prayer, but again it might be a worthwhile reminder to us if we recorded here a few more of his written pleas for such support.

"I urge you brothers, by our Lord Jesus Christ and by the love of the Spirit, to strive together with me in your prayers to God for me" (Rom. 15:30).

"On Him we have set our hope, that He will continue to deliver us, as you help us by your prayers. Then many will give thanks on our behalf for the gracious favor granted us in answer to the prayers of many" (2 Cor. 1:10,11).

"Pray also for me, that whenever I open my mouth, words may be given me so that I will fearlessly make known the mystery of the gospel, for which I am an ambassador in chains. Pray that I may declare it fearlessly, as I should" (Eph. 6:19,20).

"Pray for us, too, that God may open a door for our message, so that we may proclaim the mystery of Christ, for which I am in prison. Pray that I may proclaim it clearly, as I should" (Col. 4:3,4).

"Brothers, pray for us" (1 Thess. 5:25).

"Brothers, pray for us that the message of the Lord may spread rapidly and be honored, just as it was with you. And pray that we may be delivered from wicked and evil men" (2 Thess. 3:1,2).

Deliverance of the captives on the mission field does not come automatically just because missionaries go there and preach the gospel. No, it is equally due to the knee-work of those who are behind them (perhaps several thousand miles away) cloistered away in some room crying out to the Lord for all the spiritual supplies and munitions, and all the fruits of the Spirit needed to get the job done.

Sooner or later, almost every missionary gets to the place where he has to call out, "Father, I just can't go on any further without some more solid prayer backing." For it is usually the case that even well-begun prayer support begins to lag and needs to be periodically rejuvenated. And if our prayer partners are not quickened and renewed and kept keen, there will inevitably come a great waste of missionary time on the field, and the thousands of dollars spent to get him there and keep him there can become pretty much of a lost investment.

The Grand Finale

Now we come to the delightful part of this story—the part which has made it such an attractive oasis in the record of Kings and Chronicles in the Old Testament:

"As they began to sing and praise, the Lord set ambushes against the men of Ammon and Moab and Mt. Seir who were invading Judah, and they were defeated. The men of Ammon and Moab rose up against the men from Mt. Seir to destroy and annihilate them. After they finished slaughtering the men from Seir, they helped to destroy one another. When the men of Judah came to the place that overlooks the desert and looked toward the vast army, they saw only dead bodies lying on the ground no one had escaped. So Jehoshaphat and his men went to carry off their plunder, and they found among them a great amount of equipment and clothing and articles of value more than they could take away. There was so much plunder that it took three days to collect it."

We all love that statement, "As they began to sing and praise, the Lord set [unseen] ambushes—and they [the enemy's forces] were defeated." This should lend great inducement to us to become effective in wielding our weapon of worship. However, at the risk of being redundant, I would reiterate that their times of worship had been preceded by a voluminous time of intercession. The reason for this emphasis is that generally the common focus given to this whole chapter is on the great value of worship, while the significant groundwork of the first part is overlooked. An adequate exegesis leads us to see that whereas our prayers and petitions need to include much worship, our worship must also be accompanied by adequate intercession. On the mission field we need uplifting and enjoyable worship, but we must also learn the more arduous task of supplication. All of God's great warriors have given themselves to both.

Now let's come back to the twofold victory described in our story. The enemy was destroyed and much plunder was gathered in. These two are always related. Though the reaping of the "plunder" (a harvest of new believers) is our goal, it cannot be achieved until the enemy has been properly overcome. "How can one enter a strong man's house and plunder his goods, except he first bind the strong man? Then he can plunder his house" (Mt. 12:29).

The marvelous deliverances now taking place in the villages of Argentina, according to their own testimonies, are due to the initial victory of overcoming the Strong Man in each sector. We have not yet seen this accomplished in Taiwan. And it may take us awhile, since this island holds the reputation of being the most idolatrous nation in the world (especially in its villages).

Then too, it is hardly possible to expect *all* missionary work to proceed with the seeming ease and with such complete victory as Jehoshaphat's army experienced. Even the apostle Paul and his team encountered almost relentless counterattack and many setbacks. In most every place, he was run out of town. He was stoned, beaten, shipwrecked, spent much time in prison, etc. But the story of Jehoshaphat's outstanding victory is still meant to give us great encouragement and to point out some valuable spiritual principles.

One helpful encouragement, which we must not overlook, comes from the description of the plunder which they were able to gather. It amounted to "a great supply of equipment, garments and articles of value." If we interpret this in terms of a missionary's spiritual harvest, it speaks of the qualities and talents of the lives which are brought into the Lord's kingdom when the breakthrough comes. Into His church will come those who are equipped by the Holy Spirit to fill the necessary posts of service. Their contributions will all be of real value, and each will be wearing a new and beautiful garment of praise to the Lord.

Conclusion

Jehoshaphat didn't forget to say "thank you." In fact he saw to it that his people entered into the full experience of *several* joyous praise sessions.

"On the fourth day they assembled in the Valley of Baracah, where they praised the Lord. This is why it is called the Valley of Baracah to this day. Then, led by Jehoshaphat, all the men of Judah and Jerusalem returned joyfully to Jerusalem, for the Lord had given them cause to rejoice over their enemies. They entered Jerusalem and went to the temple of the Lord with harps and lutes and trumpets. The fear of the Lord came upon all the kingdoms of the countries when they heard how the Lord had fought against the enemies of Israel."

That valley, which just a few days before had been but a vale of fear and hopelessness, had now become a cathedral of praise and worship to their mighty, majestic, loving God. "That is why it is called the Valley of Beracah [praise] to this day." It had become a living, lasting memorial of the magnificent, joyous victory which can be won by God's people. And the sweetness of the fruits of such victories are to be savored over and over again throughout the years.

I personally am tremendously grateful for certain victories which the Lord has granted me from time to time during my missionary career. And they bring much joy and spiritual uplift every time I look back and praise Him for them. Each of these victories came as a result of a prolonged period of spiritual warfare. And they came after I learned to accompany my intercessions with worship, fastings, and a bountiful supply of "You said in Your Word..."

The ensuing triumphs were amazing to the point of being more than I had asked or thought possible. And their memories are a continual encouragement to expect more and more and greater and greater repeats of God's assured faithfulness. Jehoshaphat's God is also our God. We need to learn to seek Him as Jehoshaphat and his people did!

19

NAVAL ENCOUNTERS

There are times when some phase of the Lord's work, perhaps the project you are involved in, seems so battered about by the enemy that the whole thing is about to sink. I have experienced this more than once here in Taiwan. Any project designed to sail into "unreached" waters, which Satan considers to be his own private sea, is bound to draw heavy enemy fire. He will try desperately to sink the whole operation. The Village Gospel Mission has been on the verge of total collapse several times, even to the point that one of our executive committee meetings was called for the specific purpose of deciding how we would fold up gracefully and dispose of the various items of equipment. Our ship was shot through with gaping holes and going down rapidly. But the Lord didn't let it founder. He not only preserved it from submerging but opened our eyes to see what was really taking place and taught us many lessons in faith and militant prayer. Now the Village Gospel Mission has its hull repaired, is armed and moving ahead, withstanding the enemy's barrages, and capturing some of his craft

Most of us are landlubbers. We rather easily get seasick, especially in storms or during an enemy broadside. A rough sea, with that heavy, ceaseless wind, and those angry billows tossing our craft seem more than our sensitive make-up can handle. We much prefer the warm, cozy floating about in some friendly harbor. But the Lord Jesus, in order to pursue the extension of His kingdom, needs tough marines who have developed their sea legs and are as invincible on the sea as they are on land.

Therefore, as part of their military training, the Lord Jesus on two occasions took His disciples out on the Sea of Galilee for some encounters with their enemy. Each time it scared them half to death, and they really had little idea of what was occurring.

But they eventually began to get the picture.

These accounts of the disciples in the storms may at first appear to be mere records of the Lord's miraculous power over the forces of nature in the physical universe. But as we proceed we will begin to realize that the Lord was aware of far more taking place than His disciples ever conceived of at that time. This, of course, was usually the case. As we study the Scriptures, we like David need always to be asking the Lord to "open my eyes that I may behold those wonderful truths in Your word" (Ps. 119:18).

First Encounter—How to Maintain Peace

This first storm (Mt. 8:23-27 and Mk. 4:35-41) was no ordinary storm. Peter and his fellow fishermen had been in many squalls on the Sea of Galilee, and it is quite evident that they were not fearful men. But this time it appeared that the end had come. They were about ready to go down. And it *would* have been the end if the Lord hadn't "rebuked" the wind. The word "rebuke" here means to reprove or reprimand for a crimination. In the second storm (Mt. 14:22-23), it states that the wind was "contrary" to them. Again, the word "contrary" means against or opposed, from which comes the noun "enemy."

Their enemy Satan would have been very happy and relieved could he have succeeded in sending the whole boatload of these twelve trainees, plus their trainer, to the bottom of the lake. But one thing made that impossible. The Lord Jesus, the Son of God, the Master of all creation, was in that boat! Although He was sleeping peacefully on a pillow, He was there to take control of things at any time. In fact He was the One who had given the order to proceed across the lake in the first place.

"If the Lord is in it, it won't sink." There are times when we launch out on our own and commence some project which is purely our little idea, and then naturally we have no assurance that it won't capsize. And this again brings up the element of faith. For in the conclusion of each of these accounts, the Lord points out the disciples' *lack of faith.*

What is faith? The Scriptures give us a very clear definition. "Faith is the *assurance* of things hoped for, the *evidence* of things not seen" (Heb. 11:1). Proper faith must have assurance and evidence. If I am to be able to have faith, to be confident that the project that I am involved in will not sink, I must have the assurance that *He* is in it.

Before George Muller, that mighty man of faith, began the construction of each of his orphanages, he spent two to three months seeking the Lord's will. Once he was *assured* that the Lord was "in it," he would move ahead with perfect confidence no matter how many storms he encountered.

Before our home church accepted their present pastor, they invited him to come and speak. I shall never forget that first message. He reminded the congregation that "we *must* know God's will in this matter. If we have the assurance and evidence that *He* is calling us to accept this ministry, then we will surmount all difficulties. Otherwise we will be weak and flounder." After he and the church were both convinced that the Lord had given the orders, he came. The church has since seen some strong winds and high waves, but it has weathered each storm and is growing beautifully.

We would do well to keep handy some of the Lord's specific promises regarding His work which we can use as missiles to torpedo the enemy's craft:

"Who is the King of Glory? The Lord *strong and mighty*, the Lord *mighty in battle*...The Lord of *Hosts*, He is the King of Glory" (Ps. 24:8,10).

"*I will* build My church, and the gates of hell *shall not prevail* against it" (Mt. 16:18).

"Your will *be done* on earth as it is in heaven" (Mt. 6:10).

"Did I not tell you that if you believed [in My assurances], you would see the glory of God?" (Jn. 11:40).

"He raised Him from the dead and seated Him at His own right hand in the heavenlies, far above all principality, and might and dominion, and every name that is named...and He put *all things under His feet*" (Eph. 1:20,22).

"Christ *loved the church* and gave Himself up for her" (Eph. 5:25).

"At the *name of Jesus* every knee shall bow, of those in heaven, of those on earth and of those under the earth" (Phil. 2:10).

"*I* have set before you an open door, and *no man* can shut it" (Rev. 3:8).

"The Lamb *will overcome* them, because He is Lord of Lords and King of Kings" (Rev. 17:14).

The Lord Jesus rebuked the wind and there was a great calm. He would have *us* also learn how to bind the forces of evil, and we have already given several chapters to that.

One of Satan's common *techniques* which can quickly sink a work of God is pictured in both Matthew's and Mark's accounts. Matthew says, "There arose a great storm on the sea, so that the boat was being *swamped* by the waves." Mark makes it even more specific in his record: "A great storm of wind arose, and the waves beat *into the boat*, so that the boat was already filling." A ship in a storm is not in such serious trouble as long as the waves are outside the boat. But once those billows begin to break over into our craft, we could soon go down. The disciples knew this all too well. And you and I should know it too.

When the enemy begins to make waves *within* our church, our mission, our fellowship group, we should begin to cry to the Lord for help. And we should bail that water out of our boat as fast as we can. Many of God's useful enterprises have sunk to the bottom of the sea because waves began to beat into the boat and the storm was not quelled.

Even very spiritual organizations are not exempt. In fact these are the groups Satan most desires to sink. During my years in the Lord's service, I have seen at close range several churches, a seminary, and a godly mission go under because of the enemy's waves beating into the boat. One church which I attended for several years was growing at such a rate that before they could rebuild, the auditorium was packed and the basement overflowed with earnest worshipers. But Satan began to make waves inside the boat, and within a few months things began to splinter, and today that church is no more.

The storm (not the people involved) must be emphatically quelled at the first sign of any wave breaking over the sides. "We wrestle not against flesh and blood, but against...the spiritual forces of evil." And we can pray with great confidence for the Lord Jesus is the *King of Glory*. He will build His church, and at

His name every knee shall bow, especially those who attack His church.

We are eligible to claim these promises when we are operating according to the directives He has laid down in His Word. And He has given us a good bit of illumination on how to deal with the potential ruptures within His body. One passage reads: "Let all bitterness and wrath and anger and clamor and slander be put away from you with all malice. And be kind to our another, tender-hearted, forgiving one another, as God in Christ forgave you" (Eph. 4:32,33). These words are preceded with the warning "Grieve not the Holy Spirit of God." It is very grievous to God's Spirit when there is disharmony within His body.

This is why the Lord Jesus highly praised all efforts to calm every indication of discord among His people. He said, "Blessed are the peacemakers, for they shall be called the children of God." They have God's very nature at work in them.

Yes, as soon as we see any of Satan's waves beginning to slop over into our boat, we had better start bailing out this bilge as quickly as we can. I know of one pastor, the leader of a very large church, who prays every day for harmony among his staff of over a hundred men and women. He knows that eruption of the slightest degree of contention is a red light, a symptom of poison within the body, or a sign of a damaged hull. The boat is taking in Satan's sea water.

In Psalm 133, which is only three verses long, David wrote: "How good and how pleasant it is when brothers live together in harmony." And he ends his little poem with the benediction, "For there the Lord bestows His blessing, even life forevermore." Yes, there is blessing and abundant life when our ship is sailing on top of the waves, with no water inside it.

Second Encounter—How to Walk on Waves

In one sense we might say that the Lord Jesus was giving His students an examination when He took them out into the storms for these confrontations with their enemy. He was an excellent teacher. So, like any good instructor, He would give His pupils a few weeks of demonstrations and classroom instruction; then it was time for a test.

This second exam (Mt. 14:22-33) was decidedly more advanced than the first. This time Jesus was not physically present with them in the boat. Also the storm lasted considerably longer. The first storm was quieted within probably half an hour. This second lasted for the whole night, until about daybreak. Also the element of a "ghost" walking on the water was particularly terrifying. Again they were completely shaken up, as you and I certainly would have been.

The thing which began to quiet their fears, and which will quiet our fears too, was the word of the Lord Jesus. "Be of good cheer, it is I, don't be afraid." Then an amazing thing happened. Impulsive Peter suggested to the Lord that he climb overboard and walk on the waves to meet the Lord. And Jesus immediately said, "Come ahead!" So over the side went Peter, and he actually began to walk on top of those waves. It didn't last long, however. The churning billows and the whipping wind were just more than he could handle, so he began to go down.

In studying the various events in the four gospels, a good rule of thumb which will help us pick up the intended lessons is to examine the foibles of the disciples as compared to the magnificence of the Lord Jesus. A classic example was the chattering Peter on the Mount of Transfiguration, when the whole scene was to exhibit the glory of God's majestic Son. "He was still speaking, when *behold*, a bright cloud overshadowed them, and a voice from the cloud said, 'This is My beloved Son; *listen to Him*'" (Mt. 17:5).

Therefore, when the Lord spoke to His disciples in the midst of this storm saying, "Take heart, it is I, don't be afraid," He was seeking to calm their fears but primarily to direct their attention to Himself and what He was doing. It was as if He were saying to them, "See, I am walking on top of the waves of this storm, and I want you to learn how to do so too."

He was not particularly interested that they become able to physically walk on water, for that would be of little practical use to them and could give rise to all sorts of pride and confusion. Rather the focus in the conclusion to each of these storm stories was on their need for faith. And faith is what they were going to need in great quantities after He left them and they encountered other storms in the book of Acts.

Now faith is a very different thing from daring and bravado. Peter had plenty of these. He was extremely impulsive, very lacking in the kind of faith which he really needed to face the tempests of life which would soon be upon him.

It is significant that the book of Acts begins with "the sound of a mighty, rushing wind" and then the coming of the Holy Spirit to equip them for a ministry which would "turn the world upside down." Within the next few days after the coming of the Spirit, Peter and John had twice been arrested, locked up in prison, and beaten. A little further on Stephen was killed, James was slain, and Peter was in chains also awaiting the death sentence. Paul was in and out of prison all his life. He was stoned, beaten, threatened repeatedly, and run out of town almost every place he went.

These are all scenes of spiritual warfare, actually depicting violent naval encounters in the midst of angry waves. It would also seem that when the Lord Jesus appeared walking on the waves in the heart of the storm that day on the Sea of Galilee, He was pantomiming a picture of His own life. From the beginning of the presentation of His new kingdom, heavy opposition was kept in motion by His enemy.

The comforting part of it all, however, which is the part we need to grasp, is to hear His voice above the storm...those reassuring words, "Take heart, it is I, be not afraid." Yes, we need to hear Him saying to us today in the thick of the battle, "Don't be anxious, or downcast, I have everything well in hand. See, I am walking serenely on top of the waves. Come, take my hand, and let's walk along together!"

The Basis of Faith

This brings us back again to one of the primary rudiments of spiritual warfare, which is the basis of faith. We have already quoted above that first verse from Hebrews 11, the great chapter on faith. "Faith is the *assurance* of things hoped for, the *evidence* of things not seen." But where and how do we get this assurance and evidence? This is a very vital question.

We have also seen above that faith is not the same as daring or bravado. Peter had plenty of venturesomeness in his blood, but at that stage he didn't have much faith. And he didn't have much faith because he didn't hear what the Lord was saying to him. His ears had heard, but that was as far as it got. He didn't really perceive what the Lord had said, so naturally he didn't take it in.

When we speak of hearing what the Lord is saying, we are not referring to some special audible or inaudible voice. Such voices have come to people on rare occasions. Samuel heard the Lord's voice in such manner that the first time he thought it was Eli speaking to him. He even got up out of bed and went in and asked Eli what he wanted. Abraham, Moses and others heard God's voice with their physical ears, and in special situations certain people have heard God today as well. But this is not the usual manner by which the Lord desires to communicate His truth to us. He has promised us wisdom, but He has not promised us revelation. And there is a great difference between the two.

God's normal means of speaking to us is through His written word, a book of over a thousand pages. This is the primary source of the "evidence" and "assurance" of His will. And the basis of faith is to know *His will*. It is not enough to be convinced of His power and ability.

Although I have absolute confidence in His infinite ability to do anything, I still cannot walk on physical water as Peter did. Why? Because I do not have the evidence or assurance that this is what He wants me to do. But I do have the assurance that He desires me to be able to walk on the waves of any storm which Satan stirs up in my work, in my home, or in my spiritual life. I have this assurance, because in His Word He has made it clear again and again. In fact it is one of the main topics of Scripture.

Now coming back to our story, we need to observe a little more closely why it was that Peter went down. He started out fine, "but when he saw the wind, he was afraid, and beginning to sink he cried out, 'Lord save me!'" The Lord in His mercy reached out and saved him, but He at the same time added the vital counsel, "O man of little faith, why did you doubt?"

The latter half of that admonition from the Lord is in the form of a question: "Why did you doubt?" Doubt what? This is the issue we must deal with here. Was the Lord Jesus simply suggesting that anyone can go down to the seaside and walk on the water, if he doesn't doubt that he can do it? Not at all! Neither you nor I nor anyone else can walk on the surface of a lake, except under one condition, and that is if the Lord specifically asks him to. For only then do we have the assurance which is the essential basis of that kind of undertaking.

Now Peter had just such a specific word from the Lord, so his failure was inexcusable. The Lord had clearly invited him to come. Therefore, when He asked Peter, "Why did you doubt?", He was saying, "Why did you doubt what I *said* to you." And this is precisely where our problem lies when we begin to sink in the storms of our life and ministry.

Peter's problem was that he *forgot* what the Lord had *said* to him. His attention was drawn to the wind and waves, so he wasn't able to apply his thoughts to the basis of what could have been firm, supportive faith. And this is where we often find ourselves. The storm erases from our memory the promises, the *assurance*, which we so much need to walk on top of those very waves.

The reason the words we need are so easily erased is that they were never implanted securely in the first place. Too often we just skim over the top of some portion of God's Word, without allowing the Holy Spirit the opportunity He needs to "implant" the word deep in our hearts. Solomon, the wisest man who ever lived, in his book of Proverbs passes on to us God's strong admonition: "My son, keep my words, and store up my commands within you. Keep my commands and you will live; guard my teachings as the apple of your eye. Bind them on your fingers; write them on the table of your heart" (Prov. 7:1-3).

Mark's conclusion to the story is very revealing. "He (the Lord) got into the boat with them and the wind ceased. And they were utterly astounded, *for they did not understand about the loaves, but their hearts were hardened.*" Just previous to this storm the Lord had done that tremendous miracle of feeding the 5,000 with five loaves and two small fish. The disciples in one sense had been very much involved in this event. They heard, they saw, they handled, they ate, and they collected the leftovers.

And yet the vital significance of it all never penetrated their hearts. "They did not understand" what was really taking place. Therefore they were not ready for the next event (another storm on the sea). We must daily ask the Holy Spirit to make our study of God's Word practical and vital and inscribe the applications deep on our hearts and minds so that we will *remember* them. Then we are not so likely to sink when we find ourselves in heavy seas.

The reason the Lord wasn't able to write the needed truths very deeply on their hearts at that time was that "their hearts were *hardened.*" It is easy to engrave on a soft surface, like wax, but very difficult to make much imprint on granite. We need to ask the Holy Spirit each morning to give us receptive hearts *to take in and retain* the vital truths the Lord has for us.

David, who had to ride out many storms, learned how to walk on waves, and we can readily understand why. We often hear him praying, "Make me know thy ways, O Lord; teach me thy paths. Lead me in thy truth and teach me, for You are the God of my salvation [deliverance]" (Ps. 25:4,5). His longest psalm of 176 verses expresses his longing to comprehend and take in all God's principles and precepts. For these were his *assurances* of victory.

If we give ourselves to grasp all God's provisions, the Lord Jesus promises that the Holy Spirit will then bring them to our remembrance when we need them (Jn. 14:26).

Third Encounter—How to Win Naval Battles

Paul's life was filled with storms. He was an "old salt." He had developed tremendous faith. So let us take a look now at his performance in the midst of a fierce naval encounter (Acts 27:20-25). The enemy was doing all he could to keep Paul from reaching Rome, living in the emperor's household, and appearing before Caesar. Paul had been longing for years to get to Rome, the capitol of the empire, with the gospel, but each time he was "*hindered.*"

He finally wrote them a letter (the book of Romans) to explain the "good news," and in both the introduction and conclusion of that epistle he refers to this restraining power. In the opening chapter he writes, "I want you to know, brethren, that I have planned many times to come to you, in order that I might have a harvest among you, just as I have had among the other Gentiles, but so far have been *prevented* from doing so" (Rom. 1:13). At the close of his letter he again comes back to this element of enemy opposition. "'They shall see, who have never been told about Him, and they shall understand, who have never heard of Him.' This is the reason why I have so often been *hindered* from coming to you" (Rom. 15:21,22).

In this storm, Satan surely did everything possible to sink the ship. In fact he did manage to sink the actual vessel itself. This third sea encounter was far more fierce and prolonged than either of the first two. It lasted fifteen days! And their sturdy old freighter, which was much larger and far more seaworthy than those small boats on the lake of Galilee, was completely demolished. But not a life was lost. It was a total victory for the Lord's kingdom. The Lord landed all 276 of those aboard the ship, safely onto the island of Malta, and gave Paul three months with them and the people living on Malta. The Holy Spirit did many miracles of healing among the sick, and the whole population had their hearts opened to the truths of the gospel.

But now we must come back to the account of the storm and observe this spiritual giant, Paul, in the thick of the battle. Here is the picture as Luke records it:

"When all hope of our being saved was at last abandoned, as they had been long without food, Paul then came forward among them and said, 'Men, you should have listened to me, and should not have set sail from Crete and incurred this injury and loss. But now I urge you to keep up your courage, because not one of you will be lost; only the ship will be destroyed. Last night an angel of the God whose I am and whom I serve, stood beside me and said, "Do not be afraid, Paul, you must stand trial before Caesar; and God has graciously given you the lives of all who sail with you." So keep up your courage, men, for *I have faith in God that it will happen just as He told me*'" (Acts 27:20-25).

Here is an example of the faith the Lord is looking for. It is the kind of faith which will win all encounters. "I have faith in

God that it will happen just as he *told* me." We may not have an angel visibly stand beside us, and we may not hear an audible voice, but we do have the completed Old and New Testaments available to us. And these are filled with the assurances, the promises, and all the encouragements we need to win any battle the Lord sees fit to allow us to become involved in. If only I can remember what He *"told"* me.

Paul's victory in the ferocious sea battle led to a series of other victories on the island. As soon as they arrived on land, everyone got busy collecting materials to build a fire, because it was cold and had started to rain. Paul pitched in and gathered his bundle of sticks, and just as he placed them on the fire, a poisonous viper, driven out by the heat, fastened itself on his hand. The islanders, seeing this snake hanging from his hand, immediately (according to their superstitions) concluded that "this man must be a murderer for though he escaped from the sea, justice has not allowed him to live." But Paul just shook the snake off into the fire and suffered no ill effects. This astounding deliverance, plus Paul's calm, confident manner, caused the people to decide that he must be a god of some kind. So they were ready to hang on every word he said. And Paul had plenty to say to them!

In addition to all this, God worked a number of healings on the island which further prepared the hearts of the people for the gospel message. So it became victory upon victory for the kingdom of God, and defeat after defeat for Satan's kingdom.

Therefore, as a conclusion to this chapter on naval encounters, I trust that we can develop the firm confidence that "storms" are not to be looked upon as negative tragedies, but as opportunities for decisive advances for the kingdom of our God. The more violent the storm, the greater shall be the spoils taken from the "strong man." ..."Did I not tell you that if you would *believe* [the things I have said to you], you would see the glory of God?" (Jn. 11:40).

"Master, the tempest is raging!
The billows are tossing high!
The sky is o'ershadowed with blackness,
No shelter or help is nigh.

The winds and the waves shall obey Thy will,
Peace, be still! Peace, be still!
Whether the wrath of the storm-tossed sea,
Or demons, or men, or whatever it be,
No waters can swallow the ship where lies
The Master of ocean and earth, and skies.
They all shall sweetly obey Thy will;
Peace! Peace, be still!"

20

THE TIME FACTOR

You have probably never seen an angel. I never have. If we did, we might be so overwhelmed we would even pass out. That is exactly what happened to Daniel when the Lord allowed him a glimpse of the angel Gabriel. Now Daniel was not a person of lowly rank. He was one of the great men of the Bible. For seventy years he was prime minister of the Babylonian empire. He held that position during the consecutive reigns of four mighty kings. So Daniel was very accustomed to the atmosphere of high position and royalty. He was at home in palaces, with emperors and rulers of the highest estate. National and international affairs were his daily meat and drink. But one day God granted Daniel a vision of some of the affairs in heaven. He allowed this great man to behold something of the persons, armies and battles in the heavenlies. And Daniel's heart melted like wax. Let's take a look at what happened, and hear Daniel tell it in his own words:

"I was standing on the bank of the great river, the Tigris. I looked up and there before me was a man dressed in linen, with a belt of the finest gold around his waist. His body was like chrysolite, His face like lightning, His eyes like flaming torches, His arms and legs like the gleam of burnished brass, and His voice like the sound of a multitude. I, Daniel, was the only one who saw the vision; the men with me did not see it, but such terror overwhelmed them that they fled and hid themselves. So I was left alone, gazing at this great vision. I had no strength left; my face turned deathly pale, and I was helpless. Then I heard Him speaking, and as I listened to Him, I fell into a deep sleep, my face to the ground. A hand touched me and set me trembling on my hands and knees. ...While He was speaking, I bowed with my face toward the ground and was speechless. Then One who looked like a man touched my lips, and I opened my mouth and began to speak. I said to the One standing before me, 'I am over-come with anguish because of the vision, my Lord, and I am helpless. How can I, your servant, talk with you, my Lord? My strength is gone and I can hardly breathe'" (Dan. 10:4-10, 15-17).

Purpose of This Vision

Daniel was also a mighty man of prayer. He was the kind that James spoke of when he wrote, "The effective prayer of a righteous man can accomplish much." Daniel knew the truth of this principle, and so his biograhy is laced together with prayer. In the opening chapter it mentions how "*God* gave knowledge and understanding of all kinds" to Daniel and his prayer partners. Then it adds, "Daniel could understand visions and dreams of all kinds." In the next chapter is the account of God's deliverance of all the "wise men" of Babylon because of the prayers of Daniel and his three friends. The third chapter tells of how God miraculously protected Daniel's three friends in the midst of the roaring furnace of fire. Then we all remember the story of what God did for Daniel when he was cast into the lions' den because he refused to break his habit of three sessions of prayer each day.

In chapter 9 of the book of Daniel is recorded one of Daniel's prayers, and it is startling to see how a man of such greatness, a man from the pinnacle of royalty and earthly majesty, could humble himself before his God in confession and penitence to the degree that is manifested in this magnificent prayer. On the one hand it is a masterpiece of oratory. On the other hand it reaches to the depths of self-effacement. The burden of his soul is deliverance for his people. This great Daniel is a *captive*. Although God has blessed him, and he has gone to the top in Babylon, he can never erase from his mind what happened that day when he as a young lad in his teens, was shackled with chains, and marched with all his countrymen across the barren, dusty deserts to this heathen Babylon. But most painful of all was that he and everyone else, including all the heathen nations, knew *why* it had happened. Israel had sinned! They had sinned willingly and despicably against their God. So they were suffering miserable disgrace under the heel of their enemies.

This was Daniel's burden. They had endured the shame of their captivity for nearly seventy years now, and Daniel knew that the prophet Jeremiah had promised a return to their homeland after such a period of chastening. As the time drew near, Daniel's prayers became more intense that the Lord wouldn't have to extend the time, but that the promised deliverance would really come.

God loved Daniel very much, but Daniel was to discover that claiming promises and answers to prayer is not always as simple and instantaneous as one might desire. Daniel was a man of great faith, and we must be too, but we like Daniel must learn that great faith must still take into account the battles which are going on in the heavenlies. Our praying and our faith can greatly affect these battles. In fact, as we have touched on in previous chapters, this is what God often seems to be waiting for as the deciding factor. God is sovereign, and God is all powerful. He therefore can at any time just say the word and accomplish instantly anything He desires. But an astounding truth is that He frequently doesn't operate merely out of His own will or decrees. He involves His children. And the more mature His children become, the more He waits for them to involve themselves in heavenly affairs.

In Chapter 2 we saw how the Lord Jesus taught His disciples to pray "Thy will be done." What a tremendous kind of praying, when you stop to think about it! Of course His will shall be done! He is *God*! And yet the Lord Jesus would have His disciples to comprehend that their praying is a genuine factor. It is often the bona fide means of God's will being done. And this is precisely where Daniel found himself. As mentioned above, Jeremiah had made it clear that the people of Israel would be allowed to return to their homeland after the seventy years of captivity. Yet Daniel was concerned that something might come up which would prolong their captivity and thus postpone their return. And he was absolutely right. Something had come up which he knew nothing about, but about which he was soon to learn a great deal.

There existed mighty forces in the heavenlies which greatly opposed Israel's return. These were Satan's forces, the forces of evil which always seek to hold people captive as long as possible. God could have smashed these forces long ago, as we have seen before, but He had (and still has) chosen not to do it yet for His own good reasons. Daniel didn't know about these forces and the powers they wield. Even less was he aware of his own involvement in all that was going on in the unseen realm. And there are far too many of us today who are just where Daniel was before he saw this vision. Many Christians hold a rather mild view of prayer. They know theoretically that it is a good thing, and sometimes God hears and grants the request and that is about as far as it goes.

The purpose of this vision was to lift both Daniel and us into a whole new level of understanding as to what really happens when we pray. This vision is meant to propel our prayer life into a new and higher orbit.

Coming back to verse one of this tenth chapter of Daniel, the vision is labeled for us. We read, "Its message was true and *it concerned a great war.*" Without realizing it, Daniel's praying had set in motion a tremendous unseen battle. And your praying and mine, if it is vital, will also stir up a battle!

The Magnitude of the War

Let us now take a look at what preceded this vision. Daniel was very downcast in his spirit because he was so burdened for the deliverance of his people. Before God, this is always a very honorable kind of concern to have. Daniel's concern was so intense that he "ate no choice foods...and used no lotions for three weeks." He gave himself to earnest prayer. Yet nothing happened. Before, God usually answered his prayers within a reasonable span of time, but for this prayer vigil the heavens seemed as impervious as brass.

Then suddenly something did happen. God allowed him this shattering vision. We have already listened to his description of the angel who appeared to him, a vision which took away all his strength and left him utterly helpless. This should give us a little conception of the might and grandeur of even one angel. And there are myriads of them before God's throne. *But* there is also a staggering array of similar beings of awesome power in Satan's army. Therefore, when Daniel or you or I ask God for something which is a threat to Satan's kingdom, it immediately precipitates a battle, and sometimes it becomes a horrendous war.

Perhaps the next thing we need to observe about the vision is that it was not meant to frighten Daniel, but it was intended to make him strong. When the angel began to speak to Daniel, his first words were, "Daniel, you are highly esteemed." Then a little further on he encourages him with, "Do not be afraid, O man highly esteemed ...Peace, be strong now; be strong." People who get themselves involved in such warfare are highly esteemed by God, but they also need to gird on their armor, sharpen their weapons, and prepare themselves for a real fight.

Now we are ready to consider the time factor which so often plagues us when God seems to delay in answering our prayers. The Lord would have us learn with Daniel that most major wars are not won in a day. Verse twelve reads, "Do not be afraid, Daniel. Since the first day that you set your mind to gain understanding, and to humble yourself before your God, your words were heard, and I have come in response to them."

Here is great encouragement. "Daniel, the first time you opened your mouth to express this concern of yours, God heard your cry, and He immediately sent me to deal with the matter. *But...*" The next sentence begins with a "but." And this is a great turning point in the story. "But the 'prince' of the Persian Kingdom resisted me twenty-one days." Even though Gabriel was an arch-angel with a whole army of other mighty angels accompanying him, he met such massive resistance from one of Satan's armies (his principality in charge of Persia) that it took him twenty-one days to even get through to Daniel to give him a brief explanation of what was taking place. And the battle was by no means over; it was really only beginning! In fact Gabriel wouldn't even have made it this far were it not for the fact that as a result of the continued and persistent interceding of Daniel and his prayer partners, God sent forth another army, Michael and his forces, to assist in the conflict.

Actually the battle was still escalating, for just as Gabriel was getting into his explanations, he said, "Soon I will return to fight against the prince of Persia, and when I go, the prince of

Greece will come." Then he adds a rather sad note, which is perhaps our main challenge from the passage. He says, "No one supports me against them except Michael, your prince." It is as if he were informing Daniel that the battle is going to become more fierce and will therefore become a long, drawn-out war, unless you can get others to join you in prayer, so that God would send forth more forces to help.

How challenging this insight should become to us! Instead of giving up when there doesn't seem to come a ready response to our supplications, we ought to consider the conflict which our prayer may be causing in the spiritual realm. What is likely to be Satan's reaction to the things I have been asking for? To what degree might they really bother him? Sometimes this is a good way to evaluate our prayer life: to think through to what extent my asking is a desire to see "Thy kingdom come." This is what both God and Satan are primarily concerned about. And the more on target my prayer, the more the enemy is going to try to block it, to hinder it, to hold back the answer. If his resistance can outlast my persistence, he has won. If we don't prevail over him, he will prevail over us.

Significance of Militant Prayer

The Christian student's campus, the pastor's parish, and that heathen village that you are praying for are each ruled over by an unseen army. The sooner we realize this, the sooner our prayer life will take on the nature of battle. For the effective prayer warrior this is going to mean many victories. Doing battle in prayer will include both agony and ecstasy.

We have many such challenges and encouragements in Scripture. One verse to start with is Hebrews 1:14: "Are not all angels ministering spirits *sent* to serve those who will inherit salvation?" Yes, God sends them out to do battle when we ask Him to. How many have you had sent forth recently?

Another example is the story of that Roman centurion in Luke 7. His favorite servant was very sick, so he asked some of his Jewish friends to go to Jesus to request healing for the young man. He thoroughly instructed his representatives as to what they were to say. "First you are to tell Jesus that He need not bother himself to come to my home, for I am by no means worthy for Him to stand under my roof." This was not just polite talk. He meant it. He had a much keener awareness of the deity of the Lord Jesus than even the Lord's disciples. "Next," he said, "you are to tell Jesus that all He needs to do is say the word and the matter will be accomplished. For I am a military officer. I tell one of my men to go to a certain place and he departs immediately. I call another to come, and he is here by my side at once. I also have higher captains over me, whom I obey. Therefore, I thoroughly understand the chain of command." When the Lord Jesus heard this message, He was absolutely thrilled. "This man understands Me. I have not seen such great faith in all Israel." The centurion knew full well that the Lord Jesus had unseen armies ready at His word. He knew that this Jesus was none other than "The Lord of *Hosts.*" He was a man of penetrating insight, which equipped him with conquering faith.

An Old Testament illustration is the account of Elisha's being pursued by the king of Syria. The Syrians had been attacking Israel, but each time, the Lord would reveal their battle plan to Elisha. The prophet would then send word to Israel's king, who would make the necessary preparations, and the Syrians' attack would always be foiled. After awhile the old Syrian king became frustrated. He called his generals together and demanded to know which one of them was leaking the information. "None of us is," they replied, "but there is a prophet in Israel to whom the God of Israel is revealing all your strategies." "Well, go round up this prophet and bring him here to me!" the king commanded. Elisha at that time was staying in the little village of Dothan, so the Syrians sent an army and completely surrounded the place at night. The next morning when Elisha's servant went out and opened the front gate, he discovered the Syrian soldiers on all sides. He rushed back in, shaking with fear, to report the hopeless situation to Elisha. The prophet calmly asked the Lord to open his servant's eyes to see the *other* army involved. When his servant went back out to have another look, he "saw the hills full of horses and chariots of fire all around Elisha."

These examples should strengthen us to pray with much

confidence and expectancy, even though the battle may rage on for a time. In fact, in some pioneering mission fields the time factor may require tenacious faith coupled with prolonged, persistent battle in prayer for years until the breakthrough comes.

The expression "until" makes a very interesting word study in Scripture. One example especially pertinent to our military scene is God's word to Joshua when he attacked the fortress of Ai. The Lord charged him not to draw back his outstretched hand holding his spear "until" his enemy was destroyed (Josh. 8:18,26). Strongholds are usually torn down piece by piece. And enemy forces are usually defeated unit by unit. Things often get worse before they get better. This was surely the case with Moses before Pharaoh in Egypt, and when Satan was attacking Job. So we never ought to be discouraged. Heavy, prolonged battle is for true soldiers. "Having done all, *stand!*" Before the Lord Jesus did His first miracle of turning water into wine at a marriage feast, the situation was in a very bad way. The steward was becoming anxious and embarrassed, for their beverage was running dangerously low. But the Lord was not worried. He merely replied, "My time has not yet come." He knew when to act; He always does. And it is never too late!

The story of the labors of James Frazer among the Lisu tribe of West China should put hope in our hearts. He was one of the most spiritually gifted missionaries of the China Inland Mission. God had also given him a group of earnest, diligent prayer partners back in his homeland in England, and he kept this corps of heavy artillery well informed of the developments on the battlefield. He and they were convinced that God had not only clearly called him to this area but had positively assured him that there would be fruit and that the Lord Jesus would build His church there.

However, it was heavy plodding from the start. The people were friendly for the most part, but disinterested and uncomprehending. Not only were they deaf and blind to the message, but bound and afraid. When a seeming breakthrough did appear after a few years, it was soon stifled by uncanny attacks of a strange sickness which came upon each of the few who did profess to believe. They all recanted, and everyone else became more unreachable than before. He tried in vain for several more years, and finally came to the point that he felt this was perhaps not God's time to reach the Lisu and that perhaps he should return to other parts of China where the response was more favorable. But he felt he should make one more trip around his circuit of mountain villages before leaving. He and his prayer partners had been bombarding the enemy's forces for *nine years*, and surely such intercession would eventually drive them back. So he wrote them of his plan, and together they once again poured out their souls before the Lord of Hosts, and Frazer then proceeded on his final round. But this time it was entirely different. In each village there was a tremendous moving of the Spirit of God, and family after family turned to the Lord...some 300 families in all. Satan's empire in that area had been toppled. The Lisu churches which were established became the fastest growing, the most solid, the most zealous of any in China.

We cannot expect to come against a powerful enemy and quickly drive him out of his heavily fortified stronghold where he has been entrenched for perhaps centuries. It just doesn't work that way. God is almighty, but He would also have you and me to come to understand and appreciate the nature of some of the things that have been going on here on planet earth. He would also have us get involved, but to get involved in the right way.

If Daniel so completely collapsed after seeing a vision of just one angel, how far could he get by his own strength in a battle where two whole armies of such angels were held back for weeks by the enemy! And how far would James Frazer have gotten trying to establish the kingdom of his God against such forces in Lisuland, armed with only his seminary degree and his books on church planting, fine as these are?!

By way of conclusion we must observe that if God answered all our prayers as soon as we asked, we would never mature. We would learn nothing of spiritual warfare. We would forever be spoiled, ignorant infants. And this is certainly not God's plan for man.

Only time and experience, mixed with a generous amount of painful "failures," can produce growth, maturity and know-how. Such words as "patience," "persistence," and "endurance" are common language in Scripture. No child grows up in a day. Majors, colonels and generals are not found in the cradle. I am discovering that a missionary's first term of service out on the firing line (even after he has had a term of orientation and language study) may amount to mostly boot camp training. Our God is seeking to prepare strong, tough marines who will throughout eternity be co-laborers with the Lord Jesus in the rule and operation of His universe.

"Be strong and take heart, all you who hope in the Lord" (Ps. 31:24).

21

THE SOLDIER'S R. & R.

Every soldier needs his R. & R. A general knows that without sufficient "rest and recreation," the morale of his men will seriously deteriorate. Man's constitution has been put together in such a way that it requires several types of renewal. Our body needs its rest in sleep every night. Our thinking mechanism needs a day off once a week for recreation, plus a vacation schedule. And our spirit needs not only its daily devotional time in God's Word and prayer, but also those occasional longer periods of quiet fellowship with the Lord which are so therapeutic and refreshing. Without these, the enemy is often able to grind us down with weariness, anxiety, or even despair. Our faith, our joy, and our resilience can become so feeble that our vision turns negative, and our enthusiasm and drive are gone. One of Satan's great weapons is discouragement. He knows that this breeds weakness of all kinds.

Soldiers in the thick of the battle can especially get worn away. Warfare is very exhausting. So let us give our attention now to these three areas of need. For even though God's Word has a lot to say about power and strength, it also has a good bit to say about our sleep and our sabbaths.

Rest for the Body

The Lord Jesus was a very busy man. He often "rose a great while before day" and spent the night in prayer. *But* He didn't do this every day. In fact, He compensated for these exigencies by allowing Himself chances to catch up. He was sound asleep on the boat as they crossed the Sea of Galilee, even in the midst of a storm. He also stopped and rested on the side of the well in Samaria, while His disciples went on into town to buy supplies. Our

Lord was not a man of extremes. Although His life was quite ir-
regular, He sought to maintain a reasonable balance.

Balance is always a key to the enjoyment of God's blessing.
God's word again and again calls us to the position of rea-
sonableness. Sometimes it is named "moderation." Sometimes
"self-control" or "sober-mindedness" or "sound judgment" or
"the good and acceptable and perfect will of God." And yet, as
Principal Maxwell of Prairie Bible Institute often told his students, "Balance is the hardest thing to maintain in all our Christian life."

When Paul urges us to present our bodies to God, he immediately describes this offering as a *"living sacrifice"* (Rom.
12:1). To be sure it will involve a measure of sacrifice. But at the
same time, it is to be a *living* ministry. It is to be the type of service which is a constant testimony of *"abundant life."* And in another place he cautions us: "Be very careful, then, how you
live—not as unwise but as wise, making the most of every opportunity (redeeming the time), because the days are evil. Therefore do not be foolish, but understand what the Lord's will is"
(Eph. 5:15-17).

In order to "make the most of every opportunity," one must
maintain a clear, sharp mind. The Holy Spirit is hindered when
He has to do His work through a weary, dull mind or a half-sick
body. I learned this lesson the hard way at the beginning of my
missionary career. Soon after I acquired enough of the Chinese
language to become involved in some ministry, I convinced myself that it was "far better to burn out than to rust out," so I set
my alarm for a good early hour each morning. I drank cups of
strong tea at lunch and filled each evening with a full schedule of
worthwhile accomplishments. "Work hard, work long, and work
fast" was the advice in the books, "for the time is short." So I
made up my mind to live by the words in Psalm 126, "Those who
sow in tears will reap in joy."

After about a year of this lack of moderation, my poor body
began to complain. I visited the nearest missionary hospital and
was immediately ordered to return home from the field with a serious case of tuberculosis. The Lord had mercy, and within a year
and a half I was back on the field feeling fine. But in the mean-

time He led me on from the conclusion of Psalm 126 to the introduction of Psalm 127: "Unless the Lord builds the house, they labor in vain who build it. Unless the Lord guards the city, the watchman keeps awake in vain. *It is vain* for you to rise up early, to retire late, to eat the bread of painful labors, *for He gives sleep to those He loves.*" We are to crucify the flesh, but not our body. There is a great difference!

At times, of course, some of us may need the opposite exhortation to be diligent and to "redeem the time because the days are evil." We may find ourselves slipping into the imbalance of taking life too casually, spending more time in front of the video or in other activities, than is really needed to restore our energies for the task God has entrusted to us.

In this book we have said a good bit about prayer, with much emphasis on the quantitative aspect. And we have given a whole chapter to the qualitative element of *concern*, since the Scriptures often use such forceful words as "supplication," "beseech," "yearn," etc. Here, however, let us insert a caution in this regard. When one has been led of the Spirit to give himself to a period of heavy intercession, with those "groanings which cannot be uttered," or has become engaged in an intense "warfare" situation, he may well need to make provision for some extra time of physical rest to counterbalance.

Recreation for the Soul

God instituted the sabbath to meet another underlying requirement in man's make-up. In the Old Testament this was written into the fundamentals of the moral law. It was placed right in the center of His Ten Commandments. However, it was by no means intended to become a burden for His people. (The rabbis, scribes and Pharisees were the ones who made it hard and legalistic.) Quite to the contrary, our Lord Jesus spoke out very strongly that "the sabbath was made for man, and not man for the sabbath" (Mk. 2:27). So, in God's word we have a twofold evaluation of this weekly day off. The Old Testament emphasizes how essential it is, and the New Testament points out how free and refreshing it should be.

It would seem that the actual purpose of setting aside this one day out of seven is to provide something more than mere physical rest. It was established as we know by God Himself at the close of His six days of creation. He "rested" on the seventh day. But Isaiah tells us plainly that "the everlasting God, the Lord, the Creator of the ends of the earth, does not become weary or tired" (Isa. 40:28). Therefore, it appears that God spent that seventh day not to relieve bodily fatigue but in observing and enjoying what He had made. God set aside a day to enjoy His creation, and He has appointed a day each week for us, His creatures, to enjoy our Creator and the world He has created. A man's whole emotional system requires regular renewal. For the Christian worker whose Sunday is a day of labor and output of energy, another day should be set aside in its place to meet this need. In the Old Testament, the Lord also specified several other annual rest periods for His people. And a soldier very much needs these extra "leaves" and vacations. In the New Testament, when His disciples had undergone a period of extra strain, the Lord invited them to "come away to a quiet place and get some rest" (Mk. 6:31).

Just recently in the village work several of our workers have been overcome with battle fatigue. They gave themselves so thoroughly and steadfastly to the demands of the work that they reached a point of near collapse. We have had to rescue some of them from the conflict for awhile until they could recover their buoyancy and emotional equilibrium.

Of course we need to realize that a *hobby* or recreational activity can also get out of control and become a hindrance to God's servant rather than a means of renewal. Our spare time pursuits should be a positive blessing in our lives, and if they grow to consume more than their minimal share of our time and money, they become thieves and robbers. They can eat up valuable portions of our already limited supplies of these precious commodities. And in reality they are stealing from the Lord. I have seen this happen to missionaries.

Our missionary message is the "good news" of deliverance and salvation. We are seeking to introduce people to God's love, wisdom and power. But it all becomes a farce if the messenger himself is continually exhausted and depleted of exhilaration in his ministry or goes too far in the other direction and becomes a man of ease.

One of the most zealous of God's servants in British history was Robert Murray McCheyne. He gave himself without stint to the people of his parish, and they all loved him. He also made exhaustive trips abroad to preach the gospel. But since he allowed his physical constitution insufficient opportunity for renewal and recovery, he died at a very early age. On his death bed he said, "God gave me a message and a horse with which to deliver the message. But now I have killed the horse and can no longer deliver the message."

Spiritual Renewal

A few months ago, I had a phone call from a friend who is involved in a missionary outreach in a dark, heathen area. He announced that he would not be able to speak at a certain meeting we had arranged, and that he had canceled all his other appointments for the next eighty days in order to spend the time at Prayer Mountain. I asked why he had done this, and here is his story. "As you know," he said, "I spent a week at Prayer Mountain a year ago, and it was a great blessing to me. I was convinced at the time that I had been filled with the Spirit and His power. When I returned to my work, I did indeed have new power, and much was accomplished for a time. But then I gradually became aware that my spiritual strength was diminishing and I felt dry. So I returned to Prayer Mountain, this time for two weeks. Again, I was refreshed and encouraged, and during this period I felt definitely that I was filled with the Spirit and His power. However, this endowment, like the first, lasted for a time and then began to wane. So I have decided to do as the Lord Jesus did, to fast for forty days, and then give my physical body another forty days to recover from the fast, so that I can be truly and completely filled and empowered by the Holy Spirit."

I asked my friend if he could come to my home before he left for Prayer Mountain so we could discuss the matter. He came and we had a good talk. I feel I was able to show him that the

Scriptures picture a *frequent* need for *renewal of spiritual strength* as a very normal thing. In fact, the admonition to "wait on the Lord" is repeated twenty-eight times in God's Word. The Lord Jesus Himself retired to the mountains or the deserts *often*, to renew His strength. It is therefore not a proper concept to feel that we can become so empowered through one experience that it will be sufficient for the rest of our lives. Actually, this is a very erroneous assumption and can lead to deep dejection.

We have already mentioned that our spirits need two kinds of renewal. We must have our daily refueling from God's Word and prayer, but for most of us this is only enough to keep our heads above water. I need not only to regularly fill the gas tank in my car, but periodically I also must take it to the mechanic and leave it there for a day or so for a thorough tune-up. Military trucks which are driven hard over the rough terrain of the battlefield, carrying heavy loads, need even more frequent maintenance. A general cannot afford to have his trucks breaking down for lack of needed repairs. Those vehicles must be kept in peak operating condition. So there are times when we need the therapy prescribed in the little chorus, "Spirit of the living God, fall *afresh* on me." This manner of spiritual renewal requires a period of "waiting" in His presence. Isaiah gives us heartening assurance: "Those who wait on the Lord shall renew their strength; they shall mount up with wings like eagles; they shall run and not be weary; they shall walk and not faint" (Isa. 40:31).

Mounting Up

Let us now take a good look at this parable about the eagle. It is refreshing just to think about it. To "mount up" high, out of the smog into the clear, blue air where the lazy white clouds float by...this is the life of the eagle. We cannot live such a life all the time, of course, for we are called to be soldiers on a battlefield. But the right kind of spiritual R. & R. can do wonders for battle-fatigue of our inner man. Mounting up has many therapeutic values, one of which is that it shifts our point of reference from a shell-pocked mudhole to a vista far up in the stratosphere. As we mount up, the objects and the situations on earth take on a diminished perspective. Houses and cars look like miniature toys. The enemy's fortifications, though real, look so small as to offer little threat. Remember your first plane ride, how fascinating and exhilarating it was? God has something similar in mind for us each time we arrange for one of these flights which come from waiting on Him. He longs to take us up every now and then to see things from His standpoint, to breathe the air of assured victory. It sends us back to the battlefield with a new confidence.

In my early days as a new recruit in mainland China, I was asked by our mission to help drive a heavily loaded three-ton truck all the way from Shanghai on the coast west to the borders of Tibet. On that trip we crossed over a hundred rivers. Some of them had small ox cart bridges. Some had no bridges at all. Some had to be forded. Some had small bamboo ferries. Often it seemed an impossible situation. If at such a time I could look up and see an eagle gliding overhead, flying at perhaps a thousand feet elevation, it would always do something for me. That eagle had no problem getting across that river. And his God was my God too. My God wanted me to learn how to "mount up" just like that eagle to where none of my problems really worried me. And I must add here that the Lord helped us across every one of those rivers, all the way to the end of the journey, even though part of that period was flood season.

Let us think again for a moment about the serenity of an eagle's flight. He doesn't flap his wings like other birds. No, he just soars in perfect peace and calm. I have never ridden in a glider, but I'm told that it is very different from an airplane. There is a remarkable absence of noise. And it is said that a glider ride can be very healing to taut nerves.

This should tell us something about the content of our times of "waiting." They are not to be occasions of heavy Bible study, or exhausting, fervent prayer. We need those times too, but quiet waiting on the Lord ought more to assume the form of resting in Him, meditating on His goodness and greatness, singing hymns of praise and thanksgiving, reading an uplifting biography, etc. Then by the help of the Holy Spirit and God's promise of wisdom, I am ready to leisurely work my way out of the tangles.

At first it may sound a bit naive to suggest that while you

are relaxed before the Lord, you leisurely work your way out of
all your tangles. "Some of these enigmas have been around for a
long time," you say. "I have already spent much time in thought
and prayer for solutions to these dilemmas, and none is forth-
coming. The sky is still as bleak and dark as ever!"

I know very well where you are coming from, for I have
been there too. But some years ago, the Lord taught me a valuable lesson. I had a problem I had been wrestling with for some
time, so one Sunday afternoon I rode my bicycle to a mango
grove on the outskirts of town, and hidden away among those
trees, I spent an hour in earnest prayer, asking the Lord for wisdom as to what to do. A week later, I was still as confused as
ever, so I returned to the mango grove for another hour of seeking light and wisdom. A second week passed with no illumination on the matter, so back to the mango grove I went. This pattern continued for months until I was really discouraged. Then I
began to complain to the Lord that I didn't feel He was standing
behind His promise in James 1:5, that "if any man lack wisdom,
he should ask of God and liberal wisdom will be given him."

At that point it didn't take the Holy Spirit long to remind me
of the next two verses. "But when he asks, he must believe and
not doubt, because he who doubts is like a wave of the sea,
blown and tossed by the wind. That man should not think he will
receive anything from the Lord." Wisdom is one thing which the
Lord has promised unconditionally. "It will be given to him."
The only condition is that we see it as an unconditional promise.
We must ask in faith, without doubting. This is sometimes hard
to do, especially if the problem is a long-standing one. But God
never wants His children to remain in the dark regarding any
problem. The Lord Jesus says, "I am the light of the world; he
who follows Me shall not walk in darkness, but *shall have* the
light of life" (Jn. 8:12). The difficulty may not go away immediately, but the Lord desires to give us *wisdom* to know exactly
what we are to do about it, at least for the next step. Therefore,
no difficulty ever need weigh you down as an unsolved problem.
God *will* give me wisdom if I ask in faith.

When I saw this truth that afternoon, I realized my mistake.
I had been asking for wisdom for many months but had not once

asked in faith, claiming wisdom with absolute expectancy. So at that moment I told myself and told the Lord that I would not ask again for wisdom for that particular problem. I had already asked long enough. In fact, I became embarrassed that I had asked so many times without faith. Wisdom did not come immediately, but each time I was tempted to ask for it again, I thanked the Lord for His unconditional promise for "generous" wisdom. In a few days it became perfectly clear to me what was at the heart of my problem and what I should do about it.

Wisdom is different from knowledge. God has not promised to equip every Christian with a Ph.D. degree. Neither is wisdom the same as revelation. Waiting on the Lord is not to be like T.M. (transcendental meditation), where we sit in a fixed position with a blank mind, waiting for a vision. This is very dangerous. A blank mind opens itself to the intrusion of false spirits. No, God has not necessarily promised supernatural knowledge or revelation, but He has surely given us the assurance that He will guide our thinking until we have ample *wisdom* to know how to handle the complex items, the entanglements which the enemy would use to bind us.

With Wings

The enemy seeks to bind us with chains, but God would have us mount up with wings. An eagle has powerful wings. And we need a set of wings which are strong enough to break out of the chains and carry us up into the heavens. Have you developed such a pair of wings? How do you go about mounting up like an eagle? What is that helpful, spiritual routine which always causes you to mount up? Your wings may be a different shape and color from mine, but I will share with you the two wings which always lift me up. One is offering *thanks*. The other is asking for *wisdom*.

When we are discouraged or depressed, we are not much good as a soldier. And our problems are usually twofold. First, things have been going wrong, and second, we don't know what to do about it. We have already dealt with the second problem, which is handled by asking for wisdom. Now let us examine the first malady. Everything seems to be out of kilter. It appears the enemy is winning. This may even be true in certain areas, but he is never winning in all areas. The Lord will not allow that. God loves His children, and although He may allow us a good wrestling match with the enemy at times, He always sets limits on how far he is allowed to go. Even in the case of Job, God said to Satan, "This far and no farther!"

Therefore, you and I *always* have areas of blessing in our life, our home, our ministry, our friendships, etc., which we can gather together and for which we can offer up thanks. Perhaps singing some of your favorite hymns or choruses, or listening to your favorite praise tape, will prepare your heart to do this. It may take awhile to think through all these areas and collect your thanksgiving list, but this is a most important part of "waiting on the Lord." When things look dark, we need to start opening the windows and let some light in. As soon as we do this and get genuinely involved in praise, Satan will become very uncomfortable and have to make his exit. He cannot stand genuine praise to the Lord!

"Be anxious for nothing, but in everything *by prayer* and supplication, *with thanksgiving*, let your requests [including your need for wisdom] be made known to God" (Phil. 4:6). This basic formula has become my set of wings whereby I mount up when I wait on the Lord for renewed strength. And I want to testify that He has *never* failed me. When I begin by offering up thanksgiving, and then in faith and complete confidence ask for wisdom, He always grants the light, the strategy, I need, at least for the next step, and I can then return to the battlefront refreshed.

Running and Walking

"They shall run and not be weary, they shall walk and not faint." Life in this latter half of the twentieth century certainly keeps us on the run. Christians are just as busy as anyone, usually more so, because we need special time each day for fellowship with our Lord and time for service to others. Therefore we live full lives indeed. But Isaiah's words are very comforting to us. Waiting on the Lord is designed to provide us with ample strength and fortitude to cope with just such a full life.

All of us need help and consolation from time to time, and how glad we are when we find one of those rare individuals who always seems able and ready with a sufficient supply of warm counsel and comfort. I have a friend in Taipei whose full-time ministry is helping others with their distress. He not only has office hours all day long, but people are continually calling on the phone for help. So he has certainly had to learn for himself how to run and not be weary. His body gets weary, of course, and his spiritual batteries need recharging often, I'm sure, but he knows how to keep them well-charged.

Finally, Isaiah encourages us with the assurance that those who have developed the skill of mounting up like an eagle will also be able to *walk* and not faint. "Walking" in Scripture is used 250 times in a spiritual sense. That is, it speaks of our Christian walk as being our godly character, our loving service, our living for others. Such a life is not natural to us. It tends to become a weight because we all much prefer living for ourselves. Satan is fully aware of this and does all he can to remind us of what a burden it all is. Then he adds other burdens of guilt and pressure until the load becomes so heavy we can't walk. We stagger and sometimes even become crippled. We need to either get out from under this heavy load, or we need a lot more strength.

Both are probably true. Oftentimes a good part of our load has been placed on us by the Evil One. But just as often, we may be needing a break. We may need time to sort through our baggage and ask the Lord about each piece and also rest awhile before we shoulder our backpack again. After the Holy Spirit has helped us to adjust the straps and shoulder pads, we should be able to walk and not faint, and even help others with their loads.

Finding Time

There still remains a very practical problem, a common complaint which we now need to face up to, and that is the need for adequate time for waiting on the Lord. How much time does one need to properly mount up? We have already conceded that we are all on the run. Therefore when we start speaking of time, we are talking about a mighty scarce commodity for most of us. And some would reply that they are so weary that if they did get really relaxed and quiet, within five minutes they would be sound asleep and enjoy their slumber for hours. This is most likely the case with many of us, and it only emphasizes the need for R.& R.

We should not be ashamed of our exhaustion. It is an indication that we have been diligently involved, and perhaps that we are becoming a real threat to the enemy. Neither should we be ashamed of catching up on physical rest. We really need this before we can begin to mount up spiritually. We need a clear mind to extricate ourselves from the enemy's snares. As mentioned above, a depleted thinking apparatus can be a real hindrance in handling wisdom from above.

Now coming back to the amount of time required to do a proper job of renewal. This depends on several factors. Some people's thought processes work much faster than others. Some problems are more deep-seated. Maybe it's been a long time since you had a period of "waiting." Ask the Holy Spirit to give you some indication of what you need. It may be only a couple of hours, or it may be half a day, a whole day, two days, or longer. Experience will prove to be a good teacher.

Should you spend the time alone, or with a friend or two? This also varies. I myself do best alone. Some do better in fellowship with a close friend. Some need the help of a small group. What about the place? There are those who reserve a room in a friend's home. Some rent a motel room. Others head for a cabin in the mountains or by the sea. Some need to be out in God's beautiful, exhilarating nature. Others would be too distracted in such an environment, so they need the four plain walls of a rented room. You are there to have relaxing, refreshing, and yet insightful fellowship with your Creator. You are getting ready to return to combat, which may be even fiercer than before, so ask the Lord from the start to make it very worthwhile.

In closing, let us hear testimonies from three of God's great warriors. In Psalm 27:13,14 David says: "I would have despaired unless I had believed that I would see the goodness of the Lord in the land of the living. Wait for the Lord. Be strong, and let your heart take courage. Yes, wait for the Lord."

Jeremiah testifies: "The Lord is good to those who wait for Him; to the person who seeks Him. It is good that he waits silently for the salvation of the Lord" (Lam. 3:25,26). And finally, we hear Isaiah say: "The Lord longs to be gracious to you, and therefore He waits on high to have compassion on you. For the Lord is a God of justice. How blessed are all those who wait for Him" (Isa. 30:18).

22

OFFICERS

Following Paul's challenge to Timothy that he wage the good warfare comes this charge: *"First of all* then, I urge that entreaties and prayers, petitions and thanksgivings be made for *all men."* And then he proceeds to explain what he means when he uses the term "all men." He is not suggesting that we go down the list of every name in the phone book when we have our prayer time, but he is urging us not to fail to focus special attention on "kings and all who are in authority."

His reasoning follows in the last half of the verse, "that we may lead a quiet and peaceable life, godly and respectful in every way." Things are often anything but "quiet and peaceful" when warfare erupts in a heathen village as the gospel moves in. But there can quickly come about a real change if the magistrate or some of those "in authority" turn to the Lord. And this vital change in a life or in a situation is that which Paul has in mind. In the next sentence he adds, "This is *good* and acceptable in the sight of God our Savior, who desires all men [even mayors and managers] to be saved and come to a knowledge of the truth" (1 Tim. 2:1-4).

So when Paul says here that God desires "all men to be saved," he again is using the phrase to remind us that in our praying and evangelizing, we should not overlook those who are in positions of leadership. In fact he urges that these be "first of all," at the top of our prayer list.

There often seems to be a subconscious mental block in our minds that those in high position are somewhat beyond God's reach. Children, the poor, the sick and those in difficult straits can be reached, but those who have succeeded in life are untouchable. This is a dangerous and restricting attitude in presenting our message of salvation.

315

It is true that in his first letter to the Corinthians Paul agreed that in their assembly there were "not many wise (according to human standards), not many mighty, not many of noble birth." But by no means was he saying there were not *any*. In fact, as you read through the book of Acts and Paul's letters, you discover that there was a good sprinkling of fine leadership material in his churches, those who in society held positions of authority. In Antioch, Manaen had been brought up with Herod the Tetrarch. At Paphos, Sergius Paulus was the proconsul. In Phillipi, the merchant Lydia and the head of the prison turned to the Lord. At Athens Dionysius believed. He was a member of the most venerable and prestigious council of the Areopagus. At Corinth, Crispus had been the leader of the synagogue and Erastus was the city treasurer. Philemon of Colosse evidently was a well-to-do plantation owner. And in Rome, there were many won from Caesar's household.

Need for Officers

An army cannot function with only foot soldiers. The bulk of its forces is of course made up of privates and those of ordinary rank, but there must be that essential supply of both commissioned and non-commissioned officers. There must be leadership! Paul sent both Timothy and Titus into the churches to commission elders and deacons in every place. But there cannot be officers without officer material. This is why Paul is so forceful in his plea, "*First of all*, then, I urge that entreaties and prayers, petitions and thanksgivings be made" for such leadership material.

I feel that one of the main reasons for the stunted growth of many churches in Taiwan, especially those in the more remote and idolatrous areas, is lack of able leadership. A man will reproduce his own kind. So if the man at the top is weak and without those basic talents to shepherd the work, his flock will also be without strength. But if he is strong, the church will be strong.

There is really no lack of "those in authority" and leadership material in these villages of Taiwan. I have been amazed at the number of beautiful homes and even expensive cars which are displayed throughout these areas. Of course we realize that wealth and success do not necessarily indicate leadership ability, but often they are the result of genuine talents in management. The resources are there, but we are not tapping them. And there are a number of reasons why we are not.

We have already mentioned the unwholesome blind spots which deprive us of an aggressive approach in presenting our message to the "up and outers." So first we need to examine the cause of this blindness. I feel this is one of our enemy's tactics. He is very eager to hold on to all this leadership material. It is extremely useful to him. As long as he has those "in authority" on his side, he can keep the mass of the villagers striding along after their leaders. It is a case of the sheep following the goats.

Another reason why we are not tapping the officer material is that we are not using "entreaties, prayers, petitions and thanksgivings" to ask the Lord for them, as Paul urges us to do. "You have not because you ask not." We can become very involved in praying for Grandma Wu's backache, and little Sung-Yu's problems in school, but how intent are we in seeing the postmaster and the head of the sugar factory come to know the Lord? Paul is saying that "God desires *all men* to be saved."

Once in awhile we meet missionaries who possess the kind of vision which Paul is seeking to promote. The biography of Pastor Hsi of Shansi Province in China was a great challenge to me. In the early beginnings of the CIM, a couple of pioneer missionaries went to the city of Ping Yang. They knew no one there, but they felt led to begin their work in an effort to first of all reach some leadership. So they prepared several posters announcing a writing contest on a popular controversial subject regarding the condition of society. The Holy Spirit used this "key" to begin the process of opening the heart of a brilliant intellectual to the gospel. This man, Mr. Hsi, had been an opium addict but was beautifully converted and became the leader of a tremendous outreach for the gospel in that city and the surrounding districts. It is actually much easier to work from the top down than from the bottom up. When God's time came to begin *His own* work of evangelism, He sent the highest, most qualified Person in His universe, His only begotten Son.

Before the Lord Jesus selected His twelve officers, He spent the night in prayer. This was obviously a vital undertaking for Him. At first we may tend to feel that He chose low-grade material when He picked four fishermen, a tax collector, etc., to train as His successors. But when we examine the record, we discover that these men were natural leaders and were those already "in authority," each in his own realm. Peter's fishing enterprise included some good-sized boats and a number of hired men. Matthew was a very able government official, well-educated, and had many friends in the tax office.

Throughout the Scriptures, God chose men of special ability for the leadership of His operations. It required a talented engineer to take God's blueprint for a ship the size of the ark, as Noah did, and construct such a vessel. Abraham was a highly respected entrepreneur, with 318 servants. Moses was in line to become the pharaoh of Egypt, the highest position in the world at that time. The prophet Elijah was primarily a messenger to kings and rulers. Isaiah was a literary man of the highest rank. Jeremiah was a political leader. Daniel was prime minister of the Babylonian Empire for seventy years. Luke was a respected medical doctor, and Paul was one of the most gifted intellectuals of his day.

So if we begin our missionary efforts with requests for such leadership material at the top of our prayer list and design our missionary strategy to reach these people for our Lord, He will surely be pleased and will grant us the keys necessary to bind their captors, to unlock their fetters, and to see some of them brought into the kingdom of light. And His church from the start will have the beams and pillars necessary to support a sturdy building.

Paul as an Example

Both before and after these verses urging us to look to the Lord with confidence for adequate leadership, Paul points to himself as an example of what God can do. First he describes what a hopeless case he was. "I formerly blasphemed and persecuted and insulted Him; but I received mercy because I acted ignorantly in unbelief, and the grace of our Lord overflowed for me with the faith and love that are in Christ Jesus. The saying is sure and worthy of full acceptance, that Christ Jesus came into the world to save sinners. And I am the foremost of sinners. But I received mercy for this reason, that in me as the foremost, Jesus Christ might display His perfect patience for *an example* to those who were to believe in Him for eternal life." Then, right after our text, he adds, "For this I was appointed a preacher and apostle, a teacher of the Gentiles in faith and truth."

So if the Lord can lasso a leader like Paul with the miraculous revelation He gave him on that Damascus Road, He can get hold of anyone! There is no man who is too high-class for Him to handle. Paul recorded his own personal testimony here to build up our confidence and expectancy and vision as we move into our mission field and as we develop our strategy.

There are many other examples in our present age of how the Lord has honored the faith of His servants and brought into His kingdom some very able majors, colonels, and generals. It was certainly no small asset to the student work of Taiwan when the Lord brought Professor Chang Ming-Che into Campus Evangelical Fellowship. This man, originally the president of the Taiwan Petroleum Company, was led into the kingdom of light through the ministry of one of the Lord's humble servants, Auntie Ni. Professor Chang later became head of the Department of Chemistry at National Taiwan University, then president of Ching Hua University, and finally head of the nation's highest technical post, the Science Research Bureau. For over twenty years he gave magnificent direction and training to Campus Fellowship, so that it became a powerful and effective instrument used of the Lord to reach thousands of high school, college and university students, many of whom are now in full-time service for their Lord.

Other examples are Charles Colson, President Nixon's aide, and his prison ministry in the U.S.; Dr. Akira Hatori, the great radio evangelist in Japan; R.A. Laidlaw, the flour milling magnate of New Zealand who became a worldwide evangelist and produced that powerful little booklet "The Reason Why," which has sold twenty million copies in over thirty languages. And there are many others.

But we don't only look at these five-star generals. The Lord has brought to Himself many sergeants, lieutenants, and captains for the equally essential echelons of pastoring His churches, leading His projects, and ministering the gospel within the framework of society.

On one occasion, when village workers were seeking a location in a strongly heathen area to hold an evangelistic meeting, all doors seemed to be closed. Finally they discovered that the principal of the high school was a Christian. They went to see him, and the school auditorium was made available. One summer the number of students who signed up to join the gospel team for a certain village area were so many that housing them seemed an insurmountable problem. But then someone suggested that the manager of the large sugar factory nearby should be contacted since he was a Christian. When he heard of the need, he readily made available his company's large hostel. In another district the head of the prison was a Christian, which meant a whole series of opportunities. Paul asks us to petition the Lord to grant us just such men of position so that, as much as possible, we may be unhindered in our outreach with the gospel.

Imperative of Training

I fear that sometimes we *too quickly* give up our pursuit of such men. When the Lord Jesus informed His disciples that it was "harder for a rich man to enter the kingdom of heaven, than for a camel to pass through the eye of a needle," He then added, "but with God all things are possible." He was laying out before us both sides of a truth. It is possible to reach quality leadership, though it is not easy.

In His first parable of The Sower, He pictures four kinds of soil. And only the fourth turns out to be productive. But the indication of the parable is that we are to be prepared to give special care and attention to this "good" soil. In Paul's second letter to Timothy he reinforces this imperative. His exhortation reads, "The things which you have heard from me in the presence of many witnesses, entrust to reliable men who will be able to teach others" (2 Tim. 2:2). People who, before their conversion, are already in positions of leadership are usually "reliable men." They have developed a measure of self-discipline. They are also able to teach others, or they could not hold a position of authority. So Paul is urging us to devote our primary efforts to nurturing and training such quality converts. They should become our special "sons in the faith" whom we disciple with utmost care and diligence. It is a great loss when we allow such prize material to slip through our fingers. And yet it often happens. The common and natural tendency is to expect that all new believers will automatically become regular attenders at our church meetings like everyone else, and then eventually we can elect them to our deacon board. But the Lord has much greater expectations of us. If He entrusts to us the life and talents of a capable leader, He expects us to pour all we can into such a vessel. The Lord Jesus gave His primary attention for three years to twelve men.

We are all busy in the Lord's work, but it is good that we periodically take a day to step back and objectively evaluate our priorities. "Am I giving my strength and efforts for that which will count the most?" The word "strategy" is a military term.

I shall never forget a seminar I attended where Professor Chang Ming-Che spoke on his strategy for the student work in Taiwan. He began by making it very clear that the primary concern of his ministry was to train the *staff* of Campus Fellowship. He, a brilliant leader, knew well that the highest priority of any work is to produce other able leaders. The victories of any army depend to a great degree upon the quality and training of its officers.

The Supremacy of the Church

In a previous chapter we have looked at the responsibility of the church as a military academy for the training of Christian soldiers. And another chapter is given to the need and content of follow-up for new believers. But here I feel we give thought to the paramount position which the church is to sustain in the life of a believer, especially the new convert in an idolatrous village. This is even more urgent if this person has administrative gifts and is therefore one whom the Lord may be choosing as a leader among His flock.

It is almost impossible to overemphasize the need for a new believer in a village of Taiwan to become firmly implanted in the church. The enemy will do everything in his power to pull him in the opposite direction. Since the Evil One has held almost complete control of these villages for so long, it is for him a great loss of face for a church to be planted in his territory and a terrible pain for him to, one by one, lose his grip on his subjects. It is like the slave owners of the early days who would go to all ends to retrieve a runaway slave.

Just a week ag, we received news of a tragedy which came upon the first and most promising convert in the newly-begun outreach in the Tungshih district. This brother, about fifty years old, was so happy in his new "life." Though he had met a great deal of opposition, and even though his wife had threatened to divorce him, he still stood firm and made great strides. Finally his wife began to soften toward the gospel and was on the verge of accepting the Lord. Then during an electrical storm, she was struck by lightning. She remained in a coma for several days and was in the hospital with badly burned hands and ears and possibly other injuries.

It is true that the Lord Jesus declared that He will build His church, and the gates of hell shall not prevail against it. But in the same breath He lays on us the responsibility of "binding and loosing" and being a faithful "keeper of the keys." In both the Old and New Testaments there are a good many warnings against shepherds who do not do a proper job of shepherding. Is it possible that one reason so many new spiritual babes fall by the wayside out in these villages is that we ourselves do not realize how essential it is to fold them into the church, and how dangerous it is for them if we don't?

There are four kinds of soil, and only the fourth kind is "good soil," so we cannot expect every "decision" for the Lord to be real and truly possess new life. But until we are sure of a "stillbirth," we dare not allow a new-born lamb to be captured by the wolves.

And now, from another perspective, let us take a look at God's evaluation of His church. In Ephesians 3, Paul states that the reason God sent him to preach to the Gentiles was "in order that the *manifold wisdom of God* might *now* be made known *through the church* to the rulers and the authorities in the heavenly places...*to Him be glory in the church* and in Christ Jesus *to all generations* for ever and ever. Amen" (Eph. 3:10,21).

God considers the church to be His masterpiece here on earth for all to see and longs that through each little local church great glory will come to Him. This is the supreme goal of His eternal plan. Therefore His church in any given district is, in His eyes, the greatest institution of the whole area. Even with all its frailties, it is of infinitely greater significance to Him than any school, bank, business, or any other enterprise. He longs for us to operate with the same consuming vision and to impart that vision to every new believer and especially to any who are likely to become leaders in His church.

When God created the universe, He produced a phenomenal display of every kind of beauty and grandeur. He made the atoms, all the chemical building blocks, all the plants, insects, fish, birds, animals, stars and galaxies. When He finished with all this, then He prepared a special, unique garden, and finally He created man and put him in this garden, which He called Paradise. This first paradise had to be abandoned because of man's fall, but He is preparing another "imperishable" paradise in heaven for *His church*. And this is the great objective of all His creating, and all His planning. So we should hold a highly exalted view of His church and be prepared to build just such a majestic concept of His church in the soul, spirit and understanding of each new convert. His church at the beginning may be small and weak in some of these villages, but He still rates that little group extremely high in His scheme of things. And we need to encourage that little group to see how precious they are to Him.

Perhaps the main reason that God so highly regards His church is that it is the only institution in any village or town which has spiritual life. A school has its secular education; a bank has its money; a factory has its material products; but only His church has life. And new life, abundant life, eternal life, is the commodity He prizes!

The Function of the Church

New believers need not only to see the grandeur of God's church, but they need to see its present purpose. If God loves His church so much, then why does He not take each new believer directly to His wonderful paradise in heaven as soon as he is "born again"? Paul explains this a little further on in his letter to the Ephesians. "Christ loved the church and gave Himself up for her to make her holy, cleansing her by the washing with water through the Word, and to present her to Himself as a radiant church, without stain or wrinkle, or any other blemish, but holy and blameless" (Eph. 5:25-27).

The Lord Jesus is preparing His church to live with Him forever in that wonderful new paradise, just as a man prepares to take a young lady to himself to be his bride. There is a great difference between a newborn baby and a mature young lady. The little baby needs many years of growing up. She needs to be fed lots of nourishing food. She needs to learn to walk, talk, read and write. She needs a good many years of schooling. She needs to learn how to keep a home. And above all, she needs to learn how to love other people and to become a person of good character. In other words, the function of the local church is to fill in that very important stage between birth and marriage.

A beautiful conclusion to all of this is pictured in one of the apostle John's visions in his book of Revelation. He writes, "Let us rejoice and be glad and give Him glory! For the wedding of the Lamb has come, and His bride has made herself ready" (Rev. 19:7). Banks, schools and businesses have their worth and usefulness, but none hold any future glory to compare with the eternal bliss of the church of the living God. The folk religions of these villages in Taiwan offer little comfort to their adherents. In fact their whole operation is pretty much built on fear of the present and even greater fear of the future. But the church of our God is meant to be set in the flow of His blessing, both now and throughout all the ages to come!

Perhaps another paragraph or so is in order here before we close this section. A new leader in God's church can be challenged to much loving devotion to the Lord by His parable of the ten virgins. Five were wise, and five were foolish. The wise kept their lamps full of oil, while the foolish were careless and passive about their waiting for the bridegroom. In the end the latter were left behind. They didn't really love Him.

So our *belonging* to His church is more than attending meetings or even being baptized. It is *loving* Him and His church. And this love is shown and proven by our wholehearted service to Him. Those who are potential leaders need to understand this. They may be occupied in their business and busy with other assignments, but they must come to see that their earthly vocations are secondary, and His church is to become their primary and highest responsibility. This may at first appear to be an extreme view to them, but we must never hesitate to ask the Holy Spirit to hold up before them the glory of His church and the magnificence of truly belonging to Him. The Lord Jesus made it very clear that whoever loves father, mother, son or daughter or even his own life more than his Savior and Master is not worthy of Him. And if the Holy Spirit is truly living in that life, there will be glad acceptance of this truth, and that one will actually be delighted to be a pillar in God's house. This will all develop as the new believer learns to worship and adore his loving Lord.

Discovering and Developing Gifts

In various New Testament passages, the Lord pictures His church as His temple which He is building from His supply of "living stones." In building, we begin with a pile of rocks, sand, cement, bricks, etc. But there is a vast difference between a few piles of these raw materials, and a beautiful, magnificent cathedral. What makes the difference? In the latter, each item of the materials has been carefully fitted into its proper place and is fulfilling its intended function. In God's temple each person is a "*living stone*." He is not only there in the right place, but he is alive and serving his Lord and his Lord's church to the extent of his strength and capability.

Now it is time to give thought to the matter of *capability*. In the Scriptures this element of competence is spoken of as the "gifts" which God has given to each of His children. In each of the major passages about gifts, there is strong emphasis on the fact that each Christian has received at least one gift. Some have several.

But it is precisely at this point that things tend to break down. Our desire for church growth sometimes amounts to little more than the numerical count of heads of those attending Sunday morning services. There are Christians who attend church regularly each week, faithfully occupying their particular seat for years, without ever giving thought to any possible gift they might possess. This is a sad state of affairs.

From his first week in the assembly of believers, each new member of the body should be encouraged to give consideration to his function within the body. It will become quite natural for him to do this if every other member of the body is so gift-conscious and so service-oriented that from this new believer's initial introduction into the group they too begin to join him in seeking the Lord as to his place of ministry. It should soon become evident to each member of a congregation not only what his own gifts are but those which the Lord has given to every other brother and sister. Such a temple is truly built of "living stones" and will grow with contagious exhilaration.

The reason some may be reticent to become involved in ministry is that they might fear being asked to do something which they are not equipped to handle. But a proper understanding of "gifts" eliminates all such qualms. The Lord never forces square pegs into round holes. He only desires His children to serve Him in those capacities for which He has equipped them.

Now we are ready to turn to Paul's primary text regarding gifts. "I *urge* you therefore, brethren, by the mercies of God, to present your bodies...[for that] which is your reasonable service...that you may prove what God's will is [for you], that which is good, well-pleasing and perfect" (Rom.1 2:1,2).

So step one is to "urge" the new believer to allocate time each week when he can become involved in some ministry. Step two is to line up an assortment of different possible ministries for him to try one by one for a week or a month at a time, so that he can "prove" what God's perfect slot is for him. Perhaps the initial exercises will be to go visiting with some other member, or to assist with the children in Sunday School, or to give his testimony at a mid-week meeting. Gradually he can work up to where he can attempt leading a service, or giving a short devotional, or chairing a small group.

In all this we must be alert to detect the gifts of *leadership*. And when we do, we should be prepared to put forth extra effort in training such people. They may very well become the majors, colonels and generals in the church's militant outreach. Here we come back again to Paul's instruction to Timothy: "The things which you have heard from me in the presence of many witnesses, entrust to *reliable* men who will be *able* to teach others" (2 Tim. 2:2).

When we ask the Lord to give us leaders for our village churches, we must be prepared and equipped to provide a proper and sufficient period of preparation for these officers. It is neither a simple nor an easy undertaking to assume the command of some portion of the Lord's army, especially out on the front lines. It requires far more than merely attending a deacon's meeting once a month or enjoying the esteem of holding the position of an elder.

When the Lord Jesus urged us to "beseech the Lord of the harvest to send out laborers into His harvest," His challenge included several considerations. He was not suggesting that we only ask for professionals from overseas, or from the larger churches in the big cities, or graduates from the seminaries. He spoke these words right after He had sent out His twelve, and then another group of seventy-two, and none of these were from such specialized categories. They were just local material to whom God had given gifts of leadership. And there must have been a good many more equally suitable officers available, or He would not have prompted those seventy-two to pray for others to join them.

His exhortation to *plead* (beseech, beg) for such qualified local staff to join us should be a tremendous encouragement to our efforts out in these difficult village areas. For when the Lord so urged those seventy-two disciples to entreat Him for workers, the context indicates that He was desiring to send them out into the villages. He is mindful of the great needs of these dark areas, and He wants us to know that He is prepared to hear our prayers for more fellow-missionaries and also to raise up needed co-workers from the local scene to build His church. So we can make our pleas with glorious anticipation!

23

DELIVERANCE

"He looked down from His holy height. From heaven the Lord gazed upon the earth, to hear the groaning of the prisoners, and release those condemned to death" (Ps. 102:19,20).

God's great goal for man is PARADISE, spelled out with capital letters. But man, for the most part, has a hard time getting there! God has certainly done His share, in every possible way short of simply plucking man up and forcing him through the gate. This, God refuses to do, because man is far more than a little rag doll. Man is a living creature with a responsible free will. Therefore, each human being has to exercise his own concern and determination in the process. But there is a third element, a powerful, crafty, cruel enemy, which we have been writing about in this book. This Evil One has succeeded in blinding and binding God's human species to the point where they are rendered almost helpless...almost, but not quite. There has always been a ray of hope. God, our Maker, even from the day of Adam's fall, has always stood by, offering Himself to be man's deliverer. He has never left Himself without a witness to this fact. And this witness has become stronger and clearer throughout the world as the centuries have passed.

God's Primary Name—"Deliverer"

In the first chapter of Genesis, during the days of creation, the Creator's name was simply God ("Elohim," The Almighty One). But beginning with the very next chapter, the story of the first paradise, in the Garden of Eden, He chose to use the name "Lord God" (Jehovah Elohim) and often from then on just "Lord" (Jehovah). This was His primary title, used some 6,000 times in the Old Testament.

As God was in the process of delivering His people Israel from their slavery in Egypt, He twice asked Moses to make it very clear to the people the significance of His name "Lord" (Jehovah). "And God said to Moses, 'I AM WHO I AM; and He said, 'This is what you shall say to the sons of Israel: "I AM" (Jehovah) has sent me to you. ...This is My name forever, the name by which I am to be remembered from generation to generation'" (Ex. 3:14,15). And a little later: "God spoke further to Moses and said to him, 'I am the Lord (Jehovah), and I appeared to Abraham, Isaac and Jacob as God Almighty, but by my name "Lord" (Jehovah) I did not make myself known to them." (Actually, God had used His name "Lord" [Jehovah] many times during the days of Abraham, Isaac and Jacob, but had not yet revealed its special meaning as "Deliverer") ..."I have heard the groaning of the sons of Israel, because the Egyptians are holding them in *bondage*; and I have remembered my covenant. Say, therefore, to the sons of Israel, 'I am the Lord (Jehovah), and I will *bring you out* from under the *burdens* of the Egyptians, and I will *deliver* you from their *bondage*. I will also redeem you with an outstretched arm and great judgments. Then I will take you for my people, and I will be your God; and you shall know that I am the Lord (Jehovah), your God, who *brought you out* from under the *burdens* of the Egyptians. And I will bring you to the land which I swore to give to Abraham, Isaac and Jacob, and I will give it to you for a possession; I am the Lord (Jehovah)'" (Ex. 6:2-8). David and the prophets also spoke much about the Lord as the Deliverer.

Then 1500 years later, the greatest episode of history began to unfold. One night out in the hills of Bethlehem, a group of shepherds were awakened by a bright light in the sky, and an angel from heaven appeared to them. "And the angel said to them, 'Don't be afraid; for behold, I am bringing you good news of great joy which will come to all people; for to you is born this day in the city of David, a *Savior*, who is Christ *the Lord*." This title "Savior" comes from the Greek word "SOZO," which means to "rescue," "deliver," or "set free." This word, in its verb form "save," is used over 500 times in the New Testament, and His name "Jesus," which means the same thing (as the noun "Savior"), is used a thousand times.

A month after the baby was born, his parents took Him to the temple for their purification rights. "Now there was a man in Jerusalem called Simeon, who was righteous and devout. He was waiting for the consolation of Israel. ...Moved by the Spirit, he went into the temple courts...took the child in his arms, and praised God saying: Sovereign Lord, as you have promised, now dismiss your servant in peace. For my eyes have seen Your *salvation*'" (Lk. 2:25-30).

Another thirty years after that first Christmas season, when this Savior began his ministry in His own home town of Nazareth, "He went to the synagogue, as His custom was on the sabbath day. And He stood up to read; and there was given to Him the book of the prophet Isaiah. He opened the book and found the place where it was written, 'The Spirit of the Lord is upon Me, because He has anointed Me to preach good news to the poor. He has sent Me to proclaim *release* to the *captives* and recovering of *sight to the blind*, to *set free* those who are oppressed, to proclaim the favorable year of the Lord.' And He closed the book, and gave it back to the attendant, and sat down; and the eyes of all in the synagogue were on Him. And He began to say to them, 'Today this Scripture has been fulfilled in your hearing'" (Lk. 4:16-21). The *Deliverer* Himself had finally come to planet Earth in human form to present the message of *salvation* and *deliverance*. A short while later, on a cross, He paid the price for it all.

When Paul stood before King Agrippa, he explained his goal in life as the fulfillment of the Lord Jesus' commission to him. The Lord had said, "I have appeared to you for this purpose, to appoint you to serve and bear witness to...the Gentiles, to whom I send you, *to open their eyes, that they may turn from darkness to light and from the power of Satan to God*, that they may receive forgiveness of sins and a place among those who are sanctified, by faith in Me" (Acts 26:16-18). His commission, simply put, was to proclaim God's message of deliverance.

Phases of Deliverance

Since the primary name of our God means "Deliverer," it is not surprising that the spectrum of His various forms of deliverance covers a broad range. And it needs to, for His enemy who has operated a wicked kingdom on our planet for so many thousands of years, has wreaked havoc in so many ways. Therefore, God's Word deals with many varieties of deliverance.

The most common Old Testament references to deliverance are of those occasions when God delivered His people from the warring nations attacking them. David also speaks many times of being delivered from grievous afflictions which often plagued and harassed him.

The New Testament begins with many pictures of the Lord Jesus delivering those who were oppressed of the Devil and preaching His gospel message of deliverance from the Devil's kingdom. "If the Son shall set you free, you will be free indeed." The Epistles take up this latter theme and make it very clear that man's primary need is to be rescued (delivered) from the power and penalty of sin. Or as Paul put it, "He has delivered us from the domain of darkness, and transferred us to the kingdom of His beloved Son" (Col. 1:13).

It is rather unfortunate that the terms "deliverance," "power encounter," and "spiritual warfare" in many quarters today have been quite narrowed down to the single area of the exorcism of demonized individuals. This aspect is, to be sure, a very essential work in certain situations, but we need to see the range and scope of deliverance as comprising a much wider latitude. (And actually, since there are now so many fine sources available which deal with that particular phase of deliverance from demonic oppression, we will not go into the details of such ministry here.)

In this chapter we want to consider several facets of deliverance, and I would like to begin with a particular type of situation in our village work here in Taiwan where new converts desperately need release.

Freedom from Fetters

It is becoming increasingly evident that those who have lived all their lives in the darkness and corruption of heathendom and whose ancestors have been steeped in idolatry for countless generations often need a special measure of deliverance when they turn to the Lord. Their problem is not necessarily de-monization (though sometimes this is definitely the case), but more often it seems to be the "depraved mind" which Paul speaks of in his first chapter to the Romans.

Even though they seem to have become "new creations" in Christ, and to a certain extent "the old has gone; the new has come," yet they are still dragging their chains. It is almost as when the Lord Jesus called Lazarus forth from the tomb. Lazarus was truly alive. But the Lord still had to add, "Take off the grave clothes and let him go."

In our next chapter we will be giving our attention to the matter of follow-up, which is so necessary for every new believer. And yet those who have just come from their heavy pagan environment seem to require an intermediate step of deliverance before they can handle such nurturing. Shackles of dullness and lack of sufficient appetite for spiritual things seem to be holding them back. They are not dull mentally, or inactive as far as their business or occupations goes. In fact this is often part of the problem. They come to church when it is convenient, and they enjoy the services and the fellowship, but the world, the flesh and the Devil still have such a stranglehold on them that "discipling" soon bogs down. In a sense the Lord has made them free, but they are not yet "free indeed."

But there is hope! And as we mentioned above, that hope lies in an initial step of deliverance from all the fetters of their heathen bondage at the very beginning of their Christian life. When the Lord Jesus sets a person free, He certainly desires for him to be "free indeed." However on at least one occasion, when the Lord healed a blind man, it was a two-step process. After the first touch, the blind one could see dimly, but after the second touch he could see clearly.

Many of the areas where Paul labored on his missionary journeys were also very heathen. He reminded the Corinthians, "You were pagans, led astray to the dumb idols" (1 Cor. 12:2). Ephesus was a city completely given over to magic and idolatry (Acts 19). And in his first letter to the Thessalonians, he recalls how they "turned to God from idols" (1 Thess. 1:9). But perhaps his most perilous encounter with idolatry came when he entered the town of Lystra in Galatia. After Paul had there healed a crippled man, "the priest of Zeus, whose temple was in the front of the city, brought oxen and garlands to the gates and wanted to offer sacrifice [to him and Barnabas] with the people" (Acts 14:13). Paul, of course, refused all such attempts and began to preach to them. Within a few hours they turned on Paul and stoned him until they were convinced that he was dead.

It was later to these Galatians that he wrote his strongest treatise on bondage and slavery. It is in the midst of this epistle that he cries out, "My dear children, for whom I am *again* in *the pains of childbirth* until Christ is formed in you" (Gal. 4:19). It is one thing to be "born again." It is quite another step forward for "Christ to be formed in you." And this is the great problem in our Taiwan village churches.

Another way of approaching this problem is to look at it as a vital step in preparation for their water baptism. If they have truly believed, they have already been baptized by the Spirit (1 Cor. 12:13). But water baptism out here in these heathen villages is a mighty big step. Sometimes an opposing family will reluctantly allow their "believing" son or daughter to attend church but will utterly forbid their being baptized. They know that such a step implies full commitment. I can now understand more thoroughly why our Lord insisted that in our "making disciples of all nations," we "baptize them in the name of the Father, the Son and the Holy Spirit." Even the new converts themselves realize that they are not ready for baptism until they have been freed from their spiritual inhibitions. And they should understand full well that water baptism is a public testimony of death to all their old self-centered, worldly ways and aspirations, and a rising again to walk in complete newness of life (Rom. 6).

This requires a special working of the Spirit in their hearts. Many "believed" on the Lord Jesus during His three years of ministry, but it was not until the special convicting power of the Holy Spirit worked in their hearts on the day of Pentecost that 3,000 of them accepted their water baptism.

After Paul refers to the "depraved minds" of the heathen in his first chapter to the Romans, he then gives ten chapters explaining his gospel message. Then after that, at the beginning of chapter 12, he begins the main challenge of his book. *"Therefore, I urge* you brothers, in view of God's mercy, to offer your bodies as living sacrifices, holy and pleasing to God—this is your reasonable act of worship [service]. *Do not conform any longer to the pattern of this world,* but *be transformed* by the *renewing of your mind."*

Critical Newborns

My daughter-in-law is a nurse in a good-sized hospital, and her job is the intensive care of "critical newborns." Normal babies are ready to leave the hospital and go home with their mothers a day or two after birth. But there are a few who are hampered with minor or major defects and require very special attention for a time before they can be released for conventional home care. Babies from abnormal, deprived backgrounds are more likely to need this extra careful observation and treatment.

So it is with those spiritual infants who have come to birth out of the degenerate, idolatrous regions of heathendom. They are pitiful indeed, and most need a band of spiritual nurses and physicians who will provide some intensive care until they are "set free" to begin the normal process of growth and discipleship.

In John 8:31,32, we see the Lord Jesus faced a very similar situation. Some of the Jews had been steeped in the bondage of blind Judaism and yet had made a genuine effort to follow Him. The passage reads, "To the Jews who *believed* Him, Jesus said, *'If* you hold to My teaching, you are *really* My disciples. Then you will know the truth, and the truth will set you free.'" This was the path of normal growth, to take in His Word, become His disciples, and be set free. But this was a very difficult pattern for these new "believers" to hold to. For their background was identical to the radical, unbelieving fellow Jews who surrounded them and who were so viciously opposed to everything the Lord Jesus said and did. In the same chapter the Lord had to declare to this hate-filled mob, "You belong to your father the Devil," and they soon picked up stones to stone Him.

The Lord Jesus thoroughly understood the bewilderment of these new, but not yet unfettered, believers, so right in the midst of the awful conflict He spoke forth this encouragement, "If the Son sets you free, you will be free indeed." But as we come back now to apply these words of His to the need for special deliverance among new believers in heathen areas on the mission field, we must bring up the question of why doesn't the Son of God just go ahead and set these shackled believers free? After all, He left heaven and came to this earth for this purpose. So we know that He desperately longs for these spiritual infants to be liberated from all their bondage. But here again we are brought back to that basic spiritual principle, that He wishes to involve *us*, His fellow-laborers, in the process. He always does things when we mean business in *asking* Him to do them. It is not automatic.

Our next chapter discusses follow-up, and we will there be examining His pronouncement to His disciples: "You did not choose Me, but I chose you and appointed you to go and bear fruit—fruit that *will last*; that whatever you *ask* of the Father in My name, He may give to you" (Jn. 15:16). In this present chapter we need to look at the latter part of that verse. He is indicating that there is to be a definite connection between our *asking* and the *stability* of our fruit. He seems to anticipate clearly the problem we are facing.

In previous chapters, we have seen repeatedly that effective asking usually involves more than the casual, one-time voicing of a request. We are encouraged to "keep asking...keep seeking ...keep knocking," and to pray "with groanings too deep for words," "in His name," etc. And it is this last element of "asking the Father *in My name*" which the Lord reinforced in His statement just above. He has many names in Scripture, but the most prevalent name, used 6,000 times in the Old Testament (as we studied in the beginning of this chapter) is "Jehovah," which means "Deliverer." His most used name in the New Testament (1,000 times) is "Jesus," which means "Savior." "You shall call His name Jesus, for He shall *save His people* from their sins" (Mt. 1:21). So when we are interceding for the release of these heathen "newborns," let us make much use of His names "Deliverer" and "Savior."

In Scripture, you and I are not spoken of as nurses, but we are called "priests of God." Actually, a priest is to be a sort of spiritual nurse. In the Old Testament each high priest was to carry about, right over his heart, the twelve names of the tribes of Israel. Nurses for "critical newborns" are highly trained these days in many skillful techniques and in the employment of the latest, most functional equipment. All this is to save the physical life of that tiny infant. How much more ought we to be trained and adept in the most effective spiritual procedures, as priests of God, in the care and deliverance of His precious little babes!

Let us take much encouragement from the reminder that the Lord Jesus is their Great High Priest who is in heaven praying for them, and we here on earth are really joining in His intercessions. "He is the Savior of all men, and especially of those who believe" (1 Tim. 4:10). And we might add: "particularly of the 'critical newborns' who have just begun to believe." "Jesus lives forever; He has a permanent priesthood. Therefore He is able to *save completely* those who come to God through Him, because He always lives to intercede for them" (Heb. 7:24,25).

In the "Warfare" section of the *Prayer Companion* which accompanies this book, there are two written prayers which offer specific help in working toward the deliverance of these "critical newborns." One of these is entitled "Warfare Prayer for a New Christian in Heathen Surroundings." This prayer can be part of our equipment as his spiritual "nurse," or interceeding "priest." The other is the "Warfare Prayer to be Prayed *by* a New Christian in a Non-Christian Home." To place this in the hands of a fragile beginner who is trying to live out his new life in the midst of heathen harrassment can be a life-saver until he fully experiences deliverance.

We need to bear in mind that new converts from these heavy pagan backgrounds will be attacked again and again. Therefore to pass through a stage in which prayers such as these are used again and again by both the "nurse" and the "infant" may often prove to be both necessary and helpful.

The Hard Cases

Just this week I heard the testimony of a missionary working in South America. She stated that when she first went to the field, she was assigned to work with an impossible little church of eight members. It seemed hopeless because every one of the eight members was living in sin or involved in some form of occult practice. As a new, determined worker, she set herself to pray for this church night and day for their deliverance. However, at the end of four years she saw no improvement, so was at the point of absolute despair. She cried to the Lord to please send someone to give her light and instruction. The Lord sent a mature and experienced eighty-year-old man to her rescue. He informed her that she would never be able to tear down such a firmly imbedded enemy stronghold by herself. He urged her to find four others who would join her in the attack, and he then would give them several days of training in the tactics of spiritual warfare. Things soon began to change, and within a few months this church was delivered from the clutches of the enemy, and in a few more months had seen well over a hundred others won to the Lord and worshipping Him together.

One of the main Scripture portions this godly, elder brother shared with that committed nucleus was the familiar passage, "I tell you the truth, whatever you bind on earth shall have been bound in heaven, and whatever you loose on earth shall have been loosed in heaven. Again I tell you that if two of you on earth agree about anything you ask for, it will be done for you by my Father in heaven. For where two or three come together in My name, there am I with them" (Mt. 18:18-20).

Not only is the "you" of verse 18 in the plural, but verses 19 and 20 both emphasize this element of plurality. Verse 19 speaks of two agreeing in prayer, and verse 20 increases it to "two or three." These verses are not primarily meant to comfort us when only two or three come out to prayer meeting. Quite to the contrary, their main emphasis is to encourage us not to try to do the binding of powerful enemy forces just by ourself. What the Lord is really urging here is the unified function of the body. The more involved, the better!

We also need to give due attention to His strong emphasis on unanimity. For this is an essential factor in our binding and loosing. "Again I tell you that if two of you on earth *agree* about anything you ask for, it will be done for you by My Father in heaven." This is really one of the major tenets of the whole passage. For several generals to agree on their warfare strategy is not a simple matter. The Lord is speaking here of something far more significant and weighty than a couple of people merely saying to one another, "Let's agree now that brother Jones will be healed."

When we turn to the Greek text of this sentence, we unearth some very meaningful words and phrases. The verse should actually read something like this: "Again I say to you that if two of you here on earth shall be in accord as to the validity of the transaction they are about to make request for, it shall be done for them by My Father in heaven."

We must keep in mind that repeatedly throughout these verses we have the expression, "in heaven" and "on earth." God is in heaven; we are on earth. So from several different angles, we are being urged to make sure that our asking, (our binding and loosing) lines up with His desires (His willingness). We should mention again that the strict translation of verse 18 should read: "Truly I say to you, whatever you bind *on earth* shall be *having been bound in heaven*, and whatever you loose *on earth* shall be *having been loosed in heaven*." The New American Standard Bible translation is very close to this.

Now, if we are to be sure that our asking for a certain accomplishment to take place is indeed in accordance with His plan, He is suggesting that *several of us* pray together about it *until* we are all in agreement that such a proceeding does truly line up with what has been decided in heaven. And this may take some time. The missionary in South America encouraged the people of her church to pray for direction about major decisions for a week or two. Minor matters might not take as long. But deliverance on a large scale, or of a long-standing problem, is not something which is always accomplished in a day, or even in a month.

Perhaps a good example of the type of issues we are dealing with here is the account of Paul and his team on their second missionary journey. After they had visited those churches established in the Province of Galatia on their first journey, they considered entering the very needy, unreached Province of Asia Minor to bring their message of deliverance and salvation to that area. But "being restrained by the Holy Spirit," they next "attempted [put to the proof]" entering the province of Bithynia. But the Spirit did not "suffer it to be done."

Then an interesting thing happened. One night Paul had a dream. He saw a man from Macedonia beckoning him to come and help. This seemed to be the final confirmation they were looking for. But it is very significant to notice the unanimity of confidence they had that this was from the Lord. "After Paul had seen the vision, *we* got ready at once to leave for Macedonia, *concluding that God had called us* to preach the gospel to them" (Acts 16:10). The Lord loves to work through His healthy, well-coordinated body, especially when it is operating on His wavelength!

Delayed Deliverance

Now let us proceed to the question of the deliverance which we more mature Christians seek, from our various afflictions and harassments. Why is it that we are not always delivered immediately from these grueling problems? As we proceed to examine this rather frustrating issue, we will discover that there are a number of reasons why we are not always at once set free. But before we discuss some of these reasons, we should lay down some more foundation.

We have already established the fact that the great objective of the Father, the Son and the Holy Spirit is deliverance. The primary name of our Father God is "Deliverer." The name of His Son is "Savior." And the name of the Holy Spirit is "Helper." These three in an instant could bind Satan and all his forces and cast them into the bottomless pit or completely destroy them. They could also, in less than a second, heal every person in the world and set all of us free from every sin, every frustration, and every hang-up. But obviously this is not Their way.

Our God is a wonderful Father. He loves His children dearly, but He is not gullible. He loves His children too much to pamper them forever as helpless infants. He desires them to grow up into adult manhood. And more than that, He is prepared to permit us to learn (even the hard way) those things which are of real spiritual value. He longs to "prove" to us His own value system which is the very highest. But there is an enemy who violently disagrees with God's views, who has a totally opposite value sysem and who uses every craft and every force to combat God's way and establish his own.

Still, God does not always insist on His own way. In fact, oftentimes He doesn't even shield us from the onslaughts of this enemy. Quite to the contrary, He allows us to increasingly become involved in the warfare, so that we might develop clearer spiritual insight and a stronger spiritual physique. He knows that all this, in the end, will deepen our understanding and our appreciation for that which truly is of the greatest value, the greatest satisfaction, and the greatest beauty. We will discover for ourselves, with profound assurance, that His value system is good and lovely and that the enemy's system is rotten, ugly and painful.

So, not only does He not spare us from the battle, but He often delays when we call and plead to obtain deliverance. However, if we understand His loving heart and something of His infinite wisdom, we can still offer up our worship and thanksgiving. This, of course, calls for an element of robust faith, based on a knowledge of Him and His ways.

Actually, pain and sickness, since Adam's fall, have been some of the most effective mercies to bring people to a serious consideration of the basic realities of life. Therefore, even God's curse upon this earth contained its wise blessings. We need to preserve a healthy balance between the various tensions of Scripture. Our God would have Himself to be known as the "Deliverer," and yet for the good of our growth and maturity, He frequently delays His deliverance. Sometimes, for instance, we are confused by such verses as Ephesians 3:20,21: "To Him, who by the power at work within us *is able* to do far more abundantly than all that we ask or think, to Him be glory...forever and ever." If He is able to do such unimaginably great and wonderful things, then why does He so often refuse to do them when we ask Him as nicely as we can? The answer would seem to be that He wants "to do *more* than we ask or think." These verses need to be coupled with others, such as those in Romans 5:3,4: "Let us rejoice in our sufferings, *knowing* that suffering produces endurance, and endurance produces character, and character produces hope."

In Luke's Gospel we have encouraging verses which read, "And He said to the woman, '*Your faith* has saved you, go in peace'" (Lk. 7:50). Then again, "And Jesus said to him [the blind man], Receive your sight; *your faith* has made you well.'" But these records need to be considered also in the light of many others urging *patience* in suffering. "Count it all joy, my brethren, when you meet various trials, for you know that the *testing of your faith* produces steadfastness. And let steadfastness have its full effect, that you may be *perfect and complete*, lacking in nothing" (Jas.1:2-4).

When Hannah (the prophet Samuel's mother) was married to Elkanah, the Lord did not immediately give her a child, as was her hope. Rather He allowed her a long and painful period of barrenness. She cried unto Him for help, but her deliverance was delayed. The Lord knew that the sorrow and disgrace of it all would develop one of the most beautiful characters of all history. When she was finally granted a child, her appreciation, devotion and worship became an exquisite masterpiece. Her heart's song is recorded in 1 Samuel 2:1-10.

The Lord is a master artist and sculptor. He knows which piece of material can be worked into a choice vessel. And He knows the type of treatment which will produce the most magnificent results. "In bitterness of soul Hannah wept much and prayed to the Lord." But her delayed deliverance brought forth far more joy, adoration and genuine gratitude than if everything had proceeded normally, without any difficulties.

After one of his struggles, David writes, "It was good for me to be afflicted so that I might learn Your decrees. ...I know, O Lord, that Your laws are righteous, and in faithfulness You have afflicted me" (Ps. 119:17,75). And Paul set forth his goal in life as "That I might know Him, and the power of His resurrection, and *the fellowship of His sufferings*, being conformed to His death" (Phil. 3:10). He knew that resurrection power comes from a certain amount of wrestling with suffering and cross-bearing. As we read the various accounts of all he went through, we come to see that for Paul that "certain amount" of adversity added up to a mighty, formidable list, and yet he was able to link all his frustrations and sufferings with the mercy and wisdom of God, so that he could maintain this marvelous stand: "In all these things we are *more than conquerors* through Him who loved us" (Rom. 8:37). Yes, the mature Christian life is a victorious life. But that means it is a life of conquering many obstacles. This is what makes us strong!

Though a handicap does make some people bitter, others come to realize that it provides a protective bridle which spares them from a lot of more serious trouble and keeps them close to the Lord. My own slowness of thought and weak constitution has kept me from many a pitfall and made me more dependent on the Lord, for which I will thank Him throughout eternity. And there are others with much more serious handicaps than mine who have developed resplendent personalities and reached amazing accomplishments. So deliverance from a handicap is not always the best thing for us.

A beautiful form of Chinese art portrays the winter plum blossoms on a gnarled old branch. It bespeaks a brand of elegance which is superb. The same type of glory is suggested in the Lord Jesus' main emphasis to the seven churches of Revelation 2 and 3, which was "overcoming." To *overcome* any and all hindrances is of real value and splendor in His scale of things.

Of course there are other reasons for delayed deliverance, such as sin, pride or the need to learn a profitable lesson. Disunity within the body, unforgiveness, spiritual coldness, and a host of other maladies can block the way to God's deliverance. Also, He often desires us to use direct, practical means to help another get freed from his troubles. Wise old Solomon wrote with insight about many things. One of his proverbs reads: "Do not withhold good from those to whom it is due, when it is in *your power* to do it" (Pr. 3:27).

Degrees of Deliverance

Before closing the chapter, we need to give some thought to the various ranges or dimensions of deliverance. As the title of this book would suggest, I, for several years, prayed sincerely for all the strongholds of Taiwan to be torn down. However, I am coming to realize that this is a mighty ambitious undertaking for one person to attempt. In Paul's famous passage on spiritual warfare in Ephesians, he indicates that there are many different echelons of enemy forces. He reminds us that "we are not contending against flesh and blood, but against the *principalities*, against the *powers*, against the world *rulers* of this present darkness, against the spiritual *hosts* of wickedness in heavenly places" (Eph. 6:12).

Paul doesn't explain the magnitude of these various ranks, but he certainly indicates that there is a scale of militant force and strength, from the individual demons of one of the "hosts," all the way up to those mighty principalities.

No general would send out a single soldier with his sword or spear or bow, or even with a rifle or a machine gun, to attack a whole regiment of enemy soldiers, and certainly not to encounter an entire army. When we remember that the island of Taiwan now holds the record of being the most idolatrous country in the world, which presupposes the highest concentration of Satan's forces of any spot on the globe, it is not surprising that we have not yet seen his vast system of strongholds torn down.

Of course there have been a good many here in Taiwan praying against his bastions, but *I now see* that the magnitude of deliverance we seek must be in line with the actual strength we can muster to bring about such deliverance. One soldier can combat one or possibly a small number of the enemy's "privates," but he doesn't get far trying to dislodge or conquer a whole battalion or a division. The Lord Jesus is almighty, and He holds all authority in heaven and on earth, and we go forth in His name, and we proclaim the victory which He won on His cross. Yet His strategies of warfare are founded on sound, honest principles involving wisdom, plus the inevitable sacrifices of battle...blood, sweat and tears. When nine of His disciples (to whom He had given special power and authority) failed to cast out a certain demon, He replied, *"This kind* comes out only by prayer (and fasting)"* (Mt. 17:21).

Recently I heard the testimony of a brother from Argentina. He told of tremendous breakthroughs which are now taking place in the villages of that land, which we have referred to before. Up until about five years ago, the rural areas of the country were not only unreached, but impenetrable to the gospel. Finally some of the Lord's servants began to realize that these were nothing other than *strongholds* of the enemy. So, one by one they began to approach these bastions by gathering a sizeable company of God's people into a given sector for two or three days of fasting and prayer, and in the name, the power and the authority of the Lord Jesus, to bind the activities of the enemy and command them to leave. Tremendous things began to happen. There are now thriving churches in over half of all the village districts of Argentina.

We have been experiencing more and more encouraging victories in the village work here in Taiwan as we build up our fighting force, and several of us feel we are on the verge of some significant breakthroughs. But we can also see that there is real need to mobilize an ever greater sector of His body (His army) into active service.

As we near the conclusion of this book, let us return to our theme text. "The weapons of our warfare are not of the flesh, but are mighty through God, for the tearing down of strongholds." Whether a student, a missionary, a pastor or a housewife, we Christians are each listed in the enemy's address book. But his hope is that he can keep us occupied with mundane affairs so that we will give him no trouble. However, when he sees us turning our attention in his direction, sharpening our weapons, putting on our armor and assembling our troops, with the intent of entering his territory and establishing the kingdom of the Lord Jesus, he then gets ready for battle too. If we *continue* to press ahead, in the name, the authority and the power of our Commander, he begins to tremble. He knows full well that he is a usurper and no longer has any valid rights to his territory. When we hold up against him the cross of Jesus Christ and His blood which was there shed to purchase all of mankind, he knows he has to back away and that his defeat is just a matter of time.

So, dear brothers and sisters, fellow soldiers of the cross, let us arise and with firm confidence move in for the tearing down of his strongholds and plant the flag of our Redeemer.

24

MAINTAINING THE VICTORIES

In the early years of my missionary work in Taiwan, I learned a memorable lesson regarding the Lord's concern for follow-up. I had been involved in some evangelistic English Bible studies for college students but had not seen any great number of decisions. Then one day a young Navigator missionary came along, whom I had never met before. He was very friendly and we had a good time of fellowship. When he asked how our student work was doing, I told him of my discouragements. He immediately asked what plan I was using for follow-up for the few who did turn to the Lord. I mentioned that we had started a weekly Bible study for Christians, but the attendance was rather spasmodic, particularly with these new converts.

He at once began to point out the great need for a period of special, individual discipling for each new believer. He used the illustration of a mother hen, who after laying a dozen eggs or so, then stops laying eggs and sits on her clutch for about three weeks until they hatch. Then even after they all hatch, she doesn't go back to laying more eggs but gives herself to intimate, vigilant care for those little chicks for the next several months. Only when they are strong and mature enough to fend for themselves does the mother hen return to her egg-laying.

I was convicted and yet encouraged by my friend's insights, so I determined to do something about it. I prepared a set of follow-up lessons and then arranged for a series of weekly individual discipleship appointments for each student who accepted the Lord. The results were phenomenal. The Lord began to give me so much fruit that I couldn't handle it all. Finally my health began to break, and I had to slow down.

In chapter 1 of this book, we told the story of the grievous defeat our student village teams suffered during the first few years of outreach. We say "defeat" because most of the rescued captives were soon pulled back into the enemy's strongholds. Therefore, in chapter 2 through chapter 23, we have dealt with problems encountered in doing battle against these strongholds, overcoming the enemy, etc. And as has already been stated, it is evident, both from God's Word and from 2,000 years of missionary history, that no matter how we try, during this age we will never be able to completely dismantle all of Satan's strongholds or dispose of all his forces. Such a final clean-up will take place only after the Lord Jesus returns. He will then bind up *all* of Satan's powers and cast them into the bottomless pit. This is all yet to take place.

This being the case, it is extremely essential then, especially in dark, idolatrous areas such as these villages of Taiwan, to give much attention to equipping new believers to "stand firm against all the schemes of the devil." For if left unattended, they are like helpless lambs in the midst of ravenous wolves.

All church-planting efforts suffer from a certain amount of loss "out the back door." But if we missionaries do not exercise extra care and attention to our spiritual babies in these totally unreached, demonic regions, the loss will be much worse. Luther's battle hymn certainly applies full force in these hazardous domains of the Evil One: "For still our ancient foe does seek to work us woe. His craft and power are great, and armed with cruel hate. On earth is not his equal." His conclusion states: "*God's truth* abideth still; His kingdom is forever." And it is only a firm grounding in God's truth and the precepts of His kingdom that will cause our fruit to remain.

Another experience I had shortly after my arrival in Taiwan illustrates vividly the hostile climate existing on many mission fields. After we had settled into our home on this new field and become accustomed to the different types of fruits and vegetables in this new land, I discovered that one of my favorite fruits was not to be found here. No honeydew melons or larger cantaloupes could be seen anywhere. So I wrote my father, asking him to send an assortment of California melon seeds. He immediately mailed out packets of nine different varieties.

One Saturday afternoon as I was preparing a small patch of

ground to plant the seeds, my neighbor who was a student at the agricultural college stopped by to chat. He was intrigued, of course, with my project and began to ask questions. But his reaction was rather negative. "Your seeds will sprout," he said, "but after the plants grow and bloom and set on their tiny fruit, the baby melons will all drop off the vines!"

I felt he was far too pessimistic, for he didn't understand how easily we grow our melons "back home." But unfortunately his predictions came true. Just as he had said, my beautiful field of healthy, blooming vines lost all their fruit in the very early stage of development. And just as he could so readily and definitely predict my physical crop failure, now many years later I can as assuredly predict a spiritual crop failure in this adverse spiritual climate of Taiwan, *if there is not adequate, proper follow-up.*

Vulnerability of Converts from Idolatry

"When an evil spirit comes out of a man, it goes through arid places seeking rest and does not find it. Then it says, 'I will return to the house I left.' When it arrives, it finds the house unoccupied, swept clean and put in order. Then it goes, and takes with it seven other spirits more wicked than itself, and they go in and live there. And the final condition of that man is worse than the first" (Mt. 12:43-45). This fearsome warning was given by the Lord Jesus himself. Surely it should cause us to be absolutely unwilling to leave a new believer unattended. The apostle Peter also warns us to be alert and very careful, for "your adversary the devil is prowling around like a roaring lion looking for someone to devour" (1 Pet. 5:8).

Not only do new converts from heathenism often need a sort of preliminary deliverance from the clinging fetters of their dark, benighted background, as mentioned in our previous chapter, but it is encumbent upon us to see that every new believer is continually protected by a band of prayer supporters. For you can be sure that those evil forces which held him captive before will surely be back again and again to latch onto him if not persistently bound and forbidden to do so.

A similar warning was sounded by a brother from the States who recently made two visits to Taiwan. Having had much experience in spiritual warfare, he lectured here on the subject of demonization and helped many through his deliverance ministry. During his first visit, he met up with such a profusion of demon activity that a few months later when he returned, he gave urgent counsel to provide special care for new believers. Even though a new convert has been brought out of the kingdom of darkness, his adversary will be determined to attack him from every standpoint and to move back into his life if at all possible.

The new babe doesn't realize all this, of course, but you and I certainly should. We must be aware of the danger and step in immediately after his new birth, as a loving nurse, to see that he is fully cared for. He will need new friends; he will need to form new habits, a new life style, a new outlook; and he will need a whole new involvement with his Lord and his new Christian family. He needs to become keenly aware that he now belongs to a new kingdom and has a new Master. "If any man be in Christ, he is a new creature...*all* things have become new" (2 Cor. 5:17). The Lord Jesus made it very clear that new wine is not to be poured back into old wineskins, and new cloth is not to be used merely to patch up an old garment.

Since Christian friends are so scarce in most of these villages, the new child of God must be warmly folded into his new church family. This fresh, cleansing atmosphere is absolutely essential for his spiritual health and nurture. But all this is still no substitute for his regular, weekly, individual discipling.

Scriptural Emphasis on Follow-up

One great push toward follow-up comes from the Great Commission itself. "Go therefore and *make disciples...baptizing them...teaching them* to observe all that I commanded you" (Mt. 28:19,20). Another imperative comes from the Lord's conclusion to His parable of the vine and the branches. "You have not chosen Me, but I have chosen you, and ordained you that you should go and bear fruit, and that *your fruit should remain*" (Jn. 15:16).

The Lord Jesus also began His parable of the vine and

branches with a specialized introduction to the paramount role of the One who had sent Him. He said, "My Father is the *vine-dresser*." He would have us see our Heavenly Father as vitally concerned that His vines be properly attended. Then in the next verse (though He admits that some which may appear to be branches do not really have life), He states that He is prepared to begin a special work of pruning and tending those which do have fruit so they might become able to bear more fruit.

Paul was primarily an evangelist, and we often hear him making such statements as "Woe to me, if I do not preach the gospel." Yet only one of his thirteen epistles (the Book of Romans) is even partially evangelistic in its content. All the others are letters to his new converts. And in most of them is an obvious deep desire to ensure protection for these new ones from all malicious attacks of the enemy. He was always anxious that they become familiar with the plots and schemes of their adversary. He knew that the spiritual knowledge and understanding of the newborn is very nearly equal to *zero*! And we must also operate on this basis.

In the Lord's parable of the sower and the four soils, the two main problems He underscored were the effects of persecution and the busyness of life which chokes the Word. These are precisely the two great obstacles to spiritual growth here in Taiwan. Persecution from neighbors and relatives seems often to be more than the new convert out in a village can bear. And since the Chinese are a hard-working, diligent people, it is not easy for the new convert to add to his already full schedule ample unhurried leisure for his devotions. So the task of the discipler is by no means an easy one.

Yet we still have a key word in Scripture regarding young Christians: the verb "establish." God wants all His children to become well established in all the principles of His Word. This again confirms the fact that the responsibility for follow-up in a dense heathen area is no small item. In fact, it can soon grow in its demands to become a volume of involvement in the lives of even a few new believers which is more than we can possibly handle. But here is where we must begin to put these new ones themselves to work.

One of Timothy's assignments from the apostle Paul was follow-up. And he quite often found himself overwhelmed. But one day Paul wrote him a piece of advice which was very similar to that given to Moses when he was also overworked. "The things you have learned from me...entrust to reliable men who will be qualified to teach others" (2 Tim. 2:2). It is very good for those we are training to have the opportunity to pass on, at once, what they have learned to a younger beginner. This is one of the basic principles of good discipling. It helps greatly to reinforce each truth in their own hearts.

Need for God's Word

In the appendix of this book is a sample set of sixteen lessons which could be used in discipling sessions with a new believer. These likewise can provide him with simple, helpful material to disciple his student. It contains lessons on prayer (including worship), walking with the Spirit, service, and spiritual warfare. But the predominant emphasis is on the Word of God.

God's Word fulfills so many functions in the lives of His children that it should be viewed as the great essential for building up and establishing the man of God. It is the indispensable requisite of all supports to the Christian life. Peter likens it to the *milk* which an infant cannot do without (1 Pet. 2:2). He also declares that God's Word is living (that which sustains life) and that it is so reliable that it abides forever (1 Pet. 1:25). It can therefore serve as a firm anchor for God's child.

David, in the very first chapter of the Psalms, directs our attention to the *blessings* which will come to the one who "meditates day and night in the law of the Lord." He shall be like a tree planted by streams of water. His leaves shall not wither; he shall bear much fruit; and all he does shall prosper.

The Lord Jesus assures us that both He and His Father will *love, speak to,* and *dwell with* the one who "has My commandments and keeps them" (Jn. 14:21,23). Paul reminds us that "All Scripture is God breathed and is useful for *teaching, rebuking, correcting* and *training* in righteousness, so that the man of God may be *thoroughly equipped* for *every good work*" (2 Tim. 3:16,17).

Finally, we come to the need for God's Word in our *spiritual warfare*. It is *the sword* which the Spirit uses to do battle with our enemy. The new Christian, trying to stand in a fierce heathen atmosphere, must acquire a sharp sword and must be trained how to use it. Therefore, you will find these follow-up materials to be particularly weighted with heavy emphasis on the Word of God and how it can be used in warring with the Evil One.

In chapter 17 we viewed David's triumph over Goliath and noted that on that occasion David chose "five smooth stones" as his weapons. We urged each Christian to gather a collection of verses from God's Word which he can use to sling at his evil attacker. Follow-up Lesson 12A gives a sample selection of such verses. These should help the new believer to do battle with the sword of the word of God, declaring, "It is written." The verses include God's pronouncements concerning His Son's name, His power, His authority, His cross, and His glory. In the "Warfare Prayers" section of the Prayer Companion is included an example of how to use these "five stones"—how to develop skill in hurling them at the enemy.

Highest Priority of All

As we come to the end of this chapter and near the conclusion of this book, we must focus our attention on that which is by far more important than all else. Whether it be the new believer, or the most mature Christian, his great ever-existing need is to maintain a close fellowship with his loving, all-sufficient Lord.

The apostle John begins his gospel by introducing to us the Lord Jesus. The main point of his introduction is that "In Him was *life*, and the life was the *light* of men" (Jn. 1:4). Then twenty chapters later, he concludes his gospel with the very same message. He tells us that the one reason he wrote all these chapters and put them down in black and white was that we may "believe that Jesus is the Christ, the Son of God, and that by believing we *might have life* in His name" (Jn. 20:31).

Now we must look more closely at this statement, for he is declaring the principal theme and foremost purpose for writing his book. Since both the verbs "believe" and "have" and the participle "believing" are all in the present progressive tense, what he is really saying is: "I have written all this material so that you might be able to *sustain* a strong faith in the Lord Jesus. For He truly is the Christ (King of Kings and Lord of Lords), and He is the eternal Son of God. And as you *continue* to believe (*maintaining* fellowship with Him), you will enjoy all the new life which comes from getting to know Him better and better."

Then, proceeding in our observations of John's Gospel, we discover that all the content and substance of his book encourage the same goal. In other words, he is seeking for his readers to develop a lifestyle of *abundant fellowship with the Lord Jesus*. The key words of the Gospel of John are "light," "life," "believe" and "love." These are the keys to the growth of every Christian. So his message could be summarized simply as the truth that abundant fellowship with the Lord Jesus produces abundant light, abundant life, abundant faith, and abundant love.

John records a number of the Lord's miracles, but he also gives special attention to what the Lord himself had to say, either preceding or following each one. In most cases, His comments are on the significance of the miracles themselves—showing that each of His "mighty works" is also to be looked upon as a parable, meant to embody a vital teaching for the benefit of His disciples. He always considered the spiritual aspect of His ministry to be far more important than the performing of a miracle. In fact, throughout the Gospel of John these special works are called "signs." They were not only signs of His deity (that He was truly the Son of God), but they were also signs pointing to a very relevant spiritual truth.

Perhaps the best example of His intention that we view His miracles as teaching signs is the sermon which followed the feeding of the 5,000. This unparalleled miracle is recorded in all four gospels, but John's record in chapter 6 is expanded into an account of seventy-one verses, and the majority of these give the Lord's own discourse on the lessons He desires us to learn from what had just taken place.

The Bread of Life

The principal aim of that mammoth object lesson of feeding the 5,000 was that He might present Himself as the "Bread of Life." He introduced this application with the challenge, "Do not work for the food that perishes, but for the food that endures to eternal life, which the Son of Man will give you." Then He leads up to His declaration "I am the Bread of Life," and finally launches into that vital discussion on "eating My flesh and drinking My blood."

This latter emphasis on eating His flesh and drinking His blood was more than His Jewish listeners could handle. They had been told repeatedly in Old Testament Scriptures that in their diet they were never to touch blood. And the very thought of eating His flesh was repulsive to them. The problem was, of course, that they didn't realize the Lord was speaking in parables. But even so, *many* of the parables, as well as other teaching passages in God's Word, are hard for a beginner to comprehend. So hard, in fact, that if our new believers are not taught patience and persistence in their personal Bible study, they can easily flounder.

The passage before us, however (verses 48-68), admits that the Jews began to "grumble," and "on hearing it, many of His disciples said, 'This is a hard teaching. Who can accept it?'" And "from this time on, many of His disciples turned back and no longer followed Him." The Lord did give an explanation of the parable, which we will come to in a moment, but these frank admissions certainly reinforce the fact that it is not an easy thing for a beginner to become established in a meaningful, constructive Bible study. Yet this phase of his daily "Quiet Time" is absolutely essential to his spiritual life. For the Lord Jesus is the *Bread of Life*. And He declared right here in this sermon: "Unless you eat the flesh of the Son of Man and drink His blood, you have no life in you."

Jesus was not primarily speaking here of the loaf and cup of the communion service. No, a little further down He explained, "The Spirit gives life; the flesh counts for nothing. *The words that I have spoken to you, they are spirit and they are life.*" Therefore, a daily feeding on His Word, which is so spiritually nourishing that it amounts to "eating His flesh and drinking His blood," is indispensable for the health and growth of any believer.

The Lord Jesus firmly accentuates this truth from many standpoints in this section. At one point He states: "Just as the living Father sent Me and I live because of the Father, so *the one who feeds on Me* will live because of Me." And again, "Whoever eats My flesh and drinks My blood *abides* in Me and I in him." This last verse reminds us of His later parable of the vine and the branches, where He declared so emphatically that "without Me you can do nothing" (Jn. 15:5).

Then, on the positive side, in His parable of the Good Shepherd He asserted: "I came that they might have life and have it abundantly" (Jn. 10:10). He very much desires that His disciples (even the new babes) learn how to abide in Him and live because of Him and bear fruit. He makes it very clear that all this can only come from feeding on the Bread of Life.

Abundant Life

Not only is it far from His plan for His new disciple to be drawn back into enemy clutches; it is also far from His desire that this new one should stumble and fumble along for months or years in blindness and weakness. Abundant life means productivity. It means fruit. "Herein is My Father glorified, that you bear much fruit" (Jn. 15:8). This can only take place as there comes deliverance from the self-centered syndrome of worldliness and greed, which is also spoken of as "the lusts of the flesh, the lusts of the eyes, and the pride of life" (1 Jn. 2:16). More simply put, it is that old focus on self, which always adds up to "what I want to do; what I want to get; what I want to be."

All this fleshly bent needs turning completely around until his life is one of serving his Lord by that new pattern of caring, sharing, and serving others as He did.*This* is abundant life. It is the productive, fruitful life. It is *His* life. And since it is His life, it is only possible as the new disciple learns to feed on Him. So the new believer not only needs protection, comfort and love; he also must have daily food. He needs the "Bread of Life" to replace his former "junk food."

As we have mentioned above, he needs to develop new habits and a new lifestyle. Probably the most important new habit we must help him establish is his eating habit. This will not be easy; it takes patience and determination to teach a young child to feed himself. It can be rather messy at first, but a loving, caring parent will stick with it until that child is able to handle a good meal on his own.

Perhaps one of the best ways to clinch any new habit is to establish a program of *accountability*. This is another reason for personal weekly appointments with our new fledgling, from the very beginning. Yes, the Holy Spirit is there to help him, but we must also be willing for Him to use us as a spiritual parent to take him by the hand and lead him along until he can walk by himself.

One of the best ways to accomplish these tasks, especially the art of eating, is to assign him a suitable portion of God's Word to chew on for a week; then at the next session together see how much he was able to digest. He may need some help in discovering how better to use his spoon (or chopsticks), but continual, faithful practice is the solution. Faithfulness in practicing the elements of Bible study, Scripture memory, etc., is aided greatly by a system of accountability. Stick with him and watch him grow. If he absolutely refuses to eat, then of course there is the question as to whether he really possesses new life. But let us make sure that the problem is not one of neglect on our part.

Every missionary should make up his mind at the outset of his career that he will not be satisfied with only a few benchwarmers. Indeed, we want fruit that remains, fruit that grows, that pleases the Lord, and is a blessing to others. What we want to see is new life which is sustained by daily feeding on His life. This life will possess the strength to stand against the enemy's "strongholds," help establish His kingdom, and glorify His name.

25

PROTECTING THE HOME FRONT

In a previous section we touched on the story in the fifteenth chapter of Matthew about a Canaanite woman who came to Jesus to ask deliverance for her daughter who was being badly tormented by a demon. At first, her type of problem may seem rather irrelevant to you and me, but as we move into the end of this age, when Satan's anger is to become more and more heated, and as we ourselves become increasingly involved in spiritual warfare, we will discover more and more helpful things here in this story.

Perilous Times Ahead

Paul begins the third chapter of his second letter to Timothy with the words: "But mark this: there will be terrible times in the last days." And then he records a long list of fearsome developments which are to take place, and which have already begun to take place. Many of these have to do with attacks on the home.

One Christian brother tells of an amazing experience he encountered during a flight on a jetliner across the United States. When the stewardess came by passing out the trays for the first meal, the man sitting next to him mentioned that he would not be eating, because he was fasting. The Christian brother pricked up his ears and a little later asked the man if he were a Christian. The man replied, "No, I am a Satan worshipper, and every Wednesday we fast and pray to Satan and his forces to destroy the families of Christians, especially Christian workers."

A few days later, here in Taiwan, a fellow missionary had a similar experience while visiting a new temple being built near his home. During the conversation with one of the monks, he was told that the content of some of their new prayers now is for the

357

collapse of Christian homes. And just a couple of weeks ago I had a call from a fellow pastor stating that his son was being harassed by an evil spirit.

This sort of thing is really beginning to build up. A missionary co-worker who lived next door to a temple soon found one of his sons acting very strange at times. As this grew worse, it became evident that he was being tormented by demons. They moved away from the temple, and gradually their son recovered.

A very similar thing occurred to another friend of mine in Japan. He lived in a strongly idolatrous area, and his son became strangely disoriented. He recognized the problem and called upon God's people to pray. Eventually the boy was restored to normal health.

Satan is indeed a cruel foe. He knows that by attacking the children of God's servants he can often incapacitate their parents. I know of several missionary families who recently have had to leave the field and return home because of their children's special crises. And in the process one father developed a bleeding ulcer. Another suffered a severe heart attack.

Among the graduates of one fine training school for missionary children, one out of every hundred during the last ten years has committed suicide. And an equal number of others have attempted suicide. This is certainly appalling when we consider that the average for non-Christians in most countries in the world today is a rate of one out of every 10,000.

All this surely enjoins us to cover the home base in our conquests of prayer. Let us not only ask that our own homes be covered by the blood of the Lord Jesus, but let us also pray for one another's families, and especially for those who are serving on the front lines. You who are single could add to your prayer list the families especially close to you or others that God lays on your heart.

The Woman Came Alone

One point we should notice about this story is that the mother of the poor, suffering daughter came to Jesus by herself. Where was her husband? Well, he was probably working. Yes, all husbands have to work. This is normal and commendable. And these days many mothers work outside the home too. Still it is the mother who has the primary responsibility in bringing up the children. And it is all too common for the husband to back off in this effort of raising the family. Children need a father as well as a mother, especially when matters enter the warfare stage. It should be the father who goes to war, who most readily gets involved in the spiritual battle. And yet, sad to say, it is often left to the mother to carry the heavy end of the prayer burden along with all the rest of her family chores.

Father and mother should have set times to pray together for their home. It is *their* family, not just her family. But that mother had to come to the Lord Jesus alone. Many young mothers have come to our home for counsel about their family, and nearly every time it has been the wife coming alone. This points up a real neglect on the part of many of us fathers.

In I Timothy 5:8 God's word makes a very strong statement. "If anyone does not provide for his own, and especially for those of his household, he has denied the faith, and is worse than an unbeliever." We fathers are careful to see that our children have enough good nourishing food to eat, nice looking clothes to wear, a suitable house to live in, a proper education, etc., but what of their spiritual equipment and protection?

I distinctly remember an occasion when Satan was going hard after one of my boys while he was still quite young. I had been praying for him, but the battle raged on. One day it seemed to come through to me so clearly, that what my son needed was his own sword. So I began helping him to memorize some relevant verses of Scripture, and the victory was soon won.

Now coming back to this need for husband and wife to have regular fixed times to pray together for their family, I would encourage you with that special promise which the Lord Jesus left for us in Matthew 18:19. "If *two* of you *agree* on earth about anything they ask, it will be done for them by my Father in heaven."

When the Lord performed the first wedding in the Garden of Eden, He stressed the fact that marriage was to be a case of two people becoming one. They were to become so united, so working together as a team, that they would really function as a unit.

The New Testament also strongly confirms this thought. Although there needs to be division of labor in the physical operation of the home, yet in the spiritual realm the Lord desires a definite bonding together to call forth His blessing upon the family, and to dispel the evil attacks of the Wicked One.

Husbands ought also to pray much for their wives. The Scripture calls them the "weaker vessel," and yet they have to handle the bulk of the family routine of making decisions, coping with harassments, arbitrating quarrels and misunderstandings, and dealing out discipline. It is not just that these are often unpleasant and stressful tasks, but they are the vital stuff that homemaking is built of. The way these are handled makes the difference between a good home and a poor one, a happy home and a hectic one. Blessed is the husband who has a wife who can handle such an assignment victoriously. And blessed is the wife who has a husband who understands her plight, who is sympathetic, who appreciates all her efforts, and who prays for her regularly.

"Great is Your Faith"

The mother in this story came to the Lord Jesus with a painful problem. That evil spirit was giving her and her daughter a terrible time. But the Lord didn't solve her problem immediately. In fact He allowed her to wrestle with some unpleasant obstructions, as we discussed in a previous chapter. But in the end, it demonstrated a greatness of faith which His disciples (and we) needed to see.

Now what really is faith? First it is confidence in someone else other than yourself. Scriptural faith is confidence in God or His Son the Lord Jesus. Secondly, faith is confidence in who and what He is, and in what He has promised. He is powerful; He is wise. But great faith also is filled with the assurance of His everlasting *love*. This is why David's psalms are so beautiful, and this is why David was so pleasing to the Lord. He trusted Him. He built his life on God's "lovingkindness."

We very much need this kind of faith when we come to God in prayer for our families. Satan is relentless. He is persistent in giving us hassle, especially during these last days as we draw near to our Lord's return. He is filled with wrath, and he is a "strong man." He is a very powerful, mean, crafty foe. Along with all this, we must keep in mind the fact that our God does not always solve our problems immediately. He wants us to really enter into this spiritual warfare, to grow in spiritual stature, and increase our skill in using our weapons and our armor. But at the same time He wants us to develop our faith. He desires that our confidence in His loving concern grow to such a level that like the Canaanite woman we will still trust him and press in with great expectation, even though He may not at once give us what we ask for.

There are two main aspects of faith. One is confidence in God's ability. The other is assurance of His will. The first part is probably no problem for most of us. We have no hesitancy in believing that He is able to perform any kind of miracle whenever He desires. The second part is what slows us down. How can I know that He desires, that He is *willing* to do this thing I am asking Him to do? I know He is a God of love, but sometimes He does say "no" or "not yet."

Yes, we must every time include "not my will but Thine be done. " However, a story like the one we have just studied is surely meant to help us with this second element of faith. His love is often more *willing* than it may at first appear. The Lord Jesus was delighted for that parent to persist in supplication for her daughter. He delights for us to see in Him greater love for His children than we have for ours, even though we are so desperately concerned for their needs. In fact, many times the real problem is that we (particularly we fathers) don't exhibit nearly *enough concern* for the spiritual welfare of our children. Often, or should I say usually, we are far too passive, far too apathetic about how our sons and daughters are doing spiritually.

I know of one mother who spent the day in fasting and prayer for each of her children on their birthday. This is really only a beginning. When your child is in deep trouble, how do you express and demonstrate your concern for him? This Canaanite mother is held up to us by the Lord Jesus as exhibit A. He surely intends that we take a good long look at her concern, her persistence and her faith.

She knew how to obtain deliverance for her daughter, how to get involved in spiritual warfare when that precious child had been attacked by the enemy. She knew some things about victorious living for herself and her family.

Praying for our Teenagers

We have already touched upon the type of cruelties which evil spirits can inflict on smaller children, but Satan's approach is rather different when our young people reach their teens. The attack is usually much more subtle. Teenagers are in a vulnerable position and the enemy knows it. Their situation is quite similar to that of Adam and Eve in many ways. When God created Adam, he was an adult as far as his body was concerned, but he had no background in the ways of the "world" or the tactics of Satan. He wasn't even aware that Satan existed. Adam didn't hate God; neither do most teenagers who have grown up in a Christian home. But Satan knew that Adam and Eve were all set for some experimentation, and he knows that your teenager is also just itching to *try* a lot of new things. They know that God has forbidden them to eat of the fruit of this tree of the "knowledge of good and *evil*," but Satan points to a lot of other teenagers who have partaken of the fruit and seem to be thoroughly enjoying it, so it often doesn't require much of a push to get them plucking and eating.

When our children reach their teens, our days of preaching and teaching are pretty well over. But we can still make much use of prayer. This is what the Canaanite woman did, and it is what we surely must do. In fact, we will do well to ask the Lord to raise up special prayer partners for our children: spiritual "aunties and uncles" who know them and have a special love for them and who know how to pray.

We must not panic when we see the drift coming. Panic is lack of faith. We should be concerned, very concerned, at each sign of further drift, and keep the corps of special prayer partners confidentially informed, but we need to come to the Lord with great expectancy, as the Canaanite woman did.

There are many portions of God's Word which we can

claim and employ in praying for our teenagers, since God gives many special promises for our "offspring" and "our descendants" (see Prayer Companion). We will want to become skilled in using such weapons. Perhaps it would be helpful to refer to a few here now.

Rebellion

Our Lord's parable of the prodigal son is, I feel, intended to be of special help to parents in praying for their teenage children. Some of our children may not go as far as the young man did in Jesus' story, but as soon as we see the drift taking place, there are certain things we can begin to ask the Lord to do for them. We can ask the Lord to give them a distaste for that which is trash. Remember, it was when the prodigal began to feed on husks that he came to his senses.

The parable also mentions that when he had spent all his money, there came a severe famine in the whole country and no one gave him anything. This, of course, is a painful, pitiful situation to wish upon our child, but famine is a powerful means to bring a child back to his father's house. There are two kinds of famine. There is the actual shortage of funds, food and all the other physical needs. But there is also spiritual famine where the heart that has known a godly home is parched with grief, guilt, loneliness and despair. And the sooner a young person enters these two famine stages, the sooner he will return home.

At first this may all appear very negative to us. The thought of daring to pray for a famine to come on his land seems very harsh, but there are several thoughts we can bear in mind. This was part of the Lord Jesus' story. It was the loving Father's method. It was also God's method during the years of Ahab and Jezebel. He had Elijah call for a famine of three and a half years, which resulted in the great victory on Mt. Carmel when there was a great turning back to God.

It would seem that James is speaking to this very point as he closes his epistle: "Elijah was a man just like us. He prayed earnestly that it would *not rain*, and it did not rain on the land for three and a half years. Again he prayed, and the heavens gave rain, and the earth produced its crops. My brothers, if one of you should wander from the truth and someone should bring him back, remember this: Whoever turns a sinner away from his error will save him from death and cover over a multitude of sins" (Jas. 5:17-20).

We may tend to fear that such a famine might drive our son or daughter to become bitter and really turn against God. But we can also pray for them as the Lord did for Peter the night before his temptation. The Lord said to Peter, "Simon, Simon, Satan has desired to have you, that he might sift you like wheat, but I have prayed for you that your faith may not fail. And when you have turned again, strengthen your brothers" (Lk. 22:31,32). Peter had a terrible, humiliating crash, but the Lord had prayed that through it all his *faith* would not fail, and it didn't. It actually became much stronger and in the end the Lord was able to greatly use Peter to strengthen others. Remember also that *after* Elijah's famine, "he prayed again, and the heavens gave rain, and the earth produced its crops."

It is very comforting to note that on that same day when the Lord Jesus told the parable of the prodigal son, He preceded it with the parable of the lost sheep, which is summed up in the words, "Does he not...go after his lost sheep until he finds it?" (Lk. 15:4). And probably the key to the whole book is: "The Son of Man came to seek and save the lost" (Lk. 19:10). The word "lost" particularly refers to one who has strayed from a godly home. The Lord has special compassion and love and determination to reach such children, and we must cooperate with Him and His ways in reaching them.

Depression

There is, however, another very different type of teenage problem. Although it is usually those with strong self-confidence who tend to drift away from their Father's home, there are others with poor self-image who become discouraged and depressed. This also is one of the attacks of the Evil One. We have dealt somewhat with depression in other chapters, but it is becoming more and more of a teenage problem, so we parents need to be equipped to protect the home front with much support from the Scriptures regarding God's *favor* toward His children.

Satan's first successful ploy in the Garden of Eden was to convince Adam and Eve that God did not really have their best interests at heart, and this lie has actually brought on all the suffering of the human race. But the gospel is designed as a perfect antidote for this illness. Not only did the Lord Jesus die for us while we were yet sinners, but as Paul writes in Romans 8, "He who did not spare His own Son, but gave Him up for us all, how will He not also, along with Him, graciously give us all things." And then a little further down he adds, "In all these things (which might appear so wrong) we are more than conquerors through Him who *loved us*. For I am convinced that neither death nor life, neither angels nor demons, neither the present nor the future, nor any powers, neither height nor depth, nor anything else in all creation, will be able to separate us from the *love* of God that is in Christ Jesus our Lord." We need to deeply implant these truths in the hearts of our children from their earliest years.

The reason David's psalms are such a blessing to all of us is that even though his life was filled with much conflict and distress, he had learned how to delight himself in God's favor. When in the midst of a trial, he would think back and revel in the Lord's past deliverances. His habitual testimony was "This poor man cried and the Lord delivered him out of all his troubles" (Ps. 34:6). And again, "Many are the troubles of the righteous man, but the Lord delivers him out of them all" (Ps. 34:19).

If through the earnest, faithful intercessions of his prayer supporters, and the proper source of compassionate counsel, your teenager can be brought to see that although God's ways are not our ways, still His ways are "*higher* than our ways as the heavens are higher than the earth," then his self-image is bound to improve, and his depression evaporate. Sometimes the Holy Spirit may lead us to ask for a special friend who can "strengthen him in his God," as Jonathan did for David.

Depression is again a case of Satan desiring to have your precious teenager, but God is love, and He certainly has no desire for any young person to be so tormented. Therefore, we can pray in faith for deliverance. When we do, we *are* praying according to God's will. Let us pray with confidence and anticipation!

That Canaanite woman had a wonderful, tremendous faith in the *love* of the Lord Jesus. In fact this is the whole point of the story. This is why it was recorded, that we might see what "great faith" really is. So let us enter into the good of it, as we seek to protect our home front.

And now as we take our place in spiritual warfare, let our eyes be fixed on the Lord of Hosts, Commander of all the Armies of Heaven. And let us join David in his prayer:

"Praise be to the Lord my Rock, who trains my hands for war, my fingers for battle. He is my loving God and my *fortress*, my *stronghold* and my *deliverer*, my *shield* in whom I take refuge...Part Your heavens, O Lord, and come down; touch the mountains, so that they smoke. Send forth lightning and scatter the enemies; shoot Your arrows and rout them. Reach down *Your* hand from on high; deliver me and rescue me" (Ps. 144:1,2,5-7).